HARVARD EAST ASIAN MONOGRAPHS

72

REFORM IN NINETEENTH-CENTURY CHINA

REFORM IN NINETEENTH-CENTURY CHINA

Edited by

Paul A. Cohen and John E. Schrecker

Published by

East Asian Research Center

Harvard University

Distributed by

Harvard University Press

Cambridge, Massachusetts

and

London, England

1976

The East Asian Research Center at Harvard University administers
research projects designed to further scholarly understanding of
China, Japan, Korea, Vietnam, Inner Asia, and adjacent areas.
These studies have been assisted by grants from the Ford Foundation.

Library of Congress Cataloging in Publication Data
Main entry under title:

Reform in nineteenth-century China.

(Harvard East Asian monographs ; 72)
"Proceedings of a workshop held under the auspices of
the East Asian Research Center at Harvard University July
7–18, 1975."
Includes index.
1. China—Congresses. I. Cohen, Paul A.
II. Schrecker, John E. III. Harvard University. East
Asian Research Center. IV. Series.
DS702.R43   951'.03   76-16116
ISBN 0-674-75281-3

CONTENTS

PREFACE

This book embodies the proceedings of a workshop held under the auspices of the East Asian Research Center of Harvard University July 7–18, 1975. It differs from the usual academic publication in a number of ways, and it is important, for the sake of both the reader and the contributors, that these differences be spelled out. Before doing this, however, a few words about the workshop itself are in order.

As distinguished from most scholarly conferences, which tend to be closed, this workshop was open to all individuals actively engaged in research in the field of nineteenth-century Chinese reform (with special reference to the period from 1850 to 1900). The fifty or so people who took part came from all over the United States, as well as from Canada, Australia, Taiwan, and France. Approximately two-thirds of them were advanced graduate students and younger scholars. To assist in meeting travel and basic living costs, modest stipends were furnished to all who applied. Without such financial assistance, attendance would have been impossible for many of the workshop members.

During the two weeks that the workshop was in progress, we met regularly in the mornings for three hours and irregularly for shorter periods in the afternoons. Each session was devoted to a particular aspect of reform in China. At the morning meetings an invited discussion coordinator started things off with a general survey, a new interpretative framework, or an in-depth treatment of some facet of the topic under consideration. After a coffee break, advanced graduate students or younger scholars presented twenty-minute papers on specific themes. The sessions concluded with an hour or so of questions and informal discussion.

Describing in this skeletal fashion the structure of the workshop gives little feel for the quality of the experience. To say that it was intellectually exhilarating is to state the obvious. Much less obvious was the effect it had in breaking down the walls of isolation with which scholars often tend to surround themselves. The chance to spend two unhurried weeks thrashing out issues that were of deep mutual concern, in a "friendly, informal, and zealous atmosphere" (to quote Marianne Bastid), was for most of us an unfamiliar experience and an extremely liberating one. A warm communal feeling developed, helped along by the equally warm summer weather with which we had to contend. The resulting esprit was not unlike that which prevails among strangers thrown together on a transoceanic voyage. The only difference was that there was nothing inadvertent about the composition of this group. One could in fact argue that the success of the workshop ultimately derived from the degree of shared interest that the participants brought to it.

It would be presumptuous to try to capture in a few words the intellectual content of a workshop in which there were over thirty presentations. Nevertheless, one idea came up so often in the course of our discussions that it can fairly be regarded as central. This was the notion that reform efforts, indeed the very impulse to reform, in nineteenth-century China were part of a longstanding reformist tradition which, in its origins, its style, and much of its actual content, owed little or nothing to the West. No one was prepared to argue that the West was unimportant or that it did not in time have a significant shaping effect on Chinese reform thought and activity. But there was a strong reaction against the facile picture of reform as a subcategory of Sino-Western relations and an equally strong sense of the need to redefine, in Chinese perspective, the entire reform process and, by extension, our overall view of nineteenth-century Chinese history.

As books go, the present volume is something of an oddity. Scholarly publications customarily aim at a certain level of polish and definitiveness. Conference volumes, in particular, tend to be highly selective with respect to the papers included. They also tend to take several years to appear in print, on the theory, presumably, that there is no need to make readily available the contents of a book written for posterity.

Our thought was that, in the case of a workshop characterized by informality and tentativeness, there was something to be said for a book which also was informal and tentative. There was a risk factor involved in this, of which we were well aware. It meant some relaxation of the degree of editorial "quality control" normally exercised. It also meant a willingness on the part of the contributors to publish papers which, in other circumstances, many of them would not have brought into print so soon or in the particular form in which they appear here. Nevertheless, there was wide agreement among the workshop participants that the very tentativeness of the papers in their existing form might constitute an advantage, transfusing into the published proceedings something of the raw excitement generated in the workshop proper and conveying to a wider reading audience the sense of problem—rather than solution—that all the participants shared. On this basis, we decided to move quickly into print. Some of the papers had to be shortened. All were edited for clarity and style. But none of the contributions was revised to the point of being fundamentally different from the original presentation.

Another way in which the present book differs from most is in its freeform design. There is considerable variation in the length and format of the contributions. Some of them are accompanied by profuse documentation; others are entirely undocumented. Although most of the presentations are reproduced in full, approximately one-fifth of them appear in summary form only, as do all of the discussions. Summarized presentations are clearly identified in order to avoid confusion.

A special cautionary note must be sounded with reference to the discussion summaries. Although the discussions were taped and the summaries were carefully checked for accuracy against the tapes, there was no real way to protect the workshop members from what they themselves had said in a spirit of spontaneous, freeranging give and take or from the distortions that any process of summarization will produce. It was not feasible to circulate the edited summaries among the participants for their approval; and we did not want to eliminate names, because this would have cloaked the discussions in anonymity and detracted from the book's liveliness and interest. With the prior consent of the participants, therefore, we elected to include the summaries in their present form and to rely on our readers' good judgment and indulgence in not holding the discussants to every last word uttered or opinion ventured.

A book that records an event owes its existence to the people who made the event possible. Foremost among these was Ezra F. Vogel, Director of the East Asian Research Center, who was unfailing in his encouragement and support from the beginning and who generously made the facilities of the Center available to the workshop. Nancy Deptula and Anna Laura Rosow, also of the Center, were extremely helpful in working out financial and other arrangements and in solving the day-to-day problems an enterprise of this sort inevitably generates. Patricia Sippel, an unflappable graduate student at Harvard, in her capacity as executive assistant took care of the multitude of tasks that had to be performed while the workshop was in progress. Robert Entenmann, also a Harvard graduate student, served most ably as rapporteur. In solving the multitude of special problems involved in turning a workshop into a book, we benefited enormously from the editorial talents of Olive Holmes of the East Asian Research Center Editorial Department. Finally, we want to thank the East Asian Research Center, the American Council of Learned Societies, and the Social Science Research Council for their generous funding of the workshop's operations.

P.A.C.
J.E.S.

March 1976
Cambridge, Massachusetts

OPENING REMARKS

John K. Fairbank
OPENING REMARKS*

"Reform" is an English-language concept which does not correspond to a single idea in Chinese. This workshop, then, deals with
a whole series of Chinese concepts, approaches, and attitudes. Their
sequence forms a sort of index to the process of change in late
nineteenth-century China leading up to the Revolution. Reform
can be seen in many guises, some apparently mutually exclusive or
contradictory.

We must always bear in mind that we are dealing with an
authoritarian framework. In a highly stratified society reform is a
ruling-class activity, backed by the prestige and prerogatives of the
ruling class. This authoritarianism was a product of China's dense
population and unified state, conditions that we find increasingly
on a world-wide scale, thus making the question of reform through
an authoritarian framework a very relevant one today.

The Confucian world view included fluctuation and the interaction of *yin* and *yang,* but did not include the concept of linear
change. Reform is therefore seen as a revival of the past. It requires
a considerable effort of imagination to reconstruct the mental
framework of the late-Ch'ing literatus, his faith in the power of
exhortation and example, and his assumptions about the classical
example of the sages embodied in the emperor, about the ruling
class of the *chün-tzu,* and about the people.

Finally there is the dichotomy between the self and the
empire. On one hand there is the focus on the cultivation of the
self, *hsiu-shen,* and on the other the focus on state and society,
p'ing t'ien-hsia. Both are activities of members of the ruling class.
One question worth examining is at what point do commoners get
into the process of cultivating the self and ordering the empire.

The statecraft tradition, the "making the system work"
approach, also comes into consideration. Tseng Kuo-fan, upon
whom Kwang-Ching Liu is now working, is an example. Tseng

*A summary.

believed in virtue acquired through learning; therefore he tried to select the talented and control them through personal moral bonds. Tseng subscribed to the *san-kang* religion, and was very intent on maintaining the three bonds. Yet his policies were unsuccessful. The Hunan Army turned into a shambles. He tried to revive the status of the literati, but ignored the people. On balance, his reforms failed. Tseng and his Confucian moralism did not achieve a good enough record in practice.

John E. Schrecker
OPENING REMARKS*

The purpose of the workshop is to advance our understanding of reform in nineteenth-century China. The basic organization of the workshop is to bring together "people of talent" in a casual, open-ended discussion, to compare different perspectives and viewpoints.

The point of history is to get the story straight. This is because history is so relevant we have to try to get it as accurate as possible. A basic way of getting an accurate story of the era that concerns us is by trying at every point to get a Chinese baseline on things. There are at least two ways in which the workshop might help do that.

One way is to clarify as much as possible how nineteenth-century reform relates to what came before, how it ties to the past. We recognize the great change that occurred in late nineteenth-century China, stimulated often by Western imperialism. We must concern ourselves, however, with change and continuity, which are by no means antithetical. We can discover patterns and models of both change and continuity from what came before: reform, barbarian pressures, rebellion, all of which are involved in the nineteenth century but not unique to it.

Concern with the rectification of names can help us consciously to avoid a Western baseline and aim at a historical perspective. We should be as accurate as possible in understanding and translating terms. Take, for example, the relationship between the *ch'ing-i* movement and the reform movement of 1898. Our tendency to see one as "conservative" and the other as "radical" has obscured historical reality as well as our understanding of the Chinese approach to reform. And what about the idea of reform, itself? In the nineteenth century people spoke about *chung-hsing* in the 1860s and *wei-hsin* in the 1890s. Is the difference important? What does the progression mean?

*A summary.

5

A second way of achieving an understanding of nineteenth-century China is to appreciate a variety of different methods and approaches, but then to try to reintegrate them into a coherent story. For this reason, the program of the workshop is designed to bring together various perspectives, including economics, intellectual history, and so forth. As we think about these several approaches we should keep the task of integration in our minds.

What we do here can be of general significance. For example, a knowledge of late Ch'ing is important to an understanding of what came later, including the People's Republic. The study of contemporary China suffers from a lack of historical sense, and the workshop may be able to contribute to lessening this problem.

TRADITIONS OF REFORM

James T. C. Liu
THE VARIETY OF POLITICAL REFORMS IN CHINESE
HISTORY: A SIMPLIFIED TYPOLOGY*

I propose to discuss a simplified typology that I think might
provide a baseline for the construction of a framework that would
be helpful in substantive research.

Throughout Chinese history, continuity generally prevailed
through convention, conservatism, and conformity. Many changes
did take place, however, sometimes through an evolutionary process
(rarely revolutionary), but perhaps more frequently through involu-
tion, to borrow a term from anthropology. Involutionary change
refers to the development of certain phenomena within a larger
cultural context that is not itself undergoing significant or basic
change.

I suggest, as a working hypothesis, that a change known as
political reform is neither revolutionary nor evolutionary (except
as a background dimension), but is involutionary in nature, a process of change wherein certain ideas are put into action aimed at
immediate improvement of the existing political system. There
were many types of reform in China, much more numerous than
the textbook examples usually given. Although "reform" is an
English word, it is used here in a generic sense detached from its
Western cultural connotations. It includes the following Chinese
concepts: *keng, keng-hua* (the *hua* being the *ka* in the Japanese
Taika Reform; *keng* as used in the slogan in contemporary China,
tzu-li keng-sheng); *kai, kai-shan, kai-liang, kai-chin, kai-ko, kai-tsao,*
and *tou-p'i-kai* in the People's Republic of China. A third set of
terms includes the character *pien: pien-fa, kai-pien.* Some terms
stressed innovation in order to avoid explicit criticism of the
previous system by using the word *hsin,* thereby emphasizing the
new features in the reform: *hsin-ting, wei-hsin* (as in the Meiji
Restoration, *Meiji Isshin*), *ko-hsin.* Similar to the use of *hsin* were

* A summary.

terms like *ch'uang,* "pioneering," or *chien,* "establishing." There
were also a number of weaker terms such as *cheng-chih,* "tighten-
ing up" (*cheng-tun* in colloquial Chinese), *li-ting,* "minutely regu-
lative."

Three broad types of reforms may be suggested. First is the
system-repairing or system-adjusting type. Second is the system-
founding or system-remodeling type. These reforms are generally
incorporated into the system during the founding or consolidation
of a new dynasty. The third type, which fits in between the first
two but is closer to the second, is that of system-reorienting
reforms. These reforms are undertaken at the national or court
level, but at a midpoint in the lifespan of the dynasty, revitalizing
and rejuvenating the system, and ushering in such a marked degree
of change as to be recognized as major reforms. Perhaps only the
third category can be strictly referred to as "reform." This typology
is also applicable to the acculturative changes that take place during
nomadic conquest dynasties. Often overlooked are such changes as
the equitable land system of the Northern Wei and the regional
conscripted armies of the Northern Chou, both adopted by the
T'ang later on.

As for the first type, one finds in Chinese history an infinite
number of system-repairing, or what might also be called "metamorphic" reforms. These were limited in scope to a particular
office, institution, branch of government, or locality. Few of them
earned a major place in dynastic histories, which traditionally were
biased toward court politics. Some information nevertheless can be
found in encyclopedias, collectania, local gazetteers, private works,
and informal notes. Illustrative of this kind of reform at the local
level were relief acts and contributions to social welfare. Many
officials, for example, went beyond the call of duty in establishing
orphanages, homes for old people, and charitable cemeteries, and
in distributing medicine during epidemics. Other examples abound,
ranging from Yellow River flood control to control of clerical staff.
These metamorphic reforms were small in scale or brief in time
span but great in number. The impetus for them stemmed from
the tension between statecraft ideals and political reality.

System-founding reforms were incorporated into a viable system during the founding and consolidation of a new dynasty. Some of these reforms were innovative; others came as a result of a long evolutionary background and were an extension of earlier trends. Some endured beyond a particular dynasty and became irreversible changes, while others quickly became subject to abuses or elimination.

A great deal depended on the founding emperor, his background, personality, and skill. One example is the Sung founder, Chao K'uang-yin, a militarist and usurper, not a Confucianist at all, whose pensioning off of his generals contributed to de-emphasis of the military and expansion of a civil-service system which, as refined by his successors, paved the way for an increasing centralization and bureaucratization of the state. The Ming founder, Chu Yuan-chang, was a restless innovator who drew upon his Buddhist and peasant background as well as the Mongol precedent. Although he honored Confucianism, he scarcely paid even lip service to Confucian scholars. He left behind "ancestral instructions," which became more binding on Ming government than Confucian principles.

Finally, there is the system-reorienting type of reform, highlighted in all textbooks. There seem to have been only three clear cases of system-reorienting reforms, along with a few marginal ones. The first example is Ch'in, which changed itself from a kingdom to the first unified empire and established the model for subsequent unified dynasties. The second example is the Former Han, starting just before Emperor Wu and resulting largely from the efforts of men like Chia I and Tung Chung-shu. This reform entailed the expulsion from the court of the so-called Hundred Schools and the promotion of the Six Classics. Prior to it the Han had been a Legalistic empire modified by Taoism and Confucianism. Through the reform the empire became Confucianized. Erudites and disciples were appointed to the civil-service training schools. Much stress was placed on the education of princes, especially the heir apparent. The twin hallmarks of the reform were *fu-ku keng-hua* (restoring the ancient system through transformation) and forbidding officials to engage simultaneously in private trade.

The Hsin dynasty of Wang Mang may be characterized as a borderline case of system-founding reform, and the T'ang system of twice-a-year tax, a borderline case of system-adjusting reform. It seems that there were no further system-reorienting reforms of great magnitude until the Northern Sung, the third example.

The recent campaign to criticize Confucius and Lin Piao has once again brought attention to Wang An-shih. Wang boldly declared that "the heavenly portents are not sufficient cause for alarm" (contradicting Tung Chung-shu), that "the imperial ancestors are not sufficient basis for emulation," and that "criticism by other people is not sufficient cause for reconsideration."

After Wang An-shih's reforms and the ensuing factional strife, we find in late Southern Sung the appearance of a rigid orthodoxy. The *Tzu-chih t'ung-chien* was reduced by Chu Hsi to a doctrinaire outline, the *T'ung-chien kang-mu.* The growth of commerce and urbanization through Yuan and Ming into the Ch'ing led to an increased capacity for society to educate people in overall popular Confucian norms together with an admixture of other values. While philosophical Confucianism developed toward the metaphysics of Wang Yang-ming, the interest in statecraft waned. Yet the latter was never entirely eclipsed. By late Ming times a basic frustration was felt by many leading intellectuals who saw through the limitations of both conventional Confucianism and the idealism of Wang Yang-ming.

Under these complex circumstances, the case of Chang Chücheng in the late sixteenth century may qualify as bordering upon system-reorienting reform. Certainly, this man and his time deserve much more attention. Chang was in reality no less than a regent. He introduced many reforms without calling them such, preferring to characterize them as actions "to restore methods according to ancestral instructions."

A few generalizations may be ventured in conclusion. First of all, ruling elites in Chinese history usually welcomed system-repairing reforms, but not the other types we have noted.

Secondly, these elites, because of their intellectual and familial vested interests, as well as bureaucratic inertia, by and large failed to arrive at a consensus in support of system-reorienting reforms. Furthermore, scholar-officials were dispersed and unorganized—a handicap which the Fu-she societies of the late Ming attempted unsuccessfully to overcome. In the upshot, officials were often reduced to factional strife and personal attacks, making statecraft improvement virtually impossible.

Finally, the difficulty in carrying out system-reorienting reforms increased as time went on. In earlier periods reformers had fewer traditions to change. From the Sung on, Chinese society became much more complex, not only in landholding and rural control, but also in the development of urban classes, absentee landlordism, and population growth. Confucianism became a tired, worn-out body of thought, inadequate for the task of dealing with the interrelated multitude of political, economic, and social problems. Although the reform spirit did emerge for the last time in the late nineteenth century, it could not succeed by itself. The new age called for entirely different departures.

Hoyt Tillman
COMMENT

Mr. Liu has presented a brilliant classification of reforms, but I would like to suggest another major factor in the opposition to system-reorienting reforms. A systemic reform, like Wang An-shih's or Chang Chü-cheng's, could contain major dysfunctional elements which exacerbated fundamental problems. Because such reforms were sweeping and broad, the wake of administrative dislocation could be overwhelming. Scholars during the Southern Sung, for example, were particularly troubled by the administrative centralization and intellectual uniformity augmented by Wang's reform program. Administrative centralization weakened local administration and encumbered the central court. Even scholars, like Ch'en Liang and Yeh Shih, dedicated to utilitarianism and statecraft, voiced such criticism of Wang's reforms. Others, like Chu Hsi, although critical of the ideological orientation of Wang's reforms, also based their opposition on the dysfunctional effects of the reforms. John Watt's *The District Magistrate in Late Imperial China* points to similar major administrative and social dislocations caused by the Single Whip Reform in the Ming. An awareness of the high potential for dysfunction in systemic reforms encouraged later reformers to focus on repairing and adjusting particular parts of the system. As Brian McKnight's *Village and Bureaucracy in Southern Sung China* has demonstrated, this more piecemeal approach to reform could encompass considerable latitude for local initiative and adjustment in administrative development.

The opposition to systemic reform perhaps possessed some integrity beyond mere ideological conservatism, bureaucratic or social inertia, and financial or class interests. People with different ideological standpoints articulated similar administrative and functional critiques of systemic reforms or of a particular systemic reform. Our twentieth-century perspective gives us a natural appreciation of advocates of fundamental change in the traditional Chinese system. Nevertheless, we need a broader intellectual perspective

14

and a more comprehensive survey of traditional views in order to evaluate historically the reforms as well as the opponents to systemic reformers. Did a given systemic reform program, or even all five such reforms listed by Mr. Liu, contain dysfunctional elements that either negated or restricted the positive effect of the program? Given the limitations of power, resources, and means imposed upon a large, premodern empire, were systemic reforms inherently more dysfunctional to involutionary progress than other kinds of reforms? Answers to these questions are crucial to our evaluation of a reform program and of the bias against systemic reforms in imperial China.

DISCUSSION

Joanna Handlin elaborated on Mr. Liu's suggestion that Chang Chü-cheng's views seemed to be an outgrowth of ideals that were already current before he came to power and continued to be current after him. A principal reason for the continuity of these ideas lay in the spread of literacy to commoners, which in turn encouraged scholars to reach a commoner audience. After this period, Chinese scholars never lost their self-consciousness as to the nature of Confucian ideology. Mr. Liu agreed, adding that in this self-consciousness the tension between Confucian ideals and political realities persisted.

Esther Morrison asked how close the third type of reform—the system-reorienting type—was to revolution. Mr. Liu replied that revolution required the assault of a force from outside the established system. What reformers hoped for was a new arrangement within the broad confines of the traditional state—an involutionary rather than a revolutionary form of change.

Thomas Kennedy said that he found it hard to accept the rigid line between system-reorienting and system-repairing reforms. The system-repairing reforms of the early nineteenth century fed into the system-reorienting reforms of the mid-nineteenth century. Mr. Liu explained that his typology was a highly simplified baseline. Refinement was necessary to turn it into an analytical framework for research. Moreover, historical reality was a spectrum or continuum or stream, along which whatever types one might perceive were not to be taken as mutually exclusive categories. A typology such as the one suggested simply helped to highlight certain clusters.

James Polachek questioned Mr. Liu's generalization that autocracy favored piecemeal reforms and opposed system-reorienting ones. This generalization did not seem to apply in the case of the new policies of Wang An-shih, which were supported by the emperor. Mr. Liu replied that individual emperors were cases, whereas autocracy referred to the institution as a whole. This was the case of an exceptional emperor who by accident grew up outside the palace and continued his commitment to reform after Wang An-shih's

16

retirement. The individual cases of founding emperors also varied. Hao Chang pointed out that Mr. Liu had emphasized vested interest as a factor inhibiting reorienting reforms after the Sung period. What about the factor of neo-Confucian moralism in the personalities of members of the ruling elite—the great emphasis in particular on self-cultivation—which presumed that society could be transformed by moral force? Certainly this, too, had an inhibitory effect on institutional reform.

Joanna F. Handlin
DEFINITIONS OF COMMUNITY BY CH'I CHI-KUANG AND
LÜ K'UN

In 1827 the Tao-kuang Emperor accorded Lü K'un (1536–
1618), alone of all the scholars of the notorious late Ming, a place
in the Confucian Temple.[1] He did so because Ch'ing officials had
praised Lü as their forerunner and had admired him for having
stressed "practical government" (*shih-cheng*) and "practical learning" (*shih-hsueh*).[2] In the late nineteenth century, K'ang Yu-wei,
whose concept of "Great Unity" echoed Lü's effort to promote
feelings of "sameness" (*t'ung*), recorded in his autobiography that
his great-grandfather had followed Lü K'un's teachings.[3] Lü K'un,
who was by no means a seminal thinker, was only one of many
sixteenth-century writers who inspired nineteenth-century officials.
Equally important was the famous general Ch'i Chi-kuang (1528–
1597) who fascinated Tseng Kuo-fan and Li Hung-chang.[4]

Similarities between sixteenth- and nineteenth-century
thought were neither accidental nor haphazard. Scholar-officials
of both periods, after all, had much in common: having lost confidence in the hegemony of spiritual Confucian values, they sought
practical solutions to social problems.

The similarities between the conditions of the two periods
hardly call for an explanation. The breakdown of bureaucratic
efficiency, the incursions of the Japanese pirates, and the formation of ominous White Lotus sects alone can explain why so many
Ming officials harshly criticized the abstract philosophizing of the
private academies and turned in alarm to practical matters. That
internal rebellions and external threats made social reform urgent
during the Ch'ing needs no elaboration for this audience.

Intellectually, too, the preoccupation in both periods with
statecraft can be interpreted as nothing more than a swing of the
pendulum from self-cultivation to service to society, polar concerns
that occupied equally proper places in Confucianism.

But both the simple itemization of the conditions prompting

18

the reforms and the dismissal of practical learning as a mere shift of emphasis within an unchanging tradition obscure the precise patterns that marked the reforms. Indeed the writings of Lü K'un and Ch'i Chi-kuang suggest that practical learning involved a shift of focus, not from self to society, but from abstract principles to concrete affairs in both self-cultivation and social action. Lü K'un's concentration on concrete affairs, even when thinking about himself, is suggestive of why both men designed reforms that simultaneously promoted social unity and maximized individual self-reliance.

The shift of focus to concrete events took place during a period of intense social and intellectual alienation. The lively urban centers—where sumptuary regulations lost respect as social mobility increased and where bookstores displayed pernicious pornographic fiction alongside the revered classics—contributed to Lü's malaise. But more important, the numerous petty philosophical disputations during the sixteenth century had destroyed Lü's confidence in the cultural and moral leadership of his peers. Therefore while others gained, from their membership in the private academies, the strength to affirm Confucian values, Lü, who had grown cynical about scholarly groups and their abstract values, remained confused. He felt that "the myriad things of heaven and earth were disconnected, purposeless, and unrelated to the self."[5] Worse, without the support of either a social group or abstract principles, he could not transcend specific experiences and found himself repeatedly "mired in what is before one's eyes" (*niu yü mu-ch'ien*).[6] As fleeting and disconnected images whizzed by, Lü complained that any change of scene—whether from a familiar village to a large city, or from contemporary faces to the recorded events of past centuries—easily threw him off balance.[7] Unstable and vulnerable, Lü confessed that he feared confusion more than anything else. He explained: "If I enter the mountains with their multitudinous scenes I can wander about, [but] if I want to go somewhere, then I must not wander aimlessly. If I enter the valleys with their many flowers, I can survey them all, but if I want to break one off, then I must not let my eyes get dazed."[8]

Thus aimless and dazed, Lü struggled both to assert control over the myriad disconnected images and to restore a sense of social cohesion. For thirty years he kept track of his confusing surroundings in a diary. The very title of the diary, *Shen-yin yü* (Groaning words), aptly conveys Lü's angst, but, more important, the contents reveal that Lü's thoughts persistently revolved around concrete affairs. Unable to construct a philosophical system applicable to all incidents, Lü simply checked off, day after day, numberless unrelated events.[9]

Although Lü recognized that the multitude of choices generated his malaise, he had come to value his perceptions of concrete data as points of reference which the uneducated and educated alike could understand. Aware that his society was rapidly growing individuated and competitive, and concerned that the commoners were then restlessly participating in rebellions or simply clamoring for light reading matter to fill their leisure time, Lü accommodated the commoners by expressing his views in concrete terms that related to everyday life. To reunite his society, he tried to share actual experiences with the ignorant rather than persuade them to conform to abstract Confucian values. Concrete experiences had replaced humaneness (*jen*) as the bond among men. Even moral deficiencies were appreciated as concrete ailments, experiences shared by all, rather than condemned as deviations from abstract standards. Accordingly, many of Lü's contemporaries maintained that all men were sick; and one of Lü's seventeenth-century admirers, Lu Lung-ch'i (1630–1693), claimed that sages had won distinction not for their health but for their ability to understand and describe their ailments.[10]

Lü was so committed to his perceptions of everyday life that he defined what was important among the confusing array of choices by applying not abstract principles, but tests, or "critical situations" (*kuan-t'ou*) such as illnesses and battles. In fact, he often conjured up imaginary crises to determine what the scholar should value most. He argued: "When you rush to the city gate at sundown, you will be locked out if you are one step late. Where will you stay the night? Therefore scholars value being on time.

When hanging from a precipice, clinging to a lonely tree, you will fall if you let one hand go. Where will you fall? Therefore scholars value exertion of strength."[11]

To jolt himself out of his state of numbness, Lü struggled to keep alive a sense of urgency in times of leisure. Apprehensive that paralysis might set in, he frequently used the metaphor of bandits to connote unsuspected dangers. It is in this spirit of fearful alertness that Lü compiled a self-disciplinary record of errors. He explained: "Just as bandits attack men by taking them by surprise and enemy states make surprise raids by taking advantage of one's failure to be prepared, so do wrongs attack people by taking advantage of their ignorance. If the mind is always on the alert, sometimes edgy, sometimes fearful, then how can faults emerge?"[12]

A number of similar passages Lü wrote in his youth reveal the pattern for his actions during his mature years. In 1609, after retiring from office, Lü designed a plan for fortifying the wall of his home town. He argued that the project was necessary because the "true militia" (*chen ping*) had disintegrated, bandits threatened the area, and frequent floods made necessary the safe storage of grain within the city walls. Still fresh in his mind, furthermore, was the devastating famine of 1595, which could have been alleviated had the officials not extravagantly distributed the grain just the previous year among the people.[13]

In the light of later events, Lü's manual appears to be an obvious response to the challenges of his time. Indeed, shortly after his death, bandits did attack the district, causing its inhabitants to marvel at Lü's foresight. Yet in 1609 many had fiercely opposed Lü's plan and had belligerently asked, "Why bother with building walls in times of peace?"[14] It is not surprising, then, that accounts of the local politics, too detailed to analyze here, indicate that the actual incentive for Lü's project was a growing tension between town and country. By promising the commoners who lived outside the walls protection within the gates in exchange for their labor, Lü tried to keep united a rapidly disintegrating community.[15]

In other ways, too, Lü designed large projects to reduce social differences while maximizing self-reliance. Departing, for example, from the traditional forms of charity, Lü urged the wealthy to contribute to community-run schools in music and story-telling for the handicapped. The wealthy, Lü argued, would prevent costly crises and save much expense over the long run if they fostered the self-reliance of the poor.[16] By conjuring up specters of future disasters, Lü persuaded others to abandon their immediate interests; by advocating solutions that would, in some indeterminate future, benefit rich and poor alike, Lü won support for social change. He achieved his goals not through moral instruction, but by appealing to the self-interest of all. Significantly his projects reflect a vision of a society that was cooperative and thoroughly unified but one that consisted of self-reliant and self-centered people.

A reading of Ch'i Chi-kuang's military handbooks in the context of sixteenth-century attitudes suggests that nineteenth-century scholar-officials found Ch'i fascinating not primarily for concepts of loyalty and personal ties—as Western historians have often maintained—but for his innovative methods of mobilizing commoners with conflicting self-interests for collective enterprises.[17] Perceiving how atomized society had become and that "men's minds are as different as their faces,"[18] Ch'i repeatedly pondered, "How can I make them have one mind?"[19] To unify the commoners, Ch'i, foreshadowing Lü K'un, tried to communicate directly with the people. He compiled handbooks which, he instructed, were to be read aloud to each platoon and memorized by the troops; and he purposely wrote in a simple, often vernacular style.[20] More important, he spoke in concrete terms that all shortsighted, self-centered men could understand. Ch'i maintained, for example, that banners should not be labeled "north, south, east and west"— terms that would only confuse the ignorant—but should be labeled "left, right, forward, and back" so that all could identify the directions with "their own bodies."[21] Similarly he argued that military skills should be mastered to preserve the self rather than out of public-mindedness.[22]

Both Ch'i and Lü acknowledged that men were inevitably disconnected and could relate to one another only in reference to

external objects. Accordingly Ch'i's explanation of the meaning of
"regulations" (*chieh-chih*)—a compound which includes the character for "segment" (*chieh*)—reflects his view of collective action
performed by people who were separate but alike. Ch'i compared
regulations to bamboo, which, although hollow, can extend into a
strong, straight shoot because it has segments, or regulated spacing.
Drawing an analogy with the bamboo, Ch'i noted that regulations
can guide countless soldiers to fight as though they were one man.[23]
Similarly he elsewhere compared regulations to the rope men used
to coordinate their strength for pulling large stones or trees.
External objects had replaced humaneness as the common bond.[24]

In their desire to achieve strength by eliminating distinctions,
both Lü and Ch'i envisioned diffusing practical information and
responsibilities, or tasks, among the commoners.[25] Borrowing,
perhaps, the metaphor of the segmented bamboo, which gains
strength as it grows, Lü and Ch'i—long before T'ao Hsing-chih
(1892–1946) in the twentieth century—taught commoners to teach
commoners.[26] Ch'i even maintained that, after learning the bamboo-
like regulations, the people would be able to "fight of their own
accord" (*jen tzu wei chan*).[27] More important, in the interests of
uniformity, Ch'i was prepared to reject those with unusual talents.
He valued regulations because they insured that "the strong will
not advance alone and the weak will not retreat alone."[28] And he
instructed his recruiters to favor naive country bumpkins over
clever masters of military skills.[29]

A critical essay published in 1782 on Ch'i's *Chi-hsiao hsin shu*
(New manual of effectiveness) observed that men during the Ming
dynasty were cooperative only "if the self were in the center of
the affair," and that self-centeredness accounted for Ch'i's habit of
explaining in such detail just how the rank and file would profit
by cooperating.[30] Such comments demonstrate that if some during
the Ch'ing condemned Ch'i's self-centeredness, they at least understood that his major contribution was an expression of new ways
of mobilizing the commoners for action.

Both Ch'i and Lü claimed that their views were new. Ch'i
immodestly advertised that he supplied important details neglected

by Sun Tzu;[31] that he had rediscovered the secret, lost for a thousand years, of carefully instructing the troops;[32] and that he labeled one handbook "new" to indicate his freedom from methodology.[33] Lü K'un, long before K'ang Yu-wei interpreted Confucius as a reformer, maintained that if past sages were to be resurrected in his own time, they would interpret the classics variously.[34] Thus free from ideological commitment, both Lü and Ch'i were consciously innovative.

But I do not want to belabor the point, now so widely accepted, that many officials who were considered proper Confucian scholars interpreted the classics flexibly to support institutional change. Far more interesting, for the questions it raises, is the shift of focus from abstract principles to concrete events. During the Ming this shift reflected not only intellectual alienation but also an accommodation of the commoners. Were the nineteenth-century reformers, then, drawing on a strain of Confucianism which, although most pronounced during the late Ming, had in fact remained alive during the early Ch'ing among those who, alarmed by the endemic White Lotus rebellions or the rapidly growing population, were responsive to the commoners? How else might one explain why so many ideas that found acceptance in China during the nineteenth century fit into patterns that Lü K'un and his contemporaries worked out in response to the commoners? In addition to the pragmatism and the new forms of collective projects stressed above, these included: the use of the vernacular language, forms of popular consensus, and the comparability of men and women.[35] Is it indeed possible that the late Ming experience of eliminating barriers between an educated elite and commoners facilitated the appropriation of Western ideas in the nineteenth century?

Thus Ming writings, untainted by Western influence, suggest that the pressure of commoners contributed to nineteenth-century Chinese thought. In addition, the innovativeness of pre-Ch'ing scholars warns us to abandon assumptions about the inflexibility of Confucianism and engage in closer scrutiny of Chinese perceptions. In particular, both the simultaneous emphasis on self-reliance and cooperation and the vision of achieving strength by diffusing responsibilities among the commoners not only demonstrate the responsiveness of premodern Chinese to social change but bear significantly on contemporary Chinese thought.

Judith Whitbeck
THREE IMAGES OF THE CULTURAL HERO IN THE THOUGHT OF KUNG TZU-CHEN*

Kung Tzu-chen (1792–1841) is now hailed as a forerunner of China's modern age, a herald of imminent chaos and an outspoken advocate of radical institutional reforms; he is also remembered as an apostle of long-ignored learning: the teachings of Mo-tzu, the Legalists, and the Kung-yang commentary on the *Spring and Autumn Annals.* I propose to reconstruct aspects of Kung's thinking through an examination of three images of the cultural hero articulated in his early writings (ca. 1814 to ca. 1825): the system-founder, the historically minded critic, and the chronicler-historian.

The most honored and crucial role described by Kung was that of one who provided for the welfare of the people by bringing order to the age through equalization (*p'ing-chün*). "Of those who have had *t'ien-hsia,* none are more esteemed than those who have equalized it."** Kung credits Yao and Shun alone with this achievement. The order they established gave way to one in which people had unequal allotments of wealth. This inequality persisted through Chinese history; the work of Yao and Shun was neither repeated nor continued. After them the best system-founders were only able to bring peace to all under heaven. Of the peacemakers, Kung had the highest regard for the Duke of Chou.

Chou culture was the cornerstone of all later Chinese culture. Records remain testifying to the Chou system. The Six Classics, according to Kung, were merely the records kept by the recording officials or chroniclers. These records reveal the *tao* as put into

---

*A summary.

**Kung Tzu-chen, *Kung Tzu-chen ch'üan-chi* (The collected works of Kung Tzu-chen), ed. Wang P'ei-cheng (Hong Kong, 1974), I, 78. Wang An-shih, whose ideas Kung admired, referred to *chün-p'ing* as "the essence of *ching-t'ien*" (equal fields). See Joseph Levenson, "Ill Wind in the Well-Field," in Arthur Wright, ed., *The Confucian Persuasion* (Stanford University Press, 1960), p. 273.

practice, a concrete rather than an abstract *tao*. Outstanding
scholars were selected to discuss and interpret the regulatory laws
of the dynasty and to convey their understanding to the emperor
and the people. An important aspect of the early Chou system was
the routinization of criticism of the emperor's policies. The office
of Grand Historian was established to make periodic reports on the
condition of *t'ien-hsia*. If natural calamities occurred the emperor
would seek to remedy the situation.

In Kung's early writings the belief is expressed that no sociopolitical system has ever arisen without transformative change.
The state cannot flourish without flexibility, open-mindedness and
criticism. After a dynasty has been founded and prosperity has
been achieved, the emperor and ministers must become even more
diligent in order to sustain order. But prosperity and order bring
the threat of ossification, hedonism among the officials, and neglect of matters of state. When deterioration goes too far, not even
a sage can retrieve the situation. Knowing this, the sage not only
allows criticism but encourages it, and integrates it into the system
of government.

Kung's immediate goal was not the establishment of a new
dynasty, but extensive reform of the Ch'ing. If the system-founder
is the hero of the age of order, the apostle of open criticism is the
hero of an age of decline. The concern of the ideal critic extends
to the whole of *t'ien-hsia*—its geography, the conditions of the land
and land use, the feelings and mores of the people, the pattern of
ethical conduct, the order established by the dynastic reformer,
judicial cases, military matters, and the state of government administration. He understands the principles of the past as revealed in the
classics, literature, and historical episodes. Kung's critic, in short, is
an informed cultural historian who focuses on the contemporary
setting.

The role of the historically informed critic became the core of
Kung's identity in young adulthood. In this period he sought to
illuminate how the current situation had come about and to clarify
the implications that contemporary conditions held for the future.
In four treatises collectively entitled *Clarifying Goodness* (*Ming-*

liang lun), which he wrote in 1814, Kung indicated what he thought to be the roots of contemporary problems. These roots were to be found in the bureaucracy and the relationship between the emperor and his officials. Kung believed that rigid adherence to the seniority principle in the promotion system stifled incentive and deprived the administration of young, talented, and enthusiastic leaders. The fear of reprisals led to adherence to conventional methods and outright neglect of serious problems. Government unwillingness to take bold action undermined the people's respect for official authority and inclined them toward recalcitrance and even rebellion. The lack of adequate emolument led officials to corruption, in turn bringing about the moral and financial impoverishment of the bureaucracy. Sycophancy led to loss of integrity on the part of officials toward the emperor.

The scholar who ignored the political and social problems of the age and concerned himself merely with textual exegesis was equally responsible for social and political decline. Scholars who ignored practical problems denied the government much-needed talent. Kung later added that by remaining parochially attached to the culture of their own dynasty, they contributed to the loss both of that culture and the culture of the past.

To what extent and to what purpose should one be engaged in the study of the past? By 1825 these questions seemed to be nearing resolution in Kung's mind. In his *Investigations into History and Antiquity* (*Ku-shih kou-ch'en lun*) Kung passed judgment on the achievements of the Chou chroniclers and the work of Confucius in preserving their records. In the process he delineated the third type of culture-hero—the chronicler-historian. Chang Hsueh-ch'eng's distinction between record-keeping and historical writing is explicit in Kung's thought, though less clearly drawn. Chang was concerned with the art of historical writing; Kung was primarily concerned with insights that could be gained from the historical past and applied to the present.

The shift from Chang's emphasis is significant. Kung sees the past more as a reservoir of useful experience, to be drawn upon for the purpose of evaluating one's own age and improving it. The historian-chronicler provides the ground for the historically minded critic and reformer. One can utilize the past only to the extent that the historian-chronicler has done his job.

The problem with later periods, in Kung's view, was that nobody rose to the task of historian-chronicler. At the end of the early Chou period, the records of the Chou were already incomplete and inaccurate. Confucius, fearing that the experience of his own age would be lost to future ages, journeyed with Tso Ch'iu-ming to the state of Lu where, utilizing the Lu archives, he compiled the *Spring and Autumn Annals.* However, much of Confucius' work was in vain. After a hundred years of oral transmission of his teachings, several versions of the Six Classics emerged. When the classics were carved into wood during the Han period, not only were half of the original graphics replaced by loan characters, but the more simple script of the Han was employed as well. The final product must have been far removed from the work of Confucius.

Kung believed that the ages of Yao and Shun and the Three Dynasties represented the pinnacle of experience and that the failure to transmit a complete and systematic record of their system of government was the ultimate tragedy. What conclusions did Kung draw from this tragedy? On the one hand, it justified a turning away from an exclusive concern with classical scholarship, since the classics themselves were adulterated. On the other hand, the fragmented classical legacy justified turning to alternate sources for clues as to how present institutions might be changed. One such source was the Hundred Schools of the late Chou, embracing Mo-tzu, Han Fei, Kao-tzu, Chuang-tzu, and others. Kung granted these philosophers a legitimate place in his intellectual pantheon. To Kung the Five Classics represented the main line from the early Chou chroniclers and the Hundred Schools the cadet branch. Whereas the former had lost most of their original content, the latter retained their original integrity as texts. Thus, Kung believed one should rely more on the Hundred Schools as a source for contemporary policy making. Other sources were economic geography and direct observation of social and administrative conditions throughout the realm.

Kung came to see himself in all three of his idealized roles—
as chronicler of contemporary conditions, historically minded critic,
and system-founder in the midst of a dynasty. In setting forth his
reforms, he, like Wei Yuan and other statecraft reformers of his
time, remained committed to the survival of the Ch'ing dynasty.
According to Kung, the passing of dynasties resulted from their
failure to carry out basic institutional changes when the need arose.
He believed that one should follow the dictum of the *Book of
Changes:* "When one is obstructed, one must change. When one
changes, one can proceed freely. When one proceeds freely, one
can endure long."

DISCUSSION

John Schrecker mentioned that the late Ch'ing reformers saw Ch'i Chi-kuang and Lü K'un as people who tried to combine a sense of community with reform; he asked about the immediate political views of Lü K'un. Joanna Handlin replied that Lü did not generally approve of academies and factions, although he respected the Tung-lin Academy. Lü felt a sense of distance, detachment, and intellectual isolation from people who joined the academies. Although he believed that most men were only average, he felt that political responsibility should be diffused downward to check abuses. Mr. Schrecker pointed out that in this respect Lü seemed more advanced than K'ang Yu-wei, who often talked about the gentry, but rarely mentioned the people. Did the late Ming go beyond the late Ch'ing in some ways? Whom did Lü mean when he talked about commoners? Ms. Handlin replied that Lü included among commoners virtually all people with some degree of education and economic self-reliance. Judith Whitbeck added that a strong belief existed in the late Ming that every man could become a sage. This belief was very different from those of K'ang or Kung Tzu-chen who felt that whatever might have been the case originally, it was no longer so.

John Schrecker brought up the question of Kung's belief that one could not use the past with confidence. If one could not use history, could one use religion or myth, such as Buddhism or the mythology of the Modern Text (*chin-wen*) school? Could religion have bolstered the sense of egalitarianism? Ms. Whitbeck replied that Kung was not really a *chin-wen* thinker; nor did he have, for example, K'ang's idea of Confucianism as a religion. Kung turned to people like Mo-tzu for alternatives, and he was attracted to the nonreligious side of Mo-tzu.

James Liu mentioned the problem of rapidly changing circumstances, especially from the late Ming on. One individual, such as Lü K'un, could live through very different circumstances. Thus there is unevenness in the thought of one individual, and it

31

is hard to make generalizations that fit the entirety of a person's thought.

I-fan Ch'eng pointed out the very different intellectual climates that prevailed at different times. We must be wary of saying that some traditions were "Chinese" and others were not. Ming and Ch'ing traditions were different. In Ming times there was a tendency toward egalitarianism. Wang Yang-ming and his school encouraged a shift toward greater freeness, self-expression, and individualism, especially in urban centers. Innate goodness and self-interest were considered complementary. The position of commoners was relatively high. A Shansi merchant could tell his sons that all four occupations—scholar, peasant, artisan, merchant— were legitimate. In Ch'ing times intellectual currents were more dominated by the scholar class, and the liberalness of the Wang Yang-ming school was lost.

Hao Chang wondered whether there was any relationship between Lü K'un and the left wing of the Wang Yang-ming school, given their shared tendency to assign a more important role to commoners and to hold self-interest in greater esteem. Ms. Handlin doubted that Lü, whom she described as a mainstream Confucianist, owed a direct intellectual debt to Wang or Li Chih; he did, however, share some of their ideas.

James Polachek said that although Kung Tzu-chen saw himself as a social chronicler and critic, the first quatrain of his essays in 1814 related to government issues. Mr. Polachek wondered whether Kung was really dealing with a vision of society beyond government, whether he had any firm idea of societal problems. Hao Chang suggested that Kung did have a conception of society beyond government. However, he saw reform within an administrative framework, and was concerned with trying to readjust the social order through administrative reform. Ms. Whitbeck said that Kung saw the bureaucratic system as in some respects crushing society, and thus it was necessary to change the bureaucratic framework.

Young-tsu Wong suggested that Kung was not really revolutionary in promoting greater equalization of wealth. His aim was not to achieve social equality, but to maintain social stability.

ECONOMIC ASPECTS OF REFORM

Albert Feuerwerker
ECONOMIC ASPECTS OF REFORM*

The Prospects for Cliometrics
   I shall begin by assessing the prospects for "cliometric" study
of the economic history of late Ch'ing China. Counterfactual, "as
if" models do not appear to be of much value in such an undertaking. They are inadequate for distinguishing between necessary
causes and sufficient causes. No particular single cause is necessary;
for any one such cause can in theory be compensated for by
changes in the system as a whole. To produce an adequate historical description, we must therefore look for a sufficiency of causes,
probably through a combination of neoclassical economic theory
and cliometric data. However, we should be aware of the limitations of cliometric research; the usefulness of numerical analysis
should not be exaggerated.
   What are the prospects for doing this kind of research in late
Ch'ing economic history? One major problem is collecting the kind
of data we have for Western history; archival materials, probates of
estates, household and firm records, parish records of birth, marriage, and death are inaccessible or nonexistent. Some quantitative
work has been done on late Ch'ing economic history (for example
by Dwight Perkins and Yūji Muramatsu), and in one or two works
from the People's Republic of China (such as the research by Ching
Su on managing landlords) one can find data which can be used in
quantitative research. Very little of this kind of writing has been
done on the handicraft industries. We have collections of trade
statistics and likin data. Population data have been exploited by
Ping-ti Ho and Dwight Perkins, and Yeh-chien Wang has done a
great deal of work on quantitative data on land taxation.
   The great problem is the assembly of data, much of which
still remains buried. The recent publication of palace archives in
Taiwan seems to indicate that there were a number of memorials

*A summary.

which included detailed information on prices, crop yields, and
the like from the provinces. Local histories have been considered a
potential major source. Although they are often disappointing in
terms of economic history, Perkins was able to gather much of his
information on pre-1900 crop yields from local histories, and also
found detailed data on water-control projects.

Documentary collections published in the People's Republic
of China in the 1950s and 1960s present mostly qualitative data;
the quantitative data is very selective. Nevertheless, index numbers
published in China perhaps suggest that some holdings of materials
with quantitative information are available there.

The main implication of the existing and available resources
is that in the study of Chinese economic history, the time for
cleometrics has not yet arrived.

Economic Aspects of Self-Strengthening

In a recent article in *Ch'ing-shih wen-t'i* Thomas Kennedy
asked whether it is true that Confucian conservatism undermined
economic reform in the late Ch'ing. It is probably not true that
values are the primary obstacles to economic reform. It is not even
clear precisely how values affect policies. A particular set of basic
values might justify more than one kind of institutional structure.
However, that structure, once set up and justified by a widely
accepted ideology, is hard to upset without a sharp historical
experience.

Possibly one should look at the specific structure of the traditional economy and ask whether that structure tended to neu-
tralize the surplus product by channeling it into nonproductive
uses. The place to look might well be the structure rather than
values. When we do look at values, moreover, we should consider
the ways in which they may have served not only as positive
obstacles to growth, but also as negative obstacles. An example of
the latter may be the absence of a strong enough political system
and strong enough values to provide for economic development.
One might also argue, along the lines of Gerschenkron, that the

later the development of the economy the greater the need for
political input into economic growth.

Another question which should be asked is whether any of
the self-strengtheners were interested in agriculture. Did they consider the technological aspects or distributive problems of agriculture? Was there any understanding of the relationship between
agriculture and industry?

Finally, we should ask to what extent the self-strengthening
movement reflected the emergence of new social strata. Do we see
a greater differentiation of classes in late Ch'ing China? What social
changes were reflected in the changes in the political climate?

Models of the Nineteenth-Century Economy?

Along with studies of enterprises and the question of values
and their effect on the economic system, possibly we should
attempt to construct a model of how the nineteenth-century
economy operated, illustrating the specific relationships among
variables. Of course, models do not replace research or adequate
historical description, but they are useful in allowing one to see
the relationships between various parts of the whole economy. For
example, we talk about the progressive commercialization of agriculture in the late Ch'ing period. If this happened, how did it
happen? Was it the result of increased demand, or changes in supply?
What in fact are the relations between the urban sector and the
rural sector? What is the flow of goods, people, and ideas, and how
are they connected? In order to make sense of the scattered information available, we might need a kind of tentative model.

There is a hypothesis, for example, that commercial expansion
in pre-twentieth-century China was characterized by very slow
growth accompanied by a rapid dispersion of wealth resulting from
the division of family property (*fen-chia*). A tentative model is
needed to examine this hypothesis. Such a model would also be
helpful in coping with counterfactual ("as if") questions like the
impact of imperialism on domestic industry. Looking at the
nineteenth-century economy in Marxist terms, it could be argued

that the internal contradictions in the premodern Chinese economy
were insufficient to overthrow it from within. It is unlikely that
the productive forces ever outgrew the premodern relations of
production.

The Interface of the Economy and the Polity
    The interface between the economy and the political system
has always been central to the study of Chinese economic history,
and continues to be so today. It is necessary systematically to
comb biographical works to extract information on economic
reform activities and on the economic activities of lower-level
officials.

Imperialism
    The central question in dealing with imperialism is whether
its main effect was on the Chinese economy or on the superstructure. The Chinese economy, I would suggest, remained generally
isolated from foreign economic forces and was not much affected
by them. Distinguishing between modern and traditional societies,
we find that in modern societies the superstructure is strong while
the economy is vulnerable, while in traditional societies the
economy is strong while the superstructure is vulnerable when
challenged. Thus the economies of underdeveloped countries are
not that vulnerable. Vietnam is an example: the United States
failed to bomb North Vietnam "into the Stone Age" because the
economy was traditional and therefore resilient. However, the
superstructure in a traditional society tends to be much more
vulnerable. Quasi-Western appendages to a traditional society are
insufficient to protect it. The political system and values of such
a society are easily challenged in a new situation. Therefore, as
Mao Tse-tung has also observed, the real battle takes place in the
superstructure of men's minds, not, as in Europe, in the economic
substructure.

The Anatomy of Cities and Towns
    Local histories are a valuable source for the study of the

urban structure of China, as Gilbert Rozman's work and F. W. Mote's studies of Nanking and Soochow suggest.

Perhaps we can discover more accurately what the actual rural-urban flow of goods and people was. It would be desirable to get enough data to do demographic profiles on cities. We might then get enough information to answer the question why Chinese cities seemed less dynamic than Western cities. What information, for example, do we have on the middle strata of Chinese society? Evelyn Rawski has done some work on literacy in traditional China which indicates that literate groups—including not only scholars but merchants, priests, story tellers, and military officers—constituted a larger stratum of the population than we had previously believed. Certainly the bulk of these people lived in towns and cities.

One might possibly do a detailed sociological study of a city by looking at the building trades and architecture. The shape of the Chinese city is interesting. There is no clearly defined city center, no cathedral or town hall as in European cities. Even the yamen is inconspicuous.

Domestic Trade and Transport

A more sophisticated analysis of the traditional sector of domestic trade and transport is desirable. Possible sources include merchant handbooks, route descriptions, and accounts by Chinese travelers. The types of goods moved along the various routes should be examined more closely. We do have some very useful studies of mid-Ch'ing rice markets, such as that recently published by Han-sheng Ch'üan and Richard Kraus.

The Study of Individual Enterprises

Work still should be done on individual enterprises. This kind of study can most profitably be done in the context of other questions. There is in this kind of endeavor the possibility of finding as much systematic quantitative material as can be found anywhere.

These individual enterprises should be seen as a part of the larger whole, with special attention paid to such questions as the role of foreigners, relations between the enterprise and the polity, the location of enterprises, and their functioning within the context of domestic trade patterns.

Susan Mann Jones
MERCHANT INVESTMENT, COMMERCIALIZATION, AND SOCIAL CHANGE IN THE NINGPO AREA

Contact with the West in those areas of China that Paul Cohen has called the littoral produced a distinctive pattern of interaction between Western and Chinese institutions and life styles. Ningpo prefecture, as a coastal region, treaty-port center, and a part of Shanghai's economic hinterland, was one such area. In the late Ch'ing it produced a few leaders of national importance (Shen Tun-ho might qualify as one),[1] but for the most part its elite was a local or regional elite, a commercial elite committed not to reform and politics but to business and profits, and an elite that wrote very little about itself.

Perspectives on the Ningpo area nonetheless are primarily elite perspectives, derived from local gazetteers, newspapers, and biographies. Foreign observers also compiled substantial data, particularly important being the publications of the Tōa Dōbunkai at Shanghai and the writings of missionaries and Western China hands.

The local elite of Ningpo achieved national significance in Chinese history because of its power in Shanghai, the dominant commercial center in late Ch'ing China. The Ningpo area is also significant for our purposes because of the emergence there of a hybrid culture which gave rise to both conflict and change in local society. This change was not, prior to 1911, generally directed toward reform. Cases where reform was consciously sought by the Ningpo financiers were confined mostly to the period after 1895, and to issues of fiscal reform within the government. Rather, change took the form of economic development, commercialization, and what some would call early modernization, seen not only in improved communications and transportation, but in the growth and expansion of local economies and the emergence of specialized social and commercial organizations.[2]

New commercial wealth and private entrepreneurship assumed

41

increasing importance in the politics and society of the late Ch'ing period. Private wealth had long been accumulated by individuals operating in the sphere of public government, in a trend marked in its early stages by the inseparability of private trade from official tribute in Ch'ing foreign relations. Steady growth in the private commercial sector had its roots in the monetization of the rural economy associated with the Ming single-whip tax reforms, and was spurred in the eighteenth century following the Ch'ing conquest by the period of *pax sinica*. This century saw the emergence of the Shansi banks and the *ch'ien-chuang* (commonly translated as native banks), the proliferation of merchant guilds in major trade centers, and steady growth in the network of rural periodic markets.[3]

During the first half of the nineteenth century, this private commercial sector attracted increased attention from the central government. Tea and silk traders had begun to amass wealth rivaling that of the government-sponsored salt merchants; the growth of foreign trade at Canton began to shift the fulcrum of merchant wealth out of Yangchow and Hui-chou. In 1825 private coastal shippers were hired to transport the official grain levies to Peking during the breakdown of the Grand Canal system. Indeed the commercialization of the entire grain tribute became a subject of growing concern in Chia-ch'ing and Tao-kuang memorials. The statecraft scholars of Wei Yuan's generation, in treatises reminiscent of those of present-day postal-service reformers, were outspoken advocates of hiring out the whole operation to private entrepreneurs as a means of circumventing a corrupt bureaucracy whose patronage workers and larded payrolls impeded the existing transport network.

One critical juncture in the ascendance of private entrepreneurs to positions of political influence was the Taiping Rebellion. The importance of merchant funds (in the form of special levies and fees for purchased rank) and of the commercial likin tax in financing the pacification of the rebels is well known. Hu Kuang-yung and Yang Fang are among the most famous of the merchant elite that emerged from this period.[4] Merchant wealth and real estate were concentrated in the cities of the lower Yangtze region which were among the last sanctuaries from the Taiping assault. The

Taiping period saw a wave of eastward migration in Chekiang, as people sought refuge in seaboard towns and in the political sanctuary of Shanghai's foreign settlements. Urban facilities were strained by wildly fluctuating populations: Ningpo doubled its census (from 200 to 400 thousand, according to some estimates) between 1840 and 1860, and in the wake of the rebellion shrank to a low of 20,000.[5] From these urban centers, merchant groups organized themselves to provide aid to refugees and relief for the countryside. Likewise, money for rehabilitation and reconstruction in the wake of the rebellion poured out of these same cities. The striking ascendancy of the Ningpo merchant group in the post-Taiping period is clearly due in part to their early foothold (after 1849) in the French Concession in Shanghai, and to the protection they enjoyed as a result.[6]

One of the main ways in which merchants enhanced their power in the 1860s was by supplying credit in an economy where circulation of both currency and commodities had been disrupted by the rebellion.[7] From 1862 until the early 1880s, native banking institutions (*ch'ien-chuang*) began to multiply as domestic silk and tea production resumed. Other spurs to commercial development in the southeast were the rapid rise in the demand for Chinese cotton engendered by the civil war in the United States, and the decision of foreign banks to extend short-term loans at high interest (so-called "chop loans," *ch'e-p'iao*) to native banks.

The most powerful group of native bankers in Shanghai in the late nineteenth and early twentieth centuries came from Ningpo prefecture. Ningpo was a center of trade, not agriculture. A coastal prefecture, the area encompassed extensive salt flats. It was the seat of a flourishing fishing industry, and it had a history of shipbuilding based on a ready supply of wood from the hills of eastern Chekiang and a natural water-transport system which carried logs to centers of manufacture. Commercial crops in the area included tea and silk; these were exported in exchange for rice and sugar from Fukien and Taiwan, and beans from Shantung and Manchuria.

In the nineteenth century the center of Ningpo's commercial

elite was not Ningpo (which itself was heavily peopled with Foochow traders) but Shanghai.[8] Especially after 1870, when daily
steamers linked the two cities, the Ningpo community at Shanghai
represented as much as a third of Ningpo's total population.[9] By
1907 such estimates were running as high as one-half, and foreign
steamers were beginning to cater to affluent Chinese traveling
between the two cities. The *North China Herald* reported that
over 150,000 Ningpo people resided in the International Settlement alone at that time.[10]

Ningpo interests at Shanghai were traditionally represented
by the Ningpo Guild (Ssu-ming kung-so), named for the Ssu-ming
Mountains that curved to the west of the city at the end of the
Ch'in-ling range. Like merchants in most agrarian societies, Ningpo
entrepreneurs conducted their business away from home. But like
the gentry with whom they are frequently lumped as a class in the
early twentieth century, they retained a residential identity in their
ancestral home and formed *t'ung-hsiang* (native-place) guilds to
serve as centers of social and business life while they sojourned.
They had no other real ties to the land; they were not grain merchants, nor even large-scale producers of commercial crops. They
were middlemen who shipped, extended credit, and dealt in
wholesale markets. The more successful among them created their
own small banking houses (*ch'ien-chuang*), many of which grew in
the late nineteenth century into enterprises with credit networks
and note circulation spanning the Yangtze Valley and eastern
Chekiang, and based in Shanghai.

They were middlemen of another sort as well. These traders
and their banks became the compradors who mediated between
native production and marketing and the foreign trade.[11] They
were even middlemen in a cultural sense; unbound (indeed frequently shut out early in life) from the traditional education and
civil-service system, they formed a significant portion of the new
men who studied Western languages in the treaty ports.[12] In turn
they were the least affected by the demise of the old examination
system in 1905. However, their alienation from traditional mobility
routes did not cause them to reject the existing social system. On

the contrary, their status as an elite in local society was so well
established by the turn of the century that, in the period of rapid
change surrounding the 1911 Revolution, their leadership tended
to be moderate in scope and in impact. Even investments in Western-
style "modernization" were in essence investments in their own
future as a commercial elite.

The manner in which merchants secured and legitimized their
status in local society is reflected in their investment in the myriad
public services that fell under the rubric of "philanthropy" (*tz'u-
shan*).[13] By the early twentieth century, such services included not
only the usual care for widows and orphans, free schools for the
poor, and fire-protection brigades, but also health and sanitation
facilities, and Western-style schools and medical centers. Another
prominent feature of merchant investment in this period was the
number of charitable estates (*i-chuang*) self-consciously founded in
the Fan Chung-yen tradition and designed to yield rent income to
assist indigent members of the lineage (and in at least one case, to
provide seed money for new family business).[14]

In the Ningpo case this investment is interesting for two
reasons. First, it sheds light on the problem of the drain of talent
and investment out of rural areas into major urban centers in the
early twentieth century. Although such investment was concentrated in hsien seats, and in a few major market towns, much of it
flowed there *out* of Shanghai in a pattern that must have been
repeated by merchant investors from other local systems. Second,
and conversely, because much of this capital flowed from the
outside in, or from the top down, so to speak, and because some
of it remained oriented toward lineages rather than the general
public, the institutions it supported frequently served the interests
of the investor rather than the needs of the local populace. (This
question is worth exploring further because, for example, attacks
on modern schools by local mobs usually involved tax resistance;
were privately-sponsored schools attacked as well?)

As residents of a treaty-port city with a comprador tradition
of exporting merchant talent, the elite of Ningpo were accustomed

to contact and collaboration with foreigners. Exposure to Western culture was also shown in expressions of antiforeignism and anti-Western riots in the Ningpo area. The effects of the opening of the treaty ports were keenly felt by Ningpo business and society: the opening of Shanghai in 1842 caused a sharp reduction in the overseas trade at the port of Ningpo; and after Hangchow became a treaty port in 1896, Ningpo ceased to serve as a silk port for Chekiang. Instead the city's economy became one of a Chinese-dominated transshipping center for imports and exports via Shanghai.[15] The Western presence at Ningpo was primarily a missionary presence.[16]

Some evidence for the way in which the commercialization associated with the foreign transshipping trade acted as a catalyst for change—not only in the economy but in the society as well—may be adduced from a study of local development in Chen-hai, one of the districts that composed Ningpo prefecture. Prior to the opening of the treaty ports, Ningpo was a Janus-faced port serving the coastal trade (and overseas as far as Nagasaki and ports of Southeast Asia) on the east; and the canal trade of Chekiang, oriented toward Shaohsing and Hangchow on the west. The coastal entry to Ningpo was guarded from the east by the hsien seat of Chen-hai, at the mouth of the Yung River. The city of Ningpo (itself the seat of Yin hsien) and the hsien city of Tz'u-ch'i, midway between Ningpo and Shaohsing, were the merchant centers of the era before 1842. Accounts of trade along the Yü-yao River describe the festive air of entertainment and panoply that accompanied the traffic to and from Shaohsing. It was a thoroughfare of salt, tea, and silk merchants, and of purveyors of Shaohsing wines. After 1842 the direction of trade gradually changed, as Ningpo became a center of transshipping for goods imported through Shanghai via the Yung River, past Chen-hai to the east. The change brought with it a change in the status of the hsien city of Chen-hai, no longer a center of defense but a newly emerging focus of commercial wealth in its own right. The result of these changes was to gradually place Chen-hai in the forefront of economic development in the prefecture during the late nineteenth and early twentieth centuries.

The rise of Chen-hai is documented in a remarkable gazetteer compiled in 1924 and self-consciously divided to cover the period after 1911 in a separate volume, the *Hsin-chih pei-kao* (Complete draft of a new gazetteer). One index of local development in Chen-hai is found in the section on philanthropy, which describes the gradual economic differentiation of the Chen-hai district after 1870 from the prefecture as a whole and its establishment as an independent center capable of planning and funding its own charities.

Cooperative philanthropic projects involving all of Ningpo prefecture date (according to the gazetteer) from the founding of an orphanage at Ningpo in the Yung-cheng period, and from efforts of a Ningpo prefect to coordinate charitable projects from the city of Ningpo during the 1720s.[17] In the early Kuang-hsu reign a movement was begun in Chen-hai to keep district funds at home rather than sending them to Ningpo; between 1876 and 1879, Chen-hai established its own orphanage (*yü-ying t'ang*), a society to provide for widows of holders of the first degree in the state examinations (*sheng-yuan*), and a hospital (*kung-shan i-yuan*). Of the fifty-seven fire prevention stations in Chen-hai, thirty-eight were built during the Kuang-hsu reign or later. Most charitable organizations providing funeral expenses were founded in Kuang-hsu; a new relief organization for flood victims and a medical dispensary likewise belong to this period.[18]

A further index of Chen-hai development appears in accounts of examination lodges. Whereas (observe the editors) at one time lodges in Hangchow were maintained only by Yin and Tz'u-ch'i districts, between 1876 and 1880 a Chen-hai lodge (Chen-hai shih-kuan) was constructed at Hangchow and duly commemorated in an inscription by Yü Yueh. In Peking, where a similar situation had prevailed (that is, a lodge for Yin and Tz'u-ch'i respectively, in addition to the old Ning-po hui-kuan), a Chen-hai lodge was established as early as 1867.[19]

Here the details supplied are particularly suggestive. The Peking lodge (Ching-tu Chen-hai shih-kuan) was founded by two officials from Chen-hai (Hsieh Fu-tien and Sheng Chih-hsing, of whom the latter at least came from a merchant family) using funds borrowed from a Chen-hai merchant named Yü Hung-ch'ao. The loan was advanced with a special view to speeding construction, as the number of Chen-hai natives going to the exams had grown from an earlier average of twenty-eight to around forty.

While most gazetteer entries are not so obliging in supplying information concerning investors, the main sources of local wealth can be spotted in part by looking at an inverse form of conspicuous consumption: the charitable estate (*i-chuang*). The earliest *i-chuang* recorded in Chen-hai dates from the Hsien-feng reign and was founded by a family named Hu (background obscure). Of the remaining five estates established before 1911, four (including the two largest, which were 2,000 and 1,200 *mou* respectively) were founded by families who acquired their fortunes in trade.[20]

That merchants had a heavy hand in other projects ordinarily assumed to be the realm of the literati can be seen in the compilation of the gazetteer itself, which enjoyed the collaboration of a separate Shanghai staff (*kan-shih pu*).[21]

These findings in Chen-hai district indicate that at the local level in Ningpo prefecture, the period between 1870 and 1911 was one of steady growth and development, marked by the apparent accumulation of private capital, growth of trade, and the expansion of services in areas most accessible to foreign trade. Most important, in highly commercialized areas like these, was the assimilation of merchants into the established local elite during the last quarter of the nineteenth century. This elite in turn served as an effective culture broker for the gradual introduction of Western-style institutions to the region.

Michael R. Godley
OVERSEAS CHINESE ENTREPRENEURS AS REFORMERS:
THE CASE OF CHANG PI-SHIH

The role of the overseas Chinese in the K'ang–Liang reform movement and the revolution is an old story. It is also widely recognized that Chinese returning from sojourns abroad added a more worldly outlook to the southern coastal provinces, which may have made the task of reform a bit easier. That many individuals in foreign lands lent their expertise and capital to the cause of Chinese modernization is less universal knowledge but still probably matter of fact to the specialist. What is not generally appreciated is that a few overseas Chinese attained prominent positions from which they pressed for important changes, particularly in the area of commerce and industry, after 1900.[1]

It is axiomatic that the development of modern economies in most countries has depended on the size and efficiency of the bourgeoisie. As China struggled to modernize in the closing decades of the Ch'ing dynasty, it was extremely difficult for the traditional bureaucracy to tap the new wealth of the treaty ports. Incentives such as the lure of monopoly rights or purchased brevet rank worked for a while, but the same outside stimuli that forced the government to modify its opinion of the importance of commercial and industrial endeavors also gave Chinese businessmen a position they had never enjoyed before. Secure in Western enclaves and still suspicious of the machinations of officials who had long controlled commerce, more and more merchants felt inclined to participate in government schemes only on their own terms. In order to introduce needed capital and to stimulate China's reluctant entrepreneurial group, without completely abandoning the old system of patronage and official control, the Ch'ing leadership turned to the overseas Chinese.

By the 1890s several million Chinese lived under Western colonial administration in nearby Southeast Asia (Nanyang). Exposed to international trade and encouraged to enter commerce or the development of native economies, a small but significant number became very successful. There are some who would argue that the Nanyang environment was able to produce "Chinese capitalists" while traditional China was not. At any rate, the alien atmosphere, dominated by Western concerns, seems to have been conducive to the growth of bourgeois values. As was the case in the treaty ports, many overseas Chinese became cosmopolitan in their views. Unlike the inhabitants of coastal China, however, the immigrants were not as easily alienated from the traditional system. The China-born among the prosperous overseas business community remained socially conservative. As in previous generations on the mainland, the most respected individuals continued to be those closely associated with classical education and bureaucratic rank. Consequently, a majority of the successful overseas Chinese entrepreneurs at the turn of the century attempted to disguise bourgeois wealth with the prestige of purchased degrees, titles, and brevet posts.

There are a number of reasons for this tendency to identify with the existing elite tradition even while off in the midst of a flourishing commercial setting. For one, merchants were denied entry into the European ruling class. They were also almost exclusively of peasant background with strong ties to families in the Chinese hinterland. A traditional uneasiness about mercantile wealth also seems to have survived the move south. Furthermore, riches earned abroad still required protection at home, and this was best assured through the attainment of traditional status. For many years, returning individuals faced discrimination often tantamount to extortion at the hands of local magistrates, since to leave one's family to search for wealth in far-off places violated basic Confucian principles. To overcome both the social and the practical disadvantages of long residence abroad, prosperous overseas Chinese felt a pressure to achieve the approbation of the traditional system. Yet it must be understood that, far from representing a denial of the emerging bourgeois standards of Southeast Asia and the treaty ports, this inclination to seek gentry-bureaucrat status was complementary to the on-going transformation of the Confucian order. It was but part of a broader movement to redefine the qualifications for membership in the ruling class.

Regardless of the depth of their Western veneer, the one thing that virtually all Nanyang residents came to share by the year 1900 was an interest in the development of the China homeland. For some this simply meant continued remittances to their families or ownership of a token share in the railroad that was expected to bring affluence to their native region. Others returned home to become part of the growing Chinese bourgeoisie. A few outstanding individuals, however, took advantage of the leverage even brevet honors gave within the traditional framework, first, to protect their own interests and, then, to introduce new elements into the late Ch'ing scene. The participation of such entrepreneurial types from overseas in.the "establishment" raises a number of questions that directly address the critical issues of the period—the fate of Confucian norms and the meaning of reform in the Chinese context.

Unquestionably the foremost example of an overseas entrepreneur was Chang Pi-shih (*tzu:* Chen-hsun; 1840–1916). Born in rural Kwangtung, Chang began as a provisioner for the Dutch in Java and, by the 1890s, had utilized colonial support to make extensive investments in the Netherlands Indies. His dozen ships dominated the Sumatran coastal trade and flew the Dutch flag. He soon had an interest in almost all the major revenue farms on either side of the Straits of Malacca and was also involved in mining, banking, and large plantation farming. In the formative years of modern Chinese industry, between 1895 and 1910, he expanded his operations to China where he set an example of economic diversification for the entire country to follow. He established the famous Chang Yü Pioneer Wine Company at Chefoo, textile mills, a brick factory, and a glass-making operation. He was also connected with salt, cattle, mining, cotton, and general commerce. As one of the leading proponents of railway development, his name was associated with every railway project in the coastal provinces of Kwangtung and Fukien.[2] He was the largest private shareholder in the Imperial Bank of China and on the board of directors of this and other early financial institutions. He took the lead in the organization of chambers of commerce and by the years immediately preceding his death, Chang

was the most famous Chinese entrepreneur, honored during an
official visit by America's Wall Street.[3]

For present purposes, it is enough to say that Chang Pi-shih,
receiving varying degrees of support from a number of prominent
reformers, attained important positions of power and honor in
China. Although originally recruited into the *kuan-tu shang-pan*
(official-supervision merchant-management) system at the merchant-
managing end, a diplomatic position as consul-general in Singapore,
successive brevet ranks beginning at the *taotai* level, and an external
source of wealth beyond the touch of the government gave Chang
the weight needed to become an official supervisor. He also cata-
pulted himself ahead with several well-timed contributions, including the entire sum necessary to open a technical school. Such subscriptions netted him the first of many imperial audiences and
metropolitan rank. Eventually he was made a vice president of the
new Board of Trade. Even greater honors followed.

There would have been no place for enterprising overseas
Chinese, of course, if the Ch'ing government had not looked favorably upon their participation. As I have documented elsewhere, the
interest of the Nanyang Chinese in developing China coincided
with a well-organized campaign to attract overseas investments.[4]
Beginning with its discovery of the plight of coolie laborers, the
dynasty gradually formed a policy which ultimately granted returning entrepreneurs a major stake in economic affairs. Although such
noted reformers as Ting Jih-ch'ang, Chang Chih-tung, Hsueh Fu-
ch'eng, and Huang Tsun-hsien all influenced this course, the decisive
role was played by Chang Pi-shih.

In his conversations with the Empress Dowager and in a number of memorials, Chang repeated the same basic arguments. He
believed that the throne needed the full and active support of the
nation's commercial community, which should be given appropriate
recognition. But he warned that treaty-port and overseas merchants
would not be likely to provide such support until positive steps
were taken to purge the bureaucracy of its corruption and anti-
commerce orientation. Furthermore, he suggested that commercial
expertise was itself a qualification for office. Unquestionably,

however, the argument that most caught the attention of high
officials was his fervent belief that overseas Chinese could be
attracted back to China in large enough numbers to provide the
missing entrepreneurial thrust while gaining the confidence of the
native bourgeoisie. Nanyang Chinese, under his leadership, would
thus become the vanguard of the modernization process.

Evidently, many of Chang's proposals did find takers. Wu
T'ing-fang, for example, advised the Empress Dowager that the
Board of Trade carefully discussed his specific suggestions for
economic modernization and intended to implement most of them
under the watchful eye of an official specially appointed to
administer what might be called the "Chang plan."[5]

Probably because of his own rural origins, Chang Pi-shih maintained that the emerging bourgeois class should lead in the development of the Chinese interior as well as in the urban centers. He
proposed the appointment of commercial officers to recruit
merchant capital for the expansion of irrigation and flood control.
This would make it possible for very large companies embracing
far more than a village or two to be formed. While Chang's ideas
are somewhat sketchy, he was apparently urging the creation of
something much larger than an agricultural cooperative. What he
was promoting was the opening of the hinterland to giant syndi-
cates through which the landlord and commercial classes would
join forces to build an ever-expanding water-works system. The
association he had in mind could own land and be so grandiose
and powerful as to be self-perpetuating. Even those who did not
wish to invest would be forced by the government to pay a regular
assessment.

In a similar vein, Chang also took on the rural credit situation,
with its notorious inadequacies, and concluded that only when
merchant-funded companies institutionalized the process of loan-
making on a broad scale would there be enough capital to drive
down exorbitant interest rates. The critical point, as Chang saw it,
was to guarantee that investments made in water conservation,
credit, and capital improvements would be just as secure as the
traditional stake in land. To do so, he recommended that the

government first establish a regularized commercial law. Then urban wealth could be drawn into the interior to fund the various improvements needed to upgrade peasant life and modernize the countryside. His plan was thus directed at both the rural majority and the new bourgeoisie.

Although some might argue that his plan would only have opened the hinterland to the horrors of monopoly capital and new forms of exploitation, Chang always couched his innovations in the moral convictions of a classical Confucianist. He spoke not of great profits but of the building of a countryside free from floods, drought and famine, where the farming masses might enjoy a good life. Be this as it may, the leading figures of the utopian society envisioned by Chang were not to be the old-style mandarins but the new superior men of commerce.

This tendency to join the treaty-port and interior cultures was one of the most pronounced features of Chang's writings. He was determined to facilitate contact between the two worlds, a dream that found concrete expression in his commitment to improved roads and railways. He also sponsored modern schools and other measures to raise the peasant standard of living. But Chang refused to blame rural folk for the backward state of the nation. "Criticizing farmers," he wrote, "was like criticizing those who were not cooking because they had no rice or not weaving when they had no cloth."[6] The problem was a lack of capital and innovative example—elements that only a new elite class could supply.

The paradoxical identification with both poor peasants and wealthy urbanites is easily fathomed if one is familiar with the overseas Chinese success story in Southeast Asia. There, with the West providing the markets, protective laws, capital, and the needed example, impoverished farmers did make good. Chang was therefore quick to point out that China trailed the West for reasons other than character or cultural defect. Given the proper tools and mentors, the Chinese could match the West.

Although many reformers believed that China's efforts at modernization suffered from an absence of machines, and Chang in a sense agreed, he had the courage to trace the problem beyond

technology. There could be no real modernization, he argued, until
the negative influence of the conservative gentry had been eliminated.
As it was, local leaders complained about innovations and provoked
the common people to resist those changes which were most in their
interest, while government magistrates, unwilling to stir up trouble,
went along with the prevailing sentiment and intervened only if
heavily bribed. Chang, therefore, identified gentry intransigence and
the bureaucratic corruption that supported it as the real barriers to
economic growth, for they stifled invention and kept capital away.

True, there had been some progressive officials in the past
who recognized the ways in which the existing system discouraged
entrepreneurship. These perceptive leaders had therefore recommended "official-supervised merchant-managed" or even completely
official-run undertakings to overcome the resistance of the old
gentry. For a time, joint Sino-foreign projects had also been tried
but these enterprises only caused resentment and never served as a
real model. The problem, as Chang boldly put it, was that the
kuan-tu shang-pan formula was outmoded. As long as authority
remained in the hands of bureaucrats who did not understand the
world of commerce, few individuals would ever be willing to risk
capital anywhere but in the protected treaty ports or overseas.
When foreign funding was used, evils were only compounded.

If it was, in fact, against the national interest to invite the
Western powers in as financial sponsors and teachers, then the only
remaining way to develop the country's resources was to permit
selected Chinese businessmen to be both supervisors and managers.
There is, of course, no question that Chang knew exactly where the
throne should search for a new generation of officials who possessed needed capital and were more attuned to the demands of
the day.

Apparently willing to pay the price required to attract overseas Chinese resources, the Empress Dowager named Chang imperial
commissioner to Nanyang and also superintendent of agriculture,
industry, railroads, and mining for Fukien and Kwangtung in
November 1904. To test his ideas and prove that a few men of
talent could bring about reforms through example, he also asked

for permission to set up a model administration. He promised that with the right kind of official supervision the resultant modern enterprises, inaugurated by returning overseas Chinese, would point the way to an entirely new era. But to attract his first recruits, he requested that the throne grant Nanyang entrepreneurs the same legal status then permitted to foreign firms, including incorporation outside of China. Not only did Chang express his intention to treat businessmen henceforth as the equals of bureaucrats, he went on to suggest that the dynasty award them honorary titles to eliminate any ambiguity. Within two years, as it turned out, the regime had become so desperate for development capital that it willingly bestowed titles of nobility as well as high metropolitan rank on large-scale entrepreneurs.

For Chang and most of his principal recruits, however, brevet honor and even foreign status were no longer enough; they wanted full equality with officials and the right to represent their own projects directly to the government. The mandarin-capitalists from Nanyang were thus remarkable for their ability to exploit the traditional system. But they also took full advantage of their alien origins. Almost to a man, the big investors insisted on maintaining their permanent residence and the base of their influence in Southeast Asia. It can, in fact, be argued that in certain regards—and this was true in the case of treaty-port compradors too—the entire process was barely distinguishable from imperialism. Indeed, Chang once attempted to convince the Empress Dowager that overseas Chinese entrepreneurship could replace Western enterprise in China.

In some ways, these men really were foreigners. They frequently served adopted governments, followed Western laws, engaged in a kind of secondary imperialism in Southeast Asia which utilized small kingdoms of laborers to exploit local resources, and looked with favor upon certain Occidental pursuits. Many were even honored for loyalty by colonial masters. But, unlike foreigners, they spoke Chinese, quoted the classics, and were willing to substitute participation in the old order for the omnipresent gunboats. For these and other reasons, they gained the acceptance of the Ch'ing leadership. In the final analysis, they were, however, part of a historical movement greater than China.

One of the characteristic features of successful overseas Chinese entrepreneurs, such as Chang Pi-shih, was an ambivalence toward imperialism. While clearly opposing unequal treaties and Western intervention, they could never quite forget the opportunities that European expansion into Asia had given them. Their primary identification was therefore with an international commercial arena beyond China. Merging a strong sense of nationalism with a realization of what the outside world had to offer, they ultimately demanded that their country produce a business elite with the same power and stature as its Western counterpart.

Many scholars contend that modernizing societies produce generations of half-breeds, unsure of their identity. For overseas Chinese entrepreneurs in China it was not so simple. It may well be true that they felt inadequate in the eyes of the West and superior to native Chinese merchants. In a paradoxical way, however, traditional status at home actually provided recognition abroad. It is often forgotten that Western industrialists, as late as the turn of the century, were also struggling for social acceptance. Chinese entrepreneurs, overseas and at home, occupied a similarly awkward nouveau riche position, further tainted sometimes by contact with imperialism. Old aristocrats of both the European and Chinese variety looked down upon new wealth. Respectability required a special life style, marked (for both Westerners and Chinese) by philanthropy and classical education. It was precisely because the overseas Chinese were desirous of simultaneous recognition in two different cultural settings that they moved so freely from one to the other. Under such circumstances, there naturally emerged a common sociocultural denominator, a multinational "gentleman." Some of the attributes of this "gentleman" were borrowed from Chinese tradition while others more closely fit the West. In any case, returning entrepreneurs began to argue that their values, with all the bourgeois overtones, were not necessarily antithetical to the Chinese pattern. Increasingly they viewed triumph at commerce, properly dignified, as a legitimate avenue to native power and status. And, as with all equations, the obverse was equally compelling: China's mandarin-gowned gentleman-merchants had a valid claim on foreign respect.

The success overseas Chinese entrepreneurs had at wedding bourgeois values to traditional bureaucratic principles suggests that, contrary to what has sometimes been argued, the traditional system may not, after all, have been that inimical to capitalist purposes. In this connection, it should be remembered that the early generations of overseas Chinese in Southeast Asia got their start under some form of colonial sponsorship. The customary colonial policy of awarding exclusive rights for a commodity or vice was a continuation of Chinese practice. The fact that headmen in the Netherlands Indies, for example, usually controlled the most profitable monopolies and businesses was completely in accord with older Chinese expectations, with merchant profit tied to official favor. Thus, while Chang Pi-shih and many of his Nanyang friends certainly represented a stage in the evolution of the capitalist personality the overseas Chinese have become noted for, they appear to have felt quite at home in a China where existing tradition favored bureaucratic intervention.

In his memorials Chang therefore asked for tax incentives, developmental monopolies, and bureaucratic appointments for his associates. He viewed his coterie as an elite group, a proper replacement for the traditional gentry. As such he showed little patience with those who lacked his acumen. He suggested that the government should establish firm time limits for private Chinese to develop their land. If they failed to meet these limits, the state should call in entrepreneurs who could. All foreign activities in China were, of course, also to be divided among the commercial elite. In some ways, Chang's arguments are reminiscent of European policies toward Chinese subjects in Southeast Asia. There, Chinese were taught both the principles of free-market competition and the advantages of monopoly. And with coolie armies and government patronage given to winning bidders, Chinese contributed immeasurably to the growth of export economies.

Although terms like "reformer," "modernizer," and "entrepreneur" have been used interchangeably, it is not improper to reflect upon their significance. That Chang and those he attracted to China probably functioned as all three does not mean that their activities in these capacities were mutually reinforcing, always propelling the country in the same direction. As an entrepreneur, Chang Pi-shih provided much-needed capital and initiative. By combining official and businessman roles, he also helped surmount a major obstacle to modernization and contributed to the rise of the bourgeoisie as a critical mediator between traditional and modern China. But, in so doing, he also helped strengthen older Chinese tendencies.

Before the arrival of the mandarin-capitalists from Nanyang, the state had always meddled in commerce, freely granting monopolies and patronizing select merchants. Once able to enter the bureaucracy themselves, overseas Chinese continued to use governmental influence in a traditional manner. When merchants became officials, the door was opened to all the old abuses of power. And for another generation at least, the alliance between bureaucrats and capitalists would characterize the Chinese economy.

DISCUSSION

Sue Chung asked Michael Godley about problems overseas Chinese had with the Ch'ing government when they returned to China. Mr. Godley said that there were, indeed, problems, and that attempts were made to moderate Ch'ing restrictions on overseas Chinese. The trouble was that even when these attempts succeeded, there was great difficulty in getting local officials to enforce the new policy.

Maryruth Coleman asked if overseas Chinese investing in China could be regarded as imperialists. Did the overseas Chinese draw profits off from China or did they reinvest in China? Mr. Godley said that money flowed back and forth and was invested both in China and in enterprises in Southeast Asia. Albert Feuerwerker added that it was possible to compute the inflow of foreign investments and loans and the outflow of profits and loan payments. In the case of overseas Chinese entrepreneurs from Southeast Asia, we would probably find a net outflow of profits, but not of loan payments.

Jonathan Ocko mentioned that Susan Jones had said that in the beginning of the twentieth century Ningpo merchants who acted as cultural brokers were subject to nationalist pressure. Was this also the case with overseas Chinese in their capacity as cultural brokers? Mr. Godley said that overseas Chinese were very often active in nationalist movements. Chang Pi-shih and other prominent overseas figures were leaders in the rights-recovery movement.

Mr. Ocko asked Ms. Jones whether merchants in Ningpo ever tried to turn xenophobic pressures away from themselves by getting involved in rights recovery. Ms. Jones replied that the xenophobia was never really directed at the merchants in Ningpo and that their businesses were not much affected in anti-Western boycotts.

David Pong said that when overseas Chinese went back to China they would appear in Western dress to exploit their Western identity and obtain protection from it. However, their position was still precarious, and they were vulnerable to exploitation by

60

the bureaucracy. Mr. Pong further observed that the early
reformers admired England for the power of its merchants and for
the manner in which English merchants contributed to the wealth
and power of their country. He wondered whether knowledge of
this mutually beneficial relationship was not a factor in encouraging the Ch'ing government to extend its influence and protection
to the overseas Chinese in Southeast Asia.

Joseph Cheng mentioned that he had encountered two different terms for what seemed to be the same type of enterprise:
kuan-shang ho-pan and *kuan-tu shang-pan.* What was the difference
between the two? Mr. Feuerwerker replied that they were nearly
the same, the main difference being in the form of control. The
problem in either instance was how to encourage merchants to
invest in enterprises in which their managerial power was only
nominal.

Yeh-chien Wang asked why overseas Chinese became successful
capitalists, while Chinese at home did not. Mr. Godley replied that
he did not think that the difference lay in commercial law, since
the Chinese in many Southeast Asian areas did not have the privileges of Europeans until the turn of the century. In fact, the
Chinese in Southeast Asia played a role similar to that of merchants
in China. There were monopolies, revenue-sharing operations, and
other institutions which combined wealth and status. Under the
Dutch in the Dutch East Indies some Chinese were appointed headmen of the Chinese communities. Ms. Jones suggested that the
critical variable might have been the lack of overseas Chinese
dependence on foreign capital. Mr. Godley said, however, that
many overseas Chinese began their careers in foreign enterprises
and with foreign capital.

Suzanne Barnett asked how common it was for overseas
Chinese to convert to Christianity. Mr. Godley said the English-
educated overseas Chinese, especially those with professional train-
ing, were often nominal Christians, but few of the others. Ms.
Barnett also asked whether Chinese merchants ever invested in
Western enterprises outside of China. Ms. Jones said that there was

such investment, but it was not very successful. The 1910 rubber crisis ruined many Chinese investors.

Mary Rankin suggested that the precarious position of merchants as cultural brokers prompted them to take the lead in nationalist activities and to invest in Chinese enterprises. Some merchants emulated the life style of the gentry and identified themselves with the Chinese way of life to show that they were not foreign in culture or loyalties.

Thomas Kennedy pointed out that the basic beliefs of the self-strengtheners could justify a number of policies and said that it had yet to be proved that beliefs as such were the overwhelming factor in impeding the growth of arsenals and dockyards. Foreign influence for example was often a negative factor, in part because many of the Western advisers simply did not do a very good job. Mr. Kennedy also noted the emergence, around the 1860s, of a concept of economic growth among the self-strengtheners, especially those who had been affected by statecraft writings. These men believed in balanced, rationalized industrialization. He wondered if there was Chinese acceptance of the idea that the normal road to development followed the Western bourgeois-capitalist model. John Schrecker said that what we really needed was more information on traditional Chinese economic thought.

Saundra Sturdevant
IMPERIALISM, SOVEREIGNTY, AND SELF-STRENGTHENING:
A REASSESSMENT OF THE 1870s

The *Celestial Empire* with full load gave a shriek and whistle
and then glided out of the station amid cheers. Open country
was soon reached. The little engine pulled six carriages over
a 2 foot 6 inch gauge track at 15 miles per hour. There was no
oscillation. Country people looked up as the train passed but
then quietly resumed their labours; they had become
accustomed to another, even smaller engine, the *Pioneer,*
which had pulled ballast wagons for the previous three or
four months.

The train reached Kiangwan, half-way station, in seventeen
minutes. The one hundred and sixty-four invited passengers
alighted from the train and were greeted by an ample supply
of champagne and cake in the waiting room. Corks popped as
all nationalities toasted and drank together. Walter H. Med-
hurst, British consul at Shanghai, mounted a table and led
three cheers for Gabriel James Morrison, construction engineer.
Someone else soon shouted three cheers for Jardine, Matheson
and Company.

A half an hour was spent in such gaity before the engine was
again attached to the train and the passengers had resumed
their seats for the return trip to Shanghai. Most of the rest of
the day was spent in giving free trips to the Chinese, thousands
of whom came to get a ride. Precautions were taken by officials to see that no one was injured. Laughter and shouts of
delight prevailed in all directions.[1]

Thus did the first railway in China, the Shanghai–Wusung Railway, make its maiden trip on June 30, 1876. Neither Chinese initiative
nor Chinese capital played any role in this venture. The promoters
had not requested permission from local or central officials for a
concession. It was an example of *de facto* introduction: Westerners
proceeding without the permission of a concession and presenting

Chinese officials with a *fait accompli.* Western officials gave their
nationals full support.

In less than six months time the governor-general of Liang-
chiang, Shen Pao-chen (1820–1879), with the support of Chihli
Governor-General Li Hung-chang (1823–1901), completed negotiations with Jardine Matheson for the purchase of the Wusung–
Shanghai Railway. A year later Shen Pao-chen oversaw the dismantling of that railroad and its shipment to Taiwan. At about the same
time Shen moved to stop Western telegraph construction at
Foochow. When the lines at Foochow were taken down in 1877
and shipped to Taiwan by Ting Jih-ch'ang (1823–1882), governor
of Fukien, neither Shen, Li, nor any other official protested; on
the contrary, they supported the action. Examples of Chinese opposition to railways and telegraphs had occurred previously. In 1865
Ting Jih-ch'ang, then a *taotai* at Shanghai, sanctioned the destruction of a telegraph constructed at that port. His superior, Li Hung-
chang, supported his action.[2]

The contradiction is obvious. Li Hung-chang, Shen Pao-chen,
Ting Jih-ch'ang, together with Tseng Kuo-fan (1811–1872), were
statecraft (*ching-shih*) reformers, responsible for almost all of the
self-strengthening measures introduced from the beginning of the
T'ung-chih Restoration (1862–1874). They established arsenals,
dockyards, translation bureaus, and colleges. They sent Chinese
overseas to study and they worked for the establishment of diplomatic representation abroad, the introduction of Western science
and mathematics, and the reform of China's examination and military systems. To a considerable extent they also worked for the
reform of China's basic governmental institutions. Li, Shen, and
Ting also advocated the construction of telegraphs and railroads
and were instrumental in the introduction of Western mining
methods. Yet it was they who were responsible for the disman-
tlement of the Wusung–Shanghai Railway and of the telegraph
lines at Foochow.

In attempting to understand this contradiction, I have examined
the British Foreign Office papers, the Jardine Matheson Archives,
Robert Hart's diaries at Belfast, American consular reports, and the

papers of such merchant firms as Forbes and Heard. On the
Chinese side, the *Hai-fang-tang* (Archives on maritime defense), the
memorials of Shen Pao-chen, and the correspondence and memorials
of Li Hung-chang have been especially valuable. In the process
three questions have defined themselves. One is the nature of
Western imperialism and its effect on China. A second is the relationship of Confucian values to the modernization of China. Finally,
there is the question of timing and development of the concept of
sovereignty. Some of my assessments follow.

Chinese foreign policy was defensive. It aimed at containing
Westerners, at preventing them from gaining more "rights" than
they already enjoyed. Ultimate control was the key: it lessened the
possibility of future conflicts and concessions. A defensive posture
did not mean an unwillingness to consider the introduction of
Western innovations. It is clear that during the period under study
neither Chinese officials nor the citizens of Shanghai or Foochow
were opposed to innovations *per se.*

It is also clear that Chinese officials were more receptive to
the introduction of telegraphs than railways. Chinese policy changed
gradually from total prohibition of telegraph construction in 1865 to
the Wade–Tsungli Yamen Agreement of 1870 which provided for
the cable linkage of China to the rest of the world, but prohibited
cables from being brought ashore. (The cable ends were to be
placed on hulks of ships in the harbors at the treaty ports.) Soon
after signing this agreement, the British brought a cable ashore at
Wusung and the Americans did the same at Amoy. From that point
to stringing a land line from Wusung to Shanghai was a short step.
Then in 1874, with the Sino-Japanese confrontation over Taiwan,
the court recognized the validity of Shen Pao-chen's request—
extended on military grounds—for a cable connecting Taiwan with
the mainland and for a land line from Foochow to Amoy. It was
again only a small step to Chinese assumption of protection and
finally financial liability. The Western strategy of piecemeal *de
facto* introduction, accompanied by constant education and pressure, worked.

With railways, it was a different story. Chinese policy had not

changed fundamentally since Li Hung-chang's strong rejection in
1863 of a Western request to construct a railway between Shanghai
and Soochow. His objection centered on his determination to prevent foreign influence from spreading into China's interior. At
present, he said, foreigners controlled the major ports and had
access all along the coast. He would not allow the spread of their
influence into the interior; the right to travel there was a serious
enough evil. Li further elaborated on the economic consequences
of foreign influence in the Chinese interior: it would be of benefit
only to foreigners and a threat to China's economic control (*li-
ch'üan*). Still, Li left open the possibility of future railway construction should China some day find such a course to her advantage.
But, he added an important qualification: "If ever a railroad exists
on Chinese territory, it must be a Chinese and not a foreign undertaking."[3]

In time statecraft officials like Li Hung-chang, Shen Pao-chen,
and Ting Jih-ch'ang would call for the introduction of railways at
mines in Chihli, at the Kiangnan arsenal, and on Taiwan. And from
there, as Shanghai *taotai* Feng Chün-kuang told George Seward in
1874, it would probably be only a short step to the introduction of
railways in the interior—but always, he stressed, under Chinese control. Indeed, the theme of control, of sovereignty, was to be reiterated over and over again by officials at all levels when the question
of the introduction of railways was brought up. This issue lay at
the center of Chinese opposition to the Wusung–Shanghai Railway
and to the telegraph lines at Foochow. For example, Feng Chün-
kuang, citing precedent in Western countries and Western practices
in Japan, which were respectful of the sovereign rights of the
country concerned, defended with skill and consistency China's
dismantling of the Wusung line: "I wish to say to you that we are
quite as well posted as you are in regard to railroads in Europe and
America. We know the railroads that have been built for political
purposes and the roads that have been built for commercial purposes. We know the roads that pay and those that do not. Whenever
this empire is ready for railroads we will be prepared to introduce
them. We have taken up this Wusung Railroad for the purpose of

asserting our sovereignty, and to show these gentlemen who put it down that a like enterprise must not be attempted again."[4]

Feng Chün-kuang's words and the actions of Shen Pao-chen, Li Hung-chang, and other statecraft officials of the 1870s pose a sharp challenge to the assumption that Confucian values and modernization were inherently incompatible. The opposition of these officials to the Wusung–Shanghai Railway and to the telegraph lines at Foochow was not reflective of the conflicting claims of modernization and Confucianism, judged by Mary C. Wright to have been the reason for the failure of self-strengthening. Nor were these situations where Chinese officials failed to see the relevance of modernization to traditional Chinese problems, as Paul Cohen has written.[5] It was not necessary to have a radical change in values, as Albert Feuerwerker has intimated, before modernization could proceed.[6] My study demonstrates that Confucian values *per se,* far from being a deterrent to modernization, could actually function as a foundation of strength and assurance upon which modernization could build. The statecraft officials who removed the Wusung–Shanghai Railway and who took up the telegraph lines at Foochow operated from a solid foundation of cultural and political identity grounded in Confucian values. Their opposition was based on the fact that both of these enterprises violated Chinese sovereignty.

This bespeaks a more highly developed concept of sovereignty and nationalism than has so far been credited to the Chinese at this early date. Schrecker's description of the nationalist approach, prominent at the end of the century, also pertains to the thought, style, and emphasis of the statecraft officials in this study. On the question of the introduction of railways and telegraphs, the issue of sovereignty was central to the position of these officials from the early 1860s. Moreover, a sense of shame was not yet a motivating principle. It was an issue born of strength and pride in Chinese civilization and of a determination not to allow Westerners further economic, military, and political advantages in China.

One can speculate on what might have happened had Westerners understood the genuine interest of the self-strengthening officials in the exploitation of coal and iron for China's steamships

and for use at her arsenals and shipyards. If Westerners had
accepted that reality and had worked with those officials in introducing railways at mines, it is quite conceivable that China would
have witnessed the introduction of railways much sooner than she
did. For railways, in these circumstances, would have been introduced in conjunction with a vital Chinese interest and without an
intrusion on Chinese sovereignty.

The cooperative policy held out the promise that Western
sensitivity, and hence receptiveness, would be reflected in relationships with China. Secured by the British presence, it was the policy
of the Ch'ing and Western governments from the early 1860s
through the 1870s. During that time British foreign secretaries and
envoys—Bruce through Wade—"never wavered in their conviction
that the Chinese government must be allowed the fullest freedom,
not only from foreign military force but from the excessive pressure
of foreign advice, foreign commercial requirements, and foreign
missionary activity. The British government was prepared to sacrifice immediate interests in the hope, and even the expectation, that
the Chinese government would make the necessary adjustments
to modern problems at its own pace and on its own terms."[7]

The reality was something else. Western policy aimed at
increasing Western political and economic power in China. Although
British and American economic activities were of a different scale,
the merchants of both countries were vitally interested in the
further exploitation of the China market. Their investment in long-
term ventures such as railways, telegraphs, and public utilities,
carried the expectation of future growth and integration of China's
economy into the world economy. British and American officials
strove to create a political climate within which that economic
expansion and integration could take place. The cooperative policy
was tailored to that end, and as regards the introduction of telegraphs and railways, the method of *de facto* introduction was its
natural expression.

From the Western point of view, China's policy on the introduction of railways and telegraphs was an equivocal one and
Westerners believed if they continued to educate, to present

ingenious rationales and schemes, Chinese officials would eventually yield. Westerners were convinced that it was in China's best interests to adopt innovations and that it was only a matter of time until she did. For Western merchants, a China receptive to innovations would mean a more accessible China market, a China more receptive to Western goods. For Western officials, especially the British, China's adoption of innovations was viewed as a necessary step along the path of Progress, a sign that the cooperative policy was working. Each had a role to play. Generally, merchants initiated schemes; officials presented them, argued for them, and negotiated their introduction.

This Western approach of pressuring, educating, and initiating did not necessitate the actual use of force. In the period of accommodation under the cooperative policy, the threat of the use of force was enough. This policy worked as long as Chinese officials were cooperative. Their collaboration was necessary before the transfer of Chinese economic resources and the development of Chinese markets were possible.

Those Chinese officials—the statecraft officials—who should have been the natural allies of the Westerners in the modernization of China were the very officials who most effectively opposed Western introduction of telegraphs and railways. These men were favorable to Western innovations and saw clearly the economic, military, and political power of telegraphs and railways. Indeed, they were in favor of their introduction precisely because of the wealth and power they generated. But they realized, too, that unless China maintained ultimate control, increased commerce could only come at the expense of Chinese merchants and government enterprises. And increased political power, which these innovations generated, meant more conflicts with Westerners gaining more rights, such as travel, trade, and interior residence. Chinese officials knew well the aggressive character of the Western presence —the opium wars and resultant treaties and the distasteful experiences with arrogant Westerners during the Taiping Rebellion were events of recent experience. Continued Western pressures for concessions to build railways and telegraphs served to reenforce that reality.

In pursuing the goal of gradual modernization of China, the cooperative policy, by the very methods that it necessitated, undermined the sovereignty that it purported to uphold. At best the cooperative policy bought time for both Chinese and Western officials during which each could become sensitive to the priorities and behavior of the other. At its worst, it was a shield under which Western economic imperialism pressured, manipulated, and bullied Chinese officials for concessions. Chinese statecraft officials were caught in the contradiction of knowing this truth and at the same time realizing the need for China to adopt certain innovations to increase her wealth and power. It was a contradiction to be repeated again and again in the course of modern Chinese history.

Robert P. Gardella
REFORM AND THE TEA INDUSTRY AND TRADE IN LATE
CH'ING CHINA: THE FUKIEN CASE

Recent scholarship on the development of agriculture and
commerce in late imperial China exemplifies the need for a clearer
understanding of the nature of the involvement of littoral China
and its hinterland with foreign trade.[1] One important feature of
this involvement was the overseas export of staple commodities,
which before the twentieth century was restricted to relatively few
goods, chiefly tea and silk. In the latter half of the nineteenth
century tea and silk dominated China's trade with the West. In the
1860s and 70s tea alone constituted well over 40 percent of China's
principal exports by value. Only during the 1890s did silk finally
overtake tea as the leading export commodity.[2]

Chinese tea exports generated income for society and revenue
for the state. Growing and processing tea by traditional handicraft
methods was an important subsidiary employment in peasant households throughout central and southern China. Tea manufacture
even had a role in China's early industrialization, for among the
few modern industries established before 1895 in the treaty ports,
Russian brick tea factories were second only to shipyards in terms
of capital invested, total assets, and number of workers employed.[3]
Furthermore, the revenue from taxation of the tea trade became a
valuable source of funds to imperial authorities during the "self-
strengthening" era.

Above all, the tea industry and trade illustrates that the late
Ch'ing agrarian economy was both flexible and vulnerable. Flexible,
because of its capacity to expand production rapidly to great magni-
tudes without substantive organizational or technological change.
Vulnerable, because the organization and technology of tea production proved easily transferable to other countries, which then
emerged as competitive sources of supply for the world market.
The issue of economic reform in late Ch'ing China is thus framed
by two phenomena: the ability of the traditional economy to

71

respond to expanded economic opportunities generated by increased trade with the West and its inability to cope with a rapidly changing global economy dominated by Western colonial enterprise. In the upshot, as the following case study of the Fukien tea industry and trade during the late nineteenth century reveals, there was a good deal of change but not very much reform.

Tea cropping became particularly significant in the economic development of Fukien during the Ch'ing dynasty. The cultivation of tea was one of the few ways in which a population growing by Malthusian proportions, and confronted by a severe shortage of arable land for cereal crops, could utilize the province's all too abundant hilly and mountainous terrain.[4] Yet despite the fact that tea production for the domestic market had been a feature of Fukien's economy since the T'ang period, the slow growth of the domestic market acted to confine tea cultivation largely to one area of the province (the northwest), thus limiting its potential growth.[5]

The expansion of tea growing from the eighteenth century on was directly linked to the growth of foreign trade. The Wu-i Mountains of Fukien produced the famed Bohea tea, which together with Congou (*kung-fu*) tea increasingly found its way to Canton and the English market. In spite of the restrictions arbitrarily imposed on foreign trade by the Canton system, it is likely that as much as twenty million pounds of Fukien black tea were exported to Great Britain by the early 1830s.[6] With the opening of the ports of Amoy, Foochow, and Tamsui to foreign shipping after 1850, the growth of tea exports became so rapid that a tea boom can be said to have prevailed until the 1880s.

Fukien's black tea was now in wide demand not only in Great Britain, but also in Australia and the United States. Shipments of tea from Foochow alone rose from thirty-five to eighty million pounds between 1856 to 1857 and 1868, reaching a high point of over ninety-six million pounds in 1880. At this time China still monopolized world tea markets, and at least one-third of her yearly tea exports by volume came from Foochow.[7] Tea made Foochow an international port of call frequented by the romantic clipper ships, which raced each other halfway around the globe to bring the first crops of the season to the London auctions. In the 1870s Russian firms looked to Fukien as a source of brick tea, establishing over half a dozen small processing factories at Foochow and deep in the interior. By 1879 over a third of China's brick tea exports, or roughly thirteen and a half million pounds, came from northern Fukien.[8]

Tea growing increased throughout the province in response to the development of foreign markets. This was especially evident in areas such as northern Taiwan and northeastern Fukien, where tea had traditionally never been an important crop. American demand for Formosan oolong tea stimulated a tremendous expansion in production. Rice paddies in the T'ao-yuan Plateau were converted to large tea estates owned by wealthy landlords (such as the Lins of Pan-ch'iao) and farmed under contract by tenants. Hills surrounding the Taipei Basin were stripped of scrub vegetation and planted in small plots of tea by peasant proprietors. Exports, usually transshipped via Amoy, burgeoned from 180,000 pounds in 1865 to over 16,000,000 pounds in 1885. Tea became the major cash crop of north Formosa in the space of two decades.[9] In the Pei-ling Hills of northeast Fukien tea cultivation only began after Foochow was opened in the 1850s. Three decades later over eleven thousand families in this area collectively produced more than 3,700,000 pounds of tea per year.[10]

Labor as well as land was mobilized for tea growing, as prosperity lured immigrants to both old and new regions of tea production. Thousands of poor peasants arrived each year from neighboring Kiangsi for the spring tea picking in the Wu-i Mountains. Migrants flocked from the overcrowded southern and backward western parts of Fukien to the north and east, built rude shacks in the mountains, and hastily cleared slopeland for tea bushes. Merchants and brokers came from Canton and Amoy to Foochow and north Formosa to "raise up their families" (i.e. make their fortunes) in the tea export business.[11]

The gains from expanded tea production were not inconsequential. In northwest Fukien a picul of tea sold for over twenty taels, leaving windfall profits to the cultivator.[12] According to one account, peasants in the interior were now able to raise their living standards by substituting rice and fish for the sweet potatoes in their diets and improving their housing accommodations.[13] Since there was little demand for Western goods, thousands of foreign silver dollars were imported each year to pay for tea exports. This increased the amount of money in circulation, alleviated the severe deflation of the 1840s, and generally stimulated business activity.[14] Foochow's *ch'ien-chuang* (money banking shops), for example, owed their origins to the pressing need to handle the additional money supply generated by the post-1850 tea trade.[15]

Both the provincial and central governments also capitalized on the growth of the tea trade. Income from tea likin and tea taxes (first levied in 1853) placed the provincial administration on a sounder financial footing than before, since elastic commercial revenue now supplemented the relatively fixed land tax as a source of public finance.[16] Until the mid-1880s approximately 40 percent of Fukien's yearly internal customs revenue was derived from a series of taxes and surtaxes on tea exports.[17] In addition to these provincial levies, the central and provincial authorities shared about a million and a half taels per year in export duties on tea collected by the maritime customs.[18] Official revenues, in these circumstances, were directly subject to the vagaries of the tea trade and to annual market fluctuations.[19]

The provincial government erected a pervasive network of internal customs barriers to levy commercial taxes; by 1896 there were over two hundred such octroi stations, among which were one hundred fifteen tea-tax barriers manned only during the tea season (April to November).[20] Authorities took some pains to protect the trade from private depredations. They provided armed escorts for tea merchants venturing into the interior and policed the market-place to check occasional malpractices, such as adulteration or mis-representation of the quality of tea consignments.[21]

The income realized from tea taxation was largely devoted to the maintenance of military strength. Provincial likin and tea taxes helped to defray the cost of provincial armed forces, while the maritime customs duties went to finance Tso Tsung-t'ang's pacification of the northwest and construction of the modern dockyard and naval arsenal at Foochow.[22] Commercial taxation thus helped to make military "self-strengthening" financially feasible, and foreign trade may be said to have contributed to the wealth and strength of late nineteenth-century China, despite the fact that there was no explicit national policy of promoting commerce.

The prosperity of China's export tea trade, however, hinged ultimately upon the historical pre-eminence of Chinese tea production and the absence of alternate sources of supply. By the 1880s China's domination of the world tea trade was already coming to an end. In India from the mid-nineteenth century, and subsequently in Ceylon, British-owned and operated tea plantations had begun to cultivate tea on a massive scale. They manufactured black tea by a machine technology developed over several decades to supersede manual processing methods originally borrowed from China.[23] Plantation organization, as adapted to tea production, combined ready access to the virgin uplands of northeast India and central Ceylon, plentiful supplies of cheap Indian field labor, and joint stock capitalization to realize great economies of scale. Cheap imports of South Asian tea by 1888 surpassed Chinese exports to the lucrative United Kingdom market, and barely a year later Englishmen were consuming ninety-six million pounds of Indian and twenty-eight and a half million pounds of Ceylon tea, but only about sixty million pounds of Chinese tea (as compared to one hundred million pounds of the latter as late as 1886).[24]

Chinese tea growing, processing, and distribution traditionally rested upon the coordinated but managerially unintegrated activities of numerous peasant producers, tea-processing workers, merchant-middlemen, and brokers. As in so many other areas of late imperial economic organization, the key to this system lay in the "triadic complex" of merchant-middleman-agent which linked small-scale units of production to a large-scale international market. In dramatic contrast to the regimented, centralized operations of South Asian plantations, there was in China no single overall point at which the activities of participants in the tea industry and trade were subject to external control.[25]

Ch'ing officials recognized full well that foreign competition posed unprecedented problems for the tea-export trade. In an 1888 report to the Tsungli Yamen, Robert Hart summarized the situation. Foreign tea was now less expensive than Chinese tea and better and more uniformly prepared. China's competitors did not levy heavy transit and export duties on tea, and they organized production on a larger, more efficient scale. Tea from China was now stigmatized as carelessly grown, sloppily prepared, subject to various kinds of adulteration, and improperly packed for shipment.[26] Western critics, however, were divided over whether reform should be piece-meal, building on the existing structure of the trade, or radical, overhauling the existing structure in accordance with foreign methods. Some suggested that tea schools, model plantations, and chartered companies be established in the tea-producing provinces.[27] Hart's admonitions and policy suggestions apparently fell on deaf ears in 1888. Ch'ing officials took no action for another decade, during which time the China tea trade lost further valuable ground to foreign competitors.

In Fukien the impact of declining demand and falling tea prices was particularly acute, since the province had depended on markets now invaded by plantation-grown tea. Regions that had hitherto prospered from producing tea now languished, as this account from Yen-p'ing *fu* in northwest Fukien illustrates:

> Those who relied on tea farming for a living were not few in number: those who clear the mountains, tea pickers, those who open *ch'a-chuang* to process and package tea, tea sellers, and tea experts and selectors. After 1881 tea prices were very low. Those who opened *ch'a-chuang* and the tea chest makers went broke, and many producers could no longer depend on tea. Those with fields recultivated them, and the ones without land cut brushwood for a living. How lamentable that the people who labored to plant tea received such bitterness from it![28]

Foochow's black tea exports declined to about thirty-eight million pounds by 1900.[29] Amoy's tea trade also decreased sharply, due both to the decline in demand for tea grown in southern Fukien, and the steady loss of the re-export trade in Formosan oolong after the Japanese occupation of Taiwan in 1895.[30] Even brick tea shipments to Russia fell to about four and a half million pounds in 1900, as most of the Russian merchants had already transferred their operations to Hankow and Kiukiang.[31]

To one high provincial official, however, the end of the tea boom was good tidings. According to Min-Che Governor-General Pien Pao-ti, the expansion of tea cultivation had distorted Fukien's economy, bringing ecological damage to rice-growing lowlands and potential socioeconomic unrest in its wake:

> From the time of the [province's] opening to commerce, foreign ships have flocked [here] and the merchants have been corrupted by profit. More and more mountains have been planted over [with tea]. The greened cliffs have been cut down to the red soil, and clear streams in the valleys have become yellow-flowing [because of] reckless cultivation. In the mountains good and bad people are mingled together in the tea workshops. Not only were they unprepared for drought and floods, but also exposed to banditry. In recent years India has been producing more tea, and wealthy merchants are taking losses.[32]

Since tea markets were depressed, Pien believed that the time (ca. 1889) was ripe to prohibit tea growing and encourage cultivation of food crops and mulberry for sericulture. To this end, he admonished the gentry and officials of northern Fukien to re-educate shortsighted peasants in the need to provide for their subsistence rather than gamble their labor in tea cultivation.[33] It is doubtful, however, that Pien Pao-ti's economic moralizing had any more effect in curbing tea cultivation than Robert Hart's report had in reforming it.

By the end of the century reformers such as Cheng Kuan-ying and Ma Chien-chung were calling for the Ch'ing state to take an active role in promoting the tea industry and trade. Both strongly advocated abolition of the likin and export taxes and called for governmental intervention to improve production techniques (though neither was very specific about how this was to be done). In a world of increasing economic rivalry, Cheng cried, China must now learn to wage commercial warfare (*shang-chan*), rather than concentrate its energies on strictly military preparations.[34] In his essay "Fu-min shuo" (On enriching the people), Ma argued that "In governing a state [one] considers wealth and strength as the basis, but in seeking strength [one] aims first for wealth."[35] Thus the road to wealth and power for these "mercantile nationalists"—to borrow Yen-p'ing Hao's term—lay in removing domestic obstacles to the growth of internal and external trade.

At least some Ch'ing officials by the turn of the century seemed prepared to act on this prescription. During the *pien-fa* whirlwind of 1898, one proposal called for the establishment of tea institutes (*ch'a-wu hsueh-t'ang*) to teach proper cultivation techniques, and advocated that provincial governments encourage tea cultivation and fund *kuan-tu shang-pan* enterprises to process tea by mechanized technology. Another memorial called for regulation of tea merchants to avoid commercial malpractices and stabilize market prices, along with the establishment of an official bank to finance the trade and a mercantile company to foster cooperation among Chinese tea dealers.[36] That same year the Fukien government bestirred itself to reduce the total inland duty on tea, set during the Taiping Rebellion at 2.35 taels per picul, to 1.91 taels.[37] Four years later, at the urging of Chinese tea merchants, the central government reduced the export duty by half, to 1.25 taels per picul.[38]

Although belated changes in fiscal policy were indicative of official good intentions, they hardly constituted a reform of the tea industry, and they did not in fact spur the hoped-for revival of the export trade. The need for a more comprehensive program of reform did, however, begin to be sensed during the dynasty's final decade. Official encouragement was given to the study of tea production in India and Ceylon (a mission was actually sent there in 1905), the establishment of experimental tea plantations (one was set up near Nanking), and the creation of the aforementioned special provincial schools to improve tea growing.[39] None of these efforts bore any dramatic short-term results, but they indicate growing concern over the future of a historically important branch of Chinese agriculture and commerce. Reform of the tea industry and trade was now perceived as a complex organizational problem, increasingly defined in a nationalistic context of global economic competition for trade, wealth, and autonomy. As one concerned Fukien official, Lü Wei-ying, stated in 1908:

> Westerners apply the principle of nationalism [*min-tsu chu-i*] to the tea industry. They employ mechanization to dazzle the eyes and ears. They promote better planting to improve profits, and also [foster] the use of Indian tea ... their newspapers slander Chinese tea as unsanitary, and this arouses distaste for it in foreign markets ... If they can use nationalism to repress our markets, how is it that we cannot use nationalism to restore our reputation? The reason, quite simply, is that commercial knowledge is not disseminated among us, our commercial spirit is dissipated, and we are unable to organize internally to deal with foreign obstacles.[40]

DISCUSSION

Jonathan Ocko, in commenting on Saundra Sturdevant's paper, noted that Chinese foreign policy was basically defensive, and that Ting Jih-ch'ang, Shen Pao-chen, and others used the treaties, often with great success, to restrict the activities of foreigners. Moreover, officials who opposed railroads and other Western innovations because there was insufficient Chinese control often used popular belief in geomancy (*feng-shui*) and such superstitions as part of their argument in dealing with Westerners. Frank Lojewski added that Ting Jih-ch'ang himself did not believe in *feng-shui* but used it to explain popular attitudes toward Westerners.

Saundra Sturdevant emphasized that Chinese officials were able to use the *feng-shui* argument to good effect only because there was a real foundation in popular belief. The officials explained the belief to the Westerners, who became very concerned over it. Thomas Kennedy said that the Westerners often exaggerated the Chinese emphasis on *feng-shui*. The Chinese themselves rarely mentioned it in their own writings. Mr. Kennedy added that his own research on the arsenals and the Foochow Shipyard substantiated Ms. Sturdevant's view that Confucian attitudes were not an ideological impediment to self-strengthening.

Paul Cohen pointed out that foreign exaggeration of Chinese attitudes toward *feng-shui* was paralleled by the fact that foreigners were more inclined than Chinese to link together opium and missionaries. Ellsworth Carlson said that his work on the Foochow area revealed no examples of official writings associating the two, although the common people did. Louis Sigel added that people in the treaty ports sometimes exploited British feelings of guilt toward opium.

John Schrecker said that in the 1890s there was a growing sense of shame over China's weakness toward foreigners. At the same time, there was a greater sense of vigor in the writings of some people, such as K'ang Yu-wei, along with a new theoretical understanding of the concept of sovereignty. Ms. Sturdevant agreed that the officials of the 1890s were different from those of the 1860s. In the 1860s

there was not the same feeling of shame, only a vigorous sense of
outrage over the foreigners' presence in China. Jonathan Ocko
added that writers in the 1860s rarely used a counterpart for the
Western term "sovereignty"; instead they would tell Westerners
"the treaty says that you can't do that," without using the abstract
concept.

Richard Shek asked Robert Gardella how growth in the tea
trade helped Fukien province become financially independent of
Peking. Mr. Gardella said that the trend toward fiscal independence
began with the likin system, which gave the provinces control over
certain tax resources. Since the likin was a tax on internal commerce, as the tea trade expanded, likin revenues grew proportionally.

Yeh-chien Wang asked Robert Gardella whether he had found
any estimates of the extent of the nationwide market before the
Westerners came to China. Mr. Gardella replied that there were
very few such indications. Up to the late Ming and early Ch'ing
periods the nationwide market was primarily in luxury goods. It
then began to broaden, however. There was also, in the case of tea,
a broadening of the base of production in response to Western
demand.

Mr. Wang also asked about tea competition between China
and India. Mr. Gardella said that the East India Company smuggled
tea into India, but was unable to duplicate Chinese cultivation
methods. The British developed their own forms of production and
grew their own types of tea on plantations in India. Cutthroat competition rose between China and India. Marianne Bastid added that
good Fukien tea maintained its position for a long time, although
the poorer grades of Chinese tea fared less well in competition with
Indian tea. She also pointed out that some sectors of the tea trade,
such as the trade with Russia, continued to prosper.

Lillian Li noted that in the silk industry old and new silk-
producing areas differed, and new areas were much more likely to
introduce innovations. Mr. Gardella said that the same was generally
true in Fukien tea-producing areas. The oldest area was the Wu-i
Mountains, where very little technological change occurred. Land
was owned, often by temples, in large managerial units, and labor

discipline was exacting. This was very different from the marginal production of tea which prevailed in many other areas. Ms. Li also asked about the management and organization of tea production. Mr. Gardella said that tea production in its modern form demanded vertical integration for standardization, but vertical integration did not exist. As for merchant investment in the tea industry, merchants did buy tea land, but they did not take direct part in the management of production, which was left to labor-brokers.

Ms. Li asked about the bearing of tax policy, specifically whether reduction or elimination of the tax burden might have encouraged organizational changes within the tea industry. Mr. Gardella said that Chinese entrepreneurs were not developing any kind of mechanized technology, and there was apparently no organizational change before the beginning of the competition of Indian tea. However, tax reform might have stimulated market expansion. Ms. Li suggested that obstacles to reform of the tea industry probably existed on several levels.

Frank Lojewski suggested that production in some areas was too fragmented and small-scale to produce enough capital for technological change. He asked for elaboration of the claim that there was an increase in the living standard of peasants in the tea-producing areas. Mr. Gardella said that British diplomatic correspondence reported such an increase, but it was hard to prove. Merchants and brokers in tea were often described as being wealthy, but it was a business with high risks. Ellsworth Carlson added that missionary correspondence in the 1850s referred to greatly increased employment in tea-producing areas. Mr. Gardella said that the Nan-t'ang suburb of Foochow, and even Taipei, grew tremendously because of the tea trade, and Marianne Bastid pointed to evidence from Ch'ing memorials of the 1860s and 1870s of an increase in tax income resulting from expansion of the tea trade.

Returning to Saundra Sturdevant's remarks, Charlton Lewis observed that there seemed to be little resistance to the building of the Shanghai–Wusung Railway, a fact of some importance when considered in light of the resistance to innovations in other areas.

When examining incidents of resistance, we should focus on the arrangement of local control in each area. Who would benefit and who would lose if an innovation were introduced? Innovations could be appraised differently under different conditions. Ms. Sturdevant replied that the Shanghai–Wusung Railway was actually very complicated. Part of the railroad went through the Western concession, where Westerners were free to buy up land and put down tracks. The *taotai* was placed in a difficult position, however, when the foreigners decided to begin the railroad in the Chinese-controlled part of the route.

Thomas Kennedy said that the sovereignty issue initially took the form of a simple gut reaction against foreign control in China. Contemporary Chinese scholarship presented the self-strengtheners as lackeys of foreign imperialism. The evidence, however, controverted such a conclusion. Paul Cohen agreed that the data presented by Ms. Sturdevant called for revision not only of Mary Wright's conclusion that Confucianism and the requirements of modernization were fundamentally incompatible, but also of the "foreign lackey" analysis of Communist historians. Official opposition to Western-inspired innovation appeared, in many instances, to have been rooted less in Confucian ideology than in sensitivity to the issue of Western control.

David Pong mentioned that although money was a continual source of concern to the Ch'ing government, it somehow became available when an issue of sovereignty was involved. When the officials wanted to buy the Wusung Railway, they were able to raise the needed funds. Mr. Pong suggested that a sophisticated concept of sovereignty was emerging in China as far back as the 1860s. He wondered whether people like Li Hung-chang and Shen Pao-chen were not motivated by something approximating "Confucian patriotism." Ms. Sturdevant thought they were. Li and Shen agreed on the importance of railroads and mines. They believed in the importance of the introduction of Western technology, and felt it necessary, for example, to develop mines for coal. However, they were extremely concerned with the problem of Chinese control over these enterprises and resources.

THE POLITICS OF REFORM

Kwang-Ching Liu
POLITICS, INTELLECTUAL OUTLOOK, AND REFORM:
THE T'UNG-WEN KUAN CONTROVERSY OF 1867

It is a truism that for any large reform measure to become realized, the breakthrough must ultimately be made in the realm of politics. But is politics the only crucial factor involved in a reform movement? Isn't it also a truism that politics itself is influenced by ideological, social, economic, and other factors? Surely one of our tasks here is to inquire into the relationships among these factors as they bear upon the late Ch'ing reform movement.

I present the case study of an attempt at educational and civil-service reform during the T'ung-chih period (1862–1874). I would go so far as to say that the proposal made by the Tsungli Yamen in 1867 for the recruitment of top scholars to the T'ung-wen kuan's projected department of "astronomy and mathematics" constituted a major reform effort which anticipated some of the most radical proposals of 1898. Before I enter into the details of the 1867 case, however, I would like to refer to two relevant observations found in the writings of the organizers of this workshop, Messrs. Cohen and Schrecker. In his essay "Ch'ing China: Confrontation with the West, 1850–1900," Mr. Cohen asks us to view late Ch'ing reform efforts as having been, in part, "a response to internal Chinese power rivalries."[1] Among the statesmen who were early advocates of self-strengthening (which may be regarded as reform in a broad sense), Li Hung-chang certainly proposed the largest number of innovations. I would agree with Mr. Cohen that Li probably often had uppermost in his mind "the problem of Li Hung-chang," that one of his principal concerns was the maintenance of his own power. Yet it is also entirely plausible that Li developed a certain intellectual outlook that went beyond his taste for power. This is what I have tried to argue in my article "The Confucian as Patriot and Pragmatist: Li Hung-chang's Formative Years, 1823–1866."[2] I believe Li to have been at once a power-holder and a patriot. The fact that he was able to introduce so

many innovations in the late Ch'ing period was a reflection of the
influence he enjoyed—the political backing of the court as well as
the financial means that came with that backing. Not conscious of
any conflict between his loyalty to the reigning dynasty and his
concern for China as a country (Chung-kuo or Chung-t'u), he frequently expressed solicitude for the security and independence of
the latter. Indeed, Li may well have been moved by a kind of
"Confucian patriotism."

I would also like to draw attention to a very original point
regarding Chinese patriotism made by Mr. Schrecker in his
Imperialism and Chinese Nationalism. Mr. Schrecker sees a historical
relationship between two seemingly opposite attitudes among the
scholar-officials of the 1890s.[3] On the one hand there was the militant culturalism often associated with *ch'ing-i*—i.e., moralistic opinion
offered by middle or low-ranking literati-officials. On the other hand,
there was the nationalistic reformism of K'ang Yu-wei and Liang
Ch'i-ch'ao, which implied not only a clear recognition of the concept
of Chinese sovereignty, but also the conviction that certain aspects
of Chinese culture needed to be changed radically. The logical
question to ask is: what accounts for the transmutation from militant culturalism to reformist nationalism? Does the explanation lie
merely in the way the political winds were blowing in 1898—the
crisis created by the European occupation of Kiaochow and Port
Arthur and the fact that the Kuang-hsu Emperor had himself
declared for reform? Or did these political circumstances merely
serve as a catalyst for the final emergence of intellectual tendencies
that had been growing for some time? What, in short, was the intellectual position of "militant culturalism" in its earlier form, and
how did it gain ascendancy in the policies of the court of the
Empress Dowager Tz'u-hsi? By examining the abortive reform
efforts of 1867, I hope this paper can serve as a baseline for the
discussion of such issues.

The Political-Intellectual Background

In presenting this case study, my own assumption is that
political power is seldom purely political. Ideas and politics have a

way of being intertwined, just as politics is often influenced by vested economic or bureaucratic interests. While strong backing is necessary for any breakthrough in the direction of reform, other factors inseparable from politics may be just as crucial. If, for example, we look at the era of the mid-1860s, when the Empress Dowager Tz'u-hsi began to assert her power at court, we find that while it was indeed she who obstructed the proposed reform of 1867, just as she did that of 1898, in neither case did she act *in vacuo.* As early as the mid-1860s, there was already a body of officials in Peking who constituted a political-intellectual force— who were not only bureaucrats but, at least in the case of a number of them, also men of conviction.

To trace the intellectual flavor of the bureaucracy of the early Tz'u-hsi court, one must go back in time at least to the early years of the Hsien-feng period (1851–1861). The Hsien-feng Emperor was in fact an unusually good Confucian monarch—that is, before his personality began to disintegrate under the pressure of internal rebellion and foreign invasion and he devoted himself almost entirely to becoming an expert on the Peking opera. He had genuine respect for his tutor Tu Shou-t'ien (1787–1852), a Neo-Confucian scholar-statesman of the Ch'eng-Chu school. After his accession to the throne, he relied heavily on Tu Shou-t'ien for advice regarding personnel. It was presumably at Tu's suggestion that he promoted Ch'i Chün-tsao (1793–1866), a grand councillor without much power under the Tao-kuang reign, to be the principal grand councillor.

Ch'i was also a Neo-Confucian scholar, representing the new trend of amalgamating the introspective moral emphasis of the Sung learning with the Han learning's emphasis on accurate knowledge of the ancient classics.[4] As a grand councillor during the last decade of the Tao-kuang reign, Ch'i had been opposed to the policies of Mu-chang-a, the emperor's favorite. But Mu was now dismissed from office, and until his own retirement in 1855, Ch'i had a chance to put many friends of kindred spirit into high places in the bureaucracy—such men as Weng Hsin-ts'un (1791–1862), Chou Tsu-p'ei (1792?–1867), and Chia Chen (1798–1874). An ideologically-oriented faction of officials may be said to have been formed in the process, and it survived the coup d'état of 1861. Weng Hsin-ts'un died in 1862. But his able son, Weng T'ung-ho (1830–1904), *chin-shih* of 1856, was to continue his associations. Chou Tsu-p'ei and Chia Chen, having served as board presidents, became grand secretaries by the late Hsien-feng era and continued in this capacity into the T'ung-chih period. As grand secretaries, they had little decision-making power. Yet they were influential among the metropolitan and even provincial officials, as they often served as examiners in the metropolitan examination and the Hanlin Academy tests and could claim many officials as their "students."

It was particularly appropriate that Tz'u-hsi, whose authority depended on the fact that she was the young T'ung-chih Emperor's mother and on the Confucian principle of "filial obedience," should emulate the high moral tone of the early Hsien-feng years. Almost immediately after the coup d'état of 1861, Wo-jen (1804–1871), a famous Neo-Confucian theorist of Mongol origin, was appointed president of the Censorate. During 1862, he was promoted to grand secretary, serving concurrently as imperial tutor. Li T'ang-chieh (1798–1865), who, like Wo-jen, was known for his scholarship in Ch'eng-Chu Confucianism as well as exemplary personal rectitude, was summoned from retirement in Honan to be president of the Censorate and concurrently a grand councillor. Li was a good friend of Wo-jen and of Tseng Kuo-fan. By nature not an aggressive person, his presence on the Grand Council seems to have been chiefly symbolic of the throne's commitment to intellectual orthodoxy.

Apparently it was not until 1865, when Tz'u-hsi enlisted the help of some of the grand secretaries to deal a blow to Prince Kung's prestige, that the factional politics of her court really began. As is now well known, in an imperial edict of early April, which she drafted herself in faulty Chinese and handed to the grand secretaries (including Chou Tsu-p'ei and Wo-jen) to edit and promulgate, she dismissed Prince Kung from all offices on grounds of corruption and disrespect for the sovereign.[5] Although she relented after ten days and restored the prince to his posts as grand councillor and

head of the Tsungli Yamen, he was permanently deprived of his
title as *i-cheng wang* (deliberative prince), which he had earned by
helping Tz'u-hsi in the coup d'état of 1861. There were, to be sure,
high officials who pleaded for Prince Kung at the time, but Wo-jen
and Chou Tsu-p'ei were not among them. Tz'u-hsi's purpose was to
make clear, especially to the metropolitan bureaucracy, that Prince
Kung was not unassailable, even though she was relying on him for
the handling of vital affairs of state, including the problem of coping with the troublesome Western powers. In the winter of 1865,
Tz'u-hsi made the further move of appointing a really able conservative partisan, Li Hung-tsao (1820–1899), as grand councillor. Li had
been the principal tutor of the T'ung-chih Emperor and had had
frequent audiences with Tz'u-hsi. A Neo-Confucian of the Sung
school, he was politically astute as well as ideologically supercilious.
Henceforth he was to be the leader of a political faction whose
ideological spokesman was Wo-jen. Although during the T'ung-wen
kuan controversy of 1867 Li was on a special one-year mourning
leave, he resided in Peking and was frequently consulted by Wo-
jen's partisans.[6]

The Reform Proposal
       Although the T'ung-wen kuan had been established under the
auspices of the Tsungli Yamen as early as 1862, the original purpose
was simply to train the interpreters needed in Sino-Western diplomatic negotiations. There was no plan to introduce science and other
aspects of Western learning. However, in 1863, when Li Hung-chang
recommended that similar foreign-language schools be established in
Shanghai and Canton, he proposed that these schools should have the
broader aim of introducing foreign learning; Western mathematics
as well as sciences were to be taught. The schools at Shanghai and
Canton were inaugurated in 1864, the same year that Li made his
famous proposal to the Tsungli Yamen that a new category (*k'o*)
be established in the civil service examinations for scholars specializ-
ing in technology—a proposal that Prince Kung forwarded to the
throne but that found no response. Meanwhile, the Kiangnan
Arsenal was established in Shanghai and the more grandiose

Foochow Navy Yard was founded by Tso Tsung-t'ang in Foochow, both with the approval of the throne.

Two Western advisers, Robert Hart and W. A. P. Martin, continued to bring to the attention of the Tsungli Yamen the value of Western sciences and technology. Prince Kung and his principal colleague and counsellor, Wen-hsiang, were responsive, and in the winter of 1866–1867, they made a truly bold proposal, the radical nature of which has often been overlooked by historians. Before actually submitting this proposal, they had taken the preliminary step of authorizing Hart, when he went home on furlough in 1866, to look in Europe for science instructors to staff a department of "astronomy and mathematics" to be established at the T'ung-wen kuan. "Astronomy and mathematics," which occupied a peripheral place in Chinese scholarship, were used to camouflage such Western sciences as chemistry and mechanics, and it was for teachers of these latter subjects that Hart was asked to search. Nor was the plan of Prince Kung and Wen-hsiang limited to the introduction of a few new subjects. Its broader goal was indeed nothing less than recognition by the throne and by such citadels of orthodoxy as the Hanlin Academy of the legitimacy of Western learning.

Initially, in its memorial of December 1866, the Tsungli Yamen had proposed that scholars and officials with the *chü-jen* degree be encouraged to apply for admission to the new program. Then on January 28, 1867, Prince Kung and his colleagues further memorialized asking that holders of the *chin-shih* degree and especially members of the Hanlin Academy—including the prestigious compilers (*pien-hsiu*)—also be encouraged to apply.[7] Upon the completion of a three-year course, moreover, scholars enrolled in the new school were to be given extraordinary recommendation for official advancement (*ko-wai yu-pao*)—a great attraction even for high degreeholders and Hanlin academicians. It is perhaps not too far-fetched to suppose that, had this proposal produced the desired effects, a major reform of the Ch'ing educational and civil service system might have occurred.

Tz'u-hsi approved both the December and January memorials, but she soon learned, perhaps for the first time in such unmistakable

fashion, that the Neo-Confucian scholars she patronized, though
sometimes pliable political tools, had strong views of their own
regarding policies of reform. These strong views did not surface
immediately. The Peking bureaucracy at first acquiesced in the
Tsungli Yamen's proposal. It was only in early March that Chang
Sheng-tsao, a censor, memorialized to present his opinion that self-
strengthening depended not on guns and ships (the manufacture of
which was presumably the purpose of learning Western techniques)
but on "good and just government." The censor was particularly
worried that the emphasis on what to him were mere matters of
technique (*chi-ch'iao*) would have an adverse effect on the spirit of
the literati; technical knowledge and good moral character seemed
to him to be antithetical. Even after this attack, the throne continued to side with Prince Kung, stating in an edict that "astronomy
and mathematics are what Confucian scholars ought to know and
should not be regarded as matters of technique." Furthermore, a
fair number of scholars applied to the Tsungli Yamen to be enrolled
in the T'ung-wen kuan's new program.

On March 20, however, a second critical memorial reached the
throne, from Grand Secretary Wo-jen himself. Wo-jen, as Mr. Hao
Chang has emphasized, stood at the T'ung-chih court virtually as
the high priest of Ch'eng-Chu Neo-Confucianism.[8] The imperial
tutor declared in his memorial, in a famous passage: "The way to
uphold the foundation of the state is to emphasize propriety and
sense of duty but not expedient schemes (*ch'üan-mou*). The basic
policy of the state [is to cultivate] people's morale (*jen-hsin*) and
not technique." Wo-jen identified technology with the despised
"magical computations" (*shu-shu*). But what was of even greater
emotional appeal to the literati-officials was his allegation that the
Tsungli Yamen wanted the Chinese to "honor the barbarians as
teachers" (*feng-i wei-shih*)[9]—the very barbarians who had so recently
invaded Peking itself and who were now spreading the abominable
doctrine of Christianity. In a memorial in reply, Prince Kung and
his colleagues argued that it was simply unrealistic to expect
"loyalty and faithfulness to serve as armor and propriety and
sense of duty as shield."[10] They went on to cite the words of loyal

officials of the time who strongly advocated the introduction of
Western technology—men like Tseng Kuo-fan, Li Hung-chang, Tso
Tsung-t'ang, and Shen Pao-chen, who presumably were no less
Confucian than Wo-jen himself.

Perhaps because Prince Kung still enjoyed considerable prestige
and power, very few officials memorialized in support of Wo-jen.[11]
But the latter's two memorials were made public by the throne.
(The second one, a reply to Prince Kung's rebuttal, stressed again
the risk of losing the support of the people by subjecting the
scholars to the degradation of having barbarians as teachers.) The
two memorials so stirred up the literati-officials of Peking that
damaging rumors began to circulate concerning the Tsungli Yamen's
intentions. Scholars who had applied for admission to the T'ung-
wen kuan's new program were sneered at by "fellow provincials
and colleagues." An informal group was formed among literati-
officials pledging not to be tempted by the new opportunities
offered by the T'ung-wen kuan. In late April, Prince Kung and his
colleagues reported to the throne that since the time when Wo-jen's
memorials were made public "no more persons had come to this
yamen to apply for the entrance examination [to the new pro-
gram]."[12] The yamen had to abandon its original plan of influencing the scholar-official elite toward the study of science and
technology. It now merely requested the throne's approval that
the entrance examination for the new program be held as planned,
to accommodate "those who at present have applied."

The outcome of this controversy for the T'ung-wen kuan's
later history is well known. The entrance examination was indeed
held. Seventy-two applicants, including Han Chinese and Manchus,
appeared for the test. But they were found to be mostly unemployed middle-aged men, "broken down hacks to whom the stipend
offered by the yamen proved dearer than their reputation," as a
Western observer remarked.[13] Thirty were admitted, but only five
eventually graduated. The better students at the T'ung-wen kuan
were those who had transferred, with the throne's approval, from
the Shanghai T'ung-wen kuan, and who included the sons of merchants and gentry of that treaty port. It is worth emphasizing that

Prince Kung and Wen-hsiang did not shun the odium of honoring
the barbarians as teachers. Two of the several foreign professors
engaged by Robert Hart in Europe arrived in 1868. W. A. P. Martin,
the famous missionary, who had earlier been engaged to teach
English at the school, was appointed chief instructor (*tsung chiao-
hsi*), a title that Martin translated as president. Martin tried to
organize the T'ung-wen kuan into a "college," with an eight-year
curriculum that included one European language as well as mathematics, physics, chemistry, and geography. In 1872, an English
medical missionary was appointed to teach anatomy and physiology.
However, the dominant purpose of the school continued to be the
training of personnel for diplomatic work. The best of the students
were appointed translators at the Tsungli Yamen even before gradu-
ation, although many of the students deemed it wise to devote a
considerable part of their time to preparation for the civil service
examinations. The idea of encouraging high degreeholders and
Hanlin academicians to enroll in the T'ung-wen kuan was not
brought up again—at least not until the late 1890s.

The Obstacles to Reform: An Analysis
     In tracing the reasons why the Tsungli Yamen's reform pro-
posal of 1867 came to nothing, the observation must be made that
intellectual attitudes did represent an autonomous force. Wo-jen
stood not only for the political interests and alignment of certain
metropolitan officials, but also for a major cultural position, albeit
by no means the only one. Weng T'ung-ho's diaries noted some gut
reactions of the Peking literati-officials toward the Tsungli Yamen's
plan of having respectable scholars take lessons from the foreigners.
Sarcastic couplets in fine calligraphy were posted at the front gates
of Peking residences lamenting the idea that "disciples of Confucius"
should learn from "teachers of demonic origins." Yet even among
the friends of Weng T'ung-ho, who was Wo-jen's junior colleague as
an imperial tutor, there were those who privately voiced the view
that "after all, steamships and mathematics are things which we
have to learn, although we must hold and express the opinion that
people's morale, integrity, and sense of shame, like our basic

principles and institutions, are of fundamental importance."[14]

The nagging question remains: would Prince Kung and Wen-hsiang, with greater support from the Empress Dowager, have been able to persuade the high-degreeholders and Hanlin academicians to enroll in the T'ung-wen kuan? For, plainly, Tz'u-hsi did not accord to Prince Kung a full measure of support during this controversy. She accepted some of his suggestions in her dealings with Wo-jen. She embarrassed the great Neo-Confucian by asking him to establish a separate school with only Chinese instructors in mathematics, Wo-jen having claimed them to be available. She also appointed him a member of the Tsungli Yamen, a humiliating assignment which Wo-jen got out of only after becoming sick—having fainted and "nearly fallen down" from the horse he was riding in the Forbidden City.

The Empress Dowager had her reasons for being angry at Wo-jen at this juncture, for he and two other imperial tutors, Hsu T'ung (1819–1900) and Weng T'ung-ho, in their concern for the proper education of the young monarch, had memorialized on March 12, 1867, remonstrating against the visits of the emperor and the dowager empresses to the homes of imperial princes, where they watched operatic performances.[15] However, Tz'u-hsi did not allow her personal pique to disturb her view of what was politically advantageous to her. While defending Prince Kung's idea that "astronomy and mathematics" were not mere techniques and ostensibly giving Wo-jen a hard time, she nevertheless refrained from repeating the call for degreeholders and Hanlin academicians to enroll in the T'ung-wen kuan's new program. Her edict of April 23 merely stated that "those who at present have applied for entrance" were to be given careful examination and admitted to the T'ung-wen kuan[16]—which meant, in effect, the abandonment of that aspect of Prince Kung's proposal aiming at major reform.

One can imagine Tz'u-hsi's reluctance to go against the grain of Wo-jen's interpretation of Confucian culture, since her own position as regent, and indeed the Manchu rule itself, were dependent on Confucian morality and culture. Conceivably, Tz'u-hsi could have chosen to adhere to a more flexible—yet still correct—view of

Confucian culture, as exemplified in the memorials of such men as Tseng Kuo-fan and Shen Pao-chen. She could have accepted Prince Kung's plea that the high-degreeholders needed only to learn certain "methods" from the hired foreigners and that they were under no circumstances to "observe the rituals of disciples" to the alien teachers. But Tz'u-hsi chose not to go this far in advancing the T'ung-wen kuan's cause. In fact, she saw no harm at all in the prince's being overpowered by Wo-jen in the controversy. More than a year later, in September 1868, we find an imperial edict undoubtedly emanating from her, pointedly singling out Wo-jen and Prince Kung, *in that order,* as the two officials of the empire with the heaviest responsibilities—one as the moral guide to the throne, since he was the imperial tutor; the other as the senior member of the Grand Council.[17] Although it was quite proper to put the imperial tutor above the grand councillor, the eminence accorded Wo-jen in the context was very likely deliberate, aiming at further reduction of Prince Kung's prestige. In her issuance of this edict, as in her role in the T'ung-wen kuan controversy generally, Tz'u-hsi must have been very much aware of the political consequences of her words and decisions.

What then can we conclude from this early case of an aborted late-Ch'ing reform effort? It is plain, in the first place, that a major new policy, such as having the Hanlin academicians study Western science and technology, could not possibly be pushed through without very strong support from the throne. Tz'u-hsi's failure to provide such support was due, apparently, not to any intellectual predilection against reform. The salient fact was, rather, that her position as imperial regent forced her to lean to the side of orthodoxy, and the most authoritative spokesman of orthodoxy at the time happened to be Wo-jen. To this consideration must be added an even more political one. Because of the respect Wo-jen enjoyed among the large number of officials in the Grand Secretariat, the Censorate, and the Hanlin Academy, Tz'u-hsi saw in these sectors of the metropolitan bureaucracy a potential source of opposition to Prince Kung, whom she regarded as a rival for influence. Although she took

the occasion of the T'ung-wen kuan controversy to issue an edict
expressly warning against the growth of factionalism,[18] she was
never to forget the criticism Prince Kung received during the
episode. And many times in the next seventeen years, until the
prince's removal from office in 1884, she was to rely on the pressure generated by memorials from metropolitan officials to
restrain Prince Kung as well as his allies at court and in the
provinces. Politics and intellectual outlook thus became very much
intertwined. In the T'ung-wen kuan episode we see in fact the
beginnings of the *ch'ing-i* politics that was to develop further in
the following decade.[19]

  As to the intellectual history revealed by this episode, it may
be remarked that although Wo-jen's stand was one of pure moralism,[20] it was not completely unrealistic. His basic position was the
Ch'eng-Chu abhorrence of considerations of utility—of "expedient
schemes" that suggested a Legalist aim. Wo-jen's criticism of the
T'ung-wen kuan's plans was consistent with his view, expressed in
an admiring commentary on Chu Hsi's discussion of Legalism, that
the search for wealth and power as practiced by such ancient
schemers as Kuan Chung and Shang Yang did not actually result
in the permanent prosperity and military invincibility of their
states.[21] When pushed to consider China's modern predicament
of having to cope with the superior technology of the West, Wo-jen
went so far as to admit, in his second memorial on the subject, that
there was no harm in the Chinese learning mathematics and the
manufacture of machines—*provided* "the scholars of China would
not be used by the barbarians."[22] It was Wo-jen's conviction, however, that only those scholars who were inferior in "intention and
conduct" (*chih hsing*) would honor the barbarians as teachers. Any
effort at self-strengthening would therefore be disastrous, if it
should involve the corruption of scholars by inducements of profit
and quick promotion and by the influence of barbarians as
teachers.[23] History was to prove Wo-jen apparently in error, since
many later Chinese who mastered Western technology actually
remained patriotic, if not also Confucian. Yet considering the fact
that what was at stake in 1867 were the career goals and commit-

ment of the most esteemed literati elite—the *chin-shih* scholars and the Hanlin academicians and compilers—Wo-jen's worry that the new proposal would cost the dynasty the support of the people was not completely imaginary. It was a valid concern, since the T'ung-wen kuan's recruitment policy would entail such change in the government's personnel policy that the old controls on the gentry-literati might very well fall apart. At the very least, the abandonment of cultural pride would disappoint a great many scholars and officials who came up through the traditional examination system.

To return to Mr. Cohen's skepticism regarding the motivations of reformers among the Ch'ing officials, one may observe that in making their bold proposal for encouraging the Hanlin academicians and the highest degreeholders to learn Western sciences at the T'ung-wen kuan, Prince Kung and his colleagues were, as far as can be determined, genuinely motivated by the need for such reform. "The greatest shame in the world," they had memorialized, "is the shame of being inferior to others."[24] China's inferiority in military weapons, unforgettably demonstrated during the Anglo-French invasion of Peking in 1860, was, Prince Kung and Wen-hsiang realized, the ultimate source of the Ch'ing diplomatic weakness. It was not enough for Chinese artisans to learn Western manufacturing. "The artisan practices [the skill], while the scholar understands the principle. It is only when the principle is understood that application can be of consequence."[25] Prince Kung and Wen-hsiang undoubtedly were convinced of the desirability of respectable Chinese scholars taking up science and technology. Whether they had thought through the political implications of their proposal, one can only speculate. The one thing we can be sure of is that with Tz'u-hsi bent on holding supreme power, Prince Kung and Wen-hsiang were hardly in a position to build a new, dominant faction at court through the T'ung-wen kuan's proposed recruitment program.

To refer again to Mr. Schrecker's thesis that militant anti-foreign culturalism had the potential to transform itself into reformist nationalism, it must be pointed out that this tendency was not yet visible as of the 1860s. The fervent attention of

Wo-jen and his colleagues was still directed chiefly to the issue of
government by properly indoctrinated men and, during the T'ung-
wen kuan controversy of 1867, to the specific question of whether
Chinese scholars should honor as teachers the Westerners, who
were aggressive and bent on spreading heterodoxy. The militancy
of the Wo-jen—Li Hung-tsao faction had yet to be applied to China's
foreign policy. Soon, however, this would become a major focus,
as the so-called Tientsin Massacre brought into prominence the issue
of whether anti-Christian officials of "rectitude" should be punished
and whether the apparently righteous sentiments of the populace
should be ignored.[26] Militant culturalism—or moralism, if you wish—
had a long way to go before it really turned introspective and looked
for weaknesses within Chinese institutions themselves. It would take
some three decades of continued Western impact as well as indigenous
intellectual ferment before this deeply ideological wing of the Chinese
conservatives could accept reformism of the 1898 variety.

Sue Fawn Chung
THE IMAGE OF THE EMPRESS DOWAGER TZ'U-HSI

The image of the Empress Dowager Tz'u-hsi as a conservative, ultraconservative, or reactionary was popularized by the radical reformers and their supporters. The *North China Herald* editors, who publicly supported the radical reformers; John Otway Percy Bland, who assisted in K'ang Yu-wei's escape in September 1898; and Yun Yü-ting (1863–1918) and Lo Tun-jung (d. 1923), contributors to Liang Ch'i-ch'ao's journal *Yung-yen* (The justice), were very influential in substantiating K'ang and Liang's negative characterization of Tz'u-hsi.[1] However, daily court records, the *Tung-hua hsu-lu, Ch'ing Te-tsung Ching huang-ti shih-lu,* and *Kung-chung tang Kuang-hsu ch'ao tsou-che,* project a very different picture of the Empress Dowager. How valid is the conservative image in view of her position on reform during the period 1898 to 1900?

Contrary to what has been widely asserted, the Empress Dowager supported the idea of reform during the summer of 1898. This was acknowledged at the time by a number of foreign observers. For example, Colonel Charles Denby, American representative to China, in writing about his experiences from 1885 to 1898, stated, "It will not be denied by anyone that the improvement and progress [in China] ... are mainly due to the will and power of the Empress Regent."[2] Henry Cockburn, the Chinese-language secretary to the British Legation who interviewed K'ang Yu-wei shortly after the coup d'état, suggested that K'ang's assertions about the Empress Dowager's opposition to reform might have been unfounded or greatly exaggerated.[3] It is also important to note that Liang Ch'i-ch'ao and Wang Chao (1859–1935) never accused the Empress Dowager of being opposed to the idea of reform and tacitly acknowledged that the reform movement could not have taken place without her cooperation.[4] One of their contemporaries even stated that Tz'u-hsi once told the emperor that reform had been her own wish for a long time and that she therefore willingly approved of the initiation of the radical reform

101

movement.[5] In light of the emperor's habit, throughout the summer of 1898, of frequently visiting the Empress Dowager at the
Summer Palace for the assumed purpose of discussing recent
memorials and policy decisions with her; his continued participation in state affairs immediately after the coup d'état; and the
decision taken by the two rulers to resume a policy of moderate
reform in the period from late 1898 to 1908, it does not seem
improbable that even prior to the Hundred Days Tz'u-hsi was
already in favor of extensive reforms. The trouble was that the
reform program initiated by the emperor with K'ang's assistance
was too extreme. Adverse reaction to the radical reform movement
mounted and high officials, such as Sun Chia-nai (1827–1909),
Wang Wen-shao (1830–1908), and Liu K'un-i (1830–1902), who
had supported extensive reforms, joined the so-called "anti-radical
reform movement" because of K'ang Yu-wei's beliefs and actions.[6]
In fact, Liu K'un-i blamed all the troubles of the summer of 1898
on K'ang and criticized high officials for being so easily beguiled
by K'ang and for not guiding the inexperienced emperor.[7] The
situation became potentially dangerous to the dynasty in many
ways, so on September 21, 1898, the Kuang-hsu Emperor officially
requested that the Empress Dowager resume the reins of government as regent.

It is important to point out that although Tz'u-hsi held the
position of greater authority after September 1898, the Kuang-hsu
Emperor sat on the throne with her; issued his own personal edicts;
made comments on secret memorials, some of which eventually
were transformed into policy statements; and, according to eye-
witness accounts, not only replied to officials when addressed in
court but also initiated discussions with officials in court.[8] It is my
assumption, therefore, that except in instances in which the Empress
Dowager issued her own personal edicts (*i-chih*) to encourage or
discourage reform policies, decisions taken by the court were in fact
joint decisions. As such they clearly reflected the general approval
of Tz'u-hsi even though they may not have originated with her.

The radical reformers and their supporters created the conservative image of the Empress Dowager for many reasons, but

primarily to gain political support for their cause. They justified
the image by citing the nullification by imperial edict of most of
the radical reforms in the fall and winter of 1898. The first such
edict was issued on September 26, 1898. Historians and others
who have viewed this edict as proof of the conservatism of the
court have failed to note that the edict also reiterated the need for
new measures to meet the changing times in order "to bring wealth
and power to the country and to provide a livelihood for the
people."[9] The court clearly stated that it had decided to wipe the
slate clean of most of the radical reform edicts because of the
prejudice that had been created by the radical reformers against
the cause of reform. The nullification of the earlier edicts was a
prerequisite to the launching of an extensive self-strengthening
program involving industry, commerce, agriculture, finance,
defense, education, and so forth. Thus the September 26th edict
marked the end of the radical reforms and the resumption of a
spirit of moderate reform.

The Empress Dowager herself in the fall of 1898 personally
pleaded with officials to respond to the needs of the people by
instituting reforms. She continually stressed that "in this time of
crises, it is urgent that we plan for self-strengthening" and ordered
all officials to devise plans to achieve this goal.[10] She even severely
chastised the conservative officials, who looked upon the moderate
reform edicts as "empty words" because "old practices have been
so deeply rooted ... that it was impossible for them to break
through the barriers [of conservatism]."[11] Some of these conservative officials apparently had misinterpreted the court's nullification of the radical reform edicts as a victory for conservatism,
so the Empress Dowager felt compelled to clarify her position in
no uncertain terms. On November 16, 1898, she forcefully stated
her intentions:

> Laws and institutions are not bad when they are first estab-
> lished, but as time goes on defects accumulate, making it
> necessary to change them in order to meet the requirements
> of the time ... Day and night I labor arduously in the Palace

... A moment does not pass that I do not think about planning for self-strengthening ...

Although the customs and governmental systems of Western countries differ in more than one way from those of China, their methods and techniques ... are, as a rule, capable of [helping a country] to attain prosperity and strength ... If we can select what are good among these and apply them, putting them into use one by one, we shall be able to achieve the desired results promptly and consistently.

It is feared, however, that persons of shallow thinking interpret Our intentions wrongly, imagining that Government has decided to follow the beaten path and is no longer concerned with far-sighted plans. This would be entirely contrary to Our intention to ... achieve good administration.[12]

Thus, on this theoretical level, there can be no doubt that the Empress Dowager favored moderate reform.

One of the first and most important foci of the Empress Dowager's moderate reform program was the modernization of the military forces on the central, provincial, and local levels. This was crucial not only because of internal and external threats to the dynasty, but also because the maintenance of peace was an important prerequisite to any attempts to achieve self-strengthening goals. In Tz'u-hsi's opinion, there could be no plans to develop the wealth and power of the country without first training troops, maintaining public order, and achieving adequate food supplies in the public granaries.[13] She often said that she "pondered every day about the drilling of troops and the nourishment of the people."[14] These were matters of grave concern to her in this period.

In modernizing the country's military forces, the court created four levels of military protection. The first level was composed of the two best banner forces, the Hu-ch'iang-ying (Marksmen for the Tiger Hunt) and the Shen-chi-ying (known as the Peking Field Force), which were drilled in the Western manner, trained in the use of modern weapons, and which served as the protective cordon around the throne. The next level of military protection was a supposedly unified central government force, which was called the Wu-wei chün.

On October 11, 1898, Jung-lu (1836–1903) was appointed commander-in-chief of this force.[15] He was assisted by Nieh Shih-
ch'eng (d. 1900), Tung Fu-hsiang (1839–1908), Sung Ch'ing, and
Yuan Shih-k'ai (1859–1916). The third level was composed of the
provincial troops, but the court was limited in its influence on the
modernization of provincial forces because these troops were supported by provincial treasuries and under the command of civil
and military officials in the provinces. Finally, there was the local
militia (t'uan-lien), which was to provide protection at the local
level and help maintain peace. In general, local militia could not
modernize without the assistance of provincial officials and, in
the straitened economic conditions of the day, this kind of support was rare.

The modernization of China's military forces was an expensive and difficult task. The Board of Revenue (Hu-pu) allotted over
three million taels to the two top levels of government forces and
gave Jung-lu the power to temporarily redirect other funds into
the Wu-wei chün treasury in order to achieve modernization.[16]
However, since the central government was operating on a deficit
budget, it was forced to pressure the provincial governments for
additional funds. And, inasmuch as the provincial officials felt that
they had already contributed ample funds to the central government, this became a source of serious tension between the two
levels.[17] Thus the lack of sufficient funds seriously hindered
progress.

The need for modern equipment and weapons presented
another serious problem. Despite the tremendous amount of capital
spent on the manufacture of weapons, China's arsenals were inef-
ficiently managed and the quality of arms produced was very low.
When the court delegated several officials to test the rifles produced
at the Kiangnan Arsenal, for example, the officials found that the
rifles either did not work at all, or burned or exploded.[18] As a
result, the government was forced to turn to the importation of
weapons. Between 1898 and 1899, provincial arms imports more
than tripled and central government arms imports increased eight-
fold as compared with only a slight increase between 1897 and

1898.[19] Although the importing of foreign-made weapons was scarcely an ideal solution to China's arms problem—many of the guns and rifles sold at exorbitant prices to bribed Chinese officials by agents of foreign firms later proved to be defective or condemned weapons[20]—nevertheless, it was a major step in the direction of military modernization. Without the acquisition of modern weapons, a modern army could not be trained.

Despite the problems encountered, the military self-strengthening program achieved some success by late 1899. In mid-1899, with the exception of Tung Fu-hsiang's troops, the central government's military forces were outfitted with modern equipment and drilled in the Western style.[21] Some of the provincial armies also were able to make the transition. In the winter of 1899 the governor of Hunan, Yü Lien-san, and the governor-general of Min-Che (Fukien and Chekiang), Hsu Ying-ch'i, informed the court that the troops under their commands had changed over completely to Western-style drilling and the use of modern weapons.[22] The court proudly ordered their achievements announced to other provincial officials, who, the court felt, should follow the example of these two high officials. However, many of the provincial forces were unable to accomplish this transition because of (1) the unwillingness of their military commanders, (2) the lack of funds to buy the necessary equipment, (3) the inability, in some cases, to hire foreign or foreign-trained military instructors, and (4) the lack of cooperation from civil officials. The situation was even worse at the level of the local militia units, which seldom had access to significant quantities of modern weapons for drilling purposes.

The court did not limit its moderate reform program to defense matters. Among the many things it approved of and tried to institute in the period from late 1898 to early 1900 were: the adoption of a fixed ratio of exchange between copper cash and silver for the benefit of the farmers, the establishment of a central mint and a national uniform currency system, the planning of tax reforms and a national budget, and the end of bureaucratic and military corruption.[23] Much of this reform program failed because of the current financial crisis, natural calamities, foreign intervention or interference, the resistance of conservative officials, tension between central and provincial governments, and the interruption of the Boxer uprising. It is significant, nevertheless, that so many of the reforms that attained visibility only in the period from 1901 to 1908, as part of the so-called "Manchu Reforms," were actually approved between late 1898 and mid-1900, prior to the siege of the legations and the departure of the Manchu court to Sian.

An illustration of this was the encouragement of Western subjects in the educational curricula. One of the most controversial issues during the Hundred Days had been the abolition of the "eight-legged essay" (*pa-ku wen*), which, to many officials, virtually implied an end to the study of the Classics. On November 13, 1898, yielding to tremendous political pressure, the Empress Dowager reinstated the old examination system because it would have been politically unwise to do otherwise.[24] However, at the same time, she rejected the *Li-pu's* petition to abolish the modern schools (*hsueh-t'ang*), arguing that such subjects as astronomy, geography, military strategy, and mathematics were indispensable to the welfare of the country.[25] Her educational policy was thus a synthesis between old and new: the teaching of traditional works to provide a strong moral foundation and an emphasis on Western subjects to promote the country's welfare. Throughout 1899, despite criticisms from conservative officials, the Empress Dowager continued to praise practical Western knowledge and supported the teaching of Western subjects in the schools. Her objectives in this direction were not limited to civil education. Following the example of Li Hung-chang (1823–1901), Chang Chih-tung (1837–1909), and others, she encouraged all provincial military academies to incorporate Western technology and related subjects into their curricula, to require military cadets to achieve good marksmanship with modern weapons, and to emphasize Western-style drilling.[26] She reasoned that with officers so trained, it would be possible to expect that the common soldiers would be drilled in the Western manner and be competent in the use of modern weapons and equipment. Therefore, in these areas, the court strongly encouraged the adoption of Western ideas, methods, and techniques.

By early 1900, it seemed that the court felt the time might be right to propose the end of the "eight-legged essay" and the initiation of a civil-service examination which included testing in Western subjects. Ch'en K'uei-lung, a long-standing friend of both Jung-lu and Li Hung-chang and a Reader for the Grand Secretariat, presented a lengthy memorial which not only praised practical knowledge, but also strongly criticized the continuation of the "eight-legged essay." Ch'en bitterly attacked the old examination system because it fostered a poor attitude among aspiring officials, who, he claimed, were only interested in how to perfect their calligraphy and classical composition for the examinations. He extolled the value of practical knowledge and suggested that a new examination system be established. On February 20, 1900, the court ordered that Ch'en's memorial be circulated throughout the country and directed educational institutions at all levels to place greater emphasis on practical education.[27] By circulating this memorial, the court tacitly supported Ch'en's proposal to abolish the old examination system. The court did not openly state its inclinations on the subject because it was anxious to see how the officials and gentry would react. Unfortunately, the court became bogged down with the Boxer problem in the spring and summer of 1900 and dropped the issue of the abolition of the old examination system.

After the Boxer catastrophe, the emperor redirected the country's attention toward the issue of reform. In an edict dated January 29, 1901, he stressed the need for reform to strengthen the empire and benefit the people, criticized the superficial studying of Western ways, and praised the deeper study of practical knowledge.[28] In response to the emperor's call for reform proposals, Liu K'un-i and Chang Chih-tung presented a joint memorial on July 12, 1901, recommending the abolition of the old examination system and the adoption of a three-part examination covering (1) Chinese political and historical events, (2) general Western subjects such as politics, geography, military science, and mathematics, and (3) the Four Books and Five Classics.[29] Their proposal seems less innovative when viewed against the Empress Dowager's encouragement of the study of Western subjects and Ch'en K'uei-lung's criticism of the old examination system and praise of practical knowledge.

In this brief essay I have challenged the traditional image of the Empress Dowager Tz'u-hsi as one who opposed changes. Military modernization, the encouragement of the study of Western subjects, and the approval of the abolition of the "eight-legged essay" were just a small part of the court's moderate reform program. Some aspects of this program were very innovative while others followed the trend of generally recognized and approved changes. However, many of the reforms were thwarted either by uncooperative officials at all levels of government, insufficient government funds, internal unrest, natural calamities, external problems, or the complexities involved in the planning and execution of reforms. As a result, the radical reformers and their supporters could claim that the Empress Dowager was a conservative or reactionary by focusing upon areas such as the old civil service examination that showed no apparent transformation.

Historians have long relied upon the works of K'ang Yu-wei, Liang Ch'i-ch'ao, Wang Chao, Yun Yü-ting, and Lo Tun-jung for their information on the Ch'ing court during this period. Since all of these men were connected with the radical reform movement, their writings are very biased. Yun Yü-ting, for example, is often considered a reliable observer because he was a member of the Hanlin Academy and served as a recorder at court for nineteen years. However, his major work, "Ch'ung-ling chuan-hsin lu" (The true story of the Kuang-hsu emperor), reveals a definite hatred for the Empress Dowager and was first published in Liang's journal *Yung-yen*.[30] Lo Tun-jung, who later became a noted historian, was also a regular contributor and staff member of *Yung-yen*. Western writers, including John Otway Percy Bland and Sir Edmund Backhouse, contributed to the perpetuation of misconceptions about the Empress Dowager's position on reform and her efforts in changing the country. And yet historians still turn to these men and their associates for "objective" insight into the court's affairs. The time has come for the much maligned Empress Dowager Tz'u-hsi to be re-evaluated in terms of her accomplishments as recorded in the writings of high court officials, like Liu K'un-i and Li Hung-chang, and in court documents.

DISCUSSION

James Polachek raised the issue of ideology, which he described as undoubtedly the "sleeper" in nineteenth-century history, the real troublemaker. One conclusion that we had been moving toward in yesterday's discussion was that it had been over-rated as an obstacle to China's economic modernization. In Kwang-Ching Liu's presentation, however, we still had ideology posed as an autonomous force in the political realm. Tz'u-hsi, for example, was in a fragile position because of the fact that she had usurped the throne and was therefore more sensitive to the challenge of ideological purity.

The attributes we tended to associate with nineteenth-century ideologues, Mr. Polachek continued, were those of being supercilious and antipragmatic, thus reinforcing our view that they were obstacles to reform. He wondered, however, whether there might not have existed in China something different from the consistent and coherent world view that we in the West regarded as ideology. As a case in point, he mentioned the ideologue Ch'i Chün-tsao, who had an important effect in determining the ideologically excited tone of Hsien-feng and perhaps also early T'ung-chih politics. He began his career on the Han-hsueh side of the intellectual controversy, rather than the Ch'eng-Chu side. On assuming office as president of the Board of Revenue and chief grand councillor in 1850, however, he immediately faced the prob-lem of raising money and was not sure whether to compromise and be pragmatic or to stick to his principles. He decided on the policy of printing paper money and creating cheap currency. Opting for expediency, in the end he lost the support of his zealous followers and lost his office too when his policies failed. Mr. Polachek con-cluded by suggesting that the ideological energy of Ch'i probably did not correspond to what we would call ideology. It was not a set of principles that a man could cling to or hold to. He further suggested that what we should perhaps be looking for in studying ideology or ideological energy in nineteenth-century China was not

111

so much the specific content of this force as where in the system it was distributed, who was most affected by it, and how the distribution of ideological excitement changed over time.

Mr. Liu agreed and said that "ideas" might be a better word in this context than "ideology." What really obstructed reform, he said, was not just ideology, but ideology combined with factional politics. People who were "ideologues" on paper were forced when in power to face concrete problems and sometimes needed to compromise. Tseng Kuo-fan found it necessary to work with corrupt officials and decided that it would be best to be like a blind and deaf monk and ignore their corruption.

Mr. Polachek wondered whether ideologies tended to form factions, or whether factions found ideologies that suited them. John Schrecker said that the word "ideology" had a Western connotation of exclusivity, religious in background and overtone, which was perhaps not applicable to China. Ideology in China was just one part of politics. Mr. Liu dealt in his talk with the political motivation of Wo-jen. However, many of the policies of Prince Kung and Wen-hsiang were politically motivated, too. They were trying to get control of the educational system and thereby control the next generation of *chin-shih.*

Kwang-Ching Liu referred to Paul Cohen's article and pointed out that the reformist impulse sometimes coincided with the desire for political power. It was still reform, however, even if politically motivated. Paul Cohen said that the acid test of whether ideology could operate as an autonomous factor would be if we could find someone in nineteenth-century China who took an ideological stand that was plainly at odds with his own political interest. Sometimes people were forced into bad positions—a case in point would be Tseng Kuo-fan at the time of the Tientsin Massacre—and their actions then cut their lines of support.

Thomas Kennedy suggested that the ideology of the statecraft school was virtually a nonideology, in that its main emphasis was on being practical and broadly learned. This attitude provided a basis for intellectual accommodation without the restrictions of an ideology. Hao Chang said that whether one agreed or not depended on how one defined ideology. Was it necessarily a system of moral ideas? Or could it be defined as a system of ideas of any kind? The statecraft school had an ideology of pragmatism. Joseph Cheng suggested that we might better talk of "a framework of orientation." Frank Lojewski said that if ideology existed at all, it was a broad framework of thought, in which all agreed on the essentials. But there could still be much variation of thought within this broad spectrum. Marxism afforded a very good example.

David Pong pointed out that many of the changes of the nineteenth century had some popular or at least gentry support. It was possible for Tseng Kuo-fan to innovate because some gentry were willing to become his private secretaries (*mu-yu*). Similarly, the navy yard in Foochow was a new enterprise that attracted considerable gentry support. There seemed in these cases to be a political vested interest involved. Perhaps there was a superabundance of unemployed gentry who could perform reasonably traditional roles in new institutions. John Schrecker said that there was indeed an overabundance of unemployed gentry, partially as a result of the increasing availability of office by purchase. Li Hung-chang, for example, often employed purchasers of office who were not very well educated in the classical tradition.

Young-tsu Wong, in commenting on Sue Chung's paper, mentioned that although the image of Tz'u-hsi after her death was very negative, some writings gave her a more positive image. The magazine *Fu-nü yueh-k'an* (Women's monthly) in the 1920s and 1930s, for example, tried to upgrade her image.

I-fan Ch'eng asked whether Wen-hsiang and Prince Kung had a program for those trained by the T'ung-wen kuan. Were they to be incorporated into the civil service system? If so, this would reflect upon the naiveté of Wen-hsiang and Prince Kung, for surely the system would be destroyed if such an innovation were introduced. How could traditionalists like Wo-jen accept these people as regular officials? Kwang-Ching Liu said that Wen-hsiang and Prince Kung had not thought through all of the possible consequences of their plan; certainly it was not their intention to reform Chinese society through the establishment of the T'ung-wen kuan.

Charlton Lewis said that in order to examine the effect of ideology on the policies of reformers and their opponents, we must break down the concept of the Confucian outlook into its constituent parts. There was, for example, the polarity between cultivating oneself and governing the world. Some felt the urge to retire into their own righteousness. The issue of *li* (propriety) was important to Tseng Kuo-fan because it upheld the social structure. It also upheld the superiority of the Confucian tradition. We must analyze reformers in terms of their emphasis on different parts of the ideology. We should also consider the idea that Confucianism was for many a faith which rose above any particular political commitment. Frank Lojewski added that sharp ideological distinctions tended to be made by people out of office, but the ideologue in office had to make compromises. Paul Cohen recalled that Lloyd Eastman in his *Throne and Mandarins* argued that lower-ranking officials tended to be more ideological, and Mr. Lojewski added that Feng Kuei-fen was more ideological out of office than when he was performing practical functions as a member of Li Hung-chang's staff.

John Schrecker said that politics changed the intellectual stand of Tz'u-hsi, who came out against the reformers in 1898 partially because they were engaged in a political struggle to take away her power. Hao Chang said that ideological factors were also part of Tz'u-hsi's make-up. She was genuinely distressed when she found out that the democratic ideas in the writings of K'ang Yu-wei and Liang Ch'i-ch'ao were opposed to the *san-kang* relationships.

Kwang-Ching Liu returned to the point that James Polachek was suggesting. In the recruitment of like-minded people into a faction, intellectual outlook was often an important factor.

THE SOCIAL CONTEXT OF REFORM

Marianne Bastid
THE SOCIAL CONTEXT OF REFORM

In logical sequence, our investigation should first deal with
the social antecedents of reform and secondly with the social consequences of reform. The former range of issues centers on whether
the politics of reform are initiated by a particular social group and
whether they are linked to specific conditions in society at large.
The latter centers on the bearing of reform policies on social
organization, on group differentiation within society, and on
society's image of itself.

Sources and Methods
Before exploring these two groups of issues, let us briefly
examine the sources and methods that we have available for con-
ducting an inquiry into late Ch'ing society.
Quantitative data are meager and scattered. We do not have
ready at hand, as do European social historians, the notaries' well-
kept records of deeds, tax registers, and post-mortem inventories.
We have no long series that can be processed for computer analysis.
The kind of information given by the extant numerical data is
intermittent in both time and space.
With much care and patience the recruitment and composition
of the literati group can be reconstructed, witness the work of
Chung-li Chang and Ping-ti Ho. But this is possible only in a very
unidimensional way since the most important factor, wealth, cannot be taken into account in quantified terms. The only precise
referent available for defining social mobility and social structure
is the literati or nonliterati ancestry of degreeholders and commoners. But even here we are able to obtain satisfactory results
only for the upper strata of the literati class. Data on the family
background of lower degreeholders are inadequate. And we have
no coherent data at all for a quantitative social history of other
segments of the population.
The bulk of the available sources provides a qualitative type

of information, in the form of official records, local gazetteers, the memoirs and essays of officials and gentry, novels, and contemporary Western writings. There is a great wealth of such qualitative material. Indeed the prospective student of social change might find himself overwhelmed by it.

But the difficulty in using these sources is not just a matter of their abundance. An even greater problem is their low level of reliability as evidence of social change. The formalism of Chinese writings tends to obliterate such evidence, the same terminology being retained in the face of changing social realities. For example, the term *shen-shih* was used originally to designate the traditional Chinese gentry, but later it came to be applied also to the Western ruling classes and to groups of literati background who went into business around the turn of the century and whose characteristics departed significantly from the old gentry pattern. Another source of confusion is the compound *shen-shang,* the meaning of which changed subtly over time from "gentry and merchants" to "merchant-gentry."

If Chinese writings can be blamed for being excessively fixed or rigid in terminology, the fault of Western sources is often just the opposite. Westerners tend to amalgamate or blur Chinese and Western categories too hastily, with the result that their descriptions of Chinese social evolution are often misleading.

We should try then to devise rigorous methods of inquiry. Given the kinds of sources we have, I believe that the safest place to start is with biographical studies, as slow and painful as these may be to compile. For the elite strata, individual biographies can be constructed and must be the basis of any generalization. But in regard to the commoners, where the data are usually too meager and do not permit individual biographies, biographical information should be pooled in accordance with set criteria. We can, for example, collect information about Chinese sentenced by the foreign courts in Shanghai, or rebel groups in one place or another, or professional groups linked to a certain place or branch of trade. Such data are not sufficient to form detailed accounts of the lives of individuals. They can, however, lead to a kind of collective biography which, in turn, can supply the basis for a sound social history of the lower strata.

In working out criteria for the selection of relevant data, the crucial point is to define the indicators or indices of social change. We often talk or read about the "modernization of Chinese society" or the "modernization of elites." These are, however, very vague and approximate notions. The assumption is that people have taken up new professional activities (such as industry or journalism) or that they have received some Western education or both. But, considering that it is often difficult to draw the line between traditional and new activities and that a traditional degreeholder might through self-education be more deeply acquainted with Western learning than a product of missionary schools, the relevance of such criteria to an understanding of Chinese social evolution is questionable. Are these criteria decisive?

Marxist theory propounds a set of apparently more sophisticated and strict categories for classifying a society and defining its stage of evolution. The trouble is that these categories have never been consistently and thoroughly applied in the analysis of late nineteenth-century Chinese society. It is doubtful, moreover, whether they can be so applied except in sweeping terms or in analyses of very limited range (for instance the study by Ching Su of landlord management in Shantung province at the end of the Ch'ing dynasty).* The reason for the relative inapplicability of Marxist categories is that they are based primarily on study of the relations of production, precisely the point at which Chinese data are lacking.

Regardless of what criteria are ultimately applied in the study of social change, we need to acquire a better understanding of the point of departure, that is, the Chinese society of the early nineteenth century. We are still very ignorant on this score. But for a few pioneer studies, the social history of the century as a whole remains largely unexplored, even less well known than that of the Republican period.

*Ch'ing-tai Shan-tung ching-ying ti-chu ti she-hui hsing-chih (The social nature of managerial landlords in Shantung during the Ch'ing; Tsinan, 1959).

Shortcomings in sources alone do not account for this state of affairs. Another reason is the persistent idea that imperial China was fixed and stable, prompting people to look for social evolution only after the abolition of the monarchy.

Yet another reason for the neglect of nineteenth-century social history is the fact that revolution with a definite social program appears in China only in the twentieth century. During the second half of the nineteenth century reform programs had primarily political and, in the broadest sense, cultural content. Their social ends were, on the whole, limited and subordinate. They aimed at best to adjust the relations among various groups in society but not to upset these relations and build a new social order.

There is, to be sure, the Taiping case. From a social point of view, Taiping policy, in boldness and scope, compares favorably with twentieth-century revolutionary movements. The Taipings achieved a relatively wide and thorough reshuffling of the privileged strata. Those who acquired positions of power in society were, at least in large areas, not the same persons who had held power before. It is, however, questionable whether the Taiping Kingdom really aimed at a radical change in social structure. It has been convincingly argued that the Taiping land law, rather than departing from the traditional model of society, rationalized it and tried to make it more efficient. Actually, it is only in the *Tzu-cheng hsin-pien* (A new treatise on aids to administration) of Hung Jen-kan that arguments may be found to support the view that the very structures of society were brought under attack. Hung's essay, however, reflected his personal viewpoint, and in any case there is general agreement that the social policy of the Taipings was not put into practice.

It is usually said that a prominent feature in the success of the T'ung-chih Restoration was its reinstatement of the old social order. It is doubtful, however, whether the old order was completely restored. Chung-li Chang has shown the numerical growth of the gentry, and studies such as Philip Kuhn's point to the increased power of local elites. When coming to grips with the social context and social consequences of reform, therefore, we should keep in mind that social change was taking place independent of reform.

The Social Antecedents of Reform

The first question to be considered is whether any specific social group can be held responsible for the promotion of reform ideas and policies. If we look at the course taken by reform up to the 1880s or even the 1890s, the situation is no different from such earlier Chinese reform movements as the one at the end of the Warring States period which brought about the founding of the centralized state, or those of Fan Chung-yen and Wang An-shih in the eleventh century. That is, the very first proponents of reform ideas were scholars of national standing or potential national standing: people like Wei Yuan, Feng Kuei-fen, T'ang Shou-ch'ien, K'ang Yu-wei, T'an Ssu-t'ung. These proponents of reform found support among the high officialdom, and a few very high officials, such as Lin Tse-hsu, Tseng Kuo-fan, Li Hung-chang, and Chang Chih-tung, became the advocates and executors of a reform policy.

Of course, not all of these people were equally devoted to reform. The reformism of those who inspired them also needs qualification. But it is with the general pattern of reformism—the overall process by which reformist ideas got started, evolved, and were finally (in some cases) implemented—that my remarks are mainly concerned. The first point to be kept in mind then is that, as in times past, the initiative for reform came from the highest strata in society, from the top of the elite.

A second feature is that there was no single common social denominator differentiating those who conceived of or attempted to execute reform from their colleagues who did not embrace reform and in some instances even formed political movements of opposition to reform. One may find in the personal experience of an individual certain facts which account for his reformist attitudes. These facts may even be the same or similar for several individuals who were active in the reform movement. For example, most of the reformers of the late nineteenth century experienced the spread of the Taiping Revolution or other popular uprisings in their home provinces. All of them were acquainted with foreigners;

several of them traveled abroad. But such features are also found in the biographies of many contemporary scholars who did not advocate reform. If we look at their socioeconomic backgrounds, we notice of course such people as Cheng Kuan-ying who were engaged in modern business, but this is far from being a general rule, and it is equally noteworthy that many of the compradors, or people engaged in Western-style business, never became prominent reformists.

In the last twenty years, Chinese historians have taken great pains to separate two trends in reformism and two camps among the reformers and also to articulate the social differences between them. They define on one side the *yang-wu p'ai* ("foreign matters" faction), made up of people belonging to high official circles or closely connected with foreign imperialist undertakings, who aimed at consolidation of the old order and sought improvements in defense and an increase in government revenue under bureaucratic control, in order to strengthen their power over the people. On the other side stands the *kai-liang p'ai,* or reformist faction, made up of people ranking lower in the officialdom and holding no position of real power (*pu tang ch'üan p'ai*) or people engaged in private modern business. This reformist faction contemplated a real change of the old order—a more or less radical change—and thought in terms not only of economic reforms but also of political ones.

Although the separation between the two camps is often drawn too sharply and even artificially, the distinction is not to be wholly rejected. There are indeed two families of thought in the reform movement, even if the nineteenth-century vocabulary remains far more unsettled than Chinese historians would like it to be. (*Yang-wu,* for example, is a broad enough category to bring together in the same company those who looked at change as a means of bolstering the essentials of tradition and those who were willing to sacrifice a great deal of tradition for survival,* those more influenced by the

---

*See for instance the excellent analysis by David Pong in "Confucian Patriotism and the Destruction of the Woosung Railway, 1877," *Modern Asian Studies,* 7.4: 647–676 (1973).

T'ung-ch'eng school and those who were closer to the *chin-wen*
school.)

Are these two schools of thought rooted in really different
social backgrounds? It is true that many members of the *kai-liang
p'ai* engaged in small private business and found support from
people who ran modern enterprises, but this is a phenomenon
which appeared later on, after a policy of reform had been
adopted. It is more a social consequence of reform than an
antecedent. The fact is, when we look at the initial phase of the
reform movement, no social distinctions can be established among
the proponents of reform, and no social criteria differentiate, in an
absolute way, the reformers from the rest of the elite.

Since there are no social characteristics that clearly distinguish
reformers, we must ask whether the social antecedents of reform
are to be found in the *specific conditions of late nineteenth-century
Chinese society*. Is reform linked to a particular social context? The
answer is evidently yes.

I shall not dwell on this social context. Although it certainly
deserves more thorough analysis, its main features are well known:
population growth and increasing shortage of food supply, the dis-
rupting effects of foreign intrusion, and mounting social disorder.
As parents increasingly could not feed or educate their children
and the ruler could not protect his subjects, the moral and political
bonds so important to the working of Chinese society and to its
self-image lost their hold over people. Judicial case records, missionary accounts, and the biographies of commoners are filled with
evidence of filial and civic disobedience, crime, job instability,
unemployment among all strata, ups and downs in fortunes.

Is the social disorder of the last century qualitatively different
from that of other periods of widespread disruption, such as the
seventeenth century? Very possibly it is, partly because of the
numbers involved, and partly because of the intervention of forces
exogenous to Chinese society and tradition.

The new social context of the nineteenth century did not
affect the manner in which the reform process got started; this was
much the same as in previous eras. It did, however, have an

important shaping impact on the contents of reform programs as well as on the ways in which society was affected by reform.

As far as the contents of reform are concerned, much thought was given to the necessity of restoring the efficient exercise of political power: its capacity to exert influence on society and also to resist external pressure. The strongest emphasis, for instance, was put on opening channels of communication between the ruler and his subjects and fostering unity of minds—*i-hsin.* Possibly the means that were devised were not the best ones, and possibly the roots of the evil were not very clearly perceived. This concern with communication between ruler and ruled was, however, a direct response to the increasing estrangement of society from the state and to the disintegration of society itself.

It can also be argued that the very social factors that prompted the launching of reform programs hampered their implementation. The atomization of society into small groups, clinging to what concrete interests remained in their hands, made it very difficult to achieve any consciously planned change, as Frank Lojewski indicates in his piece.

The Social Consequences of Reform

The social consequences of the reform movement of the late nineteenth century were very largely unexpected and unplanned-for. Historians tend to disregard them and to emphasize only the intellectual and political consequences. It is generally assumed that the new social order that grew out of the turmoil of the late Ch'ing is a twentieth-century story.

Social consequences may only be side-effects of reform, but they do exist and deserve our attention. The most striking social effect of the reform movement was its contribution to the division and disintegration of the old society. Reforms helped give birth to new social groups among the elite. Broadly speaking these were the *yang-wu* experts, comprising those who had knowledge of foreign languages and learning, those with managerial capacities, those who had acquired Western technical skills—military, and so forth—and those who started modern businesses. It is of utmost significance that in the Chinese case the growth of the last-named group—the new business class—was much more a consequence of reform than an antecedent condition.

Among commoners, the growth of an urban and industrial proletariat may also be seen partly as a consequence of the reform movement.

Did the emergence of these groups widen the opportunity structure? Did it create employment? Did it foster elite circulation and social equity? Did it breathe a new spirit into society? I would argue that although the presence of new groups such as these certainly had a disturbing short-run effect on social organization, if you look at Chinese social history in long-run terms, their role can only be construed as marginal. From the perspective of the ruling class, and even perhaps of the commoners, these groups represented an abnormal growth, a development of basically peripheral significance. Alienated from the agrarian background and foundation of Chinese society, they failed to reflect the main direction toward which the bulk of society was evolving.

This interpretation and the comments that follow require much further elaboration and discussion. I present them as a working hypothesis only, in the hope that they will be challenged and induce us to look deeper into the Chinese social history of the last century. In my view, what was in the making in China, from the end of the eighteenth century onwards, was a new pattern of agrarian society. In very inadequate terms, it was the change from a feudal agrarian society (or, in French, *une société mandarinale*) into a bourgeois agrarian society or, if one prefers, from a traditional agrarian society into a modern agrarian society. What we call it is not important at this point. The important thing is the notion of a different type of agrarian society. Provisionally, let us accept the label "bourgeois" for the sake of convenience.

Broadly speaking, this new pattern of agrarian society evolved out of a more intensive use of the agricultural means of production: more was extracted from the land, from those who tilled it and from its products. This more intensive use of the agricultural means of production was not achieved merely by an improvement in agricultural techniques. It also involved a change in agrarian structures (that is, new relationships in ownership and tenancy) and a new start in the development of trade and manufacture.

A distinguishing feature of the new pattern of agrarian society was the replacement of the old rural elite or its transformation into what may be called (for lack of a better phrase) an agrarian bourgeoisie. One crucial difference between the agrarian bourgeoisie and the old rural elite is that the status of the agrarian bourgeoisie did not depend primarily on the central government's bestowal of titles and degrees. Its loyalty and indebtedness to the central government were therefore far more tenuous. Another difference is that the power of the agrarian bourgeoisie within the local community did not rest primarily on the upholding of customary bonds and the fulfillment of customary duties (such as repair of public works and mediation with government authorities). Rather, it was a matter of wealth and strength. This strength could be military, but more often coercion was applied in a more indirect fashion, landlords, in the typical case, relying on yamen runners to compel the tenants to pay their rents.

The emergence of this agrarian bourgeoisie is, in my opinion, a much more significant fact than the formation of an urban industrial business class. Acknowledging it, moreover, helps to clarify certain twists and turns in the history of the Chinese revolution. The rise of the agrarian bourgeoisie may account for the contradictory attitudes sometimes noted within the gentry, especially in the first two decades of the twentieth century. It may also be argued that China's Communist revolutionaries attained success only after they turned their guns against this new agrarian elite.

The reform movement of the late nineteenth century added impetus to a number of secular changes in Chinese society. It encouraged an improvement in the status of merchants. It contributed to the rise of the agrarian bourgeoisie, especially by eroding social bonds. It was directly responsible for the emergence of a new group of *yang-wu* experts completely outside the traditional four categories of Chinese society (scholars, peasants, artisans, and merchants). Also, the reform movement, in part through the models and standards of action set by the urban business class, fostered new values that had a direct bearing on the power and behavior of the agrarian bourgeoisie. Indeed, in coastal areas, it was not uncommon to find members of both classes, urban business and agrarian bourgeoisie, in the same family.

Inevitably the direct influence of reform also became mixed up with much broader developments taking place largely outside of the reform movement. Certain aspects of social evolution were influenced more by imperialism than by reform. One cannot, moreover, charge the reform movement with sole responsibility for the building of strong vested interests within the provincial administrations or for the large breaches made in the elaborate system of checks and controls that had been set up in the early Ch'ing. The geographic concentration of *yang-wu* expert groups, on the other hand, did indeed aggravate interregional and intraregional rivalries, bringing them to the brink of social warfare. Moreover, it was directly as a consequence of reform that the government relinquished effective control over elite social change, as the examination system lost its capacity to limit the size of the ruling elite or to curb its power.

To sum up, first we still need to work out a methodological framework for the study of nineteenth-century Chinese society. Second, while it seems difficult to view the reform movement as primarily a social phenomenon, it clearly had a disruptive effect upon society, especially upon the elite, and it contributed a great deal to the destruction of society's traditional self-image. Finally, if we are to understand the evolution of the rural elite and the important part it took in modern Chinese history, the closest attention must be paid to developments, splits, and transformations within this elite over time.

Frank A. Lojewski
LOCAL REFORM AND ITS OPPONENTS: FENG KUEI-FEN'S
STRUGGLE FOR EQUALITY IN TAXATION

One of the most pernicious abuses in rural southern Kiangsu
was the inequity in the assessment of the tribute grain tax (*ts'ao-liang*). A small but influential and economically powerful group
was able to shift a large part of its tribute grain obligations onto
another group of taxpayers, which was unable to protest this outrage and was also least able to bear the additional financial burden.
Although this inequality had persisted a long time, the turmoil of
the middle decades of the nineteenth century, epitomized by the
Taiping success, heightened the friction between the two groups
of taxpayers. By 1853 there was a danger that the underprivileged
group might join the Taiping rebels to vent its grievances.[1] However, in spite of the obvious danger to the local economy and to
social and political stability through the overtaxation of small
landowners, little was done to curb such abuses. The only notable
efforts in this direction were those of Feng Kuei-fen (*chin-shih* of
1840 and a native of Wu-hsien, Soochow prefecture), who between
1849 and 1856 repeatedly attempted to persuade the local and
provincial authorities to abolish the illegal classification of taxpayers.

An examination of the reform efforts of Feng Kuei-fen reveals
some important aspects of the local elite's economic behavior and
its sense of social responsibility. It also illuminates the effect of
local tribute-collection policies on the relationships among the
classes of taxpayers, as well as on the landlord-tenant relationship.
Finally, it sheds light on the limits of central government-sponsored
reform at the local level.

Those households that were able to evade their tax liabilities
were known as the influential households (*ta-hu*). The majority of
influential households belonged to the official-gentry, although
some members of the scholar-gentry (*chin*), and even commoners

with wealth and connections with the official-gentry, could belong
to the influential households.[2]

All those taxpayers who did not qualify as influential households belonged to the minor households (*hsiao-hu*). This tax group
embraced the "Kleinbauern," those peasants who owned at least
some of the land they cultivated. Landlords, too, including both
small landlords who cultivated part of their acreage and large landlords who lived entirely from rent and other income, belonged to
the minor households.

The classification of households for tax purposes into "influential" and "minor" was illegal. In fact, the throne, with little
apparent success, had issued edicts from time to time prohibiting
such discrimination.[3]

The basic problem was that the influential households paid
only those taxes and surcharges that had to be delivered at the
capital. Many paid less than these basic taxes, and some even paid
no taxes at all. The influential households refused to pay any of
those surcharges and extra levies necessary for the maintenance of
local government.[4]

All deficiencies incurred because of the influential households'
refusal to bear their fair share of the taxes had to be made up somehow. Although the magistrate was legally empowered to force the
influential households to pay the assessed rate and any such fees
needed to defray the expenses of the district yamen, many of the
influential households had connections with the magistrate's
superiors, which could create difficulties for a magistrate who
chose to play strictly by the rules. In these circumstances, the
magistrates simply shifted the burden to those who lacked power
to resist the depredations of the runners, namely, the minor households.[5]

During the nineteenth century a number of provincial officials
had attacked the illegal classification into influential and minor
households. The efforts of Feng Kuei-fen are of special interest
because he was a member of southern Kiangsu's official-gentry.
Thus Feng actually proposed to do away with privileges that benefited his own class. Moreover, he wrote extensively and developed

a sustained interest in helping the minor households. Feng's concern for the welfare of the minor households grew out of a commitment to his deceased mother, whose family had been ruined by tax collectors. In fact, his mother had entreated him to work for reform should he reach a position of influence in government.[6]

Since 1849 Feng Kuei-fen had urged the Kiangsu governor to support his proposals for the equalization of taxes. He needed the approval and help of the governor to gain the attention of the district magistrates and other officials, as well as the local elite.[7] Political activity without the backing of the bureaucracy was heterodox and dangerous to anyone who engaged in it. Feng never questioned this principle of Chinese politics; in fact, he wholeheartedly supported the basic premises of the Chinese political system. His reforms were designed to strengthen, not to demolish, China's way of governing. Consequently, when he appealed to the natives of Su-Sung-T'ai, he first made certain of the approval and cooperation of the high-ranking provincial officials.

Feng pointed out that the existing inequalities in the assessment of taxes were contrary to the Confucian canonical texts.[8] It must be stressed that Feng's attack was leveled against inequities in the assessment of taxes, not the inequality of general social status as permitted by the statutes. Feng was interested in reforming and strengthening the Ch'ing government, not in preaching social revolution. He fully approved of the preferential treatment of the official- and scholar-gentry in the yamen as well as in social ranking, but not in taxation. This attitude was in accord with dynastic statutes, which gave the gentry legal privileges, but not special economic rights, at least not in the payment of tribute grain. Feng clearly pointed out that the differentiation between influential households and minor households was contrary to the statutes of the reigning dynasty. Repeatedly over the past centuries edicts had been issued to prohibit preferential treatment of the influential households in the assessment of grain tribute liabilities, and the consequent shifting of the taxes to those elements of the local population who could least afford the increase.[9] Since this overburdened sector of the population constituted the majority of the taxpayers, the danger of serious revolts against the local authorities, and ultimately against the dynasty itself, was heightened.

Feng found a sympathetic listener in Governor Hsu Nai-chao, who had been appointed to his post on April 9, 1853. Governor Hsu probably was more open to Feng's suggestions because his brother had been Feng's examiner, and therefore a special relationship bound the two together. Nor must one underestimate the influence of Feng's good relationship with the governor-general, Lu Chien-ying. Evidently Governor Hsu gave his official blessing to Feng's undertaking, because Feng began to write appeals to the various local interest groups involved in the payment of tribute, appeals he would not have written without the approval and backing of the governor. He urged the groups to support the new program of equalization for the benefit of all.

In view of the absence of documentation, we can only surmise what form the governor's help took. Most probably it was through circular letters instructing the magistrates to accede to Feng Kuei-fen's proposals, at the same time reminding them that discrimination against the minor households was contrary to the statutes and that enforcement of the statutes was one of their duties as local officials.

Feng Kuei-fen's own campaign took the form of appeals to the local populace. He addressed open letters to all major groups concerned with the assessment and collection of the grain tribute on the district level (the magistrates, the gentry, and the commoners), pointing out the advantages each would reap from the proposal to equalize taxes, and the dangers that could arise from refusal to cooperate with the provincial government in the execution of equalization. In the case of the gentry, he wrote separate letters to the official- and scholar-gentry, evidently because their interests were so far apart. Judging from the texts of these letters, the majority of influential households were official-gentry families, and most families with this prestigious status evaded taxes to some degree.

Feng's appeal to the official-gentry, who made up the top stratum of the local elite, is of the greatest interest.[10] There were a number of reasons for the paramount influence of this group. For one, its members were the social peers of the magistrate, in some cases, even his superiors. For another, they enjoyed certain legal privileges that made it difficult for the magistrate, should he be so inclined, to press them to comply with the new rule of equal taxes. For example, the magistrate could not simply arrest, much less punish, a member of the official-gentry. Any proceedings against them had to be forwarded to and handled by the higher provincial authorities.[11]

A third source of official-gentry influence was the fact that they acted together as a group, to protect their privileges.[12] This was possible because of their relatively small size and because they shared political aspirations and economic interests in common. When any one was attacked, they immediately knew that unless they banded together, all would be exploited by the magistrate. Because of their connections, they could and did contact friends in higher yamens to upset the plans of the local magistrate, even when the latter had the blessing of the governor.

Another source of influence lay in the fact that the official-gentry were natives. Unlike the clerks, they were the best educated and most respected members of the community, intimately acquainted with local customs and rules. They were the ones who compiled the local gazetteers, a task requiring a thorough knowledge of all aspects of district life, including figures for arable land, tax quotas and rates, and many other things, ignorance of which placed the magistrate at a comparative disadvantage.

The magistrate, for his part, closely identified with the official-gentry, making it all the more difficult for him to buck them. In his home district he was himself a member of the official-gentry. A stranger in the district he administered, he needed social contacts, and these tended quite naturally to be with the official-gentry stratum.

Because the official-gentry were liable for a sizable part of the grain tribute, and because they were so powerful, they were in a better position than any other group to impede fiscal reform. Feng Kuei-fen was therefore particularly careful in his arguments with them.

Strangely enough, despite the thorough training of the Chinese elite in Confucian ethics and Feng's assumption elsewhere that the official-gentry abided by this moral code,[13] there is rather little preaching of Confucian standards in his appeal. Instead, most of the argument is framed in terms of the long-range interests of the official-gentry. Because official-gentry household status could only be obtained if a member of a family reached the rank of *kung-sheng* or above, or had been a member of the bureaucracy, no family could be certain that the next generation would also belong to the official-gentry. One of Feng's most powerful arguments centered on this issue: "How can I guarantee that my sons and grandsons will belong to the official-gentry? How can I guarantee that my sons and grandsons will have fields? Again, how can I guarantee that I will have sons and grandsons [i.e. that I will not be killed in a rebellion of the commoners]? Heaven's way moves constant; place yourself in a different situation and think about it. Alas! Frightful!"[14]

It was thus imperative for their own long-range survival for the official-gentry households to cooperate in the implementation of tax equalization. The hazards of social mobility could and frequently did, within one or two generations, reduce once-powerful families to the status of commoners and to conditions of abject poverty. To prevent their descendants from suffering this fate—a fate often decreed by excessive taxation and plundering by yamen personnel—Feng entreated the members of his class to help achieve tax equality.

The specter of peasant revolt also hung over the heads of the official-gentry, especially after the arrival of the Taiping movement in Kiangsu. Feng Kuei-fen alluded to this and warned the gentry that they needed to work for the good will of the commoners before it was too late. He pointed out, elsewhere, that the peasantry was generally sympathetic to the Taipings and was ready to rise against the constituted authorities and the local elite. He also argued that a link existed between the Taiping victories and the recent tax revolts in the circuit.[15]

Because of the collusion between the yamens and the official-gentry, the peasants were not making nice distinctions between the guilt of different groups. As Feng pointed out: "High and low officials and clerks have accumulated against themselves anger and deepened the hatred; [the peasants are] glaring like a tiger watching his prey, and are waiting in secret for an opportunity against us. If one morning our strength fails, it is terrifying!"[16]

Instead of simply alluding to hypothetical threats against the established order, Feng carefully documented his appeal with references to well-known uprisings and massacres in the recent past in Su-Sung-T'ai, such as the bloody revolt in Ch'ang-shu district of Soochow prefecture in 1849 and the Chia-ting and Ch'ing-p'u district uprisings in Sungkiang prefecture in 1853.[17]

Feng maintained that the loss of income for the official-gentry households owing to equalization would be rather small and well worth the security gained. He estimated that for this group, equalization would raise the assessment to two taels or four thousand cash per picul. The total sum of additional taxes per household would be only a few dozen, perhaps a hundred or so, taels, but the return on this investment would be unimaginably great. Inasmuch as the primary reason for the revolts of the commoners lay in the abuses of yamen personnel, including the officials, why should the official-gentry, who were only partially at fault, risk their lives? Equalization would lighten the burden of the minor households and they would in turn be grateful to the official-gentry. Moreover, it would curb the corruption of the magistrates, clerks, and runners, in that equal assessments would reduce the avenues for malpractices.[18] With equal rates and equitable conversion rates, the government agents would be unable to demand more than what was prescribed by the statutes.

Lastly, Feng Kuei-fen appealed to his audience's conscience. As a Confucian he could not ignore this mode of persuasion; it seems that he genuinely believed in the high ethical standards of the majority of the official-gentry. Feng thought that most members of this group were unaware of their implication in maladministration and of the misery it caused. To appeal to their conscience was of little use, however, unless he first pointed out their wrongdoing. He hammered into them that their refusal to pay more than the rate prescribed in the tax schedule was the basic cause of the existing corruption in the yamen. As gentry they had a responsibility to live up to the standards they had been exposed to in the study of the classics. As the intellectual and moral elite, it was their duty to provide the people with a proper example. Full-hearted participation in equalizing taxes was an outstanding opportunity to show their moral fiber. Feng also appealed to their local patriotism by asking them to consider the reputation of generosity and benevolence that the official-gentry of the Wu area enjoyed. He promised that they would benefit millions of people by forsaking petty profits and that the merit they would gain would offset any financial losses.

Eventually Feng Kuei-fen stopped asking officials to suppress the illegal tax status of influential households and instead proposed reforms in the structure of local government. There were, however, officials who did attempt to uproot the abuses in the assessment and collection of the tribute grain. Liu Hsun-kao, Soochow finance commissioner from 1862 to 1866, and Ting Jih-ch'ang, Kiangsu governor from 1868 to 1870, fought against the tax evasion of the influential households. In spite of intense efforts, however, both failed in the long run.[19] Neither the emperor's edicts nor the strictures of a conscientious governor could suppress the illegal practices of the elite.

The principal reason for the central government's ineffectiveness in restraining tax evasion by the district notables was the weak position of the magistrate. It was the district magistrate's duty to enforce the will of the throne, in this instance to assess the tribute grain equitably. However, he was not given the means to exercise his authority. Although asked to tax all people in a just manner and to deliver all taxes on schedule, the magistrate had only limited authority over the official-gentry, who constituted the bulk of the influential households and who could delay the payment of their share of the tribute grain. Unless he had the unqualified backing of a strong, reform-minded governor, he was therefore forced to continue the time-honored practice of squeezing the minor households.[20]

The influential households, by misusing the magistrate's weak position to further their own gain, contributed to the impoverishment of the majority of taxpayers. For the average farm enterprise, heavier taxes meant less working capital for improvements in equipment and soil, and this in turn affected output. The minor households were caught in a vicious downward spiral that could only be slowed down, or stopped, by emulating the practices of the influential households, that is, by cheating on their taxes, thus placing a heavier burden on the rest of the minor households.[21]

Tax evasion by the influential households and some minor households also had a detrimental effect on landlord-tenant relationships in southern Kiangsu. As noted, many of the minor households were landlords. Although rents were high—above 50 percent of the annual crop—the heavy tax burden considerably reduced the margin of profit of the landlords, especially those with small and medium holdings. Therefore, in times of crop failure, under the relentless pressure of the tax collectors, these landlords could not forgive their tenants' rent without endangering their own economic survival.

Although the official-gentry owed special allegiance to the state, they were also expected to act as a buffer to protect the commoners from excessive exactions by the local government. When it came to economic matters, however, this elite felt little compunction about undermining the authority of the magistrate and shifting their own tax obligation to the commoners. The resulting exploitation was a harsh one. But the local elite was so myopic that even in the face of rebellion they rigidly adhered to their illegitimate privileges.

DISCUSSION

Kwang-Ching Liu raised the question of the relationship between the gentry and the reform movement. Some people referred to the 1898 reform as the "gentry reform." But what did we mean by "gentry"? Upper gentry? Lower gentry? If lower gentry were involved in the reform process, it would be very significant. Frank Lojewski added that much depended on locality. In parts of Szechwan, the primary social movers, frequently identified as *shen,* were merchants. But in the case of Soochow there was an abnormal concentration of degreeholding upper gentry. It varied from locality to locality. Marianne Bastid agreed, adding that merchants were often more influential than literary gentry in Kwangtung. It was hard to handle the concept of upper and lower gentry, however. Some of the lower gentry were closer to the status of merchants. They had financial means, but were jealous of the more literary gentry.

Kwang-Ching Liu said that while he was sure there was a rural bourgeoisie in the twentieth century, he was less certain about the nineteenth century. Ms. Bastid emphasized that what she had presented was a working hypothesis only and that much more analysis was needed. She said that change in agrarian society had been in progress for some centuries. The Ch'ing, however, instituted a system of tight control over the ruling class, and it was only as this system began to collapse at the end of the eighteenth century that a new kind of society started to emerge. The Taiping Rebellion might be seen as a peasant reaction to a new kind of exploitation. Imperialism was another new factor, which made the system even more reactionary than it otherwise would have been.

Paul Cohen asked if there were concrete connections between foreign capital and this agrarian bourgeoisie. Ms. Bastid said that concrete connections did exist, insofar as foreign trade, for instance, stimulated such cash crops as tea and silk, and helped generate new commercial networks within which this new social class appeared. Mr. Cohen observed that Ms. Bastid's analysis seemed to controvert the view of Rhoads Murphey and others that the early treaty ports were relatively insulated from the economy of the interior. Robert Gardella pointed out that Evelyn Rawski's analysis for late Ming supported Ms. Bastid's conclusion. The interior grew very slowly or stagnated, while coastal areas grew rapidly with foreign contact.

Susan Jones pointed out that the native banks formed a buffer between the native economy and foreign trade. Native banks were dependent on foreign capital. But foreign enterprises had to deal with Chinese banks in trade with the interior.

John Schrecker asked Ms. Bastid to elaborate more fully the nature of the agrarian bourgeoisie. Ms. Bastid said that the class was very diversified, that there were many subgroups, and that there was much regional variation. Jonathan Ocko said that Evelyn Rawski's work suggested that there was no need for a great outside impact to effect great changes. Even a minimal impact could change crop patterns and land relationships.

Richard Shek asked Marianne Bastid when the new rural class began leaving the countryside and moving into the market towns as absentee landlords. Ms. Bastid said that this began in some instances early in the 1870s, after the Taiping Rebellion, but that it depended on the area.

Joanna Handlin mentioned the curious lack of development in the seventeenth- and eighteenth-century economy. In the sixteenth century many textiles were exported. Did the Manchus put a stop to such trade? Ms. Bastid said that one inhibiting factor might have been the silver problem which lasted until the 1860s or 1870s. China had been an exporter of silver. Then, when many countries including America left the silver standard, it flowed back into China causing inflation. There was a small boom around 1895.

Paul Cohen asked whether Ms. Bastid would agree that although the new agrarian bourgeoisie was reshaped after coming into contact with foreign trade, its initial emergence was a consequence of the increasing commercialization of agriculture, prior to the beginning of widespread foreign trade. Ms. Bastid said that commercialization of agriculture was only one factor, that the new agrarian bourgeoisie also tried to profit in other ways, such as concentrating land ownership, exacting more from tenants, introducing new crops, practicing usury, and investing in small handicrafts.

Shui-yuen Yim said that class development in the late Ming period was linked to growing specialization in agriculture. Silk was grown in Kiangsu, which imported rice from Honan and other provinces. Also, since insufficient food was produced in the north and rice had to be brought in from the south, a new class developed, consisting of very large rice merchants.

Lillian Li pointed out that the definition of what was rural and what was urban was difficult to make in a period of change. Did it make a difference whether absentee landlords lived in market towns or in treaty ports? Gilbert Rozman's work suggested that up until the late Ming and early Ch'ing, there was fairly even urban development, particularly as the urban structure filled out at the market town level. The treaty ports then created disjunctions. Ms. Li wondered whether it was possible to document any pattern in the movement of absentee landlords? Did they migrate to middle-level cities, market towns? Or to the treaty ports? Ms. Bastid said that there seemed to be two stages, the first generation moving to the market towns and their children going to the treaty ports. There should be better documentation of this trend, however.

Ms. Bastid added that in the early twentieth century many absentee landlords had their main residence in their home city, but also had a place in Shanghai. Susan Jones said that Ningpo merchants in Shanghai invested money in Ningpo and maintained their ties to their home region.

Joseph Cheng asked Ms. Bastid for further clarification of her use of the expression "agrarian bourgeoisie." Ms. Bastid said that she meant to refer to a class that was intermediate between the urban bourgeoisie and the rural gentry. John Schrecker suggested that the confusion over the term might result from the fact that Ms. Bastid was speaking out of a French tradition, and that, in this instance, the French and American intellectual categories differed. Ms. Bastid said that she found the American use of the word "gentry" confusing, that it reminded her of the gentry in Central Europe and Southern Italy. However, she said, there were in fact two rural ruling classes in Southern and Central Europe in the nineteenth century—the old aristocracy and something else. Mr. Schrecker wondered if one of the problems in characterizing the new group in China might be that there was no aristocracy there.

Ms. Bastid said that the new agrarian bourgeoisie was not identified with degreeholding, but was based more on wealth. Jonathan Ocko asked whether other nonliterati powerholders, such as militia (*t'uan-lien*) leaders, would fall into the new group. Ms. Bastid said that they could. Joanna Handlin suggested that perhaps there was a move in nineteenth-century China toward more rational relationships. As the use of cash spread into the hinterland, there appeared to have been a shift from patron to contractual relationships between landlord and tenant. The influence of wealth grew, while that of literary accomplishment declined.

Kwang-Ching Liu asked whether in Frank Lojewski's view there was any such thing as a landlord class. Mr. Lojewski said that there were a number of different landlord classes. In Mao's first land reform, he attempted to get rid of all of the landlords, but found it impossible. Some small landlords were nearly on the poverty level. A large landlord was defined as one with over 100 mou of land. A medium landlord would have from 50 to 70 mou, while a small landlord might have only 20. Similarly, in the nineteenth century, the interest of a landlord with over 100 mou was different from that of a small landlord who had no connections with the yamen. Therefore it was not useful to consider the landlords as one class.

Shui-yuen Yim mentioned the heavy tax burden on the *hsiao-hu* or lesser households as compared to the *ta-hu* or greater households. He said, however, that there was a mechanism of checks and balances which prevented the inequity from becoming too great. One check was the open discussion that took place over distribution of the surcharge. Taxpayers and tax collectors discussed the question between them. Another check consisted in the way in which the work of an official was evaluated; if the tax burden on the lesser households proved excessive, it could prevent his promotion.

Frank Lojewski replied that the principal means of evaluating a magistrate consisted in whether the taxes were sent in on time, with little regard to how they were collected.

THE INTELLECTUAL CONTEXT OF REFORM

Hao Chang
THE INTELLECTUAL CONTEXT OF REFORM*

I propose first to examine the intellectual background of
reform in the period 1840–1860. At this time, ideologically articulate reformism could not be found at the court, but existed largely
among the Chinese scholar-officials in the provinces. There were
two strands of reformist thought, one exemplified by Tseng Kuo-
fan, the other represented by Feng Kuei-fen and Wei Yuan.

Feng Kuei-fen and Wei Yuan are often identified as scholars
of the statecraft school. Several interesting points can be made
about this school. First of all, quite a number of prominent scholars
of this persuasion came from Hunan, although statecraft thinking
was by no means confined to that province. Second, many of the
statecraft scholars shared a *mu-yu* background, Wei Yuan, Feng
Kuei-fen, and Pao Shih-ch'en supplying three of the best-known
examples. Finally, all of these scholars had in common a great
admiration for the seventeenth-century thinker Ku Yen-wu and
regarded him as a sort of patron saint of their statecraft thinking.
As a token of their admiration, a group of statecraft scholars,
including Wei and Feng, erected a temple at Peking in the 1830s
to commemorate Ku. Feng, in particular, expressed his respect by
adopting a courtesy name which contained a reverential reference
to Ku's courtesy name.

The members of the statecraft school shared an intellectual
outlook that concerned itself with problems of order and an institutional approach to order. This concern with order was different
from that of orthodox neo-Confucianists. The latter generally conceived of order in euphoric moral and spiritual terms. Among statecraft scholars, the concern was mainly with the secular order of
state and society. This concern led statecraft scholars to pursue
order through institutional means. They tended to see statesmanship in institutional as well as moral terms. They approved of the

*A summary.

use of coercive and managerial institutions to maintain order and attempted to reform the functioning of the bureaucratic state through piecemeal institutional innovation.

Underlying their concern with secular dynastic order was an ethical outlook, somewhat different from the orthodox Neo-Confucian ethical outlook. The orthodox outlook was characterized by a variant of what Max Weber called "the ethic of absolute ends" —an outlook oriented exclusively to the moral goal of sagehood. This ethic had no place for practical statecraft concerns. The orthodox outlook was dominated by a series of dichotomies: heavenly principle versus human desires, righteousness versus profit, public concern versus private interest, and moral government versus pragmatic government. The alternatives embraced by these dichotomies were considered to be mutually exclusive and absolutely distinct.

The statecraft scholars, however, subscribed to what I call "an ethic of social orientation" which was quite different from the ethic of the orthodox elite. The members of the statecraft school recognized the primacy of individual moral commitment to the ethic of absolute ends, but they also recognized the difficulty in implementing it. This ambivalence in their ethical outlook resulted in a tendency to value utility, to regard practical achievement as something to be prized, and to assign an important place to self-interest. The resulting "ethic of social orientation" explicitly or implicitly underlay the thought of Wei Yuan, Pao Shih-ch'en, Feng Kuei-fen, and others. This ethic had the significance of providing a degree of legitimation for many ideas which had no place in orthodox Neo-Confucianism.

More influential than the school of statecraft was the reformism of Tseng Kuo-fan. Early in Tseng's life he was greatly influenced by the Ch'eng-Chu school. He tried to give life to old ideas, mainly by infusing them with a large element of moral idealism. Tseng firmly believed in the importance of moral leadership for the creation of an exemplary center. Moral idealism, however, was only a part of his formula.

Tseng added the new dimension of interest in pragmatic statecraft to his philosophy. This is seen most clearly in his emphasis on *li* (propriety, rites) as the guiding precept in Confucian statesmanship. Tseng's concept of *li,* influenced by the School of Han Learning, was very broad. It referred in his thought not only to moral and ritual propriety but also to devices of statecraft. Tseng was thus willing to use both moral and institutional force to achieve order.

Li has its core in the basic Confucian moral precepts as embodied in the doctrine of "three bonds." There is thus a built-in limitation in Tseng's reformism, which prevents it from developing in any radical direction. In this sense there is a basic element of conservatism in Tseng's reformism.

Up to the 1860s there was no major value reorientation as a result of the presence of the West. True, some peripheral values of Chinese tradition such as *li* (profit), and wealth and power, became more influential in the Chinese consciousness. But openness to the West brought little change to the central values and world views of the bulk of Chinese scholar-officials. To the extent that they responded to the West at all, their responses reflected basically the same pragmatic approach and technically rational mode of thinking they had long applied to tackling domestic problems of statecraft.

Our picture of the intellectual outlook of the self-strengtheners is dominated by the *t'i-yung* formula of Chang Chih-tung, but this was not actually formulated until 1896; and we may well question whether it is adequately descriptive of the movement.

The *t'i-yung* formula is a broad one and very complex. Kuo Sung-tao's perception of Western learning for utility was quite different from that of Li Hung-chang, and Liang Ch'i-ch'ao's perception differed from both of theirs. The *t'i-yung* formula is a kind of umbrella concept covering many different ideas, and we must go beyond it.

Levenson viewed this formula as a psychological defense mechanism, created to placate hurt cultural pride and to help preserve a sense of cultural identity. He also raised the question whether the *t'i-yung* formula was workable for modernization. Was it functional or dysfunctional?

Another interesting question concerns the intellectual profile of the conservative opposition to self-strengtheners. We have heard a lot about the background noise they made. But we still do not have enough studies of their intellectual outlooks and how these outlooks were related to their official roles and institutional contexts.

Reformism as found in the treaty ports was distinctly different from the reformism of the self-strengtheners. Although there is some question whether the reformist outlook of the latter can be adequately described by the *t'i-yung* formula, that of the treaty-port reformers certainly cannot. Wang T'ao, for instance, sometimes used the formula, but he also sometimes credited the West with *tao*. There was quite a cultural gap between the treaty-port intellectuals and the self-strengtheners.

We should consider both of these groups of reformers in the late nineteenth-century context of the littoral and hinterland cultures described by Paul Cohen. Certainly the treaty-port reformers played a role in self-strengthening; many of them actually served on the staffs of Li Hung-chang and other self-strengthening leaders.

What was the relationship between the gentry-literati and the treaty-port intellectuals? Before 1890 there was little communication between the world of the treaty ports and that of the literati-gentry. This parallels the socioeconomic analysis of the treaty ports which indicates that prior to the late nineteenth century the ports had no significant transforming impact on the hinterland. There was of course some flow of thought from the treaty ports, but not much. A great cultural gap thus existed between the intellectual world of the treaty ports and that of the gentry-literati. For example, Liang Ch'i-ch'ao studied in Canton in the late 1880s before meeting K'ang Yu-wei. He studied in three of the largest academies in Canton, but never came into contact with Western learning until he happened to come across some books on Western learning in bookstores. Chang Chih-tung, as commissioner of education in Szechwan in the 1870s, compiled a bibliography which had a wide circulation in the late nineteenth century. The bibliography did not include a single work of Western learning. The writings of important scholars of this period also showed little or no concern with the West. It is not that they rejected the West; they simply ignored it.

The situation began to change in the 1890s, when Western learning for the first time spilled out of the treaty ports into the inland cities on a large scale. This was made possible mainly by the emergence of new social institutions. Traditional academies were renovated or gave way to new schools. Curriculum reform gave a prominent place to Western learning. Educational changes were especially noticeable after the Sino-Japanese War of 1894–1895. Many voluntary associations called "study societies" appeared among scholar-officials, their number reaching over sixty between 1895 and 1898.

The most important institutional innovation at the time was elite journalism. Newspapers and magazines were founded by literati themselves. Most were politically oriented and ideologically charged. They spread beyond the treaty ports into the inland cities and had circulation agencies in almost every major city in China proper. Elite journalism helped bridge the gap between the scholar-gentry and the treaty ports and aroused nationwide interest in Western learning.

The intellectual ferment that ensued had a number of dimensions. Focusing on the new sociopolitical thought one sees a spectrum of ideas which included Chang Chih-tung and his followers on one side and K'ang Yu-wei and his sympathizers on the other. At the extreme left were T'an Ssu-t'ung, Liang Ch'i-ch'ao, Sung Heng, and others. Intellectual stances on the right were largely outgrowths of the self-strengthening position. The left, however, represented a new departure, elements of which began to challenge the ideological foundations of the traditional social and political order—the Confucian cosmological myth. The myth had been made up of a fusion of family and political ethics and was based in the cosmological belief that sociopolitical ethics were embedded in the cosmic order. In the 1890s this foundation began to face the challenge of the radical reformers. This radical reformism spearheaded an intellectual movement that was to culminate in the May Fourth Movement in 1919.

Young-tsu Wong
THE IDEAL OF UNIVERSALITY IN LATE CH'ING REFORMISM

The ideal of universality is a difficult concept in late Ch'ing reformism. It seems perplexing to find the very reformers who were obsessed with the practical problems of modernity also entertaining visionary notions of universality. Thus, Frederic Wakeman, struck by the "blood and iron" flavor of K'ang Yu-wei's political statement, on the one hand, and by his visionary *ta-t'ung* (great community) thought on the other, regards K'ang as "the most intriguing—if seemingly inconsistent—Chinese intellectual."[1] In fact, visionary *ta-t'ung* thought is an essential aspect of late Ch'ing reformism. Many other reformers also looked to the future realization of a universal world of all nations, while advocating a reformed Chinese nation-state in the present.

Indeed, universality was the ultimate goal in the reformers' evolutionary scheme of gradual change and progress. Like other thinking men, past and present, the reformers were idealistic and evinced a concern for fundamental human values. Beyond the happiness of their own countrymen, they also wished for the happiness of all mankind. Nor was this "sheer fantasy." Although universal peace lay far beyond the reality of the late Ch'ing situation, it was, in the minds of many reformers, the culminating point of historical evolution. Given their scheme of gradual change and progress, it was perfectly consistent to recognize the reality of warring nations at present and to envision a better world of universal peace in the future. Thus, K'ang Yu-wei could write of the "emerging peace" (*sheng-p'ing shih*) of his own day while turning his thought to the "great peace" (*ta-t'ung shih*) of the future. As Kung-chuan Hsiao has shown, K'ang's thinking moved on two levels and he assumed "a double role: as a practical reformer and as a utopian thinker."[2]

The reformers based their ideal of universality on the assumption that, in the realm of values and ideas, there were no impassable boundaries. All human beings living under heaven and on the earth, for instance, had a sense of respect and affection for their elders.[3] Many ethnocentric conservatives, victims of provincialism, failed or refused to see the existence of ethical precepts in the West. The reformers, however, spilt much ink in challenging this view. Wang T'ao, while he was at Dollar, Scotland, observed that the British *li*, or propriety, was perhaps even more impressive than the Chinese *li*. For Wang, so far as *li* was concerned, there was no national line.[4]

Just as human-heartedness knows no bounds, so truth also is universal. From the Chinese cultural heritage, with its doctrine of universal love and peace, the reformers readily quoted such sayings as: "the truth permeated all under heaven," or "the same principle holds good for all."[5] What was good and true, therefore, belonged to the universal system of validity: nothing was really alien. This can be most explicitly seen in the reformers' assumption that, in basic values, Confucianism was identical with Christian doctrine and vice versa: both the Christian gospel and Confucian "selfless humanness" (*jen*), for example, were essentially doctrines of universal peace and love, though Confucianism, unlike the Christian religion, was an ethical teaching.[6]

Wang T'ao made this point clearly in his essay, "Liu-ho chiang ho wei-i" (The world will become one), in which he stated that the Westerners, who knew Christianity, would readily understand the values in Confucianism and predicted that all great teachings, through a process of mutual influencing, would tend to become more and more similar.[7]

Like Wang, though in a different way, K'ang Yu-wei tended to universalize Confucius as the "prophet of an ideal commonwealth for all mankind," on the one hand, while envisioning a Confucian religion patterned after the Christian Church on the other. Accordingly, K'ang boldly asserted that the orthodox Confucian teaching was a "forgery" and called the conventional "distinction of the barbarians from the Chinese" (*i-hsia chih-pien*) a gross misrepresentation of the Master's idea.[8] Doubtless, K'ang's universalization of Confucius contained an element of "de-Confucianization" and carried some Christian flavor.[9]

Other reformers, thinking in terms of universality, anticipated that some day Confucian scholars, like Christian missionaries, would go to the West to preach their doctrine.[10] There was, however, no evidence to suggest that they intended to make Confucianism the dominant ideology of the world. As they repeatedly said, all teachings, if universally valid, would mutually reinforce instead of undermine one another. Convinced that "eastern sages and western sages have the same mind," they looked forward to future "sages" who would make a great synthesis of different cultures.[11] This was a far cry from "Sinocentric universalism." In perceiving the possibility, and indeed desirability, of attaining the cultural unity of all mankind, these thinkers gave a new meaning to the Chinese notion of "all under heaven" (*t'ien-hsia*).

Late Ch'ing reformers were not the only ones who attempted to universalize Confucianism and Christianity. Some Jesuits in the seventeenth century, such as Matteo Ricci, had wanted to establish a footing for a "Chinese Christian civilization,"[12] and in the nineteenth century, Timothy Richard and others continued along the same lines. But the impact of Richard, perhaps even Ricci, on certain of the reformers, though discernible, was not crucial. The reformers' vision of Sino-Western syncretism does not appear to point to a Chinese Christian civilization. For theirs was, to use Karl Mannheim's term, a "liberal-humanitarian" mentality rather than the missionary's "Chiliastic mentality."[13]

Besides finding a common ground between Christianity and Confucianism, the reformers sought energetically to reinterpret Chinese cultural tradition in the light of modern Western civilization. Sometimes, this led them to "discover" ideas in the Chinese heritage that appeared to be identical or similar to certain modern Western ideas, such as science and technology. On other occasions, they reinterpreted old ideas in terms of modern Western concepts, witness the attempt to relate Mencius' concern with the people to Western democracy. These efforts may justifiably be considered forced, superficial, or specious, but unquestionably they aimed at a universal stance and reflected a readjustment of Chinese tradition under the Western impact. Also unquestionably, the faith in universality facilitated intercultural borrowing: late Ch'ing reformers adopted and blended freely whatever they thought significant and valuable. As a result, the tensions and uneasiness that could have grown out of cultural interaction were minimized. In this regard, the reformers do not fit the Levensonian dichotomy of "history" and "value," with its implication that the influx of Western thought alienated Chinese intellectuals from their own cultural tradition, even while they remained emotionally committed to that tradition.[14] The belief of these men in universality simply blurred for them the dividing line between cultures. So far as they could see, both history and value belonged to the same universe.

The best effort of bivalent elucidation, as regards Chinese and Western cultures, was made by Yen Fu. Unlike most reformers, Yen had a firm footing in both the native and Western cultural traditions; yet, like the others, he believed that all peoples and cultures shared certain universally valid principles. As Benjamin Schwartz put it, Yen tended "to find universal issues of human thought which transcend the 'dichotomy' of Western and Chinese cultures."[15] For this reason, Yen argued that the sages in different parts of the world, despite geographical isolation, had independently developed many similar ideas, such as the Taoist "Way," the Confucian "Great Ultimate," the Buddhist "Isvara," and the West's "First Cause."[16] Yen's efforts to convey Western thought in Chinese terms have been admirably studied by Schwartz. Here I only wish to offer some details on Yen's attempt to expound Chinese thought in the light of Western concepts.

Yen's profound cross-cultural experiences convinced him that Western ideas were helpful for the elucidation of certain difficult terms and passages in the Chinese classics. His knowledge of logic, for example, assisted him in understanding for the first time an awkward passage in the work of Ssu-ma Ch'ien. When Ssu-ma invited his readers "to arrive at what is manifest by starting from what is obscure" (pen-yin chih-hsien), he was really expressing the concept of induction, and when he wrote that "we should infer from what is obvious in order to reach what is obscure" (t'ui-chien chih-yin), he was demonstrating the concept of deduction. Without the benefit of Western logic, Yen said, one could only understand such classical passages in highly speculative, moralistic terms.[17]

Yen also used Western concepts in his study of Taoism, identifying Chuang-tzu's *yü* with space, *chou* with time, *ch'u-neng* with potentiality, and so on. He rejected the conventional view that Taoism was essentially an otherworldly philosophy. On the contrary, he found in it not only Yang Chu's pragmatism but also ideas identical to those of Spencer, Rousseau, and Montesquieu. He compared Chuang-tzu's "noninterference of individuals" to Yang Chu's thesis of "for myself" (*wei-wo*); he placed Lao-tzu's "primitivism" side by side with Rousseau's concern for the "natural condition of existence;" he made the doctrine of "leaving the people alone" (*wu-wei*) parallel to *laissez-faire* and democracy; and he regarded Lao-tzu's notion that "nature is unkind" (*t'ien-ti pu-jen*) as being comparable to Spencer's natural selection.[18] Yen's parallelisms were, of course, farfetched at times. My only point is that, in drawing them, he implicitly committed himself to the universalistic position. Yen set a clear example of syncretism for late Ch'ing reformers; there was no doubt in his mind that the cultural traditions of China and the West could complement each other.[19]

The reformers, of course, did not ignore obvious differences between peoples and cultures, such as physical appearance and social values. But they believed, rightly or wrongly, that civilizations in the East and the West originated in the same remote source. Travel in Egypt and visits to French and British museums convinced Wang T'ao that the ancient West was far more identical to ancient China than to the modern West.[20] Although, in the view of Wang and other reformers, differences had gradually come into being because of geographical barriers and lack of communication, Sino-Western contacts in modern times inspired them to think that the now divergent cultures of East and West could once again move toward uniformity, as modern transportation broke down the barriers among nations.[21]

Because of the lack of contact in the past, China had advanced in the moral area of the *tao,* while the West had advanced in the fields of practical science and technology. The reformers also noticed, however, that the West was not really devoid of *tao,* as many Christian values were in effect mirror images of Confucian notions. Nor did China altogether lack the roots of science and technology, as evidence for which they cited passages from the major classics as well as lesser treatises in which various "scientific" ideas were presented. Some of the reformers even suspected that the highly developed Western sciences had originated in China. Ch'en Chih, for example, argued that "the Westerners who served at the Yuan court brought back Chinese firearms, and yet they improved them continuously and eventually created the formidable modern weapons."[22] T'ang Chen was still more speculative. He thought that many Western systems had their roots in the Chou system. Hence, to T'ang, China was actually inferior to its own past rather than to the modern West.[23] Hsueh Fu-ch'eng, to cite another example, argued that the Westerners had achieved great wealth and power because they had learned from and developed Kuan-tzu's mercantilism.[24]

Certainly, the reformers' claims regarding the Chinese origins of science reflected an exaggerated confidence in their own cultural heritage. But there was some validity to their argument about the existence of science in Chinese tradition. Needham and Wang have given unintentional support to the reformers by showing that "there is some evidence of transmission [of algebra] from the Arabs to the Chinese in the thirteenth and fourteenth centuries, and much more from the Chinese earlier to India and Europe."[25]

The reformers fully recognized that science and technology were highly developed in the West and that China was far behind at the present stage. But they firmly believed that the knowledge that constituted Western science and technology was as valid for all men as ethics and morality. As Hsueh Fu-ch'eng put it, science and technology stem from "common principles" that exist between heaven and earth without national boundaries (*t'ien-ti chien kung-kung chih li*). Although the Westerners are now in the lead over other peoples in the field of modern materialistic civilization, Hsueh argued, other peoples would lead in the forward march of scientific discovery in the future.[26] To use Wang T'ao's phrase, there were no ultimate differences between East and West; there were differences only in speed between junks and steamers, in power between spear and rifle, and in effectiveness between muscle and machine.[27]

The reformers' contemplation of Chinese and Western cultures in universal and syncretic terms laid the framework for their vision of a universal world in the future, which they identified with *ta-t'ung*, or the great community, an old concept in the Chinese tradition. The term *ta-t'ung* comes from the "Li-yun" section of the *Book of Rites* (*Li-chi*). For two thousand years, various Chinese scholars, as well as rebels, have been inspired by this utopian ideal. Rebels used it, usually under the banner of *t'ai-p'ing* or great peace, in response to the suffering population's longing for a "messiah" who would bring peace, justice, and happiness. The scholars often framed their utopian thought in the image of the golden era of the past, the *san-tai* ("three dynasties"), which Confucius had praised. For them, the path leading to the ideal world of *ta-t'ung* began with the "restoration" of the ancient world as it had existed under such kingly rulers as Yao and Shun.[28]

In the nineteenth century, if the Taiping ideology reflected the heritage of the rebels' utopian thinking, the reformers evidently inherited the scholarly tradition of "Confucian utopianism." But the scope of the reformers' utopian thinking was broadened to incorporate the Western world and Western culture. Even the pioneer reformer Feng Kuei-fen's utopian concept of "clan-community," though superficially identical to the "village community" founded by Ho Hsin-yin in Ming times or to Kung Tzu-chen's "land-equalization plan" of the early nineteenth century, also reflected Western influences, such as the ideas of universal education and welfare, which he drew from translated Western books.[29]

The most systematic elaboration of *ta-t'ung* thought in the nineteenth century was that of K'ang Yu-wei. Drawing on divergent sources, indigenous as well as foreign, K'ang produced the most imaginative utopian construction in Chinese intellectual history. So bold was K'ang's conception that he has justifiably been regarded as the first Chinese utopian writer to deserve a place among the great utopians of other lands.[30] K'ang called for the demolishing of slavery, the family, the state, national cultures, social classes, private property, and racial inequality. His goal was the complete transformation of human relationships and economic life, thereby creating the basis for consummate human happiness and universal peace.[31]

Although the late Ch'ing reformers' *ta-t'ung* thought was not the same as that of earlier Chinese utopian thinkers, they nonetheless shared with their predecessors a feeling of dissatisfaction with the time in which they lived. Their ideal of universality, like their reformist thinking in general, was a direct response to dynastic decline and to the Western impact.

As is well known, the reformers accepted the modern multinational world and thought it nonsense to view China, "the Middle Kingdom," as being co-extensive with "all-under-heaven," either politically or culturally. They were convinced also that, however fine China's nonmaterial culture had been, it must be joined to the material civilization—the science and technology—of the modern West in order to survive and, perhaps, enrich the future civilization of mankind. In other words, the reformers wanted to join the family of nations and become part of world civilization. But the undeniable reality, of which they were fully aware, was that if the Chinese world order was hierarchical, so also was the modern system of nation-states. The members of the international community, which the reformers often compared to the Warring States in ancient China, were far from equal. There were big nations and small, and the small nations were the victims of the big ones.[32] As Ch'en Chih put it, China as a member nation was deprived not only of its political sovereignty but also of its economic independence.[33] Most late Ch'ing reformers felt that the modern world was one in which might, not right, held sway. Dissatisfied with this situation, they hoped for a better world community in the future. Out of this hope, they developed a strong historicist belief in the inevitability of the development of social units larger than the nation-state. They perceived the nation-state as merely a temporary and instrumental stage in the evolution toward a world society. It was unthinkable to them that human progress should end in a world of perpetually competing and conflicting nations. As long as competing states existed side by side, they believed, wars would always be fought and suffering would never end. Hence, their quest for *ta-t'ung*.

How could *ta-t'ung* be realized? Most late Ch'ing reformers felt that all nations must first be made equal, rendering it impossible for one power to exploit another. Since the basis for this equality, in their view, was modern weaponry, China and other weak nations had to pull abreast of the big powers in general military capability. When this day came, the aggressive powers would be forced to "bow their heads in submission to our authority," to use Wang T'ao's phrase, or to respect the sovereignty of other nations.[34] Only then would it be possible to progress toward a "harmonious world of all nations" (*wan-kuo ho-hui*) or, to use Hu Li-yuan's terminology, toward the end of the "dictatorship of big powers" (*p'o chuan-chih*) and toward the "freedom of all nations" (*chen tzu-yu*).[35] In K'ang Yu-wei's words, all nations would then join the great community and different peoples would, as a matter of course, forget their cultural and racial differences.

When Timothy Richard proposed a ten-nation alliance and an international conference for outlawing war, many reformers responded with enthusiasm and admiration, for the reformers regarded it as a necessary step to end aggression, to unite different nations, and to lead the way to a great community. As Hu Li-yuan stated in his letter to Richard, should an international organization indeed come into existence and ensure universal peace and harmony, it would certainly be a step on the way to *ta-t'ung*.[36]

Thus, *ta-t'ung*, for the late Ch'ing reformers, was realizable; it was not an empty dream. They seriously believed that the "one world" of the future could be realized by leading mankind toward it, stage by stage. *Ta-t'ung*, as Kung-chuan Hsiao put it, was a practical ideal which could guide men's future social development.[37]

A recent writer has argued that "the homogeneity of the *ta-t'ung* conflicted with K'ang's [and other reformers'] prediction that as society developed economically, it would grow more and more specialized."[38] This conflict, however, may be more apparent than real. For it can also be argued, as Kenneth Boulding has in his *The Meaning of the Twentieth Century*, that economic development enhances the tendency toward homogeneity.[39]

The ideal of universality of the late Ch'ing reformers calls to mind Arnold Toynbee's prediction that "our own descendants are not going to be just Western, like ourselves. They are going to be heirs of Confucius and Lao-tzu as well as Socrates, Plato, and Plotinus."[40] The irony is that so many Westerners, after bringing their influence to bear on China and helping thereby to stimulate Chinese commitment to universality, were much less ready to come to such a position themselves and persisted in looking at Chinese and Western cultures as two separate and exclusive entities.

Suzanne Wilson Barnett
NATIONAL IMAGE: MISSIONARIES AND SOME CONCEPTUAL
INGREDIENTS OF LATE CH'ING REFORM

Like reform-minded scholar-officials of the 1840s, Chinese
reformers in the 1890s responded to problems of China's weakness
in the face of Western wealth and power. However, reformers in late
nineteenth-century China differed from their earlier counterparts in
one important respect: they shared a new sense of China as a nation
operating in the Western-dominated international order. The half
century from the Opium War to the era of Sino-Japanese confrontation and the climax of imperialism had brought a startling paradig-
matic change. Participating in this change were Protestant missionaries whose writings and activities helped to create a context
for new assumptions. The paradox was that while late Ch'ing
commitment to China's national political and social transformation
called to mind earlier missionary hopes for the Chinese empire, by
the end of the nineteenth century such transformation had ceased
to be a missionary priority.

One of my central concerns in recent years has been the
relationship between reform in late Ch'ing China and the presence
of Westerners in the Middle Kingdom. We can hardly agree with
D. Z. Sheffield's implication, in 1900, that the late Ch'ing reform
movement owed its existence entirely to foreign (that is, Western)
thought.[1] Still, as this workshop has shown, Western guns and ideas
were important in stimulating a transformation of Chinese perceptions and procedures during the last decades of the Manchu dynasty.
The "Western impact" was real, and it produced a complex variety
of overlapping responses among both Chinese and Westerners. In
this regard, the 1840s are as significant as the 1890s.

Aside from its shock value, what was the impact of Western
intrusion in China? I sense that the Western impact has engaged us
primarily as a negative phenomenon with a positive outcome—a
rough-and-tumble experience that eventually brought favorable
results, in this case what the missionaries (and others) called the

160

"awakening of China."[2] This perspective has the effect of neatly rationalizing Western imperialism, but somehow it falls short of encompassing the dimensions of change connected with the Western presence in China in the late Ch'ing.

Given what we are discovering about the dynamics of Confucian scholarship as a context for reform in the Ch'ing, Westerners hardly can take credit for all of China's "progressive thoughts" (Sheffield's term).[3] However, Westerners in the empire did inspire changing perceptions of China's place in the world, and this process of intellectual change had a direct bearing on Chinese receptivity to reform. Increased Western presence in China carried its own message of a Western-dominated international order, and Chinese thinkers and policy makers responded to this Western intrusion with a new awareness of two critical phenomena: (1) a non-Chinese system asserting itself with vigor and (2) a Chinese system that was not functioning very well at all. The great encounter with opium, British guns, and treaties understandably offended the sensibilities of Confucian scholar-officials committed to China's ideals of order. But the encounter also brought conceptual changes of enormous importance.

Perhaps the single most significant conceptual change (or at least adjustment) was the acquisition of a sense of national image. The encounter with Westerners brought Chinese intellectuals to comprehend national differences. This developmental process began in earnest in the late 1830s and had as its first manifestation the separate identification of England and the English. The next step was the gradual acquisition of specialized knowledge that differentiated the other Western nations. The third stage, which in fact emerged alongside these, brought a new definition of China as a nation. The transformation of China from Middle Kingdom to nation was no simple matter, and in some respects the transformation for many good reasons may yet be incomplete. Still, it strikes me that late Ch'ing reform in its post-self-strengthening phase operated increasingly on the assumption of Chinese nationhood.

I consider that this assumption was dependent on decades of graduated preparation involving missionary educators, aggressive

merchants and consuls, and concerned Chinese scholar-officials.
For all these groups, the prospect of China's nationhood generated
(or at least encouraged) reformism involving most prominently a
new attitude toward China's inhabitants. China's nineteenth-
century experience seems to show an increasing sense of administrative responsibility to inhabitants of the empire as participants in the
state. Such considerations inspired fundamental changes in the nature
of China's institutional structure.

Differentiating the Barbarians

The practice of identifying peculiarities of different maritime
countries hardly began with the nineteenth century. The list of overseas countries appended to the *Ming shih* (History of the Ming), for
example, involves a conventional arrangement by which each foreign
trading entity received individual treatment.[4] To be sure, there is
much confusion in the list, including the scrambling of France,
Portugal, and other countries.[5] Still, there is evidence of an effort
to differentiate the maritime barbarians, and this kind of effort
provided a preface to the more extensive categorizations of maritime
countries during and after the Opium War era.

Commissioner Lin Tse-hsu and later his friend Wei Yuan were
among several Chinese literati who came up with classifications of
foreign countries for purposes of maritime defense. The efforts of
these men set a basis for new Chinese understanding of international
dynamics. Materials now included in the Institute of Modern History
series on Chinese perceptions of the West give evidence of their
knowledge.[6] Such materials also may be useful as indicators of the
evolution of national images in the early nineteenth century, the
clearest single development being the individuation of the English.
Even before the opium crisis of the 1830s, some Chinese intellectuals had turned their attention to British sea expansion. (Wang
Ta-hai is perhaps the earliest critical figure here; later Yü Cheng-
hsieh and others added to Chinese literature on the English.)[7]
Increasingly the English received separate treatment in essays on
Ying-chi-li (or equivalent transliterations for "England") or *Hung-
mao* (for "Red-hairs," used in the nineteenth century almost

exclusively for the British and not, as previously, for the Dutch).[8]
The general assessment of England and the English changed little
over time: even in the pre-Opium War period the location and size
of England appear important as motivations for expansion in search
of resources and territory; the search for profit became a fixed part
of the Chinese estimation of the British character.[9]

However, as the opium crisis mounted at Canton, subtle additions to the general understanding of the British appeared. Among
these additions, which included comments on social customs and
political institutions, were statements about the British religion.
A revealing new element was the characterization of the British as
mavericks for having raised opposition in Europe to the previously
dominant *T'ien-chu-chiao* (or Roman Catholic religion).[10] The
impression conveyed by many Chinese representations of England's
pursuit of an independent religion—the *Yeh-su-chiao* of "Protestantism," particularly of British Protestantism—is one of an
independent uncontrollable (and hence unpredictable) nation. Such
an impression had far-reaching effects: it contributed to increasing
Chinese fear of the English and a concentration of Chinese anti-
foreign hostility on the English. Americans, French, and Germans
rarely experienced wrathful treatment in the Chinese prose of the
Opium War era. The British did, and it took the form of implicit
accusations about the inferiority of English culture (despite the
firepower of the British navy) and tactical suggestions for dealing
with the British.[11]

Yü Cheng-hsieh, writing in the early 1830s, almost certainly
had in mind the British in his crude denunciation of Western
barbarians as "people with no hearts or livers" (an anatomical as
well as spiritual attack).[12] Huang Chün-tsai, a little known figure I
am trying to unearth, discussed England in the 1840s in terms of
its national power becoming increasingly widespread (*kuo-shih
chin-kuang*). However, he was critical of British wealth and power
(*fu-ch'iang*) because of its dependence on the exploitation of
China's resources, especially tea. He called for firm measures,
including the prohibition of trade, to make the British submissive
and to enhance China's strength.[13]

The separate treatment accorded England in private Chinese writings helped to create an international context in which China too could find a place. The key process at work was the use of England in the definition of other countries, including China. The focus on the English brought an accompanying effort to differentiate, among others, America, which had opposed England in a previous era.[14] Ultimately China's procedures found articulation in a comparative context. As an example the English, according to what came to be conventional wisdom on the subject, did not bow or kneel when meeting friends; instead, unlike the Chinese, they removed their hats and shook hands. Taken in isolation, such efforts to define the English had little meaning; when multiplied, they led indirectly to a new definition of "Chineseness" and were important in the gradual development of a Chinese national consciousness.

Missionaries and Conceptual Change

The articulation of Chinese self-consciousness was the work primarily of Chinese intellectuals whose writings influenced policymakers and institutional change. The great writers in this connection include Wei Yuan, Hsu Chi-yü, and later Feng Kuei-fen and Wang T'ao.[15] However, associated with this development was another group, namely, the missionary-educators: Protestant missionaries who wrote materials in Chinese about the geography and history of the non-Chinese (especially European and American) world.[16] Missionary writers began by trying to bring Chinese recognition of the critical absence of Christianity in China's heritage; Chinese writers sought to identify Westerners and their behavior in relation to China. For both groups, cultural concerns gradually incorporated political issues. Again the missionaries helped set the trend by referring in their Chinese writings, as early as the 1830s, to constitutions and parliaments.[17]

In linking the missionaries in this fashion with the rise of Chinese national self-consciousness, I recognize the difficulties involved in trying to trace clear lines of historical influence. Nonetheless, I am persuaded that the Protestant missionary endeavor initiated in the 1830s to acquaint literate Chinese with the world as defined by Westerners had a profound (if fragmented) effect on Chinese perceptions of the world order. Perhaps the most remarkable feature of this endeavor is the extent to which it found neat avenues of appropriation by the Chinese. Significantly, with Wei Yuan's *Hai-kuo t'u-chih*, Western geography and history ceased to have a separate, foreign stamp in China.[18] As early as the 1840s such subject matter began to take its place as a regular part of the realm of Chinese scholarship, a legitimate area of inquiry for Confucian-oriented intellectuals. There is no better evidence of this development than the fact that missionary-educators, impressed by the "geographical" writings of men like Lin Tse-hsu and Hsu Chi-yü—and also by what they saw as alternative educational needs— turned increasingly from geography and history to mathematics and science in their Chinese-language publications.[19]

Initially the missionaries sought to encourage an expansion of Chinese knowledge of foreign geography and culture because they assumed that such knowledge would be of vital importance to their evangelistic success. Like the Jesuits before them, the early Protestants felt compelled to establish themselves as worthy not only of Chinese attention but of Chinese respect, thus to be in a position effectively to transmit the message of salvation. The motivating missionary goal was to humble the Chinese sense of superiority over foreigners and to build respect for those Western nations involved in the missionary movement. The tactic was to inform the Chinese about the outside world, with emphasis on the achievements of the various national groups at work in trade and evangelism on the China coast (above all England and the United States). Ironically the early missionary-educators produced an unforeseen, ultimately self-defeating result: China's "culturalistic" antiforeignism gradually did give way, but in its place came a new antiforeignism based on *national* loyalty and interest. Robert Hart made astute observations of this new Chinese attitude in his remarkable essays written in 1900 and published in his *These from the Land of Sinim*.[20]

Surely the pioneer American missionary E. C. Bridgman did not anticipate that his treatise on the U.S.A., first published in

1838, would contribute to rising national consciousness in both China and Japan. His goal, quite simply, was Chinese recognition of American achievements and Chinese respect for Americans. It is equally certain that K. F. A. Gützlaff, who distributed a little piece on the English during the *Amherst* voyage in 1832 and later produced a number of treatises describing Western nations, had no idea that he was contributing to China's growing self-image and an accompanying ability to deal firmly, even harshly, with Western national powers on their own terms. The fact that these men helped to achieve something that was quite different from—even subversive of—their original intention does not, however, dilute the historical value of their achievements. Insofar as the birth of a new Chinese self-image in the late Ch'ing was contingent upon expanded Chinese awareness of the rest of the world, Protestant missionaries, by contributing to this expanded awareness, played an important historical role.

National Image and Reform

How did national image and emerging Chinese national consciousness contribute to reform in the late Ch'ing period? The actors in the process play different roles here, and it is difficult to get a handle on their respective reform functions. Still, the missionaries, it seems to me, provided two conceptual contributions relating to national image and ultimately to reform. First, the missionaries in general brought out the idea of individual salvation, which builds upon some acknowledgment of individual worth. Second, the missionary-educators from the early nineteenth century pursued a commitment to China's *national* conversion, both in a religious and in a political sense.

From the beginning, Protestant missionaries expressed interest in the transformation of China's institutions, so as to prepare a context for the salvation of China's large population. This sentiment received ample expression long before the pronouncements of W. A. P. Martin and the infamous Arthur Henderson Smith. S. Wells Williams, for example, wrote in his 1848 *Middle Kingdom:*

The future is full of promise, and the efforts of the church
with regard to China will not cease until every son and
daughter of the race of Han has been taught the truths of
the Bible, and has had them fairly propounded for reception
or rejection. They will progress until all the cities, towns,
villages, and hamlets of that vast Empire have the teacher and
professor of religion living in them; until their children are
educated, their civil liberties understood, and political rights
guaranteed; their poor cared for, their literature purified, their
condition bettered in this world by the full revelation of
another made known to them. The work of missions will go
on until the government is modified, and religious and civil
liberty granted to all, and China takes her rank among the
Christian nations of the earth, reciprocating all the courtesies
due from people professing the same faith.[21]

Williams's intentions seem clear and also representative of a general
commitment among those missionaries who attacked China's
secular as well as spiritual deficiencies. Over time, however, something happened to the firmness of these missionaries' resolve.

My sense is that the notion of national transformation
gradually became less important to missionaries: as China's existing
institutional structure began to bend (or appear to bend) more to
Western demands for commercial and evangelistic advantage, there
was less need for fundamental change at the national level. As this
happened, however, the other significant actors in the formation of
a Chinese national image—Chinese literati besieged by a series of
crises challenging the very survival of the empire—seem to have
absorbed the idea of change at the national level as a vital step
toward the accomplishment of China's improvement. Recognition
of the necessity of institutional-structural change thus shifted from
the outsiders to the insiders. The assimilation of this recognition
was a critical ingredient in late Ch'ing reform.

In another respect as well, the literati and the missionaries
seemed to pass each other, moving in opposite directions. Beginning
in the 1830s and 1840s, Protestant missionaries had posited an

important connection between individuals and the national structure encompassing them. As this connection became, over time, less
critical to the missionaries, it acquired increasing importance to
Chinese writers and reformers. Indeed, much of Chinese reformism
in the late nineteenth century seemed to operate on the premise
that change in institutional structure and procedures required
attention to the individual inhabitants of the empire. Liang Ch'i-
ch'ao's focus on the new citizen is curiously reminiscent of missionary notions of individual worth and the promise of salvation.[22]
The pattern is complex, but it would appear that where the missionaries gave first priority to the individual person and his salvation and only second priority to national concerns, Chinese
reformers, in the post-self-strengthening era, placed primary interest
in national transformation and secondary interest in needs at the
individual level.

   This curious, even ironic, switch over the last six decades of the
nineteenth century brings out all the complexities of the Western
impact. It also suggests the growing importance of perceptions of
national image among Chinese literati and policy-makers. Perceptions of national image began with a Western effort to reduce
Chinese pride and to affirm the power of Western countries involved
on the China coast. The effort produced a genuine understanding of
relative national behavior and international possibilities; but it also
produced a new awareness of China, along with a new national sense
of pride. This quite modern sense of national pride—and, in certain
circumstances, its obverse, shame—necessitated the transformation
of Chinese institutions and procedures so as to gain for China a
respected place in the international order. This process involved a
new recognition of China's inhabitants and the need for altered
attitudes toward them. By the end of the nineteenth century
popular behavior had become a powerful consideration in any
reform effort, suggesting a new kind of reformism much broader in
societal scope than the defense-minded reform proposals of statecraft writers of the 1840s. Crisis politics accounted largely for this
change, but shifting perceptions of national image also figured.

   Pinpointing stages in this important developmental process is the work of further research. I regard the contributions of early Protestant missionaries as a significant source of information and inspiration, and I recognize the critical role of a Chinese intellectual community prepared to absorb these contributions. By disseminating the knowledge of the Westerners, Chinese writers helped to promote a new perception of national difference and a new awareness of popular participation. In a sense, conversion and salvation at both individual and national levels were motivating goals for Chinese reformers as well as missionaries. Moreover, the religious terminology of the missionaries aside, for both groups conversion and salvation had a profound institutional thrust. From the beginning the missionaries had secular designs on China, and the impact of their approach was far-reaching.

I-fan Ch'eng
KUNG AS AN ETHOS IN LATE NINETEENTH-CENTURY
CHINA: THE CASE OF WANG HSIEN-CH'IEN (1842–1918)

In Mary Wright's words: "The failure of the T'ung-chih Restoration demonstrated with a rare clarity that even in the most favorable circumstances there is no way in which an effective modern state can be grafted onto a Confucian society."[1] Similarly, Albert Feuerwerker, in his study of China's early industrialization, concluded: "Perhaps the most important lesson to be drawn from this checkmate is the following: one institutional breakthrough is worth a dozen textile mills or shipping companies established within the framework of the traditional society and its system of values."[2] While the more critical reader might wish to break down the concepts "Confucian society" or "system of values" into specific components such as "peace-oriented world view" or "familism-nepotism in bureaucratic practices," many would accept the premise that China's tradition was in general incompatible with "the requirements of modernization." I believe that this premise is fallacious and that in fact certain traditional values and attitudes came to be not obstacles to, but driving forces behind, China's modernization.

The orientation toward *kung* (public good), which informs Confucian conceptions in the *Ta-hsueh* (Great learning) and *Li-chi* (Book of rites), is one of the most fundamental of these values. Indeed, it was so pervasive in late nineteenth-century China that it can legitimately be called an ethos. By examining the transformation of the meaning of *kung* in the thinking of a late Ch'ing scholar, Wang Hsien-ch'ien, I will try to show how easily this abstract symbol of collectivity could be turned to express a strong nationalist concern. Also, by showing how deeply seated this new meaning of *kung* as national collectivity was in the mind of a conservative like Wang, I shall try to suggest one of the Confucian sources of the Chinese nationalism that played such an indispensable role in China's drama of modernization. In what follows I shall treat Wang as an

170

example of certain tendencies of thought, without claiming for him any special role, as an individual, in the process of modernization.

Born in Hunan in 1842 and a *chin-shih* of 1866, Wang Hsien-ch'ien held various posts in the field of national education before he was made President of the Imperial Academy (one of the most eminent positions in the field) in 1880. From 1879 to 1889, Wang followed his career in the capital as a high-ranking academic, expressing his political views in his memorials to the throne. With much the same idealistic stubbornness that Wei Yuan displayed in completing his *Sheng-wu chi* (Record of imperial military exploits) —a determination to restore people's confidence in the ruling dynasty—he finished compiling the famous *Tung-hua lu* (Records from within the Eastern Flowery Gate) in 1884. After being granted a leave in 1889 he stayed mainly in Hunan, teaching at famous local academies and active as a local cultural leader, until his death in 1918. During this period he was even more intellectually productive than before. He finished a number of important exegetical works on *Hsun-tzu, Han-shu, Yen-t'ieh lun* (Discourse on salt and iron), *Chuang-tzu,* and so on.

Unlike K'ang Yu-wei and Liang Ch'i-ch'ao, Wang did not study with any great master. After he made his own reputation, however, he was befriended by some of the best classicists and scholars of the period, such as Wang K'ai-yun and Miao Ch'üan-sun, and he made his fellow Hunanese Kuo Sung-tao his model as a concerned thinker. In the capital and at home, he had ardently supported— though without formal assignment—the court's efforts at self-strengthening, to which he contributed both as a critic and as a "Chang Chien" type of local promoter. However, his involvement in 1898 in the opposition to K'ang Yu-wei's intellectual influence in Hunan earned him a posthumous reputation as a "conservative."[3] Although this label does not seem to do him justice in light of his "liberal" tendencies and activities, we must admit that Wang was not one to accept new or exotic ideas readily.

In any case, in terms of the study of modernization and a tradition's adaptability it is just as useful to examine shifts of emphasis—in a time of crisis and transition—in the basic assumptions of a "conservative" as it is to scrutinize the thinking of revolutionaries. The interest of Wang's thought lies not in its unconventionality—almost every aspect of his ideas can be traced to some Confucian or Legalist source—but rather in what light these ideas, especially when considered as a coherent whole, can throw on the reactions of traditional Chinese to the pressures of modernization. It is from this point of view that I shall first examine Wang's views on bureaucracy and their relation to the meaning he gave to *kung* in the 1880s. Next, I shall examine the new significance which *kung* acquired for Wang in the reform days (1897–1898), and consider it in relation to his attitude toward traditional Legalism. I shall conclude with a note on the role of *kung*, both as an ethos and as a value with transformed meaning, in the process of modernization in late nineteenth-century China, with special reference to the inner source of the nationalism of Chinese intellectuals.

A moralist,[4] Wang was quick to involve himself in traditional debates on Confucian administration and the role of the emperor. In 1879 when the Ch'ing-liu (uncontaminated group) officials were aggrandizing their influence, Wang memorialized against their leaders, Chang P'ei-lun[5] and Li Fan, for the inappropriateness of their criticisms and accused them of forming a faction (*p'eng-tang*). The throne, he warned, should maintain control over the channels of communication (*yen-lu*) lest, by not taking enough initiative, it be led into misjudgment and indecisiveness.[6] While Wang's posture in this instance may lead us to see him as a believer in Yung-cheng's doctrine of limitless trust by ministers in an absolutist ruler,[7] the stands taken by him on other occasions contradict such an impression. In 1885, a year of serious flooding in the Liang-Kiang, Liang-Hu, and Liang-Kwang regions, Wang severely criticized, as extravagant spending in time of crisis, the Empress Dowager's plans for the reconstruction and beautification of sections of the Forbidden City.[8] Again, in 1888, he attacked the chief eunuch, Li Lien-ying, a favorite of the Empress Dowager, on the ground that the notorious behavior of eunuchs was detrimental to the people's social outlook.[9]

In these situations, there was no question in Wang's mind of a power confrontation between the throne and one of its ministers, involving an ideological duel between Legalist and Confucianist—a pattern Levenson described in his interpretation of "Confucian China."[10] In taking these seemingly contradictory positions, Wang assumed the existence of a common goal for both the ruler and his assistants, an objective standard that could guide people in governing. Indeed, after criticizing the Ch'ing-liu, he explained to a friend that the mechanism that operated in him—"an impartial and sincere mind" (*i-p'ien kung-ch'eng chih hsin*)—ought to be aroused in every official.[11]

The symbol *kung* is immediately reminiscent of the Tung-lin struggle in the late Ming. According to Wakeman, the Tung-lin notion of *kung*—as contrasted to Liang Ch'i-ch'ao's *"ch'ün"* (grouping, social organization)—implied, on the one hand, devotion to an ideal of loyalty and, on the other, the rejection of "factionalism" in any form.[12] Like Wang's "impartial and sincere mind," the Tung-lin sense of commitment required a devout self-screening to eliminate any bias or selfish motivation in one's thinking concerning the court administration. But Wang's conception of *kung* did not end merely in antifactionalism. Another memorial of his exemplifies this clearly.

In 1880, the same year in which he tried to impeach Tong King-sing and Sheng Hsuan-huai for their malfeasance, Wang memorialized to express his concern for bureaucratic efficiency. He saw the greatest obstacle to China's advancement as lying in the lack of any real commitment on the part of most officials to the efficient discharge of their duties. Most of them, in Wang's words, "refrained from getting involved" (*chih-shen chü-wai*).[13] This indifference to his public assignment left the official interested only in the opportunities for personal or familial gain that his post might bring him. Wang insisted that officials must "really put their hearts into their official duties" (*shih-hsin jen-shih*).[14] That is, he wanted to see in every official substantial interaction between the ego and the official business that he handled. Hence, Wang strongly urged imperial action to force the officials' attention back to their duties. Feeling the entire polity, including the self-strengthening programs, disintegrating, a Confucian scholar like Wang was able to appeal to Legalist measures to stimulate a demoralized officialdom. Wang suggested more stress on specialization in the allocation of posts and assignments. With strict supervision and ruthless, immediate reward-punishment power in the hands of the emperor, there would be no way for an official to evade his responsibilities.

As Metzger shows, warnings against "shirking responsibility" (*t'ui-hsieh*), "punishment laws" and their Legalist assumptions, and exhortations to "exhaustively devote one's spirit and energy to the matters for which one is responsible," were familiar themes in the Ch'ing bureaucratic tradition.[15] It could also be argued that it was precisely the Legalist emphasis in the Ch'ing court since Yung-cheng[16] that, by further reducing the weight of the otherwise self-respecting *chün-tzu* on the Levensonian scale (bureaucrat vs. monarch) and hence making them less willing to commit themselves to their posts, made necessary the constant exhortation in terms of *kung* to drive individual officials back to their organizational identity. *Kung* as a limit to fiery, confident individuals in the late Ming was largely superseded in the late Ch'ing by *kung* as a standing exhortation hanging before every official.

In order to facilitate our analysis of Wang's ideas about *kung* in the reform period (1897–1898), as opposed to his ideas analyzed above, two strains of *kung* in Chinese thinking should be reviewed here. As a value in classical Chinese thought, *kung* was a sociopolitical concept, meaning "public," or "society minus the 'self-ish' element." While ancient but subversive notions like "*t'ien-hsia wei kung*" ("the polity as a whole is designed to work to the interest of everybody") were consciously suppressed by Chinese dynastic rulers as values, however unverbalized, they occupied such a central position in Confucianism that idealists could not help internalizing them as part of their basic outlook. In *Ta-hsueh,* a Confucian youth's life purpose, identity, and mission were well-defined. The goal of self-cultivation did not end in oneself. There was always a larger entity with which one could identify: the family, a geographical unit in China (*kuo*) or, finally, the Chinese sociopolitical whole (*t'ien-hsia*).

What underlay the entire regimen was an orientation to serve, to devote oneself to something beyond one's physical self, but still in this world. Since the family was considered an extension of the self (*ssu*), an aspiring Confucianist often vowed his dedication to *t'ien-hsia,* the largest and ultimate object of public identification. Ku Yen-wu, for example, articulated the intimate relationship between *kung,* the public as value, and *t'ien-hsia,* the public embodied.[17]

In the Legalist tradition, *kung* was concretized in the concepts *cheng* (justice) and *wu-ssu* (impartiality), which formed the conceptual foundation for the *ch'ing-kuan* (incorruptible official) tradition. The extreme expression of this strain of thought was encapsulated in the eclectic *Lü-shih ch'un-ch'iu* (Spring and autumn of Mr. Lü): "Confucius [allegedly] said, 'Ch'i Huang-yang was indeed a man of justice! He did not avoid recommending someone, in the internal circle, who was his son (simply to avoid the accusation of nepotism); nor someone, in the external circle, who was the intended object of his vengeance.'"[18] Such an ardent belief in absolute fairness and justice has inspired numerous intellectuals since then, but a distinction must be made between the meaning of *cheng* (justice) as a social instrument, which is compatible with a Confucian stance, and its meaning as a basic value that governs other attitudes and lesser values, which can legitimately be called "Legalist."

Only with the above two strains understood can we go into what *kung* meant to Wang in the 1897–1898 period. At the height of the reformist clamor Wang was pessimistic about the possibility of implementing democracy in China. In China, he asserted, the history of imperial institutions had already generated a "selfish condition" (*ssu chih chü*). That is to say, the "sages" who owned the empire were selfishly suspicious of the people toiling beneath them, as a result of which the people were generally apathetic toward public or official affairs. This was in direct contrast to the West, where, as Wang saw it, there was an abundance of autonomy for each individual and group, and people voluntarily planned for and discussed the public good.[19] Wang, though a conservative,

admired the marvels that "public spirit" had been able to do for
the state (*kuo-chia*) in the West. What Wang had in mind here was
the idea that individuals should devote themselves to the cause of
the ultimate political community, the *t'ien-hsia*. Lacking the
Western concept of citizenry, Wang nevertheless could appreciate
a dim sense of participation, much in the mode of the traditional
Confucian orientation of *kung*.

But Wang's solution to China's problem seems to suggest that
he was equally conscious of the Legalist side of *kung*. Since the
political pattern of imperial China, in his view, had already eliminated the sociopsychological possibility of democracy, the only
alternative still available, institutionally, was to properly regulate
individuals so that maximum justice could be ensured and wrong-
doings reduced to a minimum. Besides his early advocacy of strict
supervision of the bureaucracy to encourage efficiency and honesty,
Wang openly—and hence unorthodoxly—extolled the Legalist Han
Fei for the latter's promotion of severe punishment (*yen-hsing*)
and explicit and non-negotiable laws (*ming-fa*). Indeed, in the
chaos of Han's time, Wang argued, the only honest and constructive
course was to cast aside talk of Mencian "humanity and righteousness" (*jen-i*), which had become words without content, and in
radical fashion to substitute for them "severe statutes" (*chung-
tien*).[20] Wang also admired Hsun-tzu, the transitional figure between
Confucianism and Legalism, for the latter's basic belief that individuals should conform to the rites, which in turn should serve as
explicit and universal norms for society.[21] Of course, Hsun-tzu,
like the Legalists, did not hesitate to advocate the use of coercion
when ritual persuasion failed. Wang's support even of this stance is
suggested by the frequency with which he quoted the line from
Hsun-tzu which said: "That one thing should lose its appropriate
recompense is the beginning of confusion."[22] Punishment and
coercion, therefore, were necessary.

Was this sense of justice (*kung-cheng*) or impartiality in Wang's
Legalist orientation a basic value in itself or simply an instrumental
attitude toward social problems? We know that Wang viewed traditional rites and established statutes as no more than socially

utilitarian. That is, he did not exalt rites and laws for their timeless virtue; rather, following Hsun-tzu's historicist leanings,[23] he believed the value of rites and laws to lie in their function as regulating tools in society. Hence, as society changed, it was appropriate for rites and laws also to change.

We might, then, expect Wang's *kung-cheng* attitude, as reflected in his Legalistic outlook, to have been derived from a belief in the value of social order. Accompanying such a belief, with its implicit yearning for order, was often the mirror-image conviction of the intrinsic evilness of individuals. Looking at Wang's espousal of Hsun-tzu, one might indeed be inclined to think that he adopted Hsun-tzu's principle of "innate evil." But in fact, Wang did not believe in the all-evilness of individuals; rather, he argued that Hsun-tzu perceived people as varying in degrees of goodness and evilness, and that his "evil" theory was addressed only to the evil ones.[24] Wang's sense of justice then lies neither in the immanent quality of rites and laws nor in the ultimate value of social order.

Let us consider further the relation between the individual and the social order in Wang's thought in order to decide in which dimension of *kung* Wang's basic emphasis lay. In a proposal for examination reform written between 1897 and 1898, Wang expressly agreed with K'ang Yu-wei's denunciation of the eight-legged essay. First, Wang noted the ominous fact that *t'ien-hsia* had become one of a multitude of states (*lieh-kuo*). In a unified *t'ien-hsia* (*i-t'ung chih t'ien-hsia*) the ruler might be justified in using the eight-legged examination both to limit his subjects' intelligence and to trade on their ambition for official titles, so that they would not rebel and the dynasty would last longer. But with *t'ien-hsia* in a multistate situation, if the ruler still "knows only the advantage of fettering (*shu-fu*) the people and ignores the harm in making the people useless [as a result of the examination system]," then there would be no hope of "rescuing [the collectivity in] a time of adversity and saving the life of the country" (*chiu-shih huo-kuo*).[25] Thus Wang expressed his disgust with the narrow concentration on preventing subversion and rebellion. This exclusive concern for social order was justifiable only when the collectivity was strong enough to stop foreign encroachment in a competitive international world. In order to have a strong collectivity, Wang reasoned, individual energy should not be suppressed; rather it should be released and encouraged, so as to be put to good use. Thus, we find Wang, as early as 1880, pressing for government action to encourage merchants to take over the inland international trade and to go overseas to engage in economic warfare.[26] Later, he further argued that the government should not only subsidize but systematically enhance the prestige of merchants and artisans so that young talents would be induced to devote themselves to such professions.[27] In taking this position Wang boldly denied any absolute value to the old social order, which had suppressed tradesmen, and advocated new ways for youths to use their energies, thereby explicitly rejecting the old notion that the only worthy way was the career of the scholar-official.

Wang's conception of *kung* qua value now emerges more clearly. *Kung,* in the sense of fairness, embodied in his Legalist side, depended heavily, if not exclusively, on Wang's commitment to *kung* as a basic value, centering on devotion to the collectivity. Simply put, *kung* in the sense of *cheng* (justice) propelled Wang to insist that the system regulate individuals objectively. But an objective system would be worthless (as in the case of a bad examination system) if not infused by the value of *kung,* in the sense of the public, the collectivity. To take the example of Wang's own day, there would have been no need for institutions to be changed had not *t'ien-hsia,* the physical embodiment of *kung,* been endangered. The situation being what it was, however, only after certain institutional adjustments had been made would it be possible for individual energies to be properly released and the collectivity eventually benefited.

This underlying assumption in Wang's thinking inevitably reminds us of the views of Yen Fu. Yen Fu was deeply impressed not only by the just and effective legal system of Britain, under which individuals could make use of their energies to the fullest extent, but also by the fact that in the West individual energies were put to collective use. In speculating on the fundamental difference between China and the West, Yen Fu suggested that "While China bases the whole social order on filial piety, Westerners base it on impartiality (*kung*),"[28] a view that closely parallels Wang Hsien-ch'ien's characterization of China and the West. This presents a difficult question. Why would an "enlightened" Yen Fu share the central intellectual tendencies of a "parochial" Wang Hsien-ch'ien? The short answer to the question is that, in terms of symbolic interactionism, what Yen Fu saw in England was basically determined by a *Weltanschauung* and value orientation that had been formed long before he came in contact with the foreign world.

Benjamin Schwartz observes that "One theme running through all Yen Fu's writings which cannot be clearly traced to any element of Spencerianism ... is the praise of Western 'public spirit' (*kung-hsin*)."[29] What I would suggest is that the reason for its being a "theme running through all Yen Fu's writings" is that it was an ultimate value for concerned intellectuals at the time, both of the "right" and the "left." I would further argue that *kung,* for these individuals, was the inner moral source, as distinguished from a direct experiential source (such as humiliation at the hands of foreigners), of Chinese nationalism. Schwartz rightly states that Yen Fu was nationalistic. I would object, however, to his view that one had to make a choice or priority decision between *pao-kuo* and *pao-chiao* before one became a nationalist.[30] When Wang Hsien-ch'ien argued that "if force is lacking, then there is no means by which virtue can be manifested," he could always defend himself by asserting that he was only advocating the use of Legalist methods to reinforce Confucian morality. But since this quotation was used to condemn the Han literati for believing that virtue alone would subdue the Huns, it is clear Wang believed that Legalist "force" (*li*) was valuable because it could be used for the strengthening of the nation.[31]

Wang's nationalist feelings are so adamant that it becomes hard for us to equate his dismissal of democracy with a victory of "culturalism" over "nationalism." Indeed, it was the same idea of *kung,* seen as guaranteeing the voluntary participation of every Chinese in politics, that served as K'ang Yu-wei's rationale for promoting constitutional government and condemning the selfishly conceived monarchical system.[32]

Another thinker for whom *kung* was of key importance was Liang Ch'i-ch'ao. When Liang, in exile, invented the new terms *kung-te* (public morality) and *ssu-te* (private morality), he clearly revealed his deep concern over the collective interest. At the same time, Liang's willingness to sacrifice the time-honored "private morality" suggested the shift in his attention from individual perfection to a regulated behavior pattern in a common collectivity. This shift paralleled Wang Hsien-ch'ien's earlier move from Mencian trust in the individual self to social regulation (*li*, rites) after the fashion of Hsun-tzu. It needs only to be added that Liang, like Wang, admired the potential in the Chinese Legalist tradition, witness his interest in statism.[33]

Although these thinkers emphasized alternate aspects of *kung*, all of them saw public spiritedness as being in the national interest; the difference was that the conservative Wang Hsien-ch'ien deplored its lack in China, while the liberals strongly urged its inculcation. The ease with which Wang could transform his concept of *kung* from a court virtue for ministers to a sense of participation for his compatriots may suggest the adaptability of the tradition in response to new realities; it may betoken the existence of something inherent in the notion of *kung* that equipped it to react more readily to the pressures of modernization. Whatever the case, the fact that all of these thinkers placed a high value on the national collectivity seems indicative of the motivational power of the underlying *kung* orientation buried in the *Ta-hsueh* regimen for serious and idealistic Confucian intellectuals. The traditional call for intellectuals to shoulder responsibility for *t'ien-hsia* served as a major source of Chinese nationalism.

DISCUSSION

Kwang-Ching Liu pointed out that a kind of gestation period for new ideas was implied in the papers presented. Hao Chang's talk discussed the time frame in which each current of thought became prominent. However, it was also necessary to take into consideration the time gap between the time when a value or idea was introduced and when it became influential. Missionary ideas, for example, were not politically important until the 1890s. But even as early as mid-century, Feng Kuei-fen was reading books translated by missionaries. K'ang Yu-wei's early writings in the 1880s contained the embryo of some of his later ideas. How did he come upon such new ideas in the first place? Western ideas fit new circumstances. Wang T'ao was not a great political influence in his lifetime, but he was of crucial importance in the gestation of new ideas. Thus, the thought of the reform era should be looked at from two vantage points, one being the time that ideas first originated, and the other the time that they became politically important.

Hao Chang replied that he did not mean to underestimate the importance of gestation periods or of missionary influence, but he believed that there were two respects in which the 1890s represented a new departure. One was the development of an intellectual challenge to the *san-kang* ideology. In the 1870s and 1880s, there had been increasing receptivity toward certain Western institutions, but the attack on the traditional social and political order in the 1890s was on a different scale from that of the earlier period. The second respect in which the 1890s broke new ground lay in the degree of dissemination given to new ideas. Now, for the first time, these ideas were widely discussed in public.

Thomas Kennedy, following up the point concerning gestation periods, recalled Lloyd Eastman's stress on the Sino-French War as a prenatal catalytic agent for new ideas. This even had been a watershed for those, such as Chang Chih-tung, who were concerned with industrial development. Marianne Bastid noted the parallel

181

significance of the Sino-Japanese War for a later generation.

Sung Shin raised the question of values as an impediment to industrialization. Mark Elvin's study placed the responsibility for this partially on Neo-Confucianism. Other values, however, could be seen as having had a positive effect on industrialization. How specific did Wang Hsien-ch'ien get in defining his moral values? I-fan Ch'eng replied that Elvin saw Neo-Confucianism as an impeding force not so much because of its moral orientation, but because of its *Weltanschauung*, methodology, and indifference toward technological problems. It had a strongly inward orientation. What Wang had, however, was an almost religious sense of commitment to certain values, especially that of the public good.

Mr. Ch'eng pointed out that in its first stage, reformism grew out of tradition. It was only later that receptivity to the West became a factor. Why and how did Chinese reformers become more open to the West? Hao Chang replied that Wei Yuan first published his study of the outside world in 1844. This was followed by Feng Kuei-fen's realistic perception of Western expansion. Writers such as these helped bring about the new openness toward the West.

Joanna Handlin asked what Western ideas were accepted in the 1890s. Hao Chang mentioned democratic participation, nationalism, and social Darwinism, and suggested that these ideas led people to develop a different form of thinking which in turn caused them to raise new questions and ultimately to challenge the legitimacy of the old order.

Ms. Handlin said that there had been ideas akin to democratic participation in the sixteenth century and wondered why in the nineteenth century Chinese thinkers wanted to ascribe these ideas to the West. Did the attribution to the West confer a kind of outside legitimacy useful for attacking the internal order? Suzanne Barnett saw Ms. Handlin's question as being related to the gestation problem, whereby new ideas and new vocabulary, although introduced in the 1840s, did not become important until the 1890s.

Don Price insisted on the great difference between the Sino-French and Sino-Japanese Wars. It was not until 1894–1895 that there was a sudden awareness of the weakness of the old system and widespread recognition of new values.

Peter Ch'en pointed out that although it was often said that Confucianism had a detrimental effect on modernization, this was not the case in Japan. Not only was Confucianism not a detriment in Japan, it played a crucial role. Why was this so? In part it was because of differences between Chinese and Japanese Confucianism; in part it had to do with the different objective conditions obtaining in the two countries. Japanese Confucianists also went through a soul-searching process when they began dealing with Western thought. However, there were certain values which they refused to give up, certain "non-negotiable" ideas. We might therefore ask what it was that Chinese Confucianists refused to abandon.

Nailene Chou questioned Hao Chang's assertion that Hunan was the geographic center of the statecraft school. She pointed out that Wei Yuan left Hunan early in his career, as did others, and that few statecraft thinkers were active in Hunan, Tso Tsung-t'ang being the major exception. The centers of the statecraft school were really more in Kiangsu, Chekiang, and in the capital. Mr. Chang said that he would not insist on the point.

Luke S. K. Kwong
REFLECTIONS ON AN ASPECT OF MODERN CHINA IN
TRANSITION: T'AN SSU-T'UNG (1865–1898) AS A REFORMER

On September 28, 1898, six prisoners were decapitated at
Ts'ai-shih-k'ou, normally a marketplace outside the southern Hsuan-
wu Gate of Peking's inner city. The summary executions took place
in the wake of the so-called "palace revolution" that spelled the end
to the imperial efforts at reform initiated early in June. Characterized as "martyrdom," epitomizing the triumph of militant conservatism at the Ch'ing court, the six deaths were soon assigned a
new kind of political significance, portentous of imminent changes
more radical than those the Chinese empire, as yet, had undergone.

Of the six executed, T'an Ssu-t'ung has been the name of
greatest historical familiarity. Partly through the good office of his
eloquent biographer, Liang Ch'i-ch'ao,[1] and partly through his writings and example of extreme "self-sacrifice," T'an became a source
of inspiration initially to the generation of full-fledged anti-Manchu
activists who emerged in the 1900s and subsequently to nationalist
writers, including Marxists, who have tended to locate him in the
vanguard of the forces that brought about a new phase in the
destinies of the Chinese people.

Unfortunately, the appraisals and reappraisals of T'an's
historical role have often been confined to those aspects that bear
more generally on the so-called "reform movement." Consequently,
the balance of his life, for the most part, has remained obscure. I
intend here, first, to establish the connection between T'an, the
psychologically complex individual, and T'an, the reformer, and,
second, to reconsider the meaning of reform as it was manifested
in aspects of the life and thought of T'an Ssu-t'ung.

T'an's Life to 1894

Born into the family of T'an Chi-hsun in 1865, T'an Ssu-t'ung
spent the first twelve years of his life in north China. His father, a
chin-shih of 1860, had served in several official capacities in Peking

184

and T'ung-chou before he was appointed *taotai* of Kung-Ch'in-Chieh in Kansu in 1877. Six years later (1883), he was promoted to provincial judge of Kansu, and in the following year to provincial treasurer. The crowning moment of his career came in 1889 when he was transferred to Wuchang as governor of Hupeh. Young Ssu-t'ung accompanied his father on all these official itinerant postings.

During the twelve years of his father's tour in Kansu, T'an undertook several major trips, including visits to his native district, Liu-yang, in Hunan, mostly for the purpose of his schooling, and excursions into the frontier regions adjacent to Kansu.[2] These travels, which he duly recorded,[3] contributed to the development of a nonconformist strain in his temperament. This became apparent in T'an's growing impatience with the traditional degree candidate's repressive routine.[4] It was also reflected in the activist pattern of his life, which helped incidentally to prepare him for the challenges, intellectual and physical, of involvement in contemporary affairs. Finally, T'an's nonconformism may be detected in his later rejection of all forms of sociocultural provincialism (or parochialism).

Wuchang not only provided for a radical change of pace; it also afforded T'an opportunities to pursue entirely new directions in his interests. His father's senior colleague, the governor-general of Hu-kuang, Chang Chih-tung, maintained a host of *yang-wu* specialists to implement his new "self-strengthening" policies. Young Ssu-t'ung was acquainted with a number of Chang's "tent-friends" (*mu-yu*), who were probably instrumental in introducing T'an to a much expanded knowledge of the outside world.

Public Crisis and Personal Insecurity

When the Sino-Japanese war broke out in 1894, T'an, like many literati at the time, was keenly concerned about the hostilities. But unlike the average literatus, he was better informed. Because of his special contacts, he had access to incoming official reports on the progress of the war. Outraged by the fabricated news of China's supposed victories and dismayed at the pathetic performance of the Hunanese troops in combat, T'an experienced a further dimension of China's humiliation. He recalled, in mid-1895: "occasionally, I visited the foreign firms in Hankow and met with foreigners who spoke the Chinese language. Very often they expressed their pretentious sympathies [with China] in order to tease me. Denied refuge, I became shamefully embarrassed."[5]

T'an's anguish was exacerbated by his commitment to the precepts of what might be called the "Confucian conscience." The schema for political morality outlined in the *Great Learning* establishes the vital relevance of individual moral efforts to the attainment and maintenance of "universal" peace and order. The conscientious adherent of this view held himself answerable for the calamities befalling his community and country. T'an's response to the war situation falls very much within this pattern.[6] Amid the emotional intensities created by the public crisis, he underwent a stage of personal insecurity that led to his "awakening."

T'an reached his thirtieth *sui* in March 1894 and penned his "Autobiography at 30" (*San-shih tzu-chi*) in early 1895. To some extent, T'an's autobiographical account was an act of introspection modeled after Confucius' own scheme of self-analysis, summarized in the *Analects* by the phrase "San-shih erh li." Legge's translation, "At thirty, I stood firm,"[7] does not adequately impart the sense of a moral and intellectual "breakthrough" implied in the sage's testimony. Whatever its connection with the edifying precedent commended in the Classics, T'an's experience seems to corroborate, cross-culturally and perhaps transhistorically, the view of life-cycle scholars that a further major life crisis begins to develop around the age of thirty.[8]

What were the sources of T'an's anxieties? In early 1895, he lamented over his predicament, "All his life, Ssu-t'ung has never done anything that is gratifying to himself."[9] Between 1890 and 1894, T'an made his last two unsuccessful attempts at the examinations. Altogether, he had failed five times. His father's constant concern over his son's education and career apparently aggravated T'an's self-doubt. Approaching thirty, T'an described his dilemma, "I am impatient but I despise petty achievements."[10] Ashamed to flaunt his "petty achievements," he went so far as to prevent his writings from circulating, save among his closest friends.[11] Thus, up to his thirtieth *sui,* T'an's sense of himself as a failure appeared to have some basis and it encouraged his self-commiseration.

The convergence of crisis from without and crisis from within, therefore, precipitated T'an's "awakening." He burst forth with pronouncements equivalent to a confession and with resolutions proclaiming in essence a program of personal reform. Forcefully he expounded: "When the heavens portend forthcoming crises, men of extraordinary talent arise in response. If, now, one does not restrain oneself and continues to indulge in useless play with words and rhymes, how much more corrupt can one become? Up to the age of thirty, I have exhausted practically all my energies studying philology and composing [esoteric] literature—none of this is of any good to the world."[12]

Worse still, T'an had been victimized by the examination preparations. Now he resolved that he would forsake the mediocrity of a florid essayist and styled himself Chuang-fei (lit., "soaring flight").

It is significant that T'an described the current situation as "a time when China and the foreign countries are engaged in a ruthless struggle and empty words no longer serve any purpose [and as] a mature age that determines future growth of [personal] strength or feebleness."[13]

Here, again, T'an not only touches concurrently on both problems confronting him—public and private—but also establishes a correlation between the two. By blaming China's defeat on the influence of traditional learning and the examination system, T'an seems to have rescued himself from self-mockery for his failure to succeed in activities which he had come to consider wasteful and meaningless. In this way, he bid a symbolic farewell to his own past in order to be able to venture upon a new course of action which he hoped would lead to greater self-fulfillment and self-affirmation.[14] The period of delaying his decision on a future—a kind of "psycho-social moratorium," as Erikson calls it[15]—had come to a conclusion.

T'an's Last Years

At the close of the war, together with his Hunanese friends from Liu-yang, T'an conceived of a project to transform an academy for traditional learning in his native district into a center for mathematical studies. The scheme, however, fell through in early 1896, and in pursuance of an agreement which he had earlier reached with his father,[16] T'an now proceeded to Peking to obtain an official title through purchase.

The trip to the capital via Shanghai and Tientsin, as well as the brief Peking sojourn, was filled with intellectual excitements, as T'an carefully recounted in his correspondence.[17] Upon completing the transaction for the title of expectant prefect, T'an set out for Nanking, where he later served for some time as a minor official.

Otherwise devoid of purposeful meaning, the Nanking period witnessed the fruition of T'an's vigorous intellectual interests. His life as a petty bureaucrat was much enlivened by his frequent contacts with a Buddhist scholar, Yang Wen-hui, a prominent figure in the so-called "Buddhist revival" in the late Ch'ing period.[18] T'an's occasional visits to Shanghai brought him into association with like-minded literati-reformers, with whom, as one of them put it, he freely discussed "recent developments in scientific learning which, in most cases, are found to be in subtle harmony with Buddhist principles."[19] T'an's *magnum opus, Jen-hsueh* (On universal principles),[20] penned in 1896–1897, purported, in part, to be a manifesto of the views he shared with his Nanking–Shanghai associates of this period.

Although T'an in this work no longer endorsed the earlier *Weltanschauung,* founded either on cultural pride and superiority or simply on ethnocentrism,[21] he did not substitute for it a world view on the nationalist's model. The more pressing task was, first, to revise and readjust the time-honored notion of *ta-t'ung* (great harmony) in order to accommodate new and dynamic cosmic and geographic images, and, second, to define the ultimate meaning of various major religio-cultural traditions. The thrust of *Jen-hsueh,* therefore, gravitated toward broad principles and views of a universal culture, transcending manifestations of cultural particularism.

In late 1897, partly in conjunction with a mission, on behalf of Sheng Hsuan-huai, to negotiate with Governor Ch'en Pao-chen of Hunan on coal supplies for a railroad project,[22] T'an took a leave of absence from his post (a "beggar's livelihood"). For the better part of the following six months, T'an stayed on in Hunan and Hupeh. In Changsha, in the wake of the German occupation of Kiaochow, he became involved in the promotion of "new learning" and in local reforms as precautionary measures for Hunan's survival, in the event that the powers should decide to partition China.[23] But mounting resistance from eminent gentry leaders eventually stalled all movements to transform Hunan.

T'an's disappointment in the face of this resistance soon passed, for in June he found himself among a group of "talents" summoned by the court for an imperial audience in conjunction with the throne's recent decision to institute a program of more energetic reforms. He likened this opportunity to "life revealing itself when one is despairing unto death."[24]

T'an did not arrive in Peking until late August. He had his first (and only recorded) interview with the Kuang-hsu Emperor on September 5.[25] On the same day, together with three others, he was appointed a Grand Council Assistant, rank four, specially assigned to handle all matters pertaining to reform policies. After filling that post for only nineteen days, T'an was cashiered and placed under arrest. These events occurred three days after the Empress Dowager's decision (September 21) to "tutor" the emperor once again in state affairs. Four days after his arrest (September 28), amid the helter-skelter of alleged conspiracy and counterconspiracy, T'an, along with five others, was summarily executed.

T'an's Ambivalence

From the standpoint of his "awakening" in 1894–1895, T'an's search for personal meaning and relevance was short-circuited, in that his initial social orientation after the crisis had been of a basically traditional mode. Expectant Prefect T'an, after all, had secured some sort of formal standing within the community of the traditional elite. In 1898, in Hunan, almost as a self-styled spokesman for that community, he urged the augmentation of the political role and capacity of the gentry (*shen-ch'üan*) in local government.[26] Indeed, he was even appointed by Governor Ch'en Pao-chen to be the gentry representative for the forthcoming Wu-pei hsueh-t'ang (Academy for Military Studies) in Changsha.[27]

But problems arose where T'an's ambivalent attitudes persisted Although positive steps (such as acquiring an official title and appointment) were taken by him in order to effect a proper induction into the existing sociopolitical structure, T'an disclaimed some of the essential features of that structure. Indeed, he described his *Jen-hsueh* as an endeavor to break through various kinds of "bondage" (*wang-lo*), among which were bondage to the material attractions of an official career, bondage to rulers and masters, and bondage to traditional types of human, in particular familial, relationships.[28]

Such exhortations to freedom and liberation were in stark contrast to the trammels of his own predicament. Take, for example T'an's relationship with his father. During a brief visit to Wuchang in late 1896, T'an confided to a friend, "Ssu-t'ung seeks to leave Hupeh as much as birds and animals seek to break out of their cages and confines."[29] To terminate his almost lifelong dependence on his father in order, as it were, to fly soaring into the skies (as his name of 1895, Chuang-fei, metaphorically suggested), was no doubt part of the implication. Yet throughout his life, T'an seems, at least outwardly, to have acceded to the wishes of his anxiety-ridden and perhaps authoritarian father.[30] The problem for him, therefore, was one of internal contradictions arising from his actual adherence to a behavioral pattern which he found more and more difficult to rationalize or perpetuate.

A second dimension of T'an's dilemma may be seen in connection with his determination in 1895 to pursue a line of action that would contribute to the improvement of society. To be effective in any environment requires active and in-depth participation. But, whether because of personal insecurity or because of disdain for the formidable rules and conventions he would have to encounter

T'an decided to assume his public roles while at the same time
trying to keep his distance from the indigenous establishments.

Thus, prior to his Nanking sojourn, in full anticipation of all
the corrupting and human—all-too-human—influences of bureaucratic life, T'an vowed that he would not "sell" himself. He was
determined not to exploit the personal connections of his teacher
with those in power. But when Nanking officialdom turned a cold
and indifferent eye toward him upon his arrival, despite his
avowals and earlier defensive posture, he was sensitive enough to
feel profoundly distressed.[31]

A third dimension of T'an's dilemma lay in his need for a
coherent and total image of self and society. The expansion of
psychological and intellectual boundaries, which he dramatically
experienced in 1896–1897, had no comparable or commendable
counterparts in the mundane world of practical affairs. The
proper coordination of expectations with experience had yet to
be worked out.

The Integrative Functions of Reform

The problem of coherence, of integration, was certainly a
pressing one for T'an. It will be recalled that T'an attained his
social standing through two "irregular" channels, namely, the
purchase of official title and service in several *yang-wu* undertakings.[32] Both channels had only recently been accorded a status
of more general acceptability and they may be considered as two
parameters of social change in late Ch'ing China. In this sense,
T'an Ssu-t'ung represented a new type of literatus, whose outlook
was impregnated with visions and aspirations that were fostered by
suggestive cross-cultural comparisons. The efficacy of this outlook,
in social terms, hinged, of course, upon the initiation of desired
changes in the environment.

The variety of T'an's activities in the field of educational and
social reform in 1895–1898, as well as his writings on these subjects, delineates the profile of a newly emergent society, one in
which the level of intelligence and literacy of the common people
would be improved, in which women would no longer suffer from

bound feet and inferior status, in which human existence would be
freed from such perversions as excessive drinking and lavish feasting,
and in which compassion, equality, and prosperity would prevail.[33]

To be sure, a society built upon such premises would still entail
a drastic compromise with the utopian groundwork, however frag-
mentary and impressionistic, that T'an had laid out in *Jen-hsueh,*
and with other ideas, however ambiguous, which cropped up in his
thinking now and then. A society thus renovated would nevertheless
mark a significant departure from established ways of life and, by
implication, would constitute a congenial haven where T'an would
find life more fulfilling and gratifying, and where, perhaps, his search
for personal meaning and relevance would end.

Thus, for T'an, "reform" (*pien-fa*) carried a special meaning in
that it signified possibilities for an improved social order that would
accommodate the rising expectations of a transitional generation of
literati—a potential new elite born of social change—under the "dual
legitimation"[34] of tradition and modernity. Reform efforts, in this
sense, also constituted a series of counterpoints at which social
realities and the ideas and "vital sensibility"[35] of this generation
could interact and ultimately modify one another in a sequence of
societal renewals.

Insofar as reform served as an interstice between thought and
action, ideals and realities, it furnished a viable pattern of political
behavior within the late Ch'ing context. At one point, T'an
remarked (in 1897): "To reform is to promote learning. Even if
those in high places make no attempt at reform, they still cannot
prevent learning from being promoted from below."[36]

T'an's position typifies the perspective of much of the reform
that was being carried on in the literary and educational areas.
These were the very areas of course in which the literatus-reformer
first received his vocational training. The founding of study clubs
and periodicals, therefore, not only followed the time-honored
pattern of an "educational" approach to sociopolitical issues. It
also served as a feasible response to the demand for "change from
below," a moderate alternative to, and temporary substitute for, a
more radical "theory of action."

In this connection, some writers have portrayed T'an as a protorevolutionary dedicated to subverting the imperial regime. T'an's occasional emotional excesses, manifested in his words and deeds, may be considered suggestive and supportive of such an interpretation. However, there is no conclusive evidence to associate T'an's sporadic radical outbursts with the multifaceted complexity of a revolutionary movement.[37]

The Limitations of Reform

The possibilities for social and intellectual integration, however, became lost opportunities to the extent that T'an "failed" as an effective reformer. Reflecting the sociopolitical complexities within which he operated, his "failures" resulted from conflicts of ideas as much as from incompatible styles in public administration, personal idiosyncrasies, and so on. For a short period in the early fall of 1898, T'an, as a bona fide reformer-official, had inflated hopes of a "breakthrough" in the direction of dynastic revitalization and societal betterment through imperial sponsorship.[38] In the end, however, there was a crushing of hopes and of lives, including his own.

T'an's experience exposed a dreary scarcity of resources in late Ch'ing society for coping with the challenge of a highly protean and dynamic transitional generation. For T'an, Sino-foreign encounters, with all their ramifications, attested to an emerging world ecumene and an evolving universal humankind, to a new "age of transcendence" aptly appraised by Li Hung-chang earlier (and by others almost endlessly later) as the "greatest change in the past three millennia or more."

T'an's activities in late life represent an individual attempt to respond to this "transcendence." But his attempt was precluded by his early death from producing more concrete results. Although T'an did not in any precise sense engineer the manner of his death, and thus did not "seek" martyrdom, the tragedy that struck him at the close of the Hundred Days Reform furnishes late Ch'ing annals as well as his personal chronology with a wholly new historical meaning.

Richard H. Shek
SOME WESTERN INFLUENCES ON T'AN SSU-T'UNG'S
THOUGHT

It is common knowledge among scholars on China that T'an Ssu-t'ung, the foremost radical thinker of the late nineteenth century, was an intellectual eclectic who formulated his ideas from different strains of thought. A man of extreme versatility and complexity, T'an was well versed not only in the basic Confucian classics and Neo-Confucian writings which he had studied since childhood, but also in the unorthodox thought of Wang Fu-chih, the philosophies of Mo-tzu and Chuang-tzu, the Hua-yen and Wei-shih teachings of Buddhism, Christianity, Western science, and even Chinese folk religious beliefs and the spirit of the Chinese *yu-hsia* (knights errant) and Japanese *shishi* (men of determination). To be sure, T'an was very much steeped in the Confucian tradition, and it is obvious that he used it as his philosophical base. In the final formulation of his *Jen-hsueh,* nevertheless, the non-Confucian elements played an important part. Until recently few scholars have examined the nature and scope of these non-Confucian influences on T'an and the manner in which they might have shaped his thought. I propose here to analyze one such influence, that of the West.

The study of mathematics and other scientific subjects had been an integral part of T'an Ssu-t'ung's training since his childhood. Liang Ch'i-ch'ao informs us that "as a boy T'an had studied mathematics with considerable success, and had also read exhaustively various translations in the field of what was called 'physics,' and made full use of all the scientific knowledge then available to him."[1] T'an's interest in "Western learning" (*Hsi-hsueh*) never waned; if anything, it became intensified in the 1890s. By then the West was no longer only a corpus of useful knowledge to him, but had become a repository of wisdom from which he could gain insights into more philosophical and perennial issues. In short, the West had become for him a new source of authority in the under-

194

standing of nature, man, and society. In addition to science and
technology, the Western cultural and religious traditions became
essential subjects of concern for T'an. His interest in the nonmaterial
aspect of Western civilization can be seen in his increasing appreciation of Christianity, which he tacitly regarded as the spiritual
foundation of the West. Indeed, T'an was such an ardent student
of Christianity that, at his first meeting with Liang Ch'i-ch'ao in
late 1895, he impressed the latter as one who "highly commended
Jesus' teaching of universal love, but betrayed no knowledge of the
Buddha or even of Confucius."[2] Though undoubtedly an exaggerated observation, it serves to show T'an's strong inclination
toward Christianity at the time.

Liang Ch'i-ch'ao's *Hsi-hsueh shu-mu piao* (Bibliography of
Western learning) listed several hundred books and journals that
were available to interested literati members during the 1890s,[3]
and T'an, an even more advanced and committed student of
Western learning than Liang, must have perused and studied large
numbers of them. Many of these were highly technical treatises on
science and manufacturing published by the Kiangnan Arsenal.
Others were more general works covering a large variety of subjects
published by Westerners either privately or through the School and
Textbook Series Committee (I-chih shu-hui) and later the Society
for the Diffusion of Christian and General Knowledge among the
Chinese (Kuang-hsueh hui). With the exception of John Fryer and
a few others, the dozen or so foreigners engaged in the translation
or composition of these books were Protestant missionaries who
acted as cultural transmitters in addition to being evangelicals. It
was in the former capacity that this small minority of Westerners
managed to effect profound changes in the outlook of eclectic and
reform-minded literati.

Among the large corpus of books and magazines on Western
science, society, and Christianity that T'an had read, only a few
were cited in his writings. I shall examine in detail two publications
that seem to have contributed significantly to his intellectual
development. One is the missionary journal *Wan-kuo kung-pao*,[4]
the other is John Fryer's translation of Henry Wood's *Ideal*

Suggestion through Mental Photography, which in Chinese bears
the title of *Chih-hsin mien ping fa* (The prevention of disease
through mental healing).[5]

A successor to the *Chiao-hui hsin-pao* (The church news), the
Wan-kuo kung-pao (The globe magazine, later renamed Review of
the times) was a missionary weekly which, under the able editor-
ship of the Rev. Young J. Allen, was one of the most widely circulated publications in China before 1896. It first appeared in 1874
and subsequently went through several changes in format and
content, each time turning more and more secular in its orientation.
Coverage of current events in China and abroad was gradually
expanded, and articles dealing with Western government, politics,
customs, and education appeared with increasing frequency. Its
publication was suspended between 1884 and 1888 partly because
of the withdrawal of support by a church group which viewed its
rapid secularization with alarm and dismay. When it reappeared in
1889, the magazine was the organ of the Kuang-hsueh hui, which
had been founded by the Rev. Alexander Williamson two years
earlier. The journal was now a monthly, and its secularized tone
was even more accentuated. Its increasing popularity among the
literati was evidenced by its fast-expanding circulation. K'ang Yu-
wei, Liang Ch'i-ch'ao, and T'an Ssu-t'ung were all avid readers.
They also considered it "must reading" for their friends and students. Despite its progressive secularization, however, the publication
never abandoned its Christian orientation. Discussions of Christian
beliefs and expositions of Christian ethics continued to appear with
great regularity.

To be sure, the literati readers of the journal were primarily
interested in the general and scientific knowledge it provided. Yet
some among them with strong religious sensitivities and proclivities,
T'an Ssu-t'ung being a prominent example, seem also to have taken
note of the religious messages contained within its pages. Some of
these messages were distinctly echoed later in T'an's writings. Indeed,
it is my strong conviction that these discourses on Christianity in
the *Wan-kuo kung-pao* provided one major source of T'an's
radicalism.

The most consistent and prolific writer of these religious
articles was Alexander Williamson, the Scottish Presbyterian missionary who first arrived in China in the mid-1850s and who, as
mentioned earlier, was the founder of the important Kuang-hsueh
hui. A regular contributor to the *Wan-kuo kung-pao* and its one-
time editor, Williamson wrote extensively on the Christian faith
and its attendant ethics. In addition to telling the usual Bible
stories of the Creation, the Fall, and the life of Jesus, he expounded
the Christian notions of original sin, the soul, the love of God, and
ideal human relationships. The last subject, as it turned out, was the
most appealing to T'an. Here is Williamson's exposition (drawn from
several of his articles):

> God is the Creator of the universe and the Father of mankind.
> This Fatherhood of God makes every human being an offspring
> of His. "All men are children of God irrespective of their status
> or wealth,"[6] because each has a spiritual soul (*ling-hun*)
> endowed by Him and "treasured without distinction by Him."[7]
> This intrinsic worth of the soul is the basis for human equality,
> at least in the spiritual realm. One's rulers and parents, though
> deserving one's loyalty and filial love, are children of God like
> oneself, hence they are not superior. "[It is true that] my
> father begets me, [but] without God there is no father; [it is
> also true that] my mother nourishes me, [but] without God
> there is no mother."[8] The same argument applies to the rulers.[9]
> With this basic human equality established, all men should
> treat one another with magnanimity and love, for "when Jesus
> said, 'love others as thyself,' what he meant by others is not
> [just] others in the same family, or [even] others in the same
> state, but others in the entire human community."[10]
>   The spiritual soul, representing the image of God in each
> human being,[11] not only gives him his intrinsic worth, but
> entitles him to certain inalienable rights. Each man's soul
> makes independent decisions for him,[12] and not even God can
> compel him to do good or eschew evil. This capacity to make
> free, independent choices without interference from outside
> is the basis of man's humanity; otherwise he is no more than a
> machine that is manipulated and controlled by others. Because

of this capacity, each man is ultimately held responsible for the actions he takes. As it is within his prerogative to hold independent views and make autonomous decisions, each man has the right to be his own master, or the right of personal autonomy (*tzu neng tso chu chih ch'üan*).[13]

This lucid exposition of the Protestant ideals of spiritual equality and the moral and religious autonomy of the individual carried radical implications. But like Martin Luther's radicalism, it was limited to the spiritual-religious realm. It did not call for the equalization or democratization of all human relations in the secular, social-political realm. Nevertheless, again like Luther's radicalism, such an assertion of equality and individual sovereignty, even if only on the theoretical and spiritual level, was bound to have an impact on the secular sphere. And, indeed, Williamson's Christian message proved to be a potent challenge to the Confucian code of ethics, as capsulized in the phrase *san-kang wu-ch'ang* (three bonds and five constants). It lent much support to the late nineteenth-century Chinese reformers' criticism of the hierarchical arrangements of society.

T'an Ssu-t'ung was among the first to use Williamson's line of argument in refuting that aspect of the Confucian *san-kang* which referred to the one-sided domination of the father over the son. T'an declared that "The son is the offspring of heaven, the father is also the offspring of heaven ... [hence] they are equal."[14] The concept of the right of personal autonomy was even more exciting for T'an and made a deep imprint on him. Calling it *tzu-chu chih ch'üan* (an almost verbatim adoption of Williamson's phrase), T'an unequivocally acknowledged its Christian origin. He wrote in his *Jen-hsueh:* "Jesus ... loudly proclaims [his teaching], asserting that everyone is the son of God, that everyone is a small part of heaven, and that everyone possesses the right of autonomy."[15] Elsewhere in his *Jen-hsueh* T'an also maintained that "when Christianity was first founded ... it established [the concept of] the Heavenly Kingdom (*t'ien-kuo*) which gives each person the right of autonomy, and abolished all inequalities to restore equality."[16] When every

person is his own master, the political system will reflect this state
by letting the people become the master (*min-chu*). T'an even went
so far as to make the intriguing claim that "*Min-chu* (democracy) is
the meaning of the Heavenly Kingdom."[17] This observation clearly
reveals his conviction that Christianity (that is, Protestantism) was
the liberalizing and democratizing force in Europe, as he was led to
believe that all Western countries were Christian and that all were
liberal and democratic. It is small wonder that he longed for the
appearance of a Martin Luther in China.[18]

As a matter of fact, Williamson's introduction of the concept
of basic human rights, albeit only on the spiritual level, was to have
consequences that went far beyond the simple influencing of T'an
Ssu-t'ung's thought. The notion that one could and should be one's
own master provided the strongest argument for a more democratic
form of government and a more egalitarian arrangement of society.
The absolute power of the monarch, another tenet of the Confucian
san-kang, was called into question. Chang Chih-tung, the shrewd
spokesman for the conservative camp in the 1890s, was quick to
realize the disruptive potential of this notion. In his *Ch'üan-hsueh
p'ien* (Exhortation to learning) he warned, "Should people's rights
be advocated, the ignorant would rejoice, the unruly would arise,
the social order would stop functioning and great disturbances
would occur everywhere."[19] He went on to blame those who introduced the concept of *tzu-chu chih ch'üan* for their potential disruption of society and was unequivocal in identifying Christianity
as the source of this concept. "Lately, those who dabble in Western
learning even go so far as to assert that everyone has the right of
autonomy. This is most ridiculous. The phrase [*tzu-chu chih ch'üan*]
comes from the literature of Christianity. It means that God endows
man with a spiritual nature [so that] each has intelligence and wisdom and is capable of achievement. It is most erroneous for the
translator to interpret the phrase as everyone possessing the right of
autonomy."[20]

Whether Chang Chih-tung's interpretation was valid is not our
concern here, but he was certainly right in fearing the consequence
of the popularization of such a notion as human rights, for T'an

Ssu-t'ung's associates—Ou Chü-chia, Pi Yung-nien, P'i Hsi-jui, and others—all based their argument for constitutional government and human dignity on this concept.[21] Given a suitable secular twist, this Christian idea of the freedom of conscience became a major source of T'an Ssu-t'ung's radicalism and a most important and potent political slogan for fundamental constitutional changes. The Christianity expounded by Alexander Williamson seems to have provided a powerful weapon for the undermining of the Chinese traditional cosmological myth to which Professor Hao Chang makes reference.[22]

The book *Chih-hsin mien ping fa* was equally significant in the formulation of T'an's thought. T'an was ecstatic upon finishing it, exclaiming that it was a guide to the solution of China's unprecedented crises.[23] He had such a high opinion of the work that he purchased another copy and sent it to his teacher, Ou-yang Chung-ku, recommending that he read it for inspiration. The book's original author was the American Henry Wood, a business-man-turned-mental healer who had acquired a large following because of his adeptness in the new science of psychotherapy. This semireligious, semiscientific booklet proved to be his most popular work, running through at least six editions within the first year of its publication in 1893. John Fryer's rendering of the work in Chinese, completed in 1896, was by no means a faithful trans-lation, although the major argument of the English original was retained. The Chinese version of the book was composed of two parts, the first being a treatise on the power of the mind while the second consisted of twenty-seven five-character chants, each with accompanying explanations. These chants were published in bold print and were unmistakably Christian in tone. They were sup-posed to be read, memorized, and chanted by the faithful to help build up their mental power in their pursuit of health and happi-ness. The main argument of the book can be summarized as follows:

> There is a strict hierarchical relationship between the mind and the body. The former, which is real and permanent, has absolute dominance over the latter, which is ephemeral and

transient. Yet there is also a corresponding relationship
between the two, the state of the former being reflected and
manifested in the latter. When in perfect accord with the Will
of Heaven (*t'ien-i* or *t'ien-hsin*), the mind emanates immeasur-
able and inexhaustible power, making itself invincible and
omnipotent.[24] It is when the mind is clouded and loses its
communication with the "Ultimate Vitality" that it is rendered
powerless, unable to defend the body from the corruption of
external agents. The mind, moreover, has an affective capacity.
It can communicate with, influence, and stimulate other minds.
Neither space nor distance can obstruct its affective power.
Hence the mind is the link between one person and other
persons, between mankind and the other myriad things, and
between one planet or galaxy and the other planets and
galaxies in the universe.

This assertion of the might of mental power found a ready
supporter in T'an Ssu-t'ung. In his letter to Ou-yang Chung-ku,
T'an remarked that "there may be limits to human power, but the
mind is omnipotent. The power of the mind is so immense that the
universe cannot be compared to it. Even with the immensity of the
universe, the mind can freely create it, destroy it, or reshape it."[25]
His *Jen-hsueh* is also replete with glorification of the power of the
mind, which he saw as the only hope for the salvation of China
and all humanity.

In its discussion of the power and functions of the mind, the
Chih-hsin mien ping fa touched upon several concepts that proved
to be central to T'an Ssu-t'ung's philosophy. The most important
one was the notion of ether, a term mentioned only in passing in
the English original but much elucidated in Fryer's translation.
"Lately in the West it has been learned that inside the myriad
things there is a fluid called ether. The space [between us and] the
most distant stars is not a vacuum, but is filled by this ether. This
ether is present even within the fine molecules of the air on earth
... Nowhere is it absent, and in no way can we get rid of it. Without this ether the light of the sun and the other stars cannot be
transmitted to the earth ... Irrespective of the distance or the

sensitivity of the five senses, as soon as one person conceives a thought, he activates the ether and conveys it to the mind of others, making them have the same thought."[26]

Anyone who is familiar with the content of T'an Ssu-t'ung's *Jen-hsueh* knows how prominently the idea of ether figures in that work. But few realize that T'an's understanding and usage of the term follow closely Fryer's description of it in the *Chih-hsin mien ping fa.* Not only did T'an subscribe to the assertion that the ether filled the universe and held together the myriad things, he also concurred in the view that the ether was the medium through which one mind could be stimulated by another. He declared that through electricity, which he believed to be a function of ether, "my mental power can affect others so that they will conceive thoughts similar to mine."[27]

This affective capacity of the mind was further explained by the notion of *t'ung* (linkage, communion, communication, penetration) in the *Chih-hsin mien ping fa.* One passage reads, "As man lives in the midst of the myriad things, he is related to them ... The relationship is like a wire that links (*t'ung*) the self to the myriad things. This wire constantly vibrates in the same manner as does the string of a musical instrument or an electric wire."[28] The activities and affective capacity of the mind overcome all physical obstacles, and bring all men and all things into a harmonious communion. This argument for the identification of the self with other things (*jen-wu i-t'i*) by the usage of such scientific terms as ether and electricity was echoed in T'an's *Jen-hsueh:* "Electricity links the universe, the myriad things, the human community and myself into one body."[29] The concept of forming one body with others was not new (in fact, it was respectably Confucian), but the elucidation of this concept in scientific language *was* new and clearly showed the imprint on T'an of the West.

The emphasis on the mind in the *Chih-hsin mien ping fa* undoubtedly reinforced T'an's idealistic orientation and his disparaging attitude toward the body. A part of the book reads as follows: "People are afraid of death because they [only] think of the body as the self, [reasoning that] without the body there will be no self ... [but] if they realize that the body is not the self and that the mind is, that the latter is substantive but the former is vacuous, then they will know that for the mind there is no death and whether the body dies or not is inconsequential."[30] T'an's consistent denigration of the physical body in his writings and his later heroic martyrdom found strong support and endorsement in this argument in the *Chih-hsin mien ping fa.*

I have attempted to show how certain ideas that were current in the literature of Western learning were adopted by T'an Ssu-t'ung and incorporated into his philosophy. I have singled out these ideas not because I think they are the most important, but because I can document their sources. The influence of the West on T'an is certainly not limited to these ideas. T'an's moral and philosophical relativism, for instance, can be traced partially to his studies in Western science and various Western cultural traditions.

I am not willing nor ready to judge the significance of the West relative to other strains of thought (such as Buddhism, Taoism, Mohism) to which T'an had also been exposed. Such a task can only be performed when the influence of each strain on T'an has been studied in detail. Seen in larger context, however, the heavy influx of Western secular and religious ideas into China from the last decades of the nineteenth century was a momentous event, not unlike the introduction of Buddhism more than a millennium earlier. It introduced totally new concepts and new vocabularies that permanently changed Chinese society and mentality. The more open-minded among the literati, as they became increasingly dissatisfied with their own tradition and less complacent about its validity or immutability, turned to the new culture for inspiration and for solutions. They made use of the authority of Western ideas to reaffirm what they considered to be the true core of their tradition (now greatly reduced in dimension) and to attack what they regarded as perversions and degenerations (now tremendously expanded in scope). In either case, the tradition became transformed in the process. For the change that occurred when age-old concepts like *jen* and *jen-wu i-t'i* began to be explained, illustrated, or even proved by Western science and religion was no less significant than the change resulting from more direct assaults on tradition.

DISCUSSION

Richard Orb asked how much real interaction there was between Chinese and Christian concepts in T'an Ssu-t'ung's vocabulary. In his identification of *min-chu* (democracy) with *t'ien-kuo* (Heavenly Kingdom), for example, was there truly an infusion of Christian meaning or was T'an simply using a Chinese term to articulate a Chinese conception? Richard Shek replied that he had not meant to suggest that the Christian message itself contained the concept of democracy, but rather that this concept had been given a new twist by T'an based on the Christian belief in free will. T'an turned it around to make it a political and social slogan and to facilitate its realization. *Min-chu,* incidentally, was not a traditional term but a neologism.

It was pointed out that there was a populist tradition in Confucianism, and that this might have influenced nineteenth-century thinkers, causing them to radicalize Western thought much as Western thought was radicalizing them. Hao Chang said that the concept of *min* (the people) was very prominent in Chinese culture, but in the 1890s a new dimension was added to it that was not linked to tradition. This was the idea of participation. It was added largely as a result of Western influence.

John Schrecker suggested that it might be helpful, in assessing the concrete intellectual history of the nineteenth century, to ask the counterfactual question: where would this intellectual history have gone had there been no Western influence? One trend, apparently endogenous, was a rise in religion and some disillusionment with Confucianism. Hao Chang, reframing Mr. Schrecker's question, asked what impulses to, or capacity for, change existed within the Chinese cultural tradition apart from the Western impact.

Richard Shek pointed out that there was a tradition of popular participation at the level of popular religion, the White Lotus Sect being an example. Judith Whitbeck mentioned the concern of Kung Tzu-chen over the fact that scholars were divorced from the people.

Ms. Whitbeck said she thought that the challenge to the

204

cosmological myth began in the late eighteenth century, when skepticism about the relationship between cosmology and the world of man began to be widely expressed. Hao Chang said that the idea of an alternative order and a radical challenge to the traditional ideological order could be found in the left wing of the Wang Yang-ming school, but he regarded this as very much an exception. Paul Cohen added that the challenge appeared to be confined to the intellectual realm, without any immediate political bearing.

Frank Lojewski asked whether it was necessary to change the concept of universal kingship in order to have radical reform. He mentioned Richard Chu's dissertation on the revolutionary challenge presented by the White Lotus Rebellion. The White Lotus program was immature and half-baked, but it represented a real attempt to overthrow the existing hierarchical order.

Joanna Handlin mentioned that Lü K'un, and others who were considered quite mainstream, revealed a rather cynical attitude with respect to the emperorship and engaged in serious exploration of the functions that the imperial authority had in ordering society. Ms. Handlin felt that there was a growing ambivalence in the Ming and Ch'ing periods, when many sensed that the Confucian position was becoming bankrupt.

Linda Shin asked how T'an came to his position on the equality of women. Was it a logical extension of his ideas on reform or a result of personal experience? Hao Chang said that T'an wrote like a person who had had direct experience with the problem. Luke Kwong said that sensitivity to the criticisms of foreigners was also a factor. T'an was a good friend of Dr. Alex Mackay, a Scot. He was aware that the foreigners had a low opinion of Chinese family relationships, and he was impressed by the living example of foreign family relations provided by the Mackays.

Jonathan Ocko asked whether T'an was familiar with the antifootbinding theme in *Flowers in the Mirror* (*Ching-hua yuan*) or the feminist ideas of Yuan Mei. Richard Shek said that there was no direct indication of any influence but that T'an's descriptions of the pain caused by footbinding were very reminiscent of the descriptions in the novel. Paul Cohen added that Wang T'ao wrote a preface to the novel expressing feminist ideas.

Wai-fong Loh asked how T'an used the term *min-chu*. Richard Shek said that he used it in a Western sense. He was familiar with current Western notions of democracy and constitutional monarchy. Luke Kwong said that in T'an's frequent use of the terms *min-chu* and *min-ch'üan* the "people" referred to were gentry. It was the gentry to whom responsibility was to be given. T'an believed that the intelligence of the nongentry "people" was not yet great enough for direct political participation.

Charlton Lewis brought up the question of universality. The concept of *ta-t'ung* was long suppressed. When the real significance of the concept became apparent, probably not until 1898, it seemed to many to open the gates to all kinds of heterodox ideas and thus became anathema. Young-tsu Wong said that the concept of *ta-t'ung* was known to all literati. Its significance in the nineteenth century was related to the resurgence of Kung-yang Confucianism in a time of disorder. Many discussed the concept of *ta-t'ung*, but K'ang Yu-wei was the one who gave it systematic treatment. The influence of the idea was very important. The ultimate goal of Sun Yat-sen was the achievement of *ta-t'ung;* Wang T'ao also saw the future in universalist terms and believed that Confucianism and Christianity shared common ground. Kwang-Ching Liu added that Hung Hsiu-ch'üan held the same belief. Mr. Liu wondered why earlier Chinese thinkers had not used the *ta-t'ung* concept very much. Hao Chang said that the concept was not really needed until the conditions of disorder that arose in the nineteenth century.

Judith Whitbeck addressed the question why *chin-wen* Confucianism had not become a major issue earlier. For Kung Tzu-chen and Wei Yuan it was just another way of thinking. The idea of the three ages did not have the importance for Kung that it later did for K'ang. Kung saw history moving in a cycle over and over again. As for the tie-up between *chin-wen* Confucianism and reform thinking, one could see it a little in Kung and Wei. But other *chin-wen* scholars were really not concerned with reform at all.

Susan Jones pointed out that one of the consequences of *chin-wen* Confucianism was the redirecting of attention to other texts, such as the *I-ching.* Ms. Whitbeck added that *chin-wen* thinkers also saw different things in the same texts. Mr. Chang said that the nineteenth-century *chin-wen* interest began as a debate within the school of Han learning. At first it was a purely scholarly intellectual movement, with no political aims or over-tones. *Chin-wen* scholarship was wedded to reformism only in the 1890s by K'ang Yu-wei.

REFORM AT THE LOCAL AND PROVINCIAL LEVEL

James Polachek
REFORM AT THE LOCAL AND PROVINCIAL LEVEL*

The "Success" of Local Reform

As we look into the question of local and provincial reform efforts and their contribution to China's "modernization" in the nineteenth century, we become aware of a certain degree of success. Achievements on this level were greater than has been hitherto recognized; certainly they were much greater than reform attempts at the center, which often met with disaster. A conspicuous example of the latter was the currency reform effort of the Hsien-feng period, one of the unsung failures of nineteenth-century reform. The attempt to put into circulation a unified paper currency was a fiasco, and Prince Kung's connection with this reform effort blemished his career at an early stage. Railroad construction is another example of the ineffectualness of the central government. There were debates in Peking on the building of railroads in the 1880s after the Sino-French War, but the central government failed to agree on the decisions necessary for their completion. System-wide attempts at institutional reform fared no better. The reforms of 1898 came to nought, and the post-Boxer reforms were also relatively ineffective.

The story, however, looks much more promising on the local and provincial levels. On the whole, initiatives taken at the provincial (bureaucratic) and local (extra-bureaucratic) level seem to have been much more successful in achieving their goals. Why was this so? Was there a logic to it? One explanation that ought not to be ignored is the possible advantage of smaller scale in attempting new or "high-impact" policies—at least at the earlier stages of the modernization process. Alexander Gerschenkron has taught us to think of strong central leadership as a *sine qua non* of "catch-up" modernization. This may be a logical *requirement,* but it should not blind us to the fact that, in structural terms, local or regional government

*A summary.

initiatives are often less politically "expensive" and therefore develop first. It might be possible, therefore, to see the Chinese case—short-term "failure" at the center and "success" at the lower levels—as part of a pattern of temporary energizing of leadership sectors previously excluded or limited to more modest political roles.

The "Failure" of Local Reform

It is more difficult to account for the ultimate "failure" of these local and provincial reforms to develop into something more lasting. In dealing with this enigma we often use a motivational explanation, attributing failure to the attitudes or values of the elites involved. An alternative explanation may be offered. One of the core problems might be that China failed to develop a nation-wide level of control within which elites could operate. This factor is independent of ideological and motivational shortcomings.

"Military" Modernizers

Another explanation may have to do with the origins of the provincial and local elites. The provincial elite "progressives" came out of the *mu-fu* (personal staff) apparatus of Tseng Kuo-fan and Li Hung-chang. We can assume that such persons had a certain unity of outlook and goal structure. Yet the military origins of the self-strengtheners might have been their greatest handicap as modernizers and leaders. They were burdened by the economic and political costs of having to maintain large bodies of troops, and their attempts to expand their activities into the industrial sphere were often disrupted by military emergencies. Border or "diplomatic" crises were frequent, and people whose power depended on their military indispensability occasionally seem to have manipulated them into existence. Priorities were adjusted according to self-interest. Moreover, because of the lack of leadership from Peking, there was significant organized competition, such as the rivalry for resources between Tso Tsung-t'ang and Li Hung-chang.

Local Oligarchy

It is harder to find information on the local level. One trend that can be discerned, however, is the rise of oligarchy in local elite structures. Leadership was becoming more and more formalized, and power was becoming more and more centralized in the hands of fewer and fewer people, who enjoyed higher status and greater concentration of power.

How do we account for this development? The immediate context, as shown by Philip Kuhn's work, is militarization through the self-defense *t'uan-lien* organizations. This process was not confined to areas near the front in the fight against the Taipings; it was much more widespread.

Another aspect of the problem was the localization of the political perspective of the academic elite. A common phenomenon was the *ch'ing-i* scholar who left Peking and returned to the local area. In the context of mid-century revolt and disorder, *ch'ing-i* adherents often became pessimistic over the ability of the central government to deal with its problems; and their role in local society was often premised upon this skepticism.

The success of local elites represented an erosion of central government control. The accomplishments of these elites were at the expense of and disruptive to the power of the central government. Thus the failure of the center was not necessarily entirely a shortcoming of ideology; it also resulted from organizational weakness. This weakness impaired China's process of modernization.

Local-National Linkages

A final question which should be examined has to do with the connections that link local elites to the national political structure. After defining what we mean by local elite, we must examine how local elites act and what sorts of connections they form with the national elite. Sooner or later, it might be hypothesized, in most developing countries, local elites are forced into participation in national politics because of the impact of government communications and transportation policy. This happened in China when local elites became involved in national transportation issues, especially the railroad controversies of the early twentieth century. If we examine the Chinese case in global perspective, however, we find that China is unique in the degree to which local elites rapidly and successfully mobilized themselves in the national political arena in response to government initiatives in the transportation and communications sectors. So quickly did they succeed in asserting political power that they were able to subvert the political order.

As a contrast, the Japanese popular rights movement, although active at an early stage in influencing government road-building policies through prefectural assemblies, nevertheless turned out to be a short, unimportant episode in modern Japanese history. Similarly, the Granger and Populist movements in the United States, although triggering resistance against railroad "monopolies," turned out to have little effect on the railroads themselves.

In China, however, local political activity centering around the railroad question turned into a groundswell of local participation in national politics, which eventually overthrew the old political order. Historically, therefore, the Chinese case is of interest as a rare example of local elite interests shaping—and crippling—the national political order at a moment of transition to "modernity."

Jonathan Ocko
GENTRY-OFFICIAL CONFLICT IN THE RESTORATION
KIANGSU COUNTRYSIDE

Both James Polachek and Frank Lojewski have noted that the local elite (gentry) in Kiangsu during the T'ung-chih Restoration perceived a need for a new type of leadership structure at the local level which would enable them to balance the power of the local officials and would reach directly to the people. What follows is a brief description of the subdistrict political system and of official and gentry responses to it.*

The Taiping Rebellion had spawned a variety of subdistrict officers serving in Kiangsu at various levels: *hsiang-tung* (rural district director), *t'u-tung* (precinct director), *ts'un-tung* (village director), and *sai-tung* (stockade director). The status and function of these men is not now entirely clear. The *hsiang-tung,* who most likely had at least a *chien-sheng* title, appear to have had supervisory responsibilities over the rest of the directors. The *t'u-tung,* whose degree status might have changed over time and who were sometimes selected solely on the basis of strength and wealth, were identified with the *ti-pao,* the *pao-chia* agent who controlled an area encompassing approximately 1,000 families. At the lowest level of the *ts'un-tung,* even an old farmer was considered adequate to the task of "handling the management of all officially ordered things."

Gentry and official assessments of this political situation were sharply divergent. To a man like Feng Kuei-fen, these directors were wholly unsatisfactory; they were too closely identified with officials to be trusted by the people, and yet they lacked the official status necessary to govern effectively. Hence Feng suggested the election of commoner directors for the purpose of

*For exact citations and for a fuller discussion of this point the reader should consult Jonathan Ocko, "Ting Jih-chang and Kiangsu, 1864–1870: Rhetoric and Reality in a Restoration Official" (Ph.D. dissertation, Yale University, December, 1975).

handling minor litigation, and proposed an augmentation of the number of subdistrict magistrates and their power in order to bring formal governance down to the local level. In the view of the Kiangsu governor, Ting Jih-ch'ang, it was inevitable that both these new directors and the additional subdistrict magistrates would be influenced by the gentry—and this was impermissible. For while the state accepted the gentry's intermediary functions of forwarding to officials grievances from the people and transmitting officials' orders and imperial teachings to the people, it considered imperative the prevention of gentry involvement in taxation, litigation, or policing. Indeed, asserted one official, once given free rein and allowed to look on officials with disdain, gentry would increasingly oppress the people. Ting considered it most difficult to obtain good gentry directors and moved in a number of ways to deny gentry both leadership and supervisory responsibility in the maintenance of local order.

The issue here was the same one recently contested with the Taipings: the control of the countryside. Actually, one can argue that we see two divergent currents of reform. The local elite in the 1860s and again in the 1890s saw reform as based on the devolution of formal power from the hands of the magistrate and his surrogates, the yamen underlings, into their own hands. It was decentralized local reform that was to be manned by influential village leaders and by the thousands of unemployed degreeholders. In contrast, the official reform movement was characterized by centralization, regulation, and an effort to establish direct communication between the people and the magistrate, thereby eliminating all middlemen, regardless of whether these happened to be yamen underlings or gentry. For the state to achieve these goals, exceptional local officials were required. But the state never found such men, and the gentry, almost by default, asserted their control in the countryside. Some of them, on the basis of their managerial income, eventually became members of Marianne Bastid's "rural bourgeoisie" and as a group laid the foundations for what Mark Elvin has called "gentry democracy."

Nailene Chou

THE FORMATION OF A PROVINCE: REFORM OF FRONTIER ADMINISTRATION IN SINKIANG

One of the most important legacies bequeathed by the Ch'ing dynasty to modern China was an integrated territory. Scholars have given credit to the military genius of the dynastic founders for pushing China's frontiers to their present extent. But it was the reforms instituted in the borderlands in the last decades of the Ch'ing dynasty that effectively strengthened the tie between the periphery and the Chinese political center. Thus it was not pure coincidence that at the downfall of the Ch'ing dynasty, most of the peripheral areas that had undergone reform of one kind or another stayed within the Chinese orbit.

The process of reforming frontier administration started in the reign of Kuang-hsu and lasted to the closing days of the dynasty. The circumstances attending the process varied from area to area, as did the underlying motives. In the late 1870s and 1880s, the establishment of provincial administrations was perceived by Chinese policy makers as the most promising alternative in frontier reform. The process of converting outlying areas into provinces continued right into the Republican era. The first among the new provinces created in the peripheral areas was Sinkiang in 1884.

Sinkiang was separated from the "core areas" of China by considerable physical distance and had traditionally been resistant to Chinese cultural influence. The people of Sinkiang, particularly in the southern part of the area, had a distinct culture of their own and had always been more oriented toward the Islamic world to the west. The making of Sinkiang into a province, thereby giving it the same administrative status as a division of metropolitan China, resulted from the use of traditional reformist measures to meet the new exigencies arising in this area.

In the middle of the reign of Tao-kuang, just before the outbreak of the Opium War, the focus of scholarship in China shifted from pure retrospective research to a rising concern for practical

217

affairs. At first this shift involved only a minority of scholars; gradually however it became much more widespread. The "state-craft" school, with which these scholars identified themselves, was concerned with current state affairs and the drawing up of policy proposals. Among the adherents of the school, frontier studies rapidly gained popularity. In a period of dynastic decline, the frontier afforded an opportunity to revitalize the martial spirit inspired by the military feats of the dynastic founders. The frontier's empty land and untapped natural resources also seemed to present a solution to the problems of overpopulation and impoverishment from which China was suffering. Statecraft scholars therefore urged reform of the frontier administration and tried to influence policy makers to put their proposals into practice. The most notable early works in this vein were produced by Kung Tzu-chen and Wei Yuan. Although their writings had very little impact on policy formation in their own day, through the wide circulation of such works as *Huang-ch'ao ching-shih wen pien* (Essays on administration of government during the Ch'ing dynasty) and *Sheng-wu chi* (Record of imperial campaigns), their views became widely known and a general concern for China's frontiers grew among scholars. The ideas of Kung and Wei were finally trans-lated into action by Tso Tsung-t'ang, a soldier and statesman who had long identified himself as a statecraft scholar.[1]

While frontier studies were sensitizing scholars and officials to the need for change in the border areas, the Moslem rebellion in the northwest and the Russian occupation of Ili served as catalysts for such change. In the controversy over maritime versus land defense in the 1870s, a great many officials, influenced by the frontier studies, remained committed to a strong land frontier defense. This had been the traditional focus of China's national security concern, and they considered the menace from Russia to be much more deep-seated than the challenge from the maritime countries. Here the traditional image of Russians as "land barbarians" (*hu-jen*) and the new image of them as "maritime barbarians" (*yang-jen*) combined in a curious way to make Russia the most inscrutable of China's enemies.[2] Quite apart from the fear of Russia, Sinkiang had undergone tremendous changes in the course of the suppression of the Moslem rebellion and the post-crisis rehabilitation. A predominantly Chinese administration had replaced the Manchu monopoly in the governing of the region. The western campaign itself brought about unprecedented inter-regional communication. Merchants from Hunan, Hopei, Shansi, Shensi, and Szechwan flocked into Sinkiang, following the movement of troops. The Hunan Army replaced the banner troops as the main defense of the area. The old military colony system was inadequate to cope with the new problems arising from these rapid developments. A far-reaching change was imperative.

Tso Tsung-t'ang, who was responsible for re-establishing Chinese authority in Sinkiang, was convinced that the only way to integrate the area effectively into the Chinese political community was by transforming it into a province. Tso acknowledged that the blueprint for provincial administration put out by Kung Tzu-chen and Wei Yuan some fifty years before had had considerable influence on him. His conviction was also based on his own experience of active participation in provincial administration. In the self-strengthening movement, provincial government leaders often acted as a progressive force in attempting, through the use of unprecedented means, to preserve the old political and moral edifice of the empire. Although their efforts to maintain the integrity of the Ch'ing paradoxically reinforced the centrifugal tendencies of provincial power, the restoration leaders were interested, in Mary Wright's words, "not in securing satrapies for themselves, but in assuring the survival of the Confucian order."[3] We can hardly overestimate the importance of this attitude in the formation of new provincial units. The ideological commitment to a unified state gave justification to the establishment of such units; it also had a binding force on those officials who subsequently were called on to put new provinces into operation.

For decades following the reconquest of Sinkiang, Tso Tsungt'ang remained the patron saint of the new colonizers and administrators who worked there. The latter attempted to emulate Tso and to live up to the ideals prescribed in his memorials and writings on

Sinkiang. The majority of officials sent to the province had unwavering faith in the supremacy of Confucianism and in the civilizing mission of the Chinese among borderland peoples. The resulting atmosphere, according to travelers in the early 1900s, was anachronistic. As the rest of China moved into the twentieth century, in Sinkiang the spirit of Tso still lived. The ideals of the restoration survived in almost petrified form, offering a striking contrast to the changes that were taking place elsewhere in the country.

It seems paradoxical that Sinkiang, the focal point of such progressive action in the 1880s, should, by the end of the dynasty, have become an anachronism. The trouble was that, although the governors of the new province were successful in integrating it territorially and administratively with the rest of China, for social and economic integration to take place, a much stronger government was needed, one with adequate financial resources to sponsor long-term projects, far-sighted planners, and dedicated cadres to carry out new programs. All such elements were lacking in the last decades of the Ch'ing dynasty. It would take decades before people realized the complexity of integrating ethnically distinct groups into a national community, a task requiring negotiation of the conflict between Chinese nationalism and local nationalism. This challenge was put off until the middle of the twentieth century.

On the other hand, the reform in Sinkiang in the 1880s may be viewed as a giant step toward national integration. Theoretically, integration was the very antithesis of regionalism. But in actuality, the awareness that the nation must be held together was born at the same time as regionalism and grew along with it. The waxing and waning of these two forces shaped the history of modern China for decades to come. The leaders of the 1870s, with only traditional means at their disposal, saw province-formation as the optimal choice for a China bent on achieving territorial integrity.

Mary Backus Rankin
LOCAL REFORM CURRENTS IN CHEKIANG BEFORE 1900

A nineteenth-century background favorable to the introduction of Western reformist ideas is essential to explain the vigor and independence of the nonofficial elite reform movement after 1900 in Chekiang. Although bureaucratic and nonofficial reform efforts were so intertwined that they ultimately cannot be considered separately, I should like to explore the reform activities of local and provincial elites. There are really two aspects to the problem. First is the impact of accelerated change in local elite society, partly in response to the Shanghai trade and partly stimulated by the Taiping Rebellion and T'ung-chih Restoration. Even though such change was well within traditional confines, by the end of the nineteenth century it was paving the way for reformism as well as for local elite political dominance. The second aspect pertains to the introduction of specifically Western ideas into Chekiang. How did such ideas enter the province and where? In the 1880s, and certainly in the 1890s, evidence of Western-inspired reform can be found down to the level of some large market towns. The number of people involved and the number of projects undertaken were small. However, they assume significance as forerunners of events during the late Ch'ing decade and as examples of the way reform impetus might spread from major centers.

I have only recently begun work on the pre-1900 period, and the materials accumulated so far come mainly from a few gazetteers of cities and towns in the prefectures of Huchow, Hangchow, Shaohsing, Ningpo, and Wenchow that cover events through the end of the dynasty. Most of these places were being brought directly or indirectly into the Shanghai trading sphere. Therefore, they (like similar parts of the lower Yangtze area) might reasonably be expected to be at the forefront of change. Even so, direct exposure to the West diminished rapidly as one moved away from the treaty ports.

Looking at evidence for reformism within Chekiang provides

221

a somewhat different perspective than that afforded by studies of
Shanghai, of pioneer reform scholars, or official reformers. First,
it underlines the point that there was no hard line between traditional and Western ideas and activities. In some respects, Chinese
reformist traditions and local elite functions provided an approach
to Western-derived concepts of reform. Second, Western reform
was the concern of both scholar-gentry and merchants, reflecting
the very considerable integration of these classes and the influence
of Shanghai business and trade. Third, new ideas entered smaller
cities and towns both through trade and the operation of traditional clan and native place ties. The vigor of existing social patterns and intellectual traditions could be an avenue to as well as a
barrier against Western reform.

Mid-Nineteenth-Century Changes in Elite Society

Disruption and destruction caused by the Taiping Rebellion
(dramatic in parts of Chekiang) coincided with the rapid growth of
foreign trade at Shanghai. Some established families were impoverished by the rebellion. Others, on the other hand, were able to
take advantage of the interlocking opportunities created during the
mid-nineteenth century through the Shanghai international trade,
the hazardous but continuing trade between government-held and
Taiping-occupied areas, and the provisioning of government troops.
Some examples are the Chang, Chiang, Chou, and Liu families of
the market town of Nan-hsun, Huchow,[1] the Yeh family of Chen-
hai, Ningpo,[2] and the Yen family of Tz'u-ch'i, Ningpo.[3]

These families made their fortunes in trade, although earlier
members may already have had local status as landowners and
scholars. Subsequently they acquired prestige and influence through
public and charitable activities in their home towns and Shanghai,
and through contributions to the government. Some acquired
honorary rank and held quasibureaucratic positions. Some took
part in such early modernization projects as the China Merchants
Steam Navigation Company or furthered traditional reforms like
the reconstruction of the Chekiang salt industry.

In general it can be said that these families demonstrated great ability to adjust to and take advantage of changing circumstances. They were open to both traditional and Western ideas of reform (particularly economic reform) and enjoyed high influence in their home towns as well as Shanghai as a result of their wealth and public service. At the end of the nineteenth and the beginning of the twentieth centuries one finds various members holding upper degrees, engaging in trade, promoting local educational and economic reforms, and joining in the railway and constitutionalist movements.

During the T'ung-chih period there were wide opportunities for public-spirited merchants and gentry to take part in the affairs of their home towns. Many of the tasks of the restoration were necessarily local in nature, and nonbureaucratic elites assumed considerable responsibility. Relief funds were often needed immediately after an area was recaptured from Taiping armies.[4] Seventy percent of the buildings in Nan-hsun had been destroyed and numerous bridges were in disrepair.[5] In Hangchow, all the major academies had been burned, and the sea wall around much of Hangchow Bay had to be rebuilt.[6] In a relatively small, but wealthy, town like Nan-hsun, rich merchants and gentry were more prominent than the few low-ranking officials responsible for local affairs. There, the role of elites in reconstruction is immediately evident in the gazetteer. However, gentry managers are also mentioned in Hangchow, where there were plenty of high-ranking officials to lay plans and get credit.[7] Some men like Ting Ping virtually made a career of reconstruction. Although mainly known for his efforts to recover and reprint scattered texts, Ting also founded and managed schools and headed water conservancy projects.[8]

Philip Kuhn has described how local elite power expanded during the Taiping period through gentry organization of local defense.[9] It would appear that the large amounts of elite money and time devoted to reconstruction during the T'ung-chih era resulted in a further increase in power, related now to wealth and civic function rather than militarization. Much of this growth in power simply involved a higher level of traditional informal activities. In some cases, however, it was reflected in the assumption of formal government prerogatives: a silk bureau (*ssu-yeh kung-so*), established in Nan-hsun in 1865 and managed by local elites, collected silk taxes as well as protecting mercantile interests.[10]

Introducing Reform at the Local Level

Expanding local elite activities touched upon reform in several ways. First, the traditional elite spheres of activity—academies, public works, construction, water conservancy, philanthropy— provided a framework into which educational, economic, and eventually political reform efforts in the 1890s and 1900s easily fitted. Second, one finds a layer of elites who were particularly active in local affairs and were concerned with solving practical problems of the day. In the 1860s and 1870s these problems revolved about restoring and rebuilding. However, once new problems were perceived and the intellectual climate changed in the 1890s this kind of concern seems to have expanded readily to include Western-oriented reform. Thus by the late 1890s one finds a few men founding Western-type schools or introducing other innovations as well as engaging in the usual range of local elite public activities.[11]

Third, in some cases restoration efforts shaded off into the introduction of Western practices. Negishi Tadashi suggests that the silk industry was closely involved in the 1898 reform movement because producers and traders had been forced to contemplate a degree of modernization as early as the T'ung-chih Restoration when the industry began to be affected by the competitive conditions of foreign trade.[12] At that time the Nan-hsun silk merchant, Chou Ch'ang-chih, tried to persuade merchants from market towns in north Chekiang to send silk to Soochow for manufacture before sale to Western traders.[13] A somewhat different example comes from Wu-chen and Ch'ing-chen, also in Huchow. Settlers (*k'o-min*) from Anhwei and other Chekiang prefectures who occupied barren lands after the Taiping Rebellion brought with them different methods of cultivation using oxen. This change resulted in an increase in the local cattle population, new concern with bovine health, and the eventual establishment of an anthrax vaccination station by two leading local merchants in 1892.[14]

Introduction of new influences can frequently be explained by the existence of a highly mobile segment of elite population which still retained strong clan and native place ties.[15] Men moved back and forth between local, regional, and national levels, and were active in more than one place. The consequent interplay of friendships and interchange of ideas can be abundantly illustrated. These were traditional phenomena that served many functions. In the late nineteenth century they also helped spread ideas of reform.

Much of the movement of men and ideas was trade-related. The author of the Nan-hsun gazetteer complained that when the town's silk trade became oriented to Shanghai after the Tao-kuang period merchants brought home the "extravagant customs" of foreign traders, undermining the old "sincere and simple" ways.[16] Chiang Monlin describes in his autobiography how by the 1890s Western influences and manufactures had reached the small village in Yü-yao, Shaohsing, where he grew up. Chiang's own father owed his wealth to banking interests accumulated in Shanghai during the Taiping Rebellion, and made occasional trips there to tend to business. The family was an example of local elites who were interested in Western technology and receptive to changes in education, medicine, and some social customs.[17]

The continuing interest of officials and Shanghai merchants in their clans and native areas was expressed in many ways right through the end of the Ch'ing dynasty. They visited home periodically, retired there, contributed to local projects, and established charitable estates. When one member of the family was managing affairs at home while close relatives were in Shanghai or Peking, opportunities for the introduction of new ideas were particularly strong. The first modern schools in Shaohsing and Nan-hsun were financed by Shanghai merchant money.[18] Public works, philanthropic institutions, and eventually modern schools in Chen-hai were underwritten by merchants in Shanghai. One of the merchants who established the anthrax station in Wu-Ch'ing was the manager of the traditional

local iron foundries. He and other members of the family traded in
Shanghai. Other close relatives held upper examination degrees, and
during the 1890s members of the next generation had begun to
study at the Kuang-fang yen-kuan in Shanghai to prepare for
Western-oriented careers.[19] The biographies of the brothers Hsu
Shu-lan and Hsu Yu-lan of Shan-yin, Shaohsing, and of the cousins
Sheng Ping-wei and Sheng Ping-chi of Chen-hai provide excellent
examples of the interweaving within a family of official, merchant,
and gentry strains, external and local careers, traditional and
reformist concerns in ways that resulted in promotion of reform in
those cities in the late 1890s.[20]

Traditional Scholarship and Reform

The motive behind reformism in Chekiang was basically the
same as elsewhere: an essentially nationalistic concern over China's
place in the world and fear for the country's future unless economic,
educational, and other institutional changes were introduced to
enhance its wealth and power. Except for the Ningpo area and some
coastal trade with Foochow, most direct Chekiangese contact with
foreigners before 1895 came in Shanghai. However, coastal areas
had direct experience with foreign aggression during both the Opium
and Sino-French Wars. Perhaps significantly, two Chen-hai merchants
in Shanghai who strongly defended the position of Chinese traders
during the French blockade of 1885, Yeh Ch'eng-chung and Fan
Fen, were later leading proponents of reform, locally and provincially.

More important, traditional intellectual currents could inspire
reform efforts even when there was a minimum of direct exposure
to the West. The group of reform scholars in Wenchow during the
1880s and 1890s provides the clearest illustration of this possibility.[21]
Although Wenchow was a coastal trading area, it was not one of the
most economically advanced parts of the province. It did, however,
have strong local intellectual traditions and numerous academies,
which provided the milieu in which reformers developed and
exchanged ideas.

The main figures were the philologist, classical scholar, and
educator, Sun I-jang (1848–1908), the historian and future president

of the Chekiang Provincial Assembly, Ch'en Fu-ch'en (1861–1917), the radical reformist philosopher, Sung Heng (1862–1910), the reformist scholar, Ch'en Ch'iu (1851–1903), and the reformer, official, and educator, Huang Shao-chi (1854–1908). Most of these men came from locally established families. Sun's and Huang's fathers were well-known officials. Ch'en's grandfather and Sung's father were members of the lower gentry noted for local good works. Only Ch'en Ch'iu's family was poor.

Huang Shao-chi's father had been a leading member of the Ch'ing-liu tang at the time of the Sino-French War, and he undoubtedly absorbed militant influences.[23] *Ching-shih* (statecraft) ideas were a still more important inspiration. Sun I-jang's father had been associated with the statecraft school. Statecraft concerns were a common element in many of the sources from which the Wenchow group drew their ideas. These ranged from the *Chou-li,* through the works of later Han scholars and local Chekiangese Southern Sung scholars of the Yung-k'ang school, and—unfortunately for consistency—the *I-ching* and Ch'an Buddhism.[24]

The ideas of this group were not uniform, but there were a number of common elements. These scholars were generally committed to statecraft notions of practical studies and evinced deep concern over China's future. Although only Sung Heng, in attacking the whole range of Neo-Confucian metaphysics (*li-hsueh*), fundamentally challenged the orthodox world view, all concluded that China must adopt broad educational, economic, and political reforms modeled on the West, and they particularly favored forms of elite participation in government outside the bureaucracy. These men did not consider the reforms they espoused antithetical to the Chinese heritage. The Wenchow scholars (and some other early Chekiangese reformers like T'ang Shou-ch'ien) tended to look down upon overly Westernized Chinese and were confident that through a merging of the best aspects of Chinese and Western cultures the country could be strengthened without doing violence to traditional values. Finally, several of them were strongly interested in local customs and considerably concerned with the welfare of the common people.[25]

Although some of these men were away much of the time, and all eventually developed national reputations, there was always a nucleus in Wenchow that had a concrete local impact during the 1880s and 1890s. Ch'en Ch'iu and Ch'en Fu-ch'en established a Western-style hospital and schools during the 1880s, and later (1897) experimented with a newspaper. Ch'en Fu-ch'en spread ideas of reform while teaching in local academies during much of these two decades. After the Sino-Japanese War, Sun I-jang began to promote modern education in Wenchow and Chuchow. At the same time, Western subjects were introduced into such traditional academies as the Mei-ch'i shu-yuan in Lotsing, then headed by Ch'en Fu-ch'en.

Coalescence of Reform Efforts

Before the mid-1890s examples of local Western-inspired reformism were very scattered and seemingly isolated from one another. After the Sino-Japanese War elite reform activity merged and intensified. During 1898 a good deal of the effort was centered in Hangchow with connections to national reform groups in Shanghai and Peking.[26] In the preceding year the reformist paper, *Ching-shih pao,* was established in the provincial capital by two Shaohsing reformers, along with Ch'en Ch'iu, Sung Heng, and Ch'en Fu-ch'en.[2] The first modern academy in Hangchow, the Ch'iu-shih shu-yuan, was founded by officials, but Wang K'ang-nien and other scholar-reformers had urged its founding for over a year.[28] Much the same group of scholars were responsible for establishing a sericulture society to improve methods of silk cultivation.[29] A year after Hangchow was opened as a treaty port in 1895 two merchants established a river steam launch company,[30] and in 1897 a group of merchants and gentry made the first attempt to establish a railway company.[31]

There were still other examples of reformism at the local level. Besides the schools in Wenchow, the Chung-Hsi hsueh-t'ang was established in Shaohsing in 1897.[32] Sheng Ping-wei established the Ningpo Ch'u-ts'ai School in the same year,[33] and in 1898–1899 the academy at Nan-hsun was partly modernized.[34] Educational reform tended to run ahead of economic modernization at the local level, but projects in the latter field were soon to appear. The earliest examples of local reform are not well documented and further research will presumably fill out the picture sketched here. What seems clear, at this point, is that by the end of the 1898 reform period a small but rapidly expanding base had been laid for a provincial and local elite reform movement during the last decade of the Ch'ing dynasty.

In conclusion, let me underscore a number of points that I have raised or implied but not developed very far here. First, one should not overdraw the contrast between a conservative T'ung-chih Restoration and later reformism. Second, one is immediately struck by the importance of clan and native place ties in providing a mechanism for introducing Western reform ideas on the local level. Such ties tended to blur distinctions among local, provincial, and national elites.

Third, my views on the extent of social change during the late Ch'ing and the capacity of nonbureaucratic elites for genuine reformism fall somewhere between those of Chūzō Ichiko on the one hand, and Mary Wright and Mark Elvin on the other, although they are closer to the latter. My findings of independent elite reform initiatives differ from Edward Rhoads's conclusion that in another coastal province, Kwangtung, the original impetus came from officials.[35] In Chekiang, I believe, one can trace a series of nineteenth-century changes that culminated after 1900 in a strong reformist push from without the bureaucracy. Working from the mid-nineteenth century toward 1911 thus gives a different perspective than working from 1949 back.

Fourth, although the Chekiangese situation may have been unusually favorable to Western-oriented reform, other parts of China were subject to similar intellectual and economic influences. Clan and native place ties must have functioned similarly elsewhere (even if on a smaller scale and at a somewhat later date), and the mixture of classical scholarship, traditional reformism, and Western-inspired reformism exhibited by some Chekiangese scholars in the 1880s and 1890s may have been roughly typical of their counterparts in the rest of the country.

Finally, there is the question of the extent to which my analysis meshes with Marianne Bastid's social theories, presented elsewhere in this volume. Many of the people with whom I have dealt fall roughly into her category of elites affected by Western-related social changes, although scholars such as those from Wenchow might be better described as traditional reformers who had come to believe that Western ideas and practices offered solutions to certain Chinese problems. On the other hand, Bastid's "agrarian bourgeoisie" are not in my picture. This absence raises some problems, one of which may be the existence of both types of new elites within the same family. Much more research is needed. In the meantime, it does seem to me that in Chekiang reform occupied an important part of political life after 1900, and that at least in some parts of the province sizable local influence was exercised by prominent elites who were tied to Western-type reformist developments in a variety of ways. I see no strong reason to dismiss the sincerity of their interests in reform. I feel, moreover, that the idea of a split in the late Ch'ing between urban and rural areas needs much refinement and qualification. So the question still remains as to when, how, and if there was a shift in control from one segment of the elite to another in Chekiang.

An additional consideration may be that the types of reform pursued by reformers (and suggested by the Western example as presented to them) simply were not oriented toward agrarian social problems. The reforms fitted rather easily into the existing local picture and in the end neither disrupted nor changed things fundamentally. True, traditions of elite philanthropy continued—and these had some social bearing—but they alone could not solve the mounting demographic and social crisis.

Richard A. Orb

CHIHLI ACADEMIES AND OTHER SCHOOLS IN THE LATE CH'ING: AN INSTITUTIONAL SURVEY

Chihli province during the last decade of the Ch'ing was one of the undisputed leaders in educational reform and in the establishment of new schools. In 1907 Chihli ranked highest in number of schools and size of administrative staff and surpassed all other provinces in educational expenditure. With more than 8000 teachers and 164,000 students, it ranked second in these categories only to Szechwan, which was larger and more populous; it also stood second (behind Hupeh) in total educational revenue. Rapid expansion continued. In the third national survey of education, taken in 1909 and published in the last year of the Hsuan-t'ung reign, the figures indicate that Chihli had overtaken Hupeh in educational revenue, was closing the gap between itself and first-place Szechwan in number of teachers and revenue, and was moving up on first- and second-place Szechwan and Kwangtung in aggregate school property. Chihli reported a school population for 1909 of 242,247.[1]

The reasons for this superior performance include the realization in Chihli of the serious commitment to educational reform in the capital, the vigorous encouragement and official prosecution of reform at the provincial level by Yuan Shih-k'ai, and the equally energetic involvement of large numbers of subordinate officials at the prefectural and district levels.

The Boxer uprising, the harsh realities of the Allied intervention (directly felt in many local areas), and the restrictions of the Protocol on the customary operation of local examinations in more than a score of district capitals also generated important support for educational reform. Finally, there was the traditional educational base in Chihli, which formed a point of departure for some of the school reform activity of the nineteenth and early twentieth centuries. The focus of this presentation will be on the institutional aspects of the communal and charitable schools, the role of academies, and certain aspects of gentry mobilization of support for local reform in Chihli.

231

A few of the many new lower primary schools (*ch'u-teng hsiao-hsueh-t'ang*) established after 1900 emerged from former communal, community, or village schools (*she-hsueh*). The *Chi-fu t'ung-chih* (Chihli provincial history) of 1884 supplies a list of all communal schools past and present in the hundred and fifty administrative units of the province. Of these, 136 were still in existence in the 1870s.[2] This would suggest a mean of approximately one communal school for each district or department. In actuality, however, almost two-thirds of all Chihli administrative units reported an absence of *she-hsueh* in the late nineteenth century. Many communal schools that had been established in the Ming, or in the early or middle Ch'ing, had subsequently been abolished. Communal schools by the nineteenth century had decreased in Chihli and were relatively unimportant as potential centers of reform or as a significant institutional base for the new schools after 1900.

The charitable or endowed schools (*i-hsueh*) offered greater potential and were more clearly a factor in the formation of the new lower primaries. A count of extant charitable schools in the *Chi-fu t'ung-chih* yields a total figure of 838 *i-hsueh,* averaging a little over five schools for each administrative unit.[3] Charitable schools in earlier times occasionally became academies, and Republican gazetteers indicate that they were converted into lower primary schools at the end of the Ch'ing.

An important aspect of this transformation when it occurred— a continuity with social as well as institutional implications—was the direct transference of lands and rents previously applied to an abolished charitable school to support the operating expenses of new lower primaries. The land holdings of the charitable schools and of academies often were sizable, and this made it possible for areas with several *i-hsueh* to ease the initial task of finding sites and financial resources for the new schools. The larger the number of old schools, the lighter would be the initial burden of securing private contributions or increasing surtaxes at the local level to fund new schools.

This correlation can be clearly seen in the Shu-lu district of

Paoting *fu*, the prefecture with the largest concentration of primary school students in all of Chihli by the end of the dynasty.[4] Shu-lu may have been typical of other districts in the prefecture in terms of market structure and the like, but in education it was exceptional.[5] In 1884 Shu-lu reported two *she-hsueh* and twenty-seven *i-hsueh,* the latter figure surpassed by only one other district to the north, also in Paoting.

Two decades later the Shu-lu gazetteer of 1905 locates two higher primary schools, a model primary, two lower primaries and a normal school in the district capital. Another higher primary was in one of the eighteen outlying regions (*t'uan*). But 205 additional lower primary schools were scattered throughout the district in towns, hamlets, and in many of the 314 villages (*ts'un*). By comparing the two gazetteer accounts over time it is apparent that at least three of the old *i-hsueh* became lower primaries; in addition, one of them may have become a higher primary school.

One of the twenty-seven old charitable schools was in a small *t'uan* five miles north of the district seat. This small area of four hamlets (*chuang*) and twenty-three villages had sixteen lower primary schools in 1905. One (probably the former charitable school) was in the single market town of the *t'uan* and the rest were in the surrounding settlements. Not all of the lower primaries in Shu-lu were in the villages, but there were enough that were clearly not in the district capital or the market towns to challenge the notion that the new schools were exclusively a phenomenon of the district city and marketing areas, or that they were a mere paper transformation of the relatively few former charitable schools.[6] There were too many new schools for most of them to have emerged from earlier institutions.

An unknown element is the degree of continuity between the purely private or family schools (*ssu-shu* and *chia-shu*) of earlier times and the establishment of the new lower primaries. The rate of new school formation would seem to argue for a relative lack of such continuity. Granted, it would have been a simple matter to rename quickly an old private school when a decision had been made to implement local reform. The totals for any given district

might then be expected to be relatively high in the early years of
reform and level off somewhat after 1906. Educational statistics
for Chihli from this period, however, do not follow this pattern.
Instead, they show a steady growth from 4100 lower primary
schools in 1906 to over 11,000 by 1912. The vast majority of
these, moreover, were established by district subscriptions (*kung-li*)
and were not under private auspices (*ssu-li*).[7]

The argument here for Chihli, which was one of the most successful provinces in the implementation of reform, is that there
were clearly too few *she-hsueh* and *i-hsueh* surviving from the past
to do anything more than slightly ease the initial burden of school
development in local areas, and that private and family schools,
for their part, could at best have provided a running start for the
large efforts that were made at the very end of the dynasty. The
largest debt owed to the past in launching the initial phases of a
modern school system in Chihli came not from the institutional
base, but from the general approval (at least among wealthy
Chinese) of education as a useful activity and from the existence
of established ways of mobilizing elite support and financial
contributions for local education when motivation was present.

The two institutions that were central in this latter regard at
the district level were the higher primary school (*kao-teng hsiao-
hsueh-t'ang*) and the education promotion office (*ch'üan-hsueh-so*).
The education offices, widely established in Chihli districts in
1906 and functioning as precursors to the district departments of
education, were directed by well-known members of the gentry
who received their appointments from the magistrate. The
director's responsibilities, and those of the subordinate inspectors
whom he selected, were to initiate and supervise plans for the new
school system and to secure local support and financial contributions for school development. Upon the shoulders of this man
largely rested the measure of success for whatever local development occurred, since a large portion of educational income in a
district came from public contribution (*le-chüan*).[8]

The education director in the independent department of
Chi-chou in 1906 was Chang T'ing-hsiang, a sixty-four year old

sui-kung-sheng. He had a long record of active participation in local educational affairs and had personally subscribed funds in the 1880s to help make the department academy (Hsin-tu shu-yuan) one of the eminent institutions in Chihli. Chang was also in the forefront of modern school reform, aiding in the establishment of the Chi-chou middle school in 1902 and the higher primary school the following year. Before becoming director, Chang went to Japan to investigate local educational development.[9]

In short, the *ch'üan-hsueh-so* had all the earmarks of new institutions. The staffs of these offices were intent upon extending the formal school system beyond the district capital, more deeply into the surrounding local areas than had ever before been attempted. The directors were notable and reform-minded members of the gentry who had previous experience in elite mobilization and who identified their interests with those who would most benefit from the formation of the new schools. They were very much a part of the local power structure and they exemplified growing local elite support for institutional reform, sentiment which heretofore had found expression mainly in the provincial cities of Tientsin and Paoting. Chang T'ing-hsiang regarded himself as a protégé of the T'ung-ch'eng scholar Wu Ju-lun, who had been the director in the 1890s of the leading academy of Chihli, the Lien-ch'ih shu-yuan in Paoting. Wu had been appointed dean of the faculty of the Imperial University and had just returned from an inspection tour of education in Japan at the time of his death in 1903. Many of Wu's students were prominent in Chihli reform circles after 1900, Chang T'ing-hsiang affording only one example.[10]

The other institution which was central to the new education reforms at the local level was the higher primary school. In most cases in Chihli this school was the former academy (*shu-yuan*). The academies provided an indisputable continuity between nineteenth- and twentieth-century educational reform.

Recent scholarship has devoted increasing attention to the history of academies in the late imperial age, and the subject is an important one.[11] Here, only a brief institutional survey will be attempted, mainly to confirm for Chihli the view that these academies were increasing in number. Two were established in the Sung, 17 in the Yuan, 68 in the Ming, and 154 in the Ch'ing. (See Table 2 for the Ch'ing.) Fifty-six more are of uncertain origin. The overall but probably incomplete total for all of Chihli is 299 academies.[12]

These figures do not indicate how many *shu-yuan* were in existence at any one time or how many had been abolished and when. Gazetteer accounts most often indicate dates of formation and repair and that an academy that once existed had been abolished. Records do show, however, that at least seventy-eight academies of the 299 were in existence at the end of the nineteenth century. Seventy-nine had been abolished. The remaining 142 must be identified by the last date of record in Chihli gazetteers. (See Table 3.)

The evidence is incomplete but it is likely that more academies from earlier periods survived than were abolished during the nineteenth century and that new ones persisted until the turn of the century. Furthermore, a large number of existing academies were repaired or enlarged, or given funds or new land, especially in the T'ung-chih and Kuang-hsu reigns. Although the eighteenth century has rightly been called the "*shu-yuan* era" in terms of academy formation,[13] the trend continued in Chihli during the nineteenth century and many older academies were able to sustain operations.

Although this trend of academy support and expansion is real and important, it must be placed in the proper local perspective. By the late nineteenth century it is probable that most of the 150 administrative units in Chihli had but a single academy. This would include Lun-ts'un shu-yuan in Chang-chia-k'ou *t'ing* (Kalgan, in later Chahar), established in 1878 and the region's only academy; T'ien-kuei Academy in P'ing-shan district, Cheng-ting prefecture, in the extreme southwest; Wen-yang Academy in the least populous Chihli district of Huai-jou, northeast of Peking; and Lien-ch'ih shu-yuan in Ch'ing-yuan, the only academy in a densely populated district containing the provincial capital of Paoting.

A close reading of the pertinent sections of the 1884 provincial history, over seventy district gazetteers, and the results of the survey

by Wang Lan-yin reveals that only four districts had no academy
at all by the end of the century. On the other hand, few administrative units reported the existence over time of more than two or
three academies. And where districts recorded more than one, the
chances were high that in fact all but one or two had been abolished
before 1900. Ting-hsing district in Paoting recorded six, but only
two existed by the 1870s; Yuan-shih and Ta-ming in Cheng-ting
and Ta-ming prefectures, respectively, listed six, but only one
existed in each by 1900.

The local histories examined indicate that every surviving
academy usually became the single higher primary school in the
district, or, in a few cases, a model primary, a normal school, a
middle school, or the education promotion office. The academies
were transformed in accordance with reform proposals that in some
cases went back to the 1890s. Although direct imperial sanction
was not received until the beginning of 1904, most of the academies
in Chihli made the transformation in 1902 and 1903.

The institution that had previously been the sole center of
elite teaching and semiprivate research in each district now became
the first official expression at the local level of the Manchu reforms.
The establishment of lower primaries followed, and the education
promotion offices gave more concerted direction to expansion of
the lower primaries in the countryside. The establishment of new
police bureaus and eventually the self-government associations
completed the late Ch'ing institutional innovations at the local
level. The former academies, while changed to a degree both in
structure and curriculum, remained the leading centers of formal
study in each district and continued to serve only a very small
segment of the very best educated youth. Access to the new
higher primaries, as to the former academies, was more restricted
than access to the initial levels of the examination system. The
higher primary schools were intended to be the sole entrée to the
small number of middle schools. They thus served to limit educational mobility out of the districts, very much as the academies
had done previously.

Admittance to the higher primary schools was also very much

a matter for local scholarly elite determination. The few who were enrolled tended to be those judged qualified by men like the *ch'üan-hsueh-so* director and by those whose influence was greatest in the district capital. The class background of students in the new higher primaries was akin to that of students in the former academies. Here the institutional and social continuity with the nineteenth century is most visible.

The new feature was the growing number of lower primary schools and the beginning of an alteration of the class structure at the local level. The lower primaries provided formal educational access to larger numbers than ever before, certainly to many more Chihli students than had previously attended the *she-hsueh* and *i-hsueh* of the province. But the total number of students, when compared to the total school-age population of a district, was still very small.

In the short run, the numbers of new schools and students and the degree of modernity of the primary school curriculums are less important than the backgrounds of the new students entering the schools and the new names on the subscription lists of the education directors. New avenues to local influence and prestige became available to those who responded to the call for contributions to fund local educational development. It is logical to assume that these new persons on the subscription lists fully expected some form of *quid pro quo.*

The extensive implementation of school reforms after 1900 and the attendant broadening of the social base form a sharp contrast to the situation as it existed prior to the turn of the century. Before 1900 there was little evidence at the local level of reform in education or expansion of traditional schools. Academies did increase throughout Chihli, but only enough, generally, for each district to boast of one *shu-yuan.* No proliferation of *she-hsueh* or *i-hsueh* can be documented; indeed, their numbers may well have been greater in the eighteenth century. Aside from a handful of new technical schools in Tientsin and several Western-type schools attached to mission stations in the province, relatively little institutional change can be reported. Only after 1900 did anything approaching a modern school system begin to emerge in Chihli.

Table 1

Provincial Education Statistics for China in 1907

Province	Schools and Offices	Staff	Teachers	Students	Income*	Outgo*	School Property*
Chihli	8723	9337	8460	164,172	1,754,731	2,004,304	4,772,611
Szechwan	7793	6407	12,089	244,538	1,421,242	1,444,157	7,628,783**
Shantung	4350	5748	4759	53,996	873,499	913,359	3,041,638
Shensi	2343	3672	2360	43,232	468,237	432,842	2,379,466
Hupeh	2078**	1789	3567	56,671	2,049,885	1,877,143	2,561,051
Honan	1932	4990	2396	38,804	590,913	597,265	2,238,448
Kwangtung	1607	4581	4954	75,733	1,019,621	1,283,960	6,150,316**
Fengtien	1447	1212	2356	48,865	1,226,877	1,169,763	1,403,973
Chekiang	1295	3730	4269	41,569	789,362	865,414	3,053,780
Yunnan	1246	1055	1386	36,980	547,319	573,204	1,702,605
Kiangsu	1049	3974	4114	35,570	832,279	939,334	1,330,322
Shansi	968	2101	1223	20,399	494,831	487,900	1,581,851
Hunan	849	1228	2593	30,201	715,101	705,685	2,650,267
Kiangning	767	1605	2010	20,266	907,113	959,657	2,427,116
Kweichow	635	829	984	17,678	233,404	230,248	925,060
Kwangsi	582	843	1219	22,074	388,035	355,336	918,658
Kansu	531	595	234	10,927	127,332	90,300	87,959
Kiangsi	513	1414	1399	15,134	547,077	478,258	1,703,836
Fukien	448	1445	1645	21,085	364,983	405,521	790,797
Anhwei	344	2369	1106	8,367	460,665	493,129	1,892,711
Sinkiang	103	36	112	1,187	56,373	55,041	36,804
Heilungkiang	97	190	157	3,409	425,585	198,984	532,618
Kirin	50	209	164	2,714	665,556	638,742	978,513
TOTALS	37,672	59,359	63,556	1,013,571	16,960,020	17,199,546	37,010,084

*Monetary amounts reported in or changed to silver taels (*yin-liang*).
** 1907 figure unreported; 1908 figure from the second national survey here inserted
though not included in the column total.

(Source: Hsueh-pu tsung-wu-ssu, ed., *Kuang-hsu 33 nien fen, Ti-i-tz'u chiao-yü t'ung-chi t'u-piao*, 1910)

Table 2

Academy Establishment in the Ch'ing by Reigns

Shun-chih	4
K'ang-hsi	23
Yung-cheng	5
Ch'ien-lung	63
Chia-ch'ing	8
Tao-kuang	23
Hsien-feng	4
T'ung-chih	14
Kuang-hsu	10
Total:	154

Table 3

Last Gazetteer Record of Possibly Extant Academies
by Dynasty and Ch'ing Reigns

		Shun-chih, K'ang-hsi, Yung-cheng	5
		Ch'ien-lung, Chia-ch'ing	24
Yuan	6	Tao-kuang	19
Ming	20	Hsien-feng	4
Ch'ing	99	T'ung-chih	24
Uncertain	17	Kuang-hsu	23
Total:	142	Total:	99

DISCUSSION

Suzanne Barnett asked James Polachek where reform fit in with respect to modernization, whether modernization should be equated with reform. Mr. Polachek said that a variety of local projects could be conducted by old-fashioned elites but still have pay-offs for modernization. Ms. Barnett suggested—and Mr. Polachek concurred—that such efforts should be distinguished from conscious attempts to modernize. Mary Rankin said that in any case the gap between local reform efforts and Western-inspired reforms narrowed considerably over time, one type of reform activity shading off imperceptibly into other types.

Charlton Lewis said that the crucial factor in 1898 was foreign encroachment in the Yangtze valley, which threw the officials and gentry together in an unprecedented fashion. He added that Nailene Chou's paper suggested that it was established gentry, rather than the new radical reformers, who actually got results. These people— people like Wang Hsien-ch'ien—really had national interests at heart and saw themselves as leaders who were acting in the national interest. This in turn raised the question of how provincial and national interests related to each other. Perhaps we should be less concerned with central-local rivalry and concern ourselves more with techniques by which central and local interests could be integrated. How were local elites trying to establish a new relationship with the center?

Jonathan Ocko wondered how people in one location found out what was happening elsewhere in the empire. There seemed to be a real communications problem. People sometimes read about events in the *Ching-pao* (Peking gazette) two months after the events had taken place. Charlton Lewis said that trade routes were an informal avenue for the flow of information, and Marianne Bastid added that information also was spread via the *mu-fu* system. Officials who received their degrees in the same year often were friends and communicated with each other. Jonathan Ocko pointed out that the government itself made little effort to formalize communication and was highly selective in the information it sent. Paul Cohen suggested that ignorance was a great tactic and that the government might have had a vested interest in *not* formalizing communication.

Esther Morrison said that the creation of Sinkiang province, as described in Nailene Chou's paper, seemed to be an affirmation of the provincial system. It represented a move away from the local level as a center of gravity and confirmed the viability of the provincial unit for purposes of integrating Chinese society politically

Thomas Kennedy challenged the proposition that there existed an inverse ratio between level of government and degree of success in achieving reform. Some successful reforms were carried out at the national level. Mr. Polachek, according to Mr. Kennedy, was also mistaken in giving competition between individuals major credit as a motivating factor in reform. This was true sometimes, but documented cases were relatively few. The myth created by Franz Michael and Stanley Spector died hard. The alleged competition between Tso Tsung-t'ang and Li Hung-chang over the Kiangnan Arsenal and Foochow Shipyard in 1865 was a myth that originated in the *North China Herald* in 1872. Not a shred of documentary evidence had ever turned up to support the charge. Yet it had been perpetuated to this day.

Don Price returned to the question of communication. Liang Ch'i-ch'ao saw the new journalism as something necessary not only for introducing outside ideas into China but also for circulating information within the country and drawing it closer together.

John Schrecker said that while there was no contradiction between nationalism and localism, reform was perhaps more easily undertaken on the local level. Even at the time of the revolution, there was an interest in provincial reform partly because provincial reformers thought that they could do it better.

WOMEN AND REFORM

Linda P. Shin
WOMEN AND REFORM

It is a fairly commonplace observation that great changes have occurred in the status of Chinese women during the twentieth century, and that ideas of sexual equality, the restructuring of social roles, and ideas of female emancipation have played an important part in the social revolution that has been developing in China. Although these developments may not have been central to the revolutionary process, they have been part of it to a remarkable degree. On a recent visit to China I was struck by the emphasis on women's status in the campaign to criticize Confucius and Lin Piao.

Why is there such an extraordinary emphasis on women? Conventional explanations in cross-cultural terms usually focus upon changes in family structure as a result of the impact of industrialization and urbanization. But we know enough from studies that have been done in other nations to realize that industrialization does not axiomatically bring about "liberation" of women, that a great deal hinges upon the cultural and social environment in which industrialization takes place. Likewise, there is no a priori reason why revolutions based on Marxism-Leninism should result in the elevation of the status of women, although the strain of egalitarianism in Marxism does frequently help to create an environment conducive to female emancipation.

The question of women and the restructuring of their social roles has been linked to the revolutionary process in China to a degree and in a way unprecedented in the history of world revolutions; we must begin to find out why this has been so. The focus of this workshop is a period in which some of the basic issues were laid out and a partial framework was set up for many subsequent political developments concerning women. If we are to establish a baseline for assessing twentieth-century changes in the position of women, then, we must go back at least to the nineteenth century, if not all the way to the eighteenth.

There are two broad lines of investigation which might be

followed: what women actually were doing in Chinese society and what perceptions were held of women and their social roles.

What was the role of women in the economy? What part did they take in commercialized agriculture, especially in the production of tea, silk, and cotton; in spinning, weaving, and other occupations in the textile industry? Another category of women was the class of urban women who were active outside of the household: shopkeepers, artisans, "declassed women" such as prostitutes, female slaves, and entertainers. There is the whole question of the legal status of women, not only in the Ch'ing statutes, but also in specific cases involving women and precedents established concerning them. Studies could be made of women rebels and the role of women in secret societies and heterodox sects. Another fruitful area of research is the impact of urbanization and industrialization upon women, notably the development of handicraft and cottage industries which began to transform the economic base of households in certain parts of China. Finally, there is the question of the role of women in the industrial work force as it began to develop in the early twentieth century.

The second broad line of investigation concerns perceptions of women and their social roles, including women's perceptions of themselves and male perceptions of women and their roles. Women's perceptions of themselves can probably be seen through the poems, paintings, and letters of literate gentry women.

There should be a formal cataloguing of the major traditions and conventional stereotypes of women within the Confucian framework, examining not only orthodox thought, but also other strains of thought through materials such as household manuals and children's instruction. Heterodox and non-Confucian traditions such as Buddhism and Taoist sects should also be examined in this light.

Popular images of women are also very interesting. There is the role of heroic women (nü-hsia) in stories from the oral tradition and in written fiction. Chinese notions of sexuality, perceptions of women's physiology, and conventional wisdom concerning women's bodies could also be studied. Some work has already been done on footbinding.

Another issue is how ideas about women underwent change in the late nineteenth and early twentieth centuries. What was the connection between such ideas and other ideas of the era? It would be interesting to study the relationship of men to important women in their lives—their mothers, sisters, daughters, and wives, as well as to other women with whom they were intimate. To what extent did young men identify with their sisters in common struggle against a repressive parental figure? This is a rich area for both psychohistory and the study of women.

What was the role of Western ideas and examples in this period? One point of departure for answering this question might be the missionary movement, which had numerous female participants.

The reform movement had two focal points as far as women were concerned: the antifootbinding campaign and education. Both of these concerns had century-long antecedents, and neither was really all that radical, given gentry traditions and feelings. There was a tradition of educating gentry women within the household, and sympathy for the pain suffered by women with bound feet had found wide expression, as in the Ch'ing novel *Flowers in the Mirror* (*Ching-hua yuan*).

What is significant, in any case, is that discussion of these issues took place in the context of new political and social concerns, causing a fresh challenge to be leveled against the traditional *nei-wai* distinction (men on the outside and women on the inside). As late nineteenth- and early twentieth-century political and intellectual figures began to question what Hao Chang has called "the cosmological myth" of a hierarchy of social relationships, the status of women was inevitably affected.

DISCUSSION*

Mary Rankin spoke about women and the reform movement from the 1890s to 1911. Although the education of women was becoming more accepted through the Ch'ing dynasty, it was difficult for women to play useful social roles outside of the household. Western influence was a vital factor contributing to change in this situation toward the end of the last century. Women missionaries were important as models. Nationalism also encouraged the mobilization of women for national salvation. In 1902–1904 women began taking an active role in nationalist causes. This was a phenomenon confined to the urban elite. By 1911 considerable development had taken place in the political involvement of women. Women had also entered the whole range of new professional careers.

Noriko Kamachi discussed the issue of perceptions of women. Nationalism was the primary moral justification for the education of women. The writings of K'ang Yu-wei and Liang Ch'i-ch'ao gave both moral and self-strengthening justifications for the education of women. Education before the child-bearing years was considered necessary to the building up of a healthy Chinese race. K'ang's arguments against footbinding were nationalistic as well as humanitarian. Nationalism tended to be the primary concern, and woman's issues tended to be subordinated to larger national issues. Few advocated the cause of women for its own sake.

Marianne Bastid spoke about women and educational reform. Women's education sponsored by Chinese began about 1895. The first school providing modern education for women was opened in Shanghai in 1898. Many wives of reformers were involved in the movement for female education. By 1907 there were twelve girls'

*The format of the session on women and reform differed from that of other sessions. Following Linda Shin's introductory remarks, several brief, informal talks were given by workshop participants on areas of their research which concerned the history of women in nineteenth-century China. The talks were followed by questions and discussion.

schools in Shanghai, with an enrollment of 800 students. However, the goals of these institutions were to improve women's conditions in order to enable them to fulfill specific duties. They were founded on the idea that women inculcated public virtues in their children. Nationally, by the end of the Ch'ing, only 1 percent of school-age girls were enrolled in modern schools, as opposed to 5 percent for boys. Chinese women also often found it necessary to go abroad for their higher education.

Suzanne Barnett pointed out the role of Christian missionary schools in educating women. Such schools began in the 1830s. Their goal was to promote the cause of Christianity. Inadvertently missionary schools provided a context in which managerial skills were developed, but there were no outlets for these skills once the girls left the schools. Missionary schools did advance the cause of women's education, however. Moreover, Western women missionaries provided role models for Chinese women.

Dian Murray discussed the part played by women in piratical activity off the Kwangtung coast between 1795 and 1810. From 1807 to 1810 the leader of the pirates was Cheng I-sao, a woman. She was the widow of the previous pirate chief, Cheng I. (Hence the name Cheng I-sao, "wife of Cheng I.") Under her able leadership, the pirates were welded into a formidable force. There were strict regulations governing the presence of women on pirate ships. Women often fought alongside their husbands. In 1810 Cheng I-sao accepted a Ch'ing offer of amnesty and surrendered.

Sue Chung discussed Tz'u-hsi as a female ruler. She pointed out the negative biases in the sources. The fact that Tz'u-hsi was a female ruler, according to Ms. Chung, was only one reason for her negative image. Also to be taken into account was the fact that she was the last real ruler of a dynasty which suffered the twin liabilities of being Manchu and the last dynasty of the imperial era.

Roxane Witke, acting as discussant, noted that the women authors of the late Ch'ing mentioned by Mary Rankin wrote in the same style as men, covered the same range of subject matter, and used the same modes of expression. They often wrote under male pseudonyms and generally adhered to male cultural standards. The same was true of women authors in the 1920s.

Ms. Witke agreed that women tended to make the greatest gains in times of crisis. The Taiping Rebellion afforded an example, although the gains were often paper gains. She noted that the Nien went further in actual implementation of female equality.

As for the bad image of Tz'u-hsi, the phenomenon of blaming a woman for the fall of the dynasty had a partial analogue in the situation that existed during the Cultural Revolution, where male victims tended to be criticized in their absence and only on paper, while their wives were brought to trial as scapegoats and subjected to direct, personal humiliation.

Ms. Witke noted that in modern China there had been very few women who attained independent intellectual status, few writers of note, or women painters, musicians, or scientists. Gains for women had been made on the mass level, rather than at the top. Women at the top often actively supported their husbands. Soong Ch'ing-ling was a good example. They worked for their husbands' causes, but did not have an independent political position. During the Cultural Revolution the personality cult around Chiang Ch'ing resulted from her being Mao's wife, his best student and helpmate. She did not owe her position to any independent political stance.

Suzanne Barnett wondered if there really was such a thing as women's history in China. Linda Shin commented that the problem was the same with all anonymous groups in history, such as poor people or children, for whom there were few formal sources. Joseph Cheng mentioned that Yen Fu and Chiang Kai-shek both attributed much to their mothers. Richard Shek added the examples of Mencius and Ou-yang Hsiu. Susan Jones mentioned that Margery Wolf's work dealt with the prestige accorded women in their role as mothers.

Richard Shek disagreed with Noriko Kamachi's view that women's education was promoted merely for utilitarian reasons. Some writers also asserted the theoretical equality of women.

T'an Ssu-t'ung drew some of his ideas on this subject from Buddhist sources. He maintained that the only difference between men and women was their genitals.

THE NEW COASTAL REFORMERS

Paul A. Cohen
THE NEW COASTAL REFORMERS

Who were the "new coastal reformers"? What is the point of
dealing with them as a group? Did they have important political
or economic interests in common? Or were they, to go back to
James Polachek's phrase, simply like-minded individuals, people
who had similar life experiences and who, in consequence of this,
developed similar outlooks? Finally, in what sense were the
reformers who emerged along the Chinese coast in the 1850s,
1860s, and 1870s new? How did they differ from Chinese
reformers of the hinterland? And what, if anything, can these
differences tell us about processes of change in late imperial China?
(Or, to put it somewhat differently: what roles did the new coastal
reformers play in the overall reform process in nineteenth-century
China? What roles *didn't* they play? And from the roles that they
didn't—or couldn't—play, what insights do we gain into modern
Chinese history?)

The Littoral as a Distinct Cultural Environment
    Before discussing some of the salient characteristics of the
coastal reformers, let me say something about the cultural environment within which they lived and worked, a cultural environment
that differed in fundamental ways from the culture—or cultures—of
the Chinese hinterland. The cultural contrast between the littoral—
or coast—and the hinterland—or interior—can be traced back at least
to the early sixteenth century, when inhabitants of the southeastern
littoral of China became more and more deeply involved in a new
maritime civilization of global embrace. With the establishment,
after the Opium War, of Hong Kong as a British colony and Shanghai,
Canton, Ningpo, Foochow, and Amoy as treaty ports, the differences
between littoral and hinterland widened and the culture of the large
coastal cities acquired an increasingly distinctive stamp that persisted until the middle of the twentieth century.
    The distinctiveness of the littoral culture lay not only in the

contrast with the culture of the Chinese heartland but also in the
very considerable similarities that emerged among the various components of the littoral culture itself. Indeed, it could be argued that
we are dealing here with a variety of "local history," the main
peculiarities of which were a lack of geographical compactness and
the presence of an important shaping influence of an exogenous,
nonlocal nature, the West. What I am saying, in more concrete
terms, is that by the last decade of the nineteenth century cities
like Canton, Hong Kong, Shanghai, Ningpo, Foochow, and Tientsin,
although geographically distant from each other, had come to
share a great deal in common. In physical terms this was manifested
in the heavy flow of goods and people back and forth among the
coastal ports. (Susan Jones has noted the very sizable community
of Ningpo merchants in Shanghai. The same point can be made
with reference to Shanghai merchants in Hong Kong and Cantonese
merchants in Tientsin and Shanghai.) The essential point, though,
is not the matter of movement *per se,* but the degree to which
these cities represented interchangeable parts of a highly cohesive,
self-contained environment. In the final analysis, it was the common cultural, institutional, and economic character of the littoral
that made movement within it natural.

What were some of the characteristics which gave the culture
of the littoral internal coherence and at the same time differentiated
it from the rest of China? First, the littoral was physically and culturally under direct (though highly selective) Western influence.
(This should be immediately qualified by noting that, in strictly
numerical terms, the populations of all littoral cities were over-
whelmingly Chinese.) Second, the economy of the littoral was
geared to commerce, including intertreaty port (or intralittoral)
commerce, littoral-hinterland commerce, and commerce between
the littoral and the West. Third, although there were small numbers
of Chinese and foreign officials and large numbers of Chinese
industrial and nonindustrial working people living in the port cities,
littoral society was dominated by the bourgeois values of its Chinese
and Western merchant elites. Fourth, the littoral was administratively
and legally mixed, with elements of Western sovereignty and practice

alongside of elements of Chinese sovereignty and practice. Fifth, the orientation of the littoral, in sharp contrast to the hinterland, was global and outward-looking, focusing as much on the world as on China.

The New Coastal Reformers: Salient Characteristics

The new coastal reformers who appeared from the 1850s on were products of this environment. The eight I have studied are Wang T'ao, Cheng Kuan-ying, Ma Chien-chung, Ma Liang, Wu T'ing-fang, Tong King-sing, Yung Wing, and Ho Kai. There were of course many others. Susan Jones has mentioned Hu Kuang-yung. The overseas Chinese personalities discussed by Michael Godley were also identified with the littoral.

Although the new coastal reformers differed from each other in many ways, their biographies and careers reveal common patterns, including attendance at missionary schools, study and travel abroad, knowledge of foreign languages, conversion to Christianity, employment with foreigners, and involvement in new kinds of careers (such as law, journalism, modern business). In contrast with the more orthodox elites of the hinterland, few of the coastal reformers studied for and competed in the civil-service examinations.

The new coastal reformers also shared a common world outlook. One aspect of this was their cosmopolitanism. Although some were much more Westernized than others, all of them were on close, familiar terms with Westerners and saw the West as having important contributions to make to China in both the institutional and technological realms. At the same time, they all retained commitments to Chinese culture or to the Chinese nation, the nature and depth of the commitment varying from individual to individual.

A second feature of the outlook of the coastal reformers was their nationalism. The social gulf between Chinese and Westerners in the littoral was great, and Chinese—even the most influential— seldom achieved full respectability in the eyes of the Westerners. (One is reminded of the case of Yung Wing, who had his American citizenship revoked as a result of the exclusion legislation.) The Westerners' sense of superiority was also reflected in their continual disparagement of Chinese culture and government. In the face of this assault, feelings of inferiority, shame, and anger were easily aroused in Chinese living in the littoral, and nationalism for many of them provided new access to dignity and self-respect.

Finally, the new coastal reformers shared a strong commitment to the development of Sino-Western commerce, partly (at least in some instances) for reasons of self-interest, partly because of the positive benefits that would accrue to Chinese society, and partly out of a spirit of economic nationalism (it being generally believed that commercial competition with the West would reduce the drain of Chinese wealth).

In terms of the overall process of change in nineteenth-century China, the most important contribution of the coastal reformers lay in the realm of innovation. This is seen both in the activities they engaged in and in the reforms they advocated in their writings. The cultural environment of the littoral was ideally suited to encourage innovation. It furnished a whole range of positive stimuli, in the form of new ideas, new institutions, new practices, and new technologies. Equally important, the littoral was relatively free of the taboos and constraints which, in the hinterland, often served to discourage or inhibit introduction of the new.

In stressing the pioneering role of the coastal reformers, their contribution as innovators, I do not mean to suggest that they were the first to introduce a reformist outlook into the Chinese setting. As we have seen again and again in this workshop, there was a persistent tradition of reform in Chinese history, exponents of which can be found in virtually every era and a resurgence of which was taking place in the mid-nineteenth century partly as a consequence of the Taiping Rebellion and quite independent of Western influence. Rather, I would emphasize the degree to which the coastal reformers, in attacking the dysfunctions they found in Chinese society, were prepared to learn from and emulate the West, even at the cost of fundamental changes in Chinese culture. In this respect, it seems to me, the reformers of the littoral went a good deal farther, prior to 1890, than their reform-minded contemporaries in the hinterland.

The Limitations of the Coastal Reformers

In the context of China as a whole, the coastal reformers worked under very real limitations. And for the historian looking back over this period, the limitations are extremely illuminating. They may be divided into two basic types: lack of political power and lack of social and cultural standing or legitimacy.

When I speak of the coastal reformers' lack of political power, I don't mean to suggest that they had no access to the hinterland power structure or that they were wholly without influence on the thinking and actions of the more powerful officials of the day. Quite to the contrary, among the great self-strengthening officials, from the Taiping period on, there was vigorous competition for the talents of the littoral reformers, and many of the latter served on the staffs of the former. This did not, however, translate into real power. Moreover, what the coastal reformers gained in status by working for people like Li Hung-chang, Chang Chih-tung, and Liu K'un-i, they lost in innovative potential. Frustrated in their efforts to introduce comprehensive reform, the best they could hope for was to serve as instruments of limited, defensive modernization.

In talking about the lack of social standing and cultural legitimacy of the coastal reformers, I find it helpful to focus on two facets of their life situations that seriously undermined whatever leverage they might have had for promoting change in the hinterland culture. I refer to the related, but not entirely identical, phenomena of collaboration and acculturation, both of which phenomena are especially revealing when placed in a comparative framework.

In my book on Wang T'ao I touched briefly on the psychological ramifications of collaboration. All of the littoral reformers were connected at one time or another with foreign institutions (missionary societies, commercial firms, government organs, Christian schools). "Insofar as they lived and worked with people who benefited directly from Western imperialism, they too, in some sense, became beneficiaries of this imperialism ... Such collaboration, from the standpoint of ... hinterland Chinese, was the ultimate form of 'sell-out' ... and since few collaborators were so emancipated

as to be entirely impervious to hinterland norms, feelings of shame
inevitably developed." An antidote to such feelings, for at least
some of the littoral reformers, was nationalism, which helped to
restore their lost sense of pride.[1]

Collaboration can also be viewed from the perspective of
political power and culture change. In many colonial settings, of
course, the native collaborator, in return for his collaboration, is
armed with substantial political power. He becomes part of the
ruling class. For illustration of this, one may turn to India and
certain African societies. Even China, in the Ch'ing dynasty, may
technically be viewed as a Manchu colony, the successful operation
of which was heavily dependent on native Chinese collaboration.
(An important distinguishing feature of the Manchu colony was
that, in contrast with Western colonies, the culture of the colonial
power was subordinated to that of the colonized.)

When the collaboration of the coastal reformers is viewed
from the perspective of political power, it seems clearly to have
been short-circuited. Except in Hong Kong, the littoral reformers
did not acquire political power from their Western associates. What
they got from them, aside from occasional economic advantage,
was a new cultural perspective, a new package of skills, techniques,
ideas, and knowledge. It is precisely here, of course, that collaboration becomes indistinguishable from the phenomenon of acculturation.

Here again the perspective gained from comparison with other
cultures is helpful in clarifying the Chinese case. Rhoads Murphey
poses the problem succinctly: "The treaty port Indian became without apology, and with all his fundamental Westernization, the
dominant modern Indian of independence, the spokesman to and
for nearly all politically conscious Indians; the role of the treaty
port Ceylonese, Burmese, Thais, Vietnamese, Indonesians, and
Filipinos was similar. All of these antecedents of Shanghai and
Tientsin had indeed worked a revolution. Why should not the
apparently closely similar pattern in China eventually produce
similar results?"[2]

The answer of course—and I think Murphey would agree—is

that the Chinese pattern really wasn't closely similar. Murphey's research focuses mainly on the strength and resilience of the Chinese economy. I would like to respond to the question he raises somewhat differently by looking at the relationship between acculturation and culture change. In many modernizing contexts, including non-Asian cases as well as the Asian ones cited by Murphey, there has tended to be a direct correlation between acculturation and culture change, the most acculturated people often being the prime movers in the change process. In the Chinese instance, however, although acculturation was important in the *launching* of culture change—the initial, pioneering phase of the process—the acculturated Chinese was unable to capitalize on his initial advantage. Indeed, what had been an advantage—his greater exposure to exogenous, Western-derived influences—easily turned into a liability. Too much acculturation, through contamination or through a simple process of distancing, served to handcuff the pioneer reformer of the Chinese coast.

There are implications here, also, for the difficult issue of radicalism. In my book I raised the question: who was more radical, K'ang Yu-wei or Yung Wing? Mao Tse-tung or Sun Yat-sen? My choices, unhesitatingly, were K'ang and Mao, not because they were "newer" than Yung and Sun, but because they spearheaded important attempts to integrate change with tradition (the primary mechanism for doing this, in each instance, being the identification and reinterpretation of traditions which, although authentically Chinese, had strongly unorthodox affiliations). Again, the problem of distance. It would seem that the more acculturated one became in modern China, the less chance one had to generate radical change, for acculturation, in making a person newer, also made him more remote from the native scene.[3]

If we step back and look at the limitations I've been discussing—the relative powerlessness of the littoral reformers, their abortive collaboration with imperialism, and the process of acculturation they all underwent to a greater or lesser degree—what implications can we draw? What do the constraints experienced by these men tell us about the China of their day?

First, they seem to suggest a great deal more cultural strength in the Chinese hinterland than has sometimes been posited. I am reminded of Saundra Sturdevant's argument that opposition to the Wusung Railway was grounded not in Confucian cultural resistance to innovation but in political opposition to innovations that were not under effective Chinese control. Could not the same kind of argument be extended to culture change in general? A great deal of the resistance to such change in the latter half of the nineteenth century was, I suspect, based less on absolute resistance to change than on resistance to change over which the Chinese themselves lacked control, or, following I-fan Ch'eng's analysis of Wang Hsien-ch'ien, change that took place within a context that failed to measure up to certain stringent Chinese ethical standards. The innovating men of the littoral, if one accepts this argument, suffered a crippling liability. They could innovate all they wanted to. But their acculturation had gone too far for them to gain for their innovative behavior the stamp of legitimacy.

Second, the inability of the coastal reformers to gain substantial power within the hinterland political structure suggests that here also there may have been a greater residue of strength than has generally been acknowledged. The judgment of political weakness has been occasioned, in great measure, by the observed inability or unwillingness of the Chinese government in the nineteenth century to take certain kinds of positive actions in coping with its problems. What is overlooked in this assessment is that *negative* action, the capacity to prevent certain kinds of things from happening, is also a form of political strength. The hidden significance of the fact that coastal reformers like Wang T'ao, Cheng Kuan-ying, and Wu T'ing-fang never really were able to crack the hinterland power structure is that the people in the hinterland were able to determine themselves, right down to 1912, just to whom they would give power and to whom they would not.

Third, and closely related to this last point, the inability of the coastal reformers to achieve more than they did in the last decades of the nineteenth century was a direct consequence of a

fact which everyone knows and everyone forgets, namely that
China as a whole was at no point a semicolony, that the phenomenon
of semicolonialism—or in the case of Hong Kong colonialism—was
confined, for all intents and purposes, to the urban culture of the
Chinese littoral. Had the entire Chinese empire—and not just the
littoral—come under the aegis of semicolonial domination after the
Opium War, it is a safe guess that collaboration and acculturation
would have been positive assets for the coastal reformers, enabling
them to play much fuller roles than they did in the overall process
of change.

The Role of the West in Nineteenth-Century China
    In conclusion, I should like to return to the point made at the
outset concerning the cultural cleavage between littoral and hinterland China and to offer a tentative framework for approaching the
tangled question of the role of the West in nineteenth-century
Chinese history. This seems to be another one of those areas, like
local versus central and politics versus ideology, where many of us,
partly for purposes of scholarly salesmanship, sin by defining the
importance of one locus of emphasis in terms of the relative
unimportance of another—and alternative—locus. In addressing the
question of the sources of change in nineteenth-century China, I
detect a swing among Western scholars from what was at one point
unquestionably an overemphasis upon exogenous forces toward
what I fear may become an equally excessive stress on endogenous
factors. The framework I would like to suggest is very simple and
schematic. But it has the merit of keeping in sharp focus both kinds
of factors.
    The basic premise on which my framework rests is that the
cultures of the littoral and the hinterland in nineteenth-century
China were fundamentally different. If this premise is accepted,
we can then proceed in a number of directions. We can analyze, as
many members of this workshop have done, the influences—
economic, cultural, intellectual, and so on—that flowed back and
forth between these two worlds, the manifold ways in which they
interacted over time. We can also move toward defining in more

precise language the very different parts played by the West in the two cultural environments. This is relatively easy to do in the case of the littoral, where we confront a situation that can accurately be described as semicolonial—or in the Hong Kong case colonial—and where the shaping role of the West was enormous, affecting directly or indirectly all individuals and spheres of life.

Defining the roles played by the West in the evolution of the hinterland culture is a much more demanding task, since these roles varied greatly in different places, at different levels of society, and at different times. One point which at this juncture hardly needs stressing is that the West did not introduce into the Chinese hinterland culture the impetus to change. What it did accomplish, gradually and in very subtle ways, was a transformation of the overall context within which the indigenous impulse to change operated in the nineteenth century. It did this, as far as I can see, in three basic ways. First, as has long been recognized, it generated new problems. Second—and here we have a phenomenon that is only now beginning to be studied—it supplied a new framework for the perception and understanding of old problems—problems which, in some instances, had been festering in China for centuries. And third, the West furnished, for the solution of problems both old and new, a radically different repository of ideas and technologies.

Linda P. Shin
WU T'ING-FANG: A MEMBER OF A COLONIAL ELITE
AS COASTAL REFORMER

In this brief talk I would like to discuss Wu's experiences as
a young man in Hong Kong and England before he entered the
Ch'ing civil service in 1882 at the age of 40, and then I would like
to present for discussion some of the ideas I have developed at
greater length in my draft manuscript entitled "Wu T'ing-fang,
1842–1922: Colonialism and Nationalism in Modern China." My
study of Wu is a "social portrait" of a member of an early generation of the modern Chinese bourgeoisie. I know it's risky to do
social history from the perspective of one individual, and so what
I have tried to do is to suggest ways in which Wu might be representative of a larger group, and to leave it to others to verify or
dispute my suggestions.

Wu was born in humble circumstances in 1842 in Singapore,
the son of an overseas Chinese merchant from the Canton delta
district of Hsin-hui. At the age of four *sui,* Wu returned with his
family to China and lived in a suburb of Canton, where he began
his education in the traditional mode but soon switched to a mission school. Apparently with a letter of introduction from a missionary, Wu moved to Hong Kong in 1855 at the age of 14 and
enrolled in St. Paul's College, an Anglican school established in
1843. Presumably at this time, if not earlier, Wu was baptized,
although he later rejected Christianity and had extremely harsh
words to say about Christian missionaries.

Wu was characteristic of St. Paul's alumni in that rather than
taking up a religious career, he became a translator for the English-
language newspaper, the Hong Kong *Daily Press,* upon his gradua-
tion in 1859. Two years later, in 1861, he got a job as clerk and
interpreter in the Hong Kong courts, a position he held until 1874,
when he left to go to England to obtain legal training.

Wu was also a pioneer in modern Chinese journalism. In 1860
(or 1861) he founded the first Chinese-language daily, the *Chung-*

ngoi san-po (or *Chung-wai hsin-pao*), using the London Missionary
Society's Chinese press to put out a "Chinese issue" of the *Daily
Press*. He maintained this newspaper for over a decade. Largely a
shipping sheet, it also carried translations of important documents
and news items about the Western world.

Wu also married well. His bride was Ho Miao-ling, Ho Kai's
sister, daughter of a rather famous early convert to Christianity and
wealthy businessman, Ho Fu-t'ang. Wu's wife's family financed his
studies in England and later arranged Wu's introduction to Li Hung-
chang.

A few incidents that took place during the years when Wu was
growing to maturity suggest something about the kind of society
Hong Kong was at the time:

(1) In 1857 in the midst of the Anglo-French War with China,
there was a panic when a Chinese baker was accused of attempting
to poison the entire European community. The baker was released
because of lack of evidence, but a massive press campaign condemned
the colonial administration for its supposed leniency. A number of
Chinese (representing all social classes) apparently left Hong Kong
during this crisis and returned to the mainland. Virulent anti-Chinese
feelings were mobilized by the press. I think that this contributed
to Wu's growing awareness of the power of the press in mobilizing
public opinion. It also illustrates the fundamental gulf between the
colonizers and colonized, which affected all aspects of life in the
colony, and which was most visibly symbolized by segregation in
public and private institutions throughout Hong Kong.

(2) The conditions in the courts during the decade or so that
Wu was employed there are also significant. In most governmental
agencies, Chinese clerks and shroffs did the bulk of the work and
frequently assumed great responsibilities, but advancement to the
higher ranks was generally barred to them and reserved for British
civil servants or for Hong Kong residents of European descent,
especially Portuguese. Wu's boss, for example, was R. A. Rosario,
a Hong Kong resident of Portuguese descent and the only non-
Chinese member of the Police Magistrate Court interpretation staff.
Rosario apparently was not a very good interpreter—in 1877 all the

major Hong Kong officials, including Wu himself, declared him to be honest but incompetent—yet Wu's salary and those of his Chinese colleagues were lower than Rosario's. Although Wu did not say so, it must have been galling to work harder and more efficiently for less compensation.

(3) In 1870 there was an incident involving another Chinese translator which I think must have quickened the dissatisfaction of Wu and his colleagues. A man named Ng A-ts'ün, clerk and interpreter for the Surveyor-General, applied for a two-week sick leave because he had tuberculosis. Ng was dismissed, whereupon he applied for a twelve-month leave of absence, a regular privilege for British civil servants. The governor refused to grant the leave, which he viewed as a "ridiculous privilege for a Chinese civil servant";* he also ruled that Chinese civil servants could not receive the customary bonus. Wu and other Chinese felt that the only explanation for this action was race distinction; they viewed the decision as a reprimand to Chinese civil servants for having dared to consider themselves on a par with British and European civil servants.

A rash of resignations followed this incident. Ch'en Ai-t'ing, Wu's friend and a collaborator on the *Wah-tze yat-po* (*Hua-tzu jih-pao*) resigned and later went as Chinese consul-general to Cuba. Two others also were said to have left the civil service in Hong Kong and to have joined the Ch'ing administration.

At this point in his life, Wu could have joined the staff of Ch'en Lan-pin, Minister to the United States, Spain, and Peru. Instead, however, he decided to go to England to study law at Lincoln's Inn, one of the four inns of court. In the nineteenth century the inns of court were still in some respects finishing schools for young aristocrats and places where ambitious young men hoped to form connections with the important political figures of their generation.

Why did Wu decide on this course? It did not make sense, certainly, in a Chinese context, where the only legal career to

* "Report by Dr. Eitel ... on the Supply of Interpreters," enclosed in Pope-Hennessy to Earl of Kimberley, October 31, 1880, No. 174, Great Britain: Colonial Office, 129/190.

speak of was that of *mu-yu* who specialized in law within a Confucian framework. If Wu wanted to rise in Chinese society, surely
he would have gone back to the Classics and tried the regular
official route. The course he chose made sense only in a colonial
context, where membership in the bar conferred great prestige.
Since there were few real aristocrats among the British residents of
Hong Kong, such membership was even more prestigious there than
back home in England. Indeed, together with wealthy merchants
and a smattering of other professional men, the barristers formed
an elite of high bourgeoisie who directed the affairs of the government under the various governors. For an ambitious young Chinese,
like Wu, the study of law thus offered an opportunity to escape
second-class status and acquire a measure of power and influence
in Hong Kong society.

Colonial environments such as Hong Kong engendered an early
commitment to modern nationalism among Wu and others of his
generation (Paul Cohen has shown this in the case of Wang T'ao).
For many Chinese, especially the coastal reformers, the colonial
situation brought forth a burning sense of shame and indignation
that evoked an early nationalist critique.

On the other hand I think that Wu's decision to become a
barrister also reflected his belief that membership in the bar
constituted a nonracial key to elite status. Wu appears at least in
part to have accepted the ideal vision of the British Empire and
the culture upon which it was based, in which theoretically an
impartial and justly administered law reigned supreme and upward
mobility was possible for anyone capable of attaining it.

In common with members of colonial "native" elites in other
parts of the Third World, Wu seems to have developed a split or
polarity in his perceptions of the mother country. On one hand,
the ideals of the mother country's civilization beckoned, promising
individual liberty, equality of opportunity, "the rights of man";
on the other hand he was directly confronted by the realities of
the colonial situation: segregated communities, inferior status,
restricted mobility.

In one form or another, Wu's dualism with respect to colonialism stayed with him throughout his life and was reflected in all his major political acts. I believe he never reconciled these two contrasting visions: the ideal and the social practice of Britain and the Western world.

In 1877, when Wu had just finished at Lincoln's Inn and had been called to the bar, there were two attempts made to recruit him into the Ch'ing administration, one by Kuo Sung-tao and Liu Hsi-hung upon their arrival in London to establish the new Chinese legation there, and then subsequently by Li Hung-chang, who wanted to use him as a legal and foreign affairs adviser. Wu haggled over salary with Kuo and Liu, but although they really wanted him, he was not interested in a low-ranking post. His father had died (leaving him a sizable inheritance) and he took the opportunity to decline all offers. When he returned to China, nevertheless, Li Hung-chang offered him a post at the salary he wanted, 6000 taels, and Wu appears at first to have leaned toward accepting it. He finally decided against it, however, possibly because of the backlash against Kuo Sung-tao's published diaries and the criticism of the use of foreign-trained men that developed in late 1877.

It would not be unfair, I think, to discern a certain opportunism in Wu's major career decisions. Upon his return to Hong Kong, he took up a colonial career, marked by a very close relationship with the maverick governor, Sir John Pope-Hennessy, who used Wu to promote the interests of the Chinese community against those of the local British merchants. It was a very stormy period, the highlights of which were Wu's appointment by Pope-Hennessy as the first Chinese member of the Legislative Council (legislative in name only, I might add), and his selection as the first Chinese to serve as magistrate. In 1882 Pope-Hennessy left the colony. Around the same time a speculative craze in land purchases by Chinese collapsed, leaving Wu (who had been involved) some 45,000 dollars in debt. In straitened financial circumstances and deprived of his previous political base, Wu decided to enter Li Hung-chang's *mu-fu.* From this point on, his interests and those of the Ch'ing elite merged.

Wu T'ing-fang was part of the modern bourgeoisie that grew

up within the context of colonial enterprise in China and Southeast
Asia. How did Hong Kong fit into this context? I do not think that
Hong Kong was a unique or isolated example of British colonialism
in the Chinese context, but rather its most complete expression.
The treaty ports were also colonial societies, but Hong Kong was
the most developed and institutionalized example. These societies
were characterized by a caste system based on a hierarchy of ethnic
groups, which in turn was grounded on the assumption of the
superiority of the white race.

Wu developed a kind of intellectual strategy for coping with
imperialism which reflected the special status that he and people
of his social milieu had. This strategy, which may have become more
widespread in the twentieth century, was marked by receptivity
toward British capitalist expansion and opposition to Russian territorial expansion. It included a conviction that there was a deep
historical trend toward ultimate Sino-Western harmony, in which
professional elites everywhere—the enlightened forces of commerce—
would together advance toward future fusion. He also believed in
the reciprocal contributions of Western political institutions and
Chinese spirituality as expressed in Confucian social relations.
Armed with such beliefs, Wu and others employed a strategy
designed to appeal to the consciences of the Western public and
Western decision-makers. The boycott of 1905 against American
goods was an example of this strategy, in that it reflected implicitly
Wu's confidence in the culture and institutions of the Anglo-Saxon
world.

Wu's attitude did not fundamentally challenge the framework
of imperialism, only its implementation. Wu was a social conservative
and his conservatism was linked to Chinese cultural norms and an
elite tradition. British colonial practices in Hong Kong and perhaps
elsewhere facilitated a blending of the bourgeoisie with the traditional
elite. The British encouraged a system of indirect rule by natural
leaders of the "natives," so long as no general conflict of custom
existed and so long as the natural leaders could maintain order. This
led to a situation in which bourgeois Chinese functioned, in a way
strikingly similar to that of traditional elites in China proper, as

intermediaries between the masses and the central authority. The Chinese bourgeoisie of Hong Kong performed traditional elite functions, seen most clearly in their establishment of charitable institutions and their control of clans and *hui-kuan.* This must have helped establish their legitimacy in traditional terms vis-à-vis the Chinese masses in Hong Kong. The purchase of Chinese ranks and titles further strengthened their legitimacy.

This process facilitated the blending of the bourgeoisie with the traditional gentry, perhaps providing a framework for the transformation of these classes into a new hybrid elite in the cities, part bourgeois, part bureaucrat, part landlord. Social conservatism characterized this "hybrid" elite. It had a vested interest in stability and tried to adapt as much as possible to the system as it existed.

People like Wu T'ing-fang wanted to accept the ideal vision of the colonial system because that was the only way they could be acculturated and still salvage some measure of pride and dignity. However, the colonial environment also bred new forms of national awareness, and Wu began to have a sense of himself as part of a nation with a long unified history and cultural tradition, as well as a well-defined elite heritage. However marginally, Wu was linked from the start to an existing Chinese elite and a functioning Chinese political system. At no point was he forced to function as a complete outsider.

Wu was a member of a generation of colonized Chinese who were the first to have intimate knowledge of the West and to communicate this knowledge to their contemporaries. After the Sino-Japanese War, new political and intellectual figures, seeing no reason to accept the inevitability of imperialist domination, developed new tactics and strategies to deal with it. Increasingly, as the revolutionary process unfolded, Wu T'ing-fang's generation were left as bystanders.

Louis T. Sigel
FOREIGN POLICY INTERESTS AND ACTIVITIES OF THE
TREATY-PORT CHINESE COMMUNITY

As Kwang-Ching Liu very succinctly noted in his presentation,
the breakthrough in reform comes with the ideas being realized
through power in the political sphere. In this context, it behooves
us to reassess the significance of the radical reform movement of
1898 and the ideas and writings of K'ang Yu-wei and Liang Ch'i-
ch'ao. It has been claimed that the reform movement led by K'ang
Yu-wei initiated a major change in the Chinese approach to international affairs by developing a nationalistic foreign policy and
that during the last decade of the Ch'ing the reformers' nationalistic
conception of foreign affairs became almost universally accepted.[1]
During this decade, Chinese foreign policy was indeed characterized
by a firm ideological commitment to the realization of full sovereignty for China and not simply to restricting those foreign activities which posed potential or actual threats of foreign control.
However, to speak of "policy" in the late Ch'ing, whether domestic
or foreign, is to becloud the issue. This kind of Western political
mechanism is largely absent; the norm tends to remain an emphasis
on the man rather than the means. Men generally gained high office
and were assigned to deal with particular problems facing the
dynasty because they were believed to possess the ability to effectively cope with the difficulties at hand.

It is therefore relevant to associate officials with the policies
they propose and administer, and it is important to identify the
Chinese diplomats and negotiators involved in the struggle to
reassert China's national rights. Among these foreign affairs experts
who demanded foreign recognition of Chinese sovereignty, one is
hard put to identify the intellectual influence of K'ang Yu-wei and
Liang Ch'i-ch'ao. This is not surprising since K'ang and Liang had
only a superficial knowledge of the West and their roots were deep
in the Confucian tradition.

The foreign policy approach of the radical reformers was

essentially a product of the impact of Western ideas and Western theories of international law. Although it is true that the radical reformers adopted the Western notion of sovereignty and assigned great importance to foreign relations, they were not the first nor were they the most important group to bring these ideas into political realization. Cheng Kuan-ying, the foremost representative of the period of intellectual innovation leading up to the radical reform movement and possibly the most influential reform writer of the early 1890s, was much more familiar with Western institutions and practices. His essays reflected the attitudes of the developing mercantile class in the treaty ports and it was this community that played the most prominent role in the adoption and implementation of a more nationalistic conception of foreign affairs. Also significant, in people like Cheng Kuan-ying, there was a social as well as intellectual continuity from the self-strengtheners' *mu-fu* of the nineteenth century to the post-Boxer reform diplomats active in rights recovery.

Cheng Kuan-ying's reform program represented a coalescence of the political and economic interests of the comprador-merchant community of the littoral with China's national interest. The members of this community thus viewed their call for the adoption of Western institutions by China as a means of achieving national strength and prosperity as well as of pressing their own advantage. The same logic prevailed in their quest for active government support to overcome the trade advantages enjoyed by their foreign competitors and in their advocacy of the elimination of the restrictions of the traditional economy.

It was also the Chinese treaty-port society that first generated a call for far-reaching reforms to regain China's legitimate prerogatives. They called for the abolition of extraterritoriality and for the return of economic sovereignty through Chinese tariff autonomy and the exclusion of foreign vessels from domestic shipping. Their proposals stressed industrial development and urged government protection for Chinese private initiative in railway, mining, banking, and manufacturing enterprises. The treaty-port community also protested against the injustices and humili-

ations suffered by Chinese at the hands of foreigners and called for
a Chinese government strong enough to prevent the Westerners
from committing offenses forbidden by Western law.

Individuals from the comprador-merchant sector had been
working to safeguard and recover China's national rights since the
middle of the nineteenth century. The early projects for industrial
development to which the pioneer comprador-entrepreneurs
devoted their wealth were seen as challenges to the threat of foreign domination in shipping, mining, insurance, and railways. The
emphasis consistently was on the need for China to preserve her
economic sovereignty or, as Cheng Kuan-ying put it, "to wage
commercial war." The comprador-merchants felt that control over
China's wealth was of vital concern particularly in the development
of railways and mining. With the founding of the Kaiping Mines
and the T'ang-shan railway, T'ang T'ing-shu (Tong King-sing) set
the example by his efforts to deny foreign ownership entirely and
to minimize foreign participation in management.

One area of concern in the minds of treaty-port merchants
was the problem of frontier defense and the need to safeguard
China's borderlands. In the late 1860s and early 1870s Cheng
Kuan-ying proposed that the Ch'ing government should change
the traditional policy of relative noninterference in the internal
administration of the tributary states and should establish effective
control under the guise of sending high officials to these states to
advise them on the means to achieve wealth and power. China
should take the lead in providing funds for reform, to be repaid on
a yearly basis, and in providing training for officials and officers,
so as to assist the tributary states in protecting themselves. By
having these states accept mutual assistance, China could make
them mutually dependent.[2]

During the 1880s, pressure on the tributaries came from
France in Vietnam and from Japan in Korea. Prominent treaty-
port men participated in both crises and urged the Chinese government to adopt the policies and techniques of the European imperial
powers to achieve and institutionalize Chinese colonial control.

They sought the assertion of Chinese authority in these previously autonomous kingdoms.

The treaty-port community was particularly active in the effort to gain dominance over Korean affairs in the 1880s and 1890s. In September 1882, Li Hung-chang and Ma Chien-chung became concerned with the possible political consequences of the loan agreements the Japanese Minister to Korea was attempting to conclude and sought alternative Chinese loan funds to assist the Korean authorities. T'ang T'ing-shu proposed the negotiation of a loan from rich Chinese merchants who would jointly pledge shares and be guaranteed repayment from customs revenues and Korean mineral wealth.[3] Subsequently, in early October, T'ang arranged to provide Korea with a loan of 500,000 taels drawn from the funds of the China Merchants Steam Navigation Company (Chao-shang-chü) and the Kaiping Mining Company to send people into the Korean interior to carry out mining surveys. After the selection of sites for mining development, these people were to request permission from the Korean government and negotiate regulations according to Sino-Western precedents. If the Koreans desired to undertake mining development themselves, they would utilize mining experts from the Kaiping Mines. The Koreans could also develop mines jointly with the China Merchants Steam Navigation Company and the Kaiping Mining Company.[4]

Subsequently in December of 1882, T'ang T'ing-shu accompanied P. G. von Möllendorff and his younger clansman, T'ang Shao-yi, to Korea where they were to set up a maritime customs service. On arrival in Korea, T'ang T'ing-shu rode into the interior together with an English engineer named Burnett to visit the native mines.[5] T'ang subsequently submitted a report advising the encouragement of industrial enterprise by means of mines and railways and the securing of a monopoly interest in this development for China. As loan negotiations proceeded in Shanghai, T'ang demanded full control over the use of the money and wanted to give the money only on the guarantee of the Chinese government. Because of these delays it was not until the end of January 1883 that the first installment of the loan funds could be raised by the China Merchants Steam Navigation Company.[6]

During the next several years in Korea, the Japanese and Chinese were engaged in an active mercantile competition for control of the Korean trade. Both encouraged the expansion of their merchant firms into the ports of Korea. Chinese traders came to play a leading role in Korean commercial life during this period, aided by the extension of China Merchants Steam Navigation Company steamship routes to encompass Korea. The Chinese authorities sought protection for Chinese merchants in Korea and the commercial efforts were so effective that Korean merchants staged a boycott in the late 1880s to support the demand that Chinese firms leave Seoul and relocate in Inchon.[7] Subsequently in 1892 when an additional loan was required to assist the Korean government in purchasing a German steamship, funds were provided by the Korean branch of a large Cantonese trading firm based in Shanghai.[8]

During the decade 1884 to 1894, when there was relative success in transforming Korea into a Chinese protectorate, key administrative and advisory roles were played by young officials with close links to the treaty-port community. T'ang Shao-yi was the chief adviser to Yuan Shih-k'ai during these years and served as Acting Resident during both of Yuan's furloughs in China. T'ang's first cousin, Liang Ju-hao, and Hsu Jun's brother-in-law, Ts'ai Shao-ch'i, both played prominent roles in Yuan's bureaucratic network. T'ang Shao-yi also helped Yuan in the recruitment of foreign-educated experts, as in the case of his fellow clansman T'ang En-t'ung. Thus, both in the commercial warfare to control the Korean economy and in the political effort to establish a Chinese "imperialist" presence within the Korean government, Chinese from the treaty-port sector took prominent parts.

Treaty-port Chinese also played an interesting, if less successful, role in the Chinese effort to resist French encroachments in Vietnam in the 1880s. In the deliberations over Vietnamese policy in the face of an anticipated French advance on Tongking, the need for a better understanding of the state of military affairs in

Vietnam and for a close liaison with the Vietnamese authorities was soon recognized. At the suggestion of Governor Ch'ing-yü of Kwangsi, it was decided to use the China Merchants Steam Navigation Company as a cover for a Chinese mission to inform the King of Vietnam of the imminent French attack and to formulate a coordinated defense policy. *Taotai* T'ang T'ing-keng, the Canton branch manager of the Chao-shang-chü, received orders for a company agent to proceed to Vietnam using a grain shipment as cover for a mission of espionage and diplomacy. He responded energetically, organizing a small but effective team comprising three military men and three Chao-shang-chü assistants. T'ang received his instructions on January 15, 1882 and by January 18 was in Hong Kong awaiting a ship bound for Vietnam. From one of the steamship captains of the China Merchants Steam Navigation Company in Hong Kong, he learned of recent changes in French naval deployment and decided to send one of the military agents with a company manager as cover to assume charge of the Saigon branch office of the China Merchants Steam Navigation Company and have them send reports of all they learned to Canton.[9]

Although never directed to do so, T'ang decided it was important to go to Tongking and Haiphong in person to assess French military strength and to gain other information useful for defense. From Haiphong, he dispatched another of the military agents, accompanied by a company manager, to proceed to Laokay to make inquiries about Liu Yung-fu and French activities in that region. He instructed these subordinates to make careful surveys of the riverine routes and report to the authorities in Canton as soon as possible. This agent was then to proceed to the Lang-son-Cao-bang region to continue his intelligence work.[10]

T'ang finally arrived in Hue on the morning of February 11, 1882 for negotiations with the King of Vietnam over a coordinated defense. Although unable to meet with the King personally he negotiated with Nguyen Van Tuong, the president of the Vietnamese Board of Revenue and one of the most powerful officials in the Hue court. The Vietnamese were unable to come

up with any means of defense of their own and sought substantial
Chinese assistance and protection. Before leaving Vietnam, T'ang
left instructions for his subordinates to compile detailed and accurate
maps of Vietnam in Chinese characters and to spy on French military activities. The China Merchants Steam Navigation Company
offices in Haiphong, Saigon, and Hue were to use their contacts and
facilities to assist in observing the French and to keep China quickly
and accurately informed of developments in Vietnam through the
home branches of the firm.[11] They served this important function
from the summer of 1882 to the autumn of 1883.

A more positive role in encouraging Chinese action to resist
Western imperialism was played in the 1880s by T'ang T'ing-shu,
the elder brother of T'ang T'ing-keng and one of the acknowledged
leaders of treaty-port society. In the summer of 1883, T'ang T'ing-
shu went on a mission to Europe ostensibly to purchase modern
machinery for the Kaiping Mines. He also sought to investigate the
trade potential for Chinese products on the European market and
to evaluate European industries that might serve as examples for
China. Traveling by way of the Suez Canal and Beirut, T'ang kept
a close watch on reports about Vietnam appearing in the English
and French wire services. Sensitive to the threat that a French
protectorate in Vietnam would pose to Yunnan and Kwangtung,
he wired his congratulations and sense of relief on learning in Rome
that Li Hung-chang had been appointed commander-in-chief of the
military forces of the three frontier provinces and commissioner
for dealing with the Franco-Vietnamese matter. T'ang further
offered Li his services if he could assist in the affair. In Milan,
while surveying the raw silk trade, T'ang received a reply from Li
accepting his offer and asking him to assess French public opinion
on the question of sending troops to Vietnam and to discover the
attitudes of the other foreign countries. After carefully studying
foreign newspapers and discussing the situation with various civil
and military officials in Italy, T'ang sent Li his assessment.[12]

T'ang T'ing-shu arrived in Paris on the evening of June 7 and
started collecting information that he thought might be of use to
Li Hung-chang. He renewed his acquaintance with a French bank

director he had known in China and discussed the situation in Vietnam. Through this friend, T'ang had an interview with the French War Minister, who reportedly had reservations about France's Indo-Chinese involvement. Brooding over the immoral behavior of the French in Vietnam, T'ang wanted "to cause the people of the world to know how the French are oppressing Vietnam, what kind of grievous disgrace Vietnam is, how it is a tributary of China, and the reasons given by China for sending troops in order to shut the mouths of the troublemakers and to strengthen the hearts of the righteous. If the letters from the King of Vietnam to the Board of Rites, to Li Hung-chang, and to Liang-kwang were published in the newspapers, so that England could make use of them to angrily attack [France], the French will blush with shame. But then we have to be resolved to persevere and not to start making excuses."[13] T'ang claimed that the effect of publicizing the letters would be to encourage the French opposition, which was unwilling to wage war against China. T'ang notified Li that public opinion was being aroused in France and that it was not yet definite that more French troops would be sent. He told him that "if China is firm then France will have to yield."[14] When rumors circulated through Paris in late June of 1883 that Li had already concluded a settlement with the French, T'ang immediately advised: "If China can pluck up her courage, she can thereby guarantee that France will not start war. They think that 5,000 men can attack and quickly occupy the whole of Tongking, otherwise they will negotiate for peace. My humble opinion is that Chinese troops ought to get to Tongking first to defend it. If the enemy gets there first and establishes a base, then I am afraid the situation will not be easy to handle."[15]

To T'ang T'ing-shu the interests of his company were closely related to the interests of China. As he noted in his letter of June 20: "I hope that before this reaches you the Vietnam situation will have proceeded in due course [to a solution], because the good fortunes of China and Vietnam are also the good fortune of the China Merchants Steam Navigation Company."[16]

I would like in concluding to take the opportunity to respond

to the challenging working hypothesis concerning Chinese social
history presented by Marianne Bastid. According to her analysis,
the *yang-wu* types, the business and managerial types, those who
possessed technical expertise, were a new group with a disturbing
effect, but they were simply parasitic excrescences on Chinese
society which, because they were not indicative of the main direction of Chinese social development, did not constitute a significant
phenomenon. Actually, from the viewpoint of social history, I do
not disagree with this assertion. From the viewpoint of the political,
and particularly diplomatic, history of late Ch'ing China, however,
Chinese from the treaty-port sector played a crucial role. They
played such a role, moreover, precisely because they were comparatively detached from their native roots and had acquired the
ability to imitate the West and deal with it on its own terms.

If Professor Feuerwerker is correct, as I believe he is, in his
assessment that the main influence of imperialism was in the
political and ideological spheres of the superstructure rather than
in the economic realm, then I think the significance of the Sino-
Western hybrid community cannot be relegated to the status of
warts on the face of the Chinese body politic. The members of the
new coastal community played a key role in the acquisition, adap-
tation, and implementation of Western concepts. Treaty-port
Chinese were particularly active as investors and as writers in the
flourishing publishing industry of late Ch'ing China. They initiated
important coastal newspapers which popularized their versions of
Western ideas and institutions. In the last decade of Ch'ing rule,
moreover, the examples they set in the negotiations concerning
China's frontiers and in their handling of China's railway and
mining affairs helped to spread a deeper understanding of Western
practice in foreign relations.

On the other hand, precisely because the urban commercial
class was so small in number and played a relatively peripheral
role in China's economic life, it was only rarely in a position to
assume an independent status in the political sphere. The mercantile sector remained embedded in a political system where others
were the main actors and participants. Chinese from the coastal

fringe therefore could do little more than assist in the realization of goals that coincided with their own interest or attempt to impede courses of action with which they disagreed.

From a broader perspective, it should be clear that we are dealing in late Ch'ing reform with different currents that sometimes ended up flowing in the same direction. Different groups came to reform with varying rationales, conditioned by different families of thought. One of the most important groups in late Ch'ing reform was the newly developing urban, commercial class—a class whose attitudes were shaped by an environment and intellectual context very different from those of other reform groups.

DISCUSSION

Marianne Bastid said that she believed that a case could be made for the early emergence of an independent outlook among merchants in the treaty ports. For example, in 1886 Chinese merchants in Shanghai petitioned to be allowed into the Shanghai public park. She then asked whether T'ang T'ing-shu was operating in an independent or merchant capacity when he went to France, or whether he was sent there as a sort of nonofficial, informal envoy. Louis Sigel said that he was not sent as an agent of the Ch'ing but took the initiative himself when he saw what was developing. He tried to push Li Hung-chang into more active involve ment in Annam. But Li was not anxious to become entangled there.

Paul Cohen pointed out that Wang T'ao, in his book on the Franco-Prussian War, noted with admiration that Prussian merchants abroad, out of a sense of patriotism, had subscribed to their country's war effort. Wang would have been gratified to see T'ang, a Chinese, acting in much the same way in the Vietnam matter.

James Polachek suggested that perhaps the coastal reformer types were not so much merchants urging changes as prisoners of their own expertise. Many became *mu-yu.* As a patriot one would expect T'ang to move away from Li Hung-chang out of disillusionment, but he was bound by the ties of *mu-yu* loyalty.

Thomas Kennedy returned to the question of the first generation of new coastal reformers and pointed out that Yung Wing, for example, acted with great selflessness as a Chinese businessman. In buying machinery for the Kiangnan Arsenal on behalf of Tseng Kuo-fan, he argued for buying capital equipment because it was more in the national interest. He was later instrumental in promoting the Chinese educational mission aimed at strengthening China. Paul Cohen, referring to James Polachek's comment, cautioned that not all coastal reformers were of one type. Thus, Yung Wing was very much a free agent culturally, too acculturated to be significantly bound by traditional sanctions. It was doubtful that

282

his relationship with Tseng was anything like the relationship
between T'ang and Li Hung-chang.

Kwang-Ching Liu said that he agreed with the concept of
hinterland and littoral cultures but believed that the concept could
be carried still further. In the hinterland there were some people,
such as Li Hung-chang, who were littoral-minded or littoral-
oriented. The littoral-minded hinterlanders, because of their special
experience in the treaty ports, perhaps represented a new departure
from the statecraft school. Feng Kuei-fen was exposed to the littoral,
witnessed the defense of Shanghai, and was impressed by Western
science and commerce. Apparently some hinterlanders were capable
of arriving at the same conclusions as the littoral reformers even
though they were not full participants in the culture of the littoral.
Finally, Mr. Liu added that although some of the littoral reformers
were nominal Christians, others like Ts'ai Erh-k'ang were genuine
Christians.

Paul Cohen agreed with much of what Mr. Liu said, but he
felt it important to stress that "littoral-minded hinterlanders" like
Li and Feng had in fact been directly influenced by the culture of
the littoral. The really interesting question was why some hinterlanders proved much more open than others to the influence of
the littoral.

Jeffrey Kinkley warned against having too preconceived a
notion of where the hinterland/littoral boundary lay. Some cities
such as Changsha and Chengtu lay somewhere between the two
cultures. There were different areas, moreover, within the hinterland. In between major gentry cultural centers such as Changsha
and Chengtu and the countryside there was a graduated scale of
cities ranging from the provincial capitals on down. Mr. Kinkley
said that the term "hinterland" was generally used by geographers
in the context of an urban-rural split, with the rural areas providing certain support functions and the urban areas acting as nodal
centers through which new cultural influences diffused, passing
from larger cities to lesser cities and finally out to the countryside. Paul Cohen accepted certain of Mr. Kinkley's qualifications

but said that the word "hinterland" could be used in different ways. Mr. Cohen used it to refer to the Chinese heartland, to areas far removed from the coastal culture. In time, however, some urban centers in the hinterland, like Changsha, became influenced by the littoral culture. This was particularly so with the advent of modern communications. Mr. Cohen added that he was not sure how far the distinction between littoral and hinterland could be pushed into the twentieth century. He felt, however, that as long as it was seen, at least to some extent, as a polarity between two ideal types, it remained useful for analytical purposes.

Hao Chang suggested that some littoral reformist positions may have been developed by hinterland reformers because of the statecraft tradition. There was an ambivalence within the statecraft school. There had always been some emphasis on self-interest and profit, but it took the Western impact to transform these from peripheral into central concerns.

Joseph Cheng pointed out that one difference between state-craft scholars and littoral reformers was that the former were more concerned with making Western ideas compatible with Chinese ways through syncretic modes of thinking.

Saundra Sturdevant suggested that reformers such as Li Hung-chang and Ting Jih-ch'ang were similar to the transitional figures of the Meiji Restoration who tried to carry out reform through the system. Their whole concept of reform was very rationalized. Kwang Ching Liu pointed out that the early littoral reformers like Wang T'ao also worked within the system in a sense.

Ellsworth Carlson said that he liked the littoral/hinterland con-cept but felt that there were different kinds of littoral and hinter-land cultures. Even in the region around Foochow there was a kind of hinterland in which missionaries were more successful than in Foochow proper. Paul Cohen agreed that there was considerable variation within both the littoral and hinterland cultures. He emphasized that the littoral was not to be construed as "Western," but rather as a hybrid cultural environment. In this connection he referred to the point made by Rhoads Murphey and others that the major treaty ports, like Foochow, were not created *de novo* in the nineteenth century but had, prior to the Opium War, already occupied important positions in the traditional society and economy. The treaty-port culture did not evolve in a vacuum; it was super-imposed on a pre-existing Chinese cultural foundation.

THE REFORM MOVEMENT OF 1898

John E. Schrecker
THE REFORM MOVEMENT OF 1898 AND THE *CH'ING-I*:
REFORM AS OPPOSITION

I would like, today, to discuss reform in nineteenth-century
China by presenting a specific point. That is, that there was a close
connection between the *ch'ing-i* movement which began in the
1870s and the reform movement of 1898. Such a connection would
significantly alter our understanding of reform and of the late nineteenth century in general. For in the standard view the two groups
are considered antithetical: the *ch'ing-i* is seen as a conservative,
xenophobic force and the reformers of 1898 as a progressive
faction, open to strong Western influences. I hope that by drawing
the connection between the two I can also demonstrate the value
of studying a major event such as the reform movement from different perspectives (political as well as intellectual, for example) as
a way of integrating and advancing our knowledge of late Ch'ing
China.

In my work on imperialism I found suggestive ties between
the *ch'ing-i* and the reformers in terms of ideology and political
style. I won't emphasize these today. What I want to bring out,
rather, are the more purely political and social connections, the
links in terms of personnel and constituency. My overall conclusion is that the *ch'ing-i* and reform movements formed an unbroken
opposition movement within the government and elite from the
late 1870s to at least 1898. In what follows I have relied heavily
on the writings of Professor Min Tu-ki of Seoul National University
who has done superb work on the subject of this talk. I have also
found particularly stimulating and useful the work of Mr. T'ang
Chih-chün, perhaps the leading scholar in China of the reform
movement. Among those present who will particularly recognize
my debt to them is Mr. Huang Chang-chien.[1]

Let me begin by giving you a sense of the *ch'ing-i* movement
and then turn to how it became metamorphosed into the reform
movement. *Ch'ing-i* literally means "pure talk" and it is a difficult

term to translate. I will use the Chinese word. If forced to a translation, however, I think something like "movement for renovation" would be appropriate. It cuts across terms like conservative and radical which are inappropriate to the historical context of the *ch'ing-i* and reform movements.

The term *ch'ing-i* implies sincere and scholarly literati working outside of the centers of power for a change in policy. Related to this—and this is often overlooked—it implies that these literati form a coherent opposition movement locked in a power struggle with the group of officials who dominate the government. There were several famous *ch'ing-i* movements toward the end of earlier dynasties. The most recent one had been in the late Ming and involved groups like the Fu-she and the Tung-lin. The Ch'ing was very strict in suppressing such groups; indeed, it did not tolerate any sort of political organization of scholars.

The *ch'ing-i* movement that concerns us got going in the late 1870s and was an important element in politics in the eighties and nineties. The rank and file members tended to be younger officials, men in their thirties and forties. They held middle- and lower-level positions in the government, generally of the third rank and below. They had very sound literary training and came to office by the regular (examination) route rather than the irregular route of purchase. When they acquired fame, it was as members of the Hanlin or as censors, a group generally selected out of the Hanlin.

The leadership of the *ch'ing-i* movement was the so-called Ch'ing-liu p'ai or Ch'ing-liu faction. The Ch'ing-liu p'ai changed membership over time, but was basically made up of the same sort of people as the *ch'ing-i* rank and file. Only the very top leaders— patrons might be a better word—were high officials. The patron saint of the Ch'ing-liu p'ai was Wo-jen. He is famous to us as the opponent of the T'ung-wen kuan. But he was better known to his contemporaries as an educational reformer. Wo-jen emphasized revitalizing the local academies (*shu-yuan*) as a way of achieving political renovation. He failed in his efforts because of the close government control of the academies in the Ch'ing. He died in 1871.

When the *ch'ing-i* movement got going, the leaders remained men famous for their educational activities. In the late 1870s and early eighties the two chief figures were Li Hung-tsao and Chang Chih-tung. In the late eighties another leader emerged, Weng T'ung-ho. He seems to have nudged Li aside a bit, though the latter remained important. Weng and Chang often cooperated, but they also competed for leadership of the *ch'ing-i* constituency.

Turning from personnel to ideology and political style, I should note that everything to be said holds for the reform movement as well as for the *ch'ing-i.* I will not repeat these points when I turn to the reform movement, but given what is generally known about the reformers, the similarities should be evident. These similarities, especially those of style, are extremely important in indicating the continuity between the two movements.

Overall, there was a striking harmony between the ideals of the *ch'ing-i* movement and its role as an opposition, a movement of outsiders. In their own minds, the members saw no split between idealistic goals and a desire for power. In Western political theory, I think we tend to sever the notions of power and virtue, pragmatism and idealism and, in fact, often see them as antitheses. This was not the tradition of these men. They believed, at least consciously, in the Confucian sense that power increases and does not decrease the virtue of a virtuous person.

In its general approach, the *ch'ing-i* movement emphasized the primacy of internal politics. *Ch'ing-i* people felt that the way to solve China's problems of internal decline and foreign aggression was to create a *shih-feng,* or a great national revival and, in particular, the revival of a dedicated public spirit among officials and gentry. The *ch'ing-i* group saw itself as the beginning of this *shih-feng* and wanted to expand it to others. This would increase both its power and theirs. As a way of developing the *shih-feng,* members of the movement particularly stressed morality in government. They attacked corruption on the central and local level, preached frugality, and opposed such specific practices as the sale of office.

On a more concrete level of political action one of the *ch'ing-i* trademarks was the use of the *yen-lu* and an insistence that the *yen-lu* be kept open. *Yen-lu* literally means paths of communication to the throne. Keeping the *yen-lu* open meant a willingness on the part of the throne to receive general memorials on the overall situation. (Normally, officials were only supposed to memorialize on specific matters relating to their administrative sphere.) It also implied imperial willingness to receive memorials from those comparatively low in the government, either directly or transmitted by higher officials. This emphasis on the *yen-lu* clearly fit the need of the *ch'ing-i* as a movement of outsiders. But also, by "uniting above and below," as they put it, opening the *yen-lu* contributed to the creation of the *shih-feng.* A second political trademark of the *ch'ing-i* was its constant urging of the throne to find and encourage young talent by promoting capable men outside of the rules of seniority. Clearly this emphasis fit both perspectives of the movement. A third trademark was the use of a very emotional writing style, particularly when attacking opponents.

In foreign affairs *ch'ing-i* partisans were militant and patriotic and generally constituted the war party. Their attitude toward borrowing from the West changed over time. Some remained adamantly against it; but by the late eighties many of them, including the leaders, had undergone a reversal of opinion. Nevertheless, the *ch'ing-i,* in general, opposed the *yang-wu* (foreign matters) movement. This was not because the latter favored borrowing from the West. Rather, it was because, from the point of view of the *ch'ing-i,* the *yang-wu* people emphasized the wrong things: foreign, not domestic affairs, technique, not morality. Furthermore, Li Hung-chang, the leading figure in the *yang-wu p'ai* was one of the chief political opponents of the *ch'ing-i* movement.

This raises the question of whom the *ch'ing-i* people opposed. The *ch'ing-i* view of its opponents was not necessarily accurate and clearly had a strong political motivation; but understanding it is essential to uncovering the ties to the reform movement. Overall, the *ch'ing-i* movement opposed the establishment. After the French war this meant, in particular, the Empress Dowager and the high officials. From the *ch'ing-i* point of view, these people were corrupt, pragmatic, and even profligate.

The empress had to be criticized indirectly. One of the favorite symbols for her was the Summer Palace. She was having it built in the late eighties and early nineties and the *ch'ing-i* attacked the construction constantly as wasteful, corrupt, and leading to the sale of office. Among the high officials the favorite *ch'ing-i* targets were Li Hung-chang, the most powerful provincial official, and Sun Yü-wen, who controlled the Grand Council for the empress between the French and Japanese wars.

After 1889 when the Kuang-hsu Emperor officially took control of the government, the *ch'ing-i* supported him. In fact, one might say that a key purpose of *ch'ing-i* politics from 1888 on was to bolster the emperor and to encourage him to act to solve China's problems. The *ch'ing-i* people hoped, by uniting with the emperor, to circumvent the high officials. He, in turn, found them congenial. For he was looking for young talent to use as allies against the empress and the senior officials whom she controlled. As a result, the later Ch'ing-liu p'ai overlapped considerably with the so-called emperor's party which opposed the so-called empress's party.

The *ch'ing-i* movement was continuously active, but there were also important spurts of effort. The first one in the period that concerns us came during the Sino-French War of 1884–1885. The next was in 1888–1889, when the *ch'ing-i* saw the retirement of the empress and the accession of Kuang-hsu as a chance for action. Finally, there was very vigorous *ch'ing-i* activity in 1894–1895 during the Sino-Japanese War.

Let me say a word about this last period, for it provides a crucial juncture between the *ch'ing-i* and reform movements. In 1894, *ch'ing-i* people became very active in opposing the accommodating attitude which they believed Li Hung-chang was displaying toward Japan. Among other things, Weng T'ung-ho and Chang Chih-tung pushed for war and two members of the Ch'ing-liu p'ai, Chang Chien and Wen T'ing-shih, led the war party in Peking. They wrote memorials, encouraged others to do so, and had officials, especially in the Hanlin and Censorate, send group petitions and organize protest meetings. One particularly noteworthy thing Wen T'ing-shih did was to organize discussion meetings of influential people in the *ch'ing-i* movement to plan political strategy. These meetings took place at the Sung-yun an, a place of great symbolic significance. It was the family shrine of the late Ming patriot Yang Chi-sheng, who died in prison because he had opposed the powerful Yen Sung by urging a tougher stance against the Mongols under Altan Khan.

All of this activity proved disastrous to the Ch'ing-liu p'ai. Virtually everyone involved left or was forced to leave the government. Only Weng T'ung-ho, Chang Chih-tung, and Li Hung-tsao kept their positions; and Weng lost his most important post, the Imperial Tutorship. Chang Chien quit Peking and Wen T'ing-shih was cashiered after being censored by Yang Ch'ung-i, the father-in-law of Li Hung-chang's son.

Let us now turn to the reform movement. What I want to do is to go through its history chronologically, hitting some of the high points, to demonstrate the links to the *ch'ing-i.*

If one examines K'ang Yu-wei's activities before the Sino-Japanese War, what emerges is that his closest political links in the government were to the Ch'ing-liu p'ai and that he was basically a member of the *ch'ing-i* movement. If one makes a list of the twenty or so names most closely associated with the *ch'ing-i,* it turns out that K'ang had close ties with over half of them by the time he got his own movement underway in 1895. The percentage is even higher if one excludes those *ch'ing-i* members who shifted politically or died.

K'ang entered the national scene in 1888 when he came to Peking; by then he had already had extensive contacts with Ch'ing-liu members, including, among others, Chang Chih-tung, who had asked K'ang and Wen T'ing-shih to establish a translation bureau. Most of K'ang's connections to the *ch'ing-i* group came in the usual way, through educational contacts and examination ties in the Hanlin and Kuo-tzu chien.

When K'ang got to Peking in 1888 he threw himself into the *ch'ing-i* activities surrounding the accession of the emperor. For example, he wrote memorials for *ch'ing-i* members on their favorite topics. A typical memorial criticized the Summer Palace, called for

opening the *yen-lu,* and attacked the sale of office. Another supported the railway plans of Chang Chih-tung against those of Li
Hung-chang. The Ch'ing-liu censor, T'u Jen-shou, was even cashiered
because of a memorial K'ang wrote for him.

K'ang's most famous act of the year was his own memorial to
the throne. It is generally viewed as his first great memorial on
reform, which it was. What is significant politically, however, is
that it was also part of the *ch'ing-i* activity of the year. First of all,
what caused the greatest stir at the time was not the contents of
the memorial but the fact that it was written by a *sheng-yuan,* a
person with the lowest degree, and a man not even in the government. One of the last times this had happened was when the Ch'ing-
liu adherent, Wu Ta-ch'eng, had tried to submit a memorial.
Secondly, the basic theme of K'ang's memorial was not specific
reform. Rather, it was a plea to the emperor, now coming to power,
to solve China's domestic and foreign problems by fostering a
dedicated spirit among the literati. Specifically, he was urged to do
this by opening the *yen-lu* and issuing a great decree. Thirdly, the
memorial is a passionate document which criticizes the usual
ch'ing-i targets, such as the Summer Palace and corruption and
neglect of duty among the high officials. Finally, the people who
worked unsuccessfully to get the memorial to the throne were all
associated with the Ch'ing-liu p'ai: Huang Shao-chi, Shen Tseng-
chih, Sheng-yü, and T'u Jen-shou.

Between 1889 and 1895 K'ang continued his typical *ch'ing-i*
activities. What he did is well known, but not generally understood
in this context. Thus, he founded an academy for local gentry (the
Wan-mu ts'ao-t'ang), and did serious philological work with a
political intent (his investigations of *chin-wen* Confucianism). He
also kept up ties with *ch'ing-i* people and met some new ones. For
example, one of the leading Ch'ing-liu members from Kwangtung,
Teng Ch'eng-hsiu, told his disciple, Ou Chü-chia, to study with
K'ang. He described K'ang as "the most prominent of all Cantonese
scholars in statecraft and letters."[2] When the governor of Kwangtung banned *Hsin-hsueh wei-ching k'ao* (The forged classics of the
Hsin) K'ang escaped punishment because his Ch'ing-liu friends in

Peking, including Wen T'ing-shih, intervened.

Overall, K'ang's views of these years, set down in 1895, were vintage *ch'ing-i:*

> Meanwhile the construction of the palaces and parks went on, and the graft and corruption of the officials continued unchecked. Sun Yü-wen and Li Lien-ying dominated the government, while the officials not only kept their mouths shut but suppressed the expression of public opinion. The lower officials had to offer bribes, while the high officials, as soon as they left the court, indulged themselves in drinking and banqueting in the company of prostitutes and actors . . . Under these conditions not only was political reform out of the question, but even the old form of government and its discipline were trampled upon. These conditions presaged China's defeat in *chia-wu* [by Japan].[3]

The next phase of K'ang Yu-wei's activities was 1894–1895, the period that marked the beginning of the organized reform movement. Once again, if one looks at K'ang's politics in the context I am presenting, they emerge as part of the *ch'ing-i* activities of these years. Among other things, he again wrote memorials for *ch'ing-i* allies and undertook organizational activities among literati and examination candidates. An example of the latter is the famous *Kung-chü shang-shu* (Petition from the degree candidates). The meeting where the petition was organized was held at the Sung-yun an, where Wen T'ing-shih had held his political gatherings. The overall point of the petition was the same as K'ang's memorial of 1888. On the main issue of the day it supported the war policy of the *ch'ing-i* group against Li Hung-chang. It even cited Chang Chih-tung and the militant Li Ping-heng as the sort of officials who could save the empire.

Kang's major organizational effort of 1895 was the Ch'iang-hsueh hui (The Society for the Study of National Strengthening). Its main branch was in Peking and the people involved in establishing and running it were not only Ch'ing-liu members or their associates, but, for the most part, the very same people who had

met earlier with Wen T'ing-shih. For example, the patrons were
Weng T'ung-ho and Li Hung-tsao. Other high officials gave money,
but when Li Hung-chang offered some, it was pointedly refused.
The director of the society was Ch'en Chih, who had met earlier
with Wen and was very close to Weng T'ung-ho. The vice-director
was a disciple of Li Hung-tsao's, Chang Hsiao-ch'ien. One secretary
was the Ch'ing-liu censor Wang Ta-hsieh; the other was K'ang's own
disciple, Liang Ch'i-ch'ao. Other leading members were also in the
Ch'ing-liu p'ai and included Wen T'ing-shih himself. The first
meeting may have been held at the Sung-yun an.

There are no membership lists for the Ch'iang-hsueh hui, but
descriptions of the society sound typically *ch'ing-i.* The members
were younger and lower-ranking figures in the Peking bureaucracy,
especially Board secretaries, Hanlin compilers, and censors. Indeed,
the *North China Herald* called the society the "Hanlin Reform
Club."[4]

The Shanghai branch of the Ch'iang-hsueh hui had similar
ties to the *ch'ing-i* movement. The patron was Chang Chih-tung
and he named as director his disciple, Wang K'ang-nien. This is
how Wang, who later edited the *Shih-wu pao,* came in contact with
the reformers. Prominent members were again from the Ch'ing-liu
p'ai and included Chang Chien, Huang T'i-fang, Liang T'ing-fen,
and Ch'en Pao-ch'en.

The documents of the Ch'iang-hsueh hui also suggest a
strong stylistic connection to the *ch'ing-i.* For example, K'ang's
opening statement for the society was extraordinarily militant. It
ended: "You closed-door scholars, are some of you coming to the
point of speaking about respecting the emperor and driving out
the barbarians? Only then will the teachings of the sacred Ch'ing
dynasty, the two emperors, the three kings, and Confucius, as well
as the four-hundred million people of China have something to
rely upon!"[5] This could have been written by Wo-jen, and, in fact,
Wo-jen is praised by name in the statement.

The end of the Ch'iang-hsueh hui was also closely linked to
the decline of the *ch'ing-i* movement in 1895. The government
closed the society after it was censored by Li Hung-chang's relative,

Yang Ch'ung-i, the same man who later brought about the downfall of Wen T'ing-shih. Through the intervention of Wen and Li Hung-tsao, the reformers did manage to salvage an official publications office from the remains. T'an Ssu-t'ung wrote two letters shortly after the society broke up which neatly expressed the sense of the organization as a *ch'ing-i* activity. In one he said, "K'ang Yu-wei led the Ch'iang-hsueh hui. Its patron in Peking was Weng T'ung-ho and in the provinces Chang Chih-tung." In the other, he wrote, "The banning of the Ch'iang-hsueh hui was due to the impeachment by Li Hung-chang's relative by marriage, the censor Yang Ch'ung-i. Yang knew that Li Hung-tsao would be certain to support the Ch'ing-liu, and so he took advantage of Li Hung-tsao's absence in P'u-t'o-yü to send in his impeachment."[6]

Between 1896 and 1898 the attention of the reform movement centered on establishing clubs, schools, and newspapers. All of this had the imprint of *ch'ing-i* activity and the reformers emphasized the similarity between their efforts and the *ch'ing-i* movement of the late Ming. The clubs were formed to create a new spirit of dedication among the literati and to help them gain political influence. The schools were established for the same purpose and to create educational facilities free of government control. The purpose of the newspapers was to spread the word of an organized literati movement and to increase its power.

Turning now to 1898, the basic point I want to bring out is that the reform politics of that year can be seen as a continuation of the *ch'ing-i* opposition. It was, in fact, a particularly important moment for the movement, for K'ang Yu-wei made a determined effort finally to bring the *ch'ing-i* to power. This becomes evident both from the sort of people involved in the reform movement and from the nature of the power struggle in 1898.

The leadership of the reform group presents a typical *ch'ing-i* cross-section. Examining the fourteen core members of the reform party, one finds that they had strong literary connections, all but two in fact holding higher degrees (eight had the *chin-shih* and four the *chü-jen*). They occupied middle and lower ranks, mainly as censors, Board secretaries, and Hanlin compilers. Only one had second rank or higher and this was Liang Ch'i-ch'ao's brother-in-law, Li Tuan-fen. They were young; the average age was 39. The same picture emerges if one examines those who worked with the reformers in early 1898 in such political activities as the Pao-kuo hui (Society to Preserve the Nation).

The patrons of the movement among the high officials were Weng T'ung-ho and Chang Chih-tung. Li Hung-tsao died in 1897. Weng's connection is famous and needs no amplification. Chang Chih-tung, despite disagreements, had remained close to the *Shih-wu pao,* the paper which grew out of the Shanghai Ch'iang-hsueh hui. He also supported the reform activities in Hunan in the years after the Sino-Japanese War. Three of the six martyrs of September 1898, Liu Kuang-ti, Yang Jui, and Yang Shen-hsiu, were actually closer to Chang than to K'ang Yu-wei and would be considered his disciples but for their execution in 1898. Partly for ideological and partly for political reasons, both Weng and Chang eventually broke with K'ang, but they were crucial to his initial success. As Chang Ping-lin wrote, K'ang rose to power "on the fervor of his seven memorials and by using the power of Weng T'ung-ho in Peking and the assistance of Chang Chih-tung in the provinces."[7]

The first thing to note about the power struggle of 1898 is that both sides viewed it in terms of the classic *ch'ing-i* confrontation of the lower officials and the emperor against the high officials and the empress. This is the basic interpretation of Liang Ch'i-ch'ao's *Wu-hsu cheng-pien chi* (Account of the coup of 1898). The emperor failed, Liang wrote, because he "was limited by the empress at the top and blocked by the great officials below."[8] It is also the thrust of K'ang Yu-wei's memorial of late 1897, which launched the reformers' efforts. The memorial blamed China's crisis on years of mismanagement by the high officials, the inadequacies of the *yang-wu* movement, and the foreign policies of Li Hung-chang and Prince Kung. Its overall assessment of those in power was very harsh: "The disaster grows daily. The end is at hand. To say that it can be postponed and that the old can escape is to fool oneself; it is the stupidest form of self-deception. It is as if a great house were burning and one didn't fetch water or raise an alarm, but pleased that the house wasn't yet completely destroyed, went in and stole jewels ... So I say that the officials are not creating a loyal or patriotic plan, but only scheme for themselves." On the other hand, K'ang praises the earlier opposition movement. Despite the impending destruction of China, he writes, "the *yen-lu* are tongue-tied and the officials simply hang their heads. It is not only different from the period of the Sino-French War, but also from the time of the Japanese War."[9]

The opponents of the reform movement saw things the same way. For example, in his famous memorial attacking K'ang Yu-wei, the censor Wen-t'i emphasized that the reformers had formed a clique which was "conniving with the censors" to dominate the government.[10] At one point in the summer, when the grand secretaries of the Boards were developing plans to move against the reformers, one is even said to have bemoaned, "What possible way is there to deal with this *ch'ing-i*?"[11]

K'ang wanted not only to bring the opposition to power and to institutionalize its control, but to do so as rapidly as possible. The evidence for this comes basically from the original documents and events of the One Hundred Days. For in their later writings, the reformers tended to downplay their strong political motivations.

One sees the reformers' drive for immediate power in their direct attacks on the high officials as a group and their vigorous demand that these officials be punished and removed. There is a very Legalist emphasis on rewards and punishments in their writings. For example, in June, Yang Shen-hsiu memorialized:

> The conservatives say that the new laws should be stopped. Those who are enlightened say that old practices should be swept aside ... The two groups are like fire and water, they hate each other as enemies. I say that you cannot allow such divided principles, there can be no neutrality. Without a fixed national policy, there is no way of showing the officials and people the proper direction; without making rewards and

punishments clear there is no way for the government to carry out its plans ... Now, you have issued repeated decrees to implement the new policies. But the high officials treat these decrees with indifference as if they hadn't heard anything. Sometimes they shelve them and don't proclaim your will. Sometimes they proclaim your will but don't carry it out and sometimes they carry it out but with no zeal. This is all because the national policy has not been set and because rewards and punishments are not clear ...

It has been six months since the loss of Kiaochow. It was not cut off by a powerful enemy but by the conservatives who mutinied against our own government. And, basically that happened because the national policy was not set and rewards and punishments were not clear ...

The conservatives fear that the new laws will bring great changes for officials of long standing and this would be very inconvenient for their plans for riches and honor. So they use all their efforts to block the new policies and to create rumors to upset them. The enlightened people understand internal and foreign affairs. But there are few of them and their influence is very weak. The conservatives inherit old customs. There are many of them and their power is very great ... You see the current situation abroad and understand feelings at home. How can you be responsible for the throne and the fate of the people and accede to the plans of the conservatives for their own riches and honor. Now if the current situation wasn't dangerous then this aimless drift would not be a problem. But actually after the Kiaochow incident, the crisis has grown steadily more desperate. If one looks for the basic reason, it is that there is more than one attitude, that the national policy has not been fixed and rewards and punishments have not been made known. As a result, the conservatives have been allowed to prosper and the new policies have not been carried out.[12]

Yang then supplied historical examples to show that rulers who made changes, like the Meiji Emperor, Peter the Great, and King Chao of Liang, were tough. In a memorial from the same period, K'ang also cited King Chao and used the allusion to suggest that the emperor deal firmly with the Empress Dowager.

The reformers' drive for immediate power is also evident in their emphasis on the need for the emperor to collect talent and appoint new men to high position without regard to seniority. Here is Hsu Chih-ching in late June:

> Your Majesty has fixed the fundamental directives for reform but their implementation is entrusted entirely to the hands of conservatives. Now if we do not reform we cannot strengthen ourselves, but if we do not use new people we will not be able to reform. At the beginning of the Meiji Restoration the emperor specially promoted low officials and provincial samurai ... They were used without regard to rank and all used their talent to the utmost ...
>
> I have heard that the sources of Western wealth and strength are deep and complex and cannot be mastered without thorough study. Today our high officials—beginning with the heads of the Boards in Peking and the governors in the provinces—have all been selected on the basis of seniority ... In normal times appointing people by seniority blocks competition for office. But if this method is used in a difficult period it will fail to meet the situation. To carry out extraordinary policies, you must have extraordinary talent.[13]

Finally, one sees the drive for a rapid political shift in the policies which the reformers advocated and the decrees the emperor issued. For example, throughout 1898 K'ang Yu-wei's plans centered on the creation of a Bureau of Reform. If such an organ had been established following K'ang's suggestions, it would, in fact, have meant a nationwide shift of power to the reformers within three months and at all levels from the Grand Council down to the hsien. Similarly, the reformers particularly emphasized the need to open the *yen-lu* as a means of weakening the political monopoly of the high officials and of discovering fresh talent. There were repeated decrees on the matter and by September the *yen-lu* were theoretically open to everyone.

In fact, decrees in all areas show a similarly political intent.

For example, the educational decrees are full of plans to be carried out in three months, plans which would have shifted power from the educational establishment in the Board of Rites to new institutions under the control of the reformers. The element of short-term politics is one reason why the decrees came so fast, for the emperor and the reformers stressed that those who did not carry out the new policies would be removed from office and punished. The very number of decrees, in other words, provided a test of who was loyal and an occasion for moving against the opposition.

Few proved loyal, of course, and the coup came. When the empress moved, she claimed that she was reacting to plans for a coup against her. I have not yet come to a final judgment on this very controversial point. Clearly, however, the reformers were working as fast as possible to undermine Tz'u-hsi and her power base. In light of past *ch'ing-i* developments it is interesting to note that the intermediary between the Peking officials and Jung-lu when the coup was planned, the man who then led the official delegation to the Summer Palace to ask the empress to resume control, was none other than Li Hung-chang's relative, Yang Ch'ung-i.

There are a number of conclusions one can draw from this story which relate to broader themes brought up in this conference. First, why was there the steady rise of an opposition movement from the 1870s onwards? On a narrow level, the most suggestive fact we have is that there was much less chance for promotion among lower bureaucrats in this period. This was primarily because so many younger men had moved ahead quickly during the Taiping Rebellion and the T'ung-chih Restoration. These men still dominated the high positions in the central and provincial governments and so blocked promotion.

On a broader level—and this, I think, suggests links with the social history of the period—there is much information to suggest that there was very low morale among literati on the regular route to office as opposed to the irregular route. The basic reason for this was that by the 1870s there was considerably less chance for official position by the regular route than in earlier periods. This

was because the increase in examination quotas after the Taiping
Rebellion had enlarged the pool of those seeking jobs by the
regular route. At the same time, the tremendous rise in the sale of
office had reduced the number of positions available.

Understanding the opposition as an expression of discontent
by literati on the regular route fits much that we know about the
ch'ing-i and reform movements. One link which may not be immediately evident is that the opposition movement continually
attacked the quality of local government and sought more power
for the local literati. Local government was a stronghold of those
who had purchased office. At the same time, many of the new
positions created by the *yang-wu* movement were staffed by men
who had purchased degrees. It is not insignificant that one difference between the new specialists under Li Hung-chang and
those under Chang Chih-tung was that the latter often came from
the regular route.

With the nature of the opposition movement in mind, one
can then link the political story to the well-known intellectual
history of the reform movement. In particular, one can ask why,
beyond reasons of abstract morality and national defense, the
opposition movement became interested in borrowing from the
West? It would appear that this was because liberalism, Western
education, and other new institutions provided new ways for an
opposition to influence the government and even to take it over.
I should emphasize that by providing this political perspective on
the reform movement I am far from intending to denigrate its
sincerity. In fact, the plight in which China found itself and the
reformers' sense that they had the answers to the nation's problems made their desire for influence and their inability to get it
all the more frustrating and all the more understandable.

On a broader level, if one links the political and intellectual
aspects of the reform movement, it suggests that our normal over-
view of late nineteenth-century reform may be in need of revision.
More precisely, our periodization, which moves from the self-
strengthening movement to the reform of institutions, may obscure
as much as it reveals. The self-strengthening movement and the
reform movement, from a political point of view, from the point

of view of the constituencies involved, may have actually represented opposing groups. Or, looked at from the point of view of intellectual history, Chang Chih-tung's *t'i-yung* ideas, often said to be opposed to the ideas of the reformers, may have actually been appealing to the same literati constituency. Such interpretations may seem strange at first, but this could well be a product of our de-emphasis of political history in the study of late nineteenth-century China. In American history, by contrast, we have no difficulty in accepting the proposition that the *laissez-faire* policies of Herbert Hoover and the activist policies of Richard Nixon may have been appealing to the same constituency.

As far as the longer sweep of Ch'ing history is concerned, what comes across is that the late nineteenth-century movement of opposition was also a reaction to the earlier tendency of the Manchus to use the Han literati but not to trust them. It is significant that the Ch'ing was the first dynasty to make the sale of office a full-fledged system; and it did this almost from the start, not just as a way of raising money, but also to control the Han literati. For literati politics often centered on educational connections and the irregular route provided a balance of personnel. The irregular route also gave Manchus, who often purchased positions, more chance for office. This then returns us to the late nineteenth century and one may wonder how much anti-Manchu sentiment was hidden in the *ch'ing-i* opposition to "barbarians."

Finally, one can look ahead in time rather than back. A sense one increasingly has of the history of communism in China is that it is somehow both very radical and very traditional. This may relate to the fact that radicalism in twentieth-century China had its roots in a *ch'ing-i* movement. Or to reverse this, one can suggest that *ch'ing-i* provides a paradigm of Chinese radicalism. The study of contemporary China needs models from the past. With this in mind think of the *ch'ing-i* movement of the late 1960s. The ruler united with those below (by which he now meant the whole population). He did this by opening the *yen-lu* (of wall posters). The purpose of the movement was to encourage virtue and oppose those in power, and the result often was to promote young talent without regard to seniority.

Huang Chang-chien
ON THE HUNDRED DAYS REFORM

Mr. John Schrecker has asked me to speak briefly on my views on the Hundred Days Reform. I feel greatly honored.

I recall when I studied modern Chinese history in college, I read Liang Ch'i-ch'ao's *Wu-hsu cheng-pien chi* (A full account of the coup in 1898). My reaction, then, was one of profound admiration for the patriotic efforts of K'ang Yu-wei and Liang Ch'i-ch'ao to save the country. But they were condemned and persecuted as traitors by the Ch'ing court. I sympathized with them to such an extent that tears even came into my eyes. By that time, I had read K'ang Yu-wei's *Wu-hsu tsou-kao* (Draft memorials of 1898) and had come to hold K'ang in great respect. Of course, I was not aware that most of these "draft memorials" were, in fact, unauthentic.*

At that time, I also read Liang Ch'i-ch'ao's *Ch'ing-tai hsueh-shu kai-lun* (Intellectual trends in the Ch'ing period) and came across Liang's reference to the revolutionary activities in 1898 in Hunan which he and T'an Ssu-t'ung organized. But I did not take note of the fact that Liang's remarks in this work contradicted his other statements in his *Wu-hsu cheng-pien chi.*

To study the political activities of K'ang and Liang in 1898, one must not overlook Liang's account in *Ch'ing-tai hsueh-shu kai-lun.* Nor can one afford to ignore the confidential letters of K'ang and Liang that fell into the hands of their political antagonists in Hunan and were later reproduced in *Chueh-mi yao-lu* (Essential writings for awakening the misled).

In my own work,** I have pointed out that K'ang and Liang became favorably disposed toward revolution as early as 1895. However, they abandoned this position in 1898 in order to support

---

*See my *K'ang Yu-wei wu-hsu cheng tsou-i* (The authentic memorials of K'ang Yu-wei in 1898; Institute of History and Philology, Academia Sinica, Taipei, 1974).
** *Wu-hsu pien-fa shih yen-chiu* (Studies on the history of the reform of 1898; Institute of History and Philology, Academia Sinica, Taipei, 1970).

the Kuang-hsu Emperor in carrying out reform. Later, in the face of the tremendous resistance to reform, they decided to strike a hard blow at the core of antireform conservatism by planning to besiege the Summer Palace where the Empress Dowager resided.

I feel that if these changing themes in the political activities of K'ang and Liang are identified and adequately explained, the history of the "reform movement" will become clearer.

There is one basic difference in approach between the K'ang group and Sun Yat-sen. Sun overtly advocated revolution by associating himself with the secret societies and by pooling the resources of the secret societies in subsequent armed uprisings. K'ang Yu-wei and Liang Ch'i-ch'ao, on the other hand, did not. They were *chin-shih* and *chü-jen* degreeholders, respectively. Their associates were mostly members of the literati class. As a result, K'ang and Liang could only, by organizing study societies and publishing periodicals, agitate for reform and for the institution of "popular rights" (*min-ch'üan*) and "parliamentary assemblies" (*i-yuan*). They were, of course, committed to the idea of revolution. But to actualize this idea, they had to rely on like-minded associates who had maintained contact with the secret societies. This factor largely explains why K'ang and Liang decided to carry out their revolutionary scheme only after T'an Ssu-t'ung and T'ang Ts'ai-ch'ang, both Hunanese, had joined their group.

The K'ang group launched their revolutionary campaigns in Hunan in the winter of 1897. By late spring of 1898, however, their efforts were obstructed by local gentry opposition. At this juncture, in June, the Kuang-hsu Emperor summoned K'ang Yu-wei for an audience—a gesture suggesting to the K'ang group that the emperor had succumbed to K'ang's persuasion and would rely heavily on K'ang in implementing nationwide reforms. This new development led the K'ang group to abandon their revolutionary stand and to emerge as supporters of the throne. They hoped that the power of the Kuang-hsu Emperor could be used to effect radical change from above. Unfortunately, documentary evidence of the group's earlier revolutionary activities in Hunan had by now gotten into the hands of Tseng Lien, a *chü-jen* from Hunan. Through him, this evidence reached the inner court. In desperation, the K'ang group devised a plan to besiege the Summer Palace in order to secure power by military means.

When the K'ang group approached Yuan Shih-k'ai with the anti-Empress Dowager plot, the argument they advanced was the protection of the Kuang-hsu Emperor. It was the very same argument that provided the basis for the *pao-huang* (protect-the-emperor) campaign which K'ang, Liang, and others organized shortly after the coup.

Two years later, in 1900, T'ang Ts'ai-ch'ang, leader of the uprising in Wuchang, proclaimed the goal of the insurgents to be the restoration of the Kuang-hsu Emperor. But, at the same time, T'ang refused to consider the Manchu regime legitimate. This incongruity reflected not real loyalty to the Kuang-hsu Emperor but the desire of the K'ang group to make the emperor a puppet monarch should the uprising turn out to be a success.

The sharp distinction between the political objectives of the K'ang group and those of Sun Yat-sen developed largely after the failure of the T'ang Ts'ai-ch'ang affair.

Liang Ch'i-ch'ao's *Wu-hsu cheng-pien chi* was written between late 1898 and early 1899 and was published in book form about May or June, 1899. Since K'ang and Liang were at this time publicizing their intention to protect the emperor, they found it imperative not to allude in the book to their previous revolutionary activities in Hunan. Similarly, since, in his *Jen-hsueh,* T'an Ssu-t'ung took an anti-Manchu stand, in Liang's biography of T'an, no mention was made of the content of T'an's *Jen-hsueh.* One other pertinent point is that the last chapter in Liang's *Wu-hsu cheng-pien chi,* entitled "Kuang-hsu sheng-te chi" (On the saintly disposition of the Kuang-hsu Emperor), was in fact written by K'ang Yu-wei. K'ang's own draft of this chapter has recently been discovered in Taiwan and will be published shortly along with other new materials on K'ang. This discovery leads to the conclusion that K'ang Yu-wei and Liang Ch'i-ch'ao collaborated on *Wu-hsu cheng-pien chi.* However, since the first chapter of the work was entitled "Kuang-hsu hsiang-yung K'ang shih-mo" (A full account of the Kuang-hsu

Emperor's favors bestowed on K'ang Yu-wei), K'ang felt it unwise to attach his name to the work as co-author.

In their printed works intended for the general public, K'ang and Liang consistently and emphatically dismissed allegations of their conspiratorial designs in 1898. Nevertheless, just recently, I have gained access to a letter written by Liang Ch'i-ch'ao to K'ang Yu-wei, which further substantiates the charge that, in 1898, K'ang and Liang did indeed adopt the drastic measure of staging a military coup against the Empress Dowager.

In my opinion, in studying modern Chinese history, we should pay attention to three trends: the rise of nationalism, the rise of the idea of popular rights, and the rise of various kinds of socialist thought. The political activities of K'ang and Liang form part of these trends.

Sung Wook Shin
REFORM THROUGH STUDY SOCIETIES IN THE LATE
CH'ING PERIOD, 1895–1900: THE NAN HSUEH-HUI

The line between reform and revolution in China became
gradually thinner in the last decade of the nineteenth century. The
sense of urgency created by the Opium War and the Taiping Rebellion reached its culmination after the Sino-Japanese War. It eventually radicalized the reform movement, pushing it toward revolution. After the Sino-Japanese War, the guiding principle of the
self-strengthening movement, as exemplified by Chang Chih-tung's
celebrated formula, "Chinese learning for the substance, Western
learning for application," was reformulated in a new context.
Chang's new formula was "enlightenment and mobilization" of
the Chinese masses against imperialism. It expressed the spirit of
the Ch'iang hsueh-hui as the new vehicle of the self-strengthening
movement. The study societies that came after the Ch'iang hsueh-
hui were further developed and became more radicalized. For
example in Hunan the main vehicle of provincial reform was the
Nan hsueh-hui. It was motivated by the new ideas of popular
enlightenment and popular rights. The Nan hsueh-hui was an
experiment in a new form of local government unconnected to the
central government. It thus represented both the last stand of
reform efforts by the late Ch'ing elite and the inception of the
revolutionary movement of the twentieth century.

It is important to remember, first, that the Nan hsueh-hui,
although concerned with national politics, worked for provincial
reform instead of reform at the court level; second, that the Nan
hsueh-hui was one of the major reform organizations of the late
1890s; third, that although it was a gentry reform organization, it
tried to unite the gentry with the people; and finally, that Western
ideas, in particular the idea of *min-ch'üan* (popular rights), played
a great role in the Nan hsueh-hui.

Although the Nan hsueh-hui helped provide background for
the revolutionary consciousness of 1911, historians have ignored

310

this aspect of the organization's history and have often interpreted it too conventionally within the general context of the 1898 reform.

The notions of popular enlightenment (*min-chih*) and popular rights were directly reflected in the goals of the Nan hsueh-hui. The association had both political and social goals. Its main political goals were to enlighten the Chinese people and mobilize them: "If we want to unite the people's hearts (*ch'ün-hsin*), to enlighten their knowledge, to promote their energy (*ch'ün-ch'i*), to create their talent (*ch'ün-ts'ai*), and thus to penetrate popular feelings (*ch'ün-ch'ing*), there is no other means but the study society."[1] The Nan hsueh-hui further aimed at experimenting in local self-government (*ti-fang tzu-chih*). Through the practice of local government, its members hoped to establish a representative form of government in China: "Every [Western] nation has a senate and a house of representatives which discuss political matters publicly. Under our political system (*kuo-chih*), people dare not interfere with political matters. However, as our meetings at the *fu* (prefecture), *hsien* (district), *shih* (city), and *ts'un* (village) levels elect the members, our study society already emulates the Western system."[2]

Along with the promotion of popular enlightenment and popular rights, the Nan hsueh-hui also had the secondary goals of creating a new spirit of equality in society, inspiring new social customs, and promoting the public welfare of the people. The Nan hsueh-hui strove to bring a new spirit of equality to the Chinese people. As P'i Hsi-jui said at a lecture meeting: "Now, our Hunan province has organized the Nan hsueh-hui. At each lecture, officials, gentry, scholars, and commoners all attend. How wonderful it is! There are no divisions; higher and lower are all one body. Alas! The matter of equality (*p'ing-teng*) originally never appeared like this in China. However, now equality is the basis of all matters affecting Hunan. If Hunan promotes the spirit of equality, it also establishes the beginning of equality for other provinces. This spirit of equality is certainly what Westerners enjoy."[3] The Nan hsueh-hui also aimed at promoting a new "spirit of public interest" (*kung-i wei chu-i*) and inspiring new customs, so that the Chinese people could eliminate such evil practices as footbinding, opium addiction, gambling, alcoholism, and so on.

The political and social goals of the Nan hsueh-hui were thus designed to renovate both the political system of China and the social customs of the Chinese people. These goals were explicitly advocated in the first clause of the general organizational charter of the Nan hsueh-hui: "Our study society extends human capacity (*neng-li*) and promotes a spirit of public interest through enlighten- ment. Furthermore, whoever becomes a member of our association must eradicate the old evil customs and prejudices."[4]

The political and social goals of the Nan hsueh-hui were directly reflected in its programs and activities. These programs can be divided into two major areas: the enlightenment of the people and social welfare. The enlightenment programs consisted of a newspaper (the *Hsiang-pao*), a library (*ts'ang-shu ch'u*), and lectures (*chiang-i*).

The *Hsiang-pao* was one of the major means by which the Nan hsueh-hui conducted its enlightenment campaign. It was founded in December 1897 and produced its first issue in January 1898. The publisher was Hsiung Hsi-ling; the editors were T'an Ssu-t'ung and T'ang Ts'ai-ch'ang. Because of its importance in the enlightenment program, the *Hsiang-pao* had its own bylaws which consisted of nineteen rules governing the purpose, content, and management of the newspaper.[5]

The *Hsiang-pao* covered a broad range of subject matter, inclu ing editorials, memorials, treaties, translations of Western books, reform programs, and the activities of Hunan and other provinces. However, as an official newspaper of the Nan hsueh-hui, it empha- sized the propagation of new ideas of the founding members that would enlighten the people of Hunan. It therefore published politic views on current affairs, public letters, lectures, discussions of the members, as well as bylaws and revisions of the bylaws of the asso- ciation. The *Hsiang-pao* was a four-page paper issued daily (except Sunday). The paper was distributed by the members of the branch offices and reached the people at the village level. The funding of the paper was based on income from advertising and subscriptions. The *Hsiang-pao* was published until the coup d'etat of September 1898, at which point it changed its name to *Hui-pao*. Although the documents do not show how many copies were issued daily and who subscribed to the paper, it is a certainty that the political ideas in the *Hsiang-pao* were carried to the general public.

The second important means of enlightenment was the Bureau of Book Collection (*ts'ang-shu ch'u*) or public library, which was open to the public. The Bureau of Book Collection had a separate organizational charter containing detailed regulations about its purposes and management.[6] The purpose of the bureau was to collect Chinese as well as Western books, to make a catalogue, and to open a reading room to the public. The bureau was managed by the secretary-treasurer (*tung-shih*) of the association and two librarians (*kuan-shu jen*). The books were largely collected by means of donations of the members and purchases by the associa-tion. There is no way of knowing which library catalogue system was used. The bylaws simply indicated that the books were arranged by title. The library was operated according to strict rules. For example, the bureau issued library cards (*k'an-shu p'ing-tan*) either yearly or monthly which were required by the members as well as the public in order to use the library. The members obtained one-year cards automatically, but the public could obtain cards (either monthly or yearly) only on the recom-mendation of members. The books could not be checked out, and people were encouraged to use the reading room. It was open every day from 10:00 a.m. until 4:00 p.m. except Sunday when there was a lecture. Eating, drinking, smoking, and talking were all absolutely forbidden in the library. The reason for establishing a modern library with a catalogue system and a large reading room was to give the members as well as the public a chance to acquire new ideas.

The third feature of the enlightenment program was the lec-ture system. Apparently this was the very core of the program. For it was mainly through lectures and discussions that the founding members advocated new ideas, particularly new political ideals and the notion of popular sovereignty. The first lecture program, accord-ing to the account of P'i Hsi-jui (the first chairman of the associa-tion), was held on February 1, 1898. The lectures were given by

Ch'en Pao-chen, Huang Tsun-hsien, T'an Ssu-t'ung, and P'i Hsi-jui. There was a large audience of three hundred people.[7]

The general organizational charter of the Nan hsueh-hui provided detailed regulations for the lecture program.[8] The lectures were to be given every Sunday and to be open to all members the public could attend with a free admission card (*p'ing-tan*). Although the documents do not tell us how many and what type of people heard the lectures (except in the case of the first one), it is clear that by holding the lectures on Sundays and issuing free admission tickets, the association hoped to recruit large audiences.

The lecture program was operated under the auspices of the lecture committee which was composed of elected members. The organizational charter also stipulated that the lectures were to be given by the members of the lecture committee. However, other members and guest lecturers were often invited. Each lecture session was divided into a lecture and then a seminar-type discussion. The lectures covered Western as well as Chinese subjects. In general, these were divided into four areas, each placed under the supervision of a member specialist. For example, P'i Hsi-jui was in charge of learning or science (*hsueh-shu*), Huang Tsun-hsien was in charge of politics and government, T'an Ssu-t'ung of astronomy, and Tsou Tai-chün of geography.[9]

Political subjects were the main focus of the lecture program. Current political events and the principles of political institutions and administration were often treated. From this it is quite clear that the main purpose of the program was to enlighten the people politically, so that they might learn how to participate in local self-government. Liang Ch'i-ch'ao later described the subjects and purposes of the lectures in his *Wu-hsu cheng-pien chi* (Record of the 1898 coup d'etat): "Once a week the association gave a lecture. The Governor and Educational Commissioner led officials to attend the lectures. Huang Tsun-hsien, T'an Ssu-t'ung, Liang Ch'i-ch'ao and the dean gave lectures in turn on the current political affairs of China and the West, and on the principles of political institutions and administration. Thus these lectures helped the people to preserve the national religion (*pao-chiao*), helped

promote patriotism and furthermore helped to develop their ability
to participate in local self-government (*ti-fang tzu-chih*)."[10]

While the political program of the Nan hsueh-hui promoted
popular enlightenment and popular rights, there was also a social
welfare program. The organizational charter of the central association (*tsung-hui chang-ch'eng*) gave detailed descriptions of this
program and of the role of the members in it.[11] Concerned with
the problem of popular education at the local level, the association,
by means of the authority of the governor, provided for the establishment of local public schools (*hsueh-t'ang*) and designated local
members to manage them. It also initiated programs for study
abroad. Qualified students were selected by the association and
were sent to Japan for study, under the direct supervision of gentry
members appointed by the governor. In addition, the organizational
charter of the Nan hsueh-hui stipulated that exceptional members
of the branch associations were to be recommended by the governor
to the Ministry of Foreign Affairs and the Grand Council. Such
persons were then entitled to take a special examination for an
official appointment.

It is not easy to tell to what extent these programs were
actually implemented. Nevertheless, it is clear that local education
was strongly emphasized by the association. It is no wonder that the
leaders of Confucian academies energetically opposed these new
school systems and educational programs.

The association was also vigorously engaged in general public
service. According to the organizational charter, the members of
the branch associations were to perform public services that were
essential to the economic and political stability of their locales.
From the scope of these services, which embraced such areas as
public works, famine relief, local defense, legal disputes, the prison
system, and so forth, it seems quite clear that the association hoped
to have its own members gradually replace the local gentry in local
public services. Local members of the association were also appointed
to study local administration in general and to report back to the
governor with proposals for reform. Thus, the Nan hsueh-hui in fact
functioned as an advisory body to the Hunan provincial government,

thereby laying a basis for the development of local self-government bureaus (*tzu-i chü*).

The Nan hsueh-hui, in its political and social programs, its organizational format, and its ideology, pointed the way toward a new political consciousness, one which aimed not only at uniting the elite but also at forging links with the people. Perhaps this was the critical step away from elitist reform and toward revolutionary consciousness. It is significant that, with the dissolution of the Nan hsueh-hui, T'ang Ts'ai-ch'ang, Ts'ai O, Pi Yung-nien, and other members immediately became engaged in revolutionary activities.[12]

The Nan hsueh-hui's basic orientation was toward local self-government, and one of its functions as a study society was to give practical training to its members so as better to fit them for leadership roles in local activities. Furthermore, the association functioned as an advisory body to the governor. Finally, in its emphasis on *min-ch'üan* and *min-chih,* which represented a radical departure from other study societies, the Nan hsueh-hui contributed to the ideological climate within which the movement culminating in the provincial assemblies was nurtured.

Daniel H. Bays
CHANG CHIH-TUNG AFTER THE "100 DAYS": 1898–1900 AS
A TRANSITIONAL PERIOD FOR REFORM CONSTITUENCIES

The Ambiguity of the 1898–1900 Period

The most important feature of the September 1898 coup was
the resumption of direct rule by the Empress Dowager. The summary execution of the "six martyrs" on September 28 showed that
she was in no mood to make generous allowances for what she had
come to view as a threat to her (and to the dynasty's) political position. Besides the six who died, in the next few weeks some thirty
men were variously arrested, imprisoned, dismissed from office, or
banished to the frontier, and for a time there were rumors that the
purge would extend to hundreds more.[1] But the purge went no
further, and its overall effect certainly was not to root out reform
sentiment within the government, but only to make its proponents
more cautious.

After the execution or removal from office of some of those
thought to be associated with K'ang Yu-wei, the most important
measures of the first weeks after the coup reaffirmed the rights of
those who had felt threatened during the summer and halted the
extension of political participation to the lower reaches of the
bureaucracy and to the gentry class. Some, though not all, sinecures
were re-established, and the councils of officials and gentry set up
to advise the throne were abolished. The right to memorialize the
throne (the opening of the *yen-lu*), which had been given to all
lower officials and common citizens in the late summer, was
rescinded, as were the various reforms of the examination system.[2]
Many of the summer edicts were allowed to stand, however, especially those providing for more effective administration of industrial and commercial affairs, structural expansion of the nation's
school system, and military reforms.[3]

It should be noted that some important elements of journal-
istic opinion were receptive to Tz'u-hsi's resumption of direct rule
and did not equate it with total reaction. For example, Wang K'ang-

317

nien's Shanghai daily, the *Chung-wai jih-pao,* which had commented favorably on most of Kuang-hsu's reform edicts, welcomed her return. At the same time the paper made it clear that it did not expect a rollback of reforms, but a more united and stronger China.[4]

The reform consensus which emerged after the defeat by Japan in 1895 and which characterized the 1895–1898 period can be seen as continuing in some respects, despite the events of the "100 days" and the September coup. A specific index is the great popularity of Chang Chih-tung's personal reform platform which he had written in the spring of 1898, *Ch'üan-hsueh p'ien.* Opponents and critics of K'ang Yu-wei were of course quick to appreciate Chang Chih-tung's attacks on K'ang's theories and his defense of orthodoxy. But the work as a whole can scarcely be called a conservative apology and in fact devotes most of its space to justifying needed institutional changes in all spheres of Chinese life, excepting only politics. Thus its continued popularity and acceptance indicate how far issue-conscious Chinese had come since 1895 in accepting the need for widespread national reforms.

Nevertheless, the political atmosphere between late 1898 and 1900 was not very conducive to progressive innovation. At Peking, the most hidebound Manchu and Chinese figures were dominant around the court, and those parts of the Kuang-hsu Emperor's reforms that they dismantled were precisely the most significant ones, those that had tried to open up the political structure.

Moreover, the political situation was tense and uncertain. It is likely that foreign pressure, or the court's fear of it, was a major factor inhibiting further extension of the purge among officialdom, and there were recurring rumors of plots at court to depose or otherwise do away with the Kuang-hsu Emperor.[5] It is true that the Empress Dowager did not satisfy the desires of the most reactionary court elements and indeed encouraged some innovations in the 1898–1900 period. But, on the other side, if one went too far in the direction of reform, it was easy to incur charges of being sympathetic to K'ang Yu-wei and Liang Ch'i-ch'ao, and officials like Chang Chih-tung were keenly aware of this.[6]

The Position of Chang Chih-tung

After the Empress Dowager's September coup, Chang Chih-tung's position was undoubtedly in some danger. As governor-general of Hupeh and Hunan, Chang had had very extensive connections with many major figures in both the Hunan and Peking reform programs, and it is possible that, had the purge been extended further, Chang would have gotten the axe. On September 28, the Hupeh judicial commissioner Ch'ü T'ing-shao, then in Peking, underwent very sharp and detailed questioning from Tz'u-hsi concerning the situation in Hupeh. And the Japanese consul-general in Shanghai, a well-informed and astute observer of Chinese politics, reported later in 1898 that immediately after the coup in September it was widely believed that Chang would be removed from his post, or at least degraded in rank.[7]

It is likely that the purge came closest to Chang in early October 1898, when several of those who had directed the Hunan reform movement—Governor Ch'en Pao-chen, his son Ch'en San-li, and others—were cashiered. Perhaps only Chang's long and close personal relationship with the Empress Dowager saved him from demotion at this time.

Some further insight into the political dynamics of the times can be gained from an examination of Chang Chih-tung's relations with the *pao-huang* (protect the emperor) group of K'ang Yu-wei and Liang Ch'i-ch'ao in the 1898–1900 period. During this time, the Ch'ing government used every device at its disposal to capture, assassinate, or forbid sanctuary to the former leaders of the radical reform movement and their followers abroad. K'ang, Liang, and their associates were pursued much more eagerly than were Sun Yat-sen and his band of revolutionaries during this time. Those around K'ang, being literati and former officials, were seen as a more serious threat—a sort of government in exile—than were Sun and his lower-class cohorts.

Chang Chih-tung was in the forefront of this fight against the reformer-exiles. He was tireless in his efforts to have them thrown out of Japan, and it was even rumored that the supervisor of students sent to Japan by Chang in the fall of 1898 had secret orders to assassinate K'ang and Liang if he could.[8] However, Chang was not simply currying favor with the court by his efforts; he had two very specific reasons for working against the exiles in Japan. The first was that their presence in Japan was an obstacle to his plans for close cooperation with the Japanese in his own Hupeh reform program, which he was continuing to carry out. The second was because they were rivals for the same "reform constituency" to which Chang himself looked for support, and they had begun actively to contest him for this constituency by attacking Chang personally in their publications.

In the late fall of 1898, Chang had plans to send significant numbers of Hupeh students to Japan, in addition to those he had already sent earlier in the year, and to hire several Japanese instructors for his new schools in the Wuhan cities.[9] Yet he was afraid of proceeding as long as the exiled radical reformers seemed welcome by the Japanese government. He argued this point very forcefully with the Japanese consul-general at Shanghai, Odagiri Masunosuke, late in 1898, claiming that his hopes of cooperation with the Japanese would be stymied until they took some action against the exiles. Chang also requested the Japanese government to broach with the Peking government the subject of sending more Chinese students to Japan, since he feared denunciation if he took the initiative himself.[10]

Interestingly, the Japanese government was responsive. Foreign Minister Aoki agreed to take up directly with Peking the subject of sending more students to Japan, and promised to try to get K'ang Yu-wei out of the country, which was finally done in March 1899.[11] Accordingly, Chang now revived his program of cooperation with Japan. He hired a small Japanese military mission to teach at his new Noncommissioned Officers' School, and sent several officers and senior enlisted men to Japan to study military organization and to observe field maneuvers. The Peking government reaffirmed its approval of sending students abroad during the summer of 1899, and Chang responded quickly, sending at least twenty-seven more students to Japan in October 1899.[12]

As K'ang Yu-wei's departure from Japan became imminent, Chang pressed for the ouster of Liang Ch'i-ch'ao and others who also remained there. He occasionally contacted Consul-General Odagiri in Shanghai on this matter, and invariably mentioned it to Japanese visitors whom he saw in Wuchang.[13] A major reason for his continued ire was a direct attack upon him by the exiles early in 1899.

In December 1898, Liang Ch'i-ch'ao began his long and influential career as journalist-in-exile with the founding of the *Ch'ing-i pao* in Yokohama. Liang's style, as well as the substance of his writings, soon won the paper a wide readership among Chinese abroad and in China as well. In the fifth issue, dated February 2, 1899, there was an article blasting Chang Chih-tung. It recounted the manner in which Chang had helped various reformers before Tz'u-hsi's coup, and accused him of being cowardly in not joining Liu K'un-i and others in protesting the alleged plan to do away with Kuang-hsu afterwards.[14]

Chang did not welcome public reminders of his past associations with the purged reformers. His own position was still such that he may have wanted to avoid raising questions in the minds of the ultraconservatives in Peking. Thus, after the attack on him, he tried to have the *Ch'ing-i pao* closed down, or at least to prevent its circulation in China. In late February and March 1899, he complained about the paper to Japanese diplomats; he also memorialized the Tsungli Yamen, requesting it to put pressure on the Japanese Foreign Ministry to shut down the newspaper and deport the reformer-exiles still in Japan.[15]

This was only the first skirmish in what would eventually (in 1900) develop into a full-scale verbal battle between the *Ch'ing-i pao* and Chang Chih-tung. At a more profound level, the clash between Chang and the exiled reformers signified their rivalry over the legacy of the 1895–1898 reform effort. To Chang, K'ang and Liang were mortal enemies, because they could claim to be the rightful owners of this legacy. They provided potent competition for the bureaucratic reform constituency which had surfaced during those years, a constituency that Chang wanted to keep identified with a moderate dynastic reform program.

The Appearance of a Nonbureaucratic Reform Constituency

At this point I would like to introduce the notion of a changing and expanding social-economic-political constituency for reform, appearing for the first time in early 1900. In the 1895–1898 period, there had been an impressive growth of study and discussion societies, as well as of the new journalism. But there was as yet no organized political action outside of what might be called the "bureaucratic community"—officeholders and their peers among the national elite of literati or gentry. In early 1900, however, for the first time a discernible extrabureaucratic public opinion made its appearance.

The occasion was the announcement, on January 24, 1900, that P'u-chün, Prince Tuan's son, was to be heir apparent to the T'ung-chih Emperor. Many observers at the time, and scholars since, concluded that this was a hesitant first step toward deposing Kuang-hsu, a kind of trial balloon that would allow the court, before proceeding further, to gauge both foreign reaction and the reaction of Liu K'un-i, who had protested apparent moves against Kuang-hsu in 1898 and 1899.[16]

In response to the January 24 edict and its possible implications, large numbers of lower officials, urban gentry, merchants, students, and overseas Chinese registered their opposition. Groups of people in Tientsin, Hangchow, Wuchang, and Shanghai turned in complaints to officials to be forwarded to Peking. Lower officials petitioned higher ones to join them in protest. Most Chinese newspapers were against the court's action, and overseas Chinese telegraphed not only the Tsungli Yamen, but also the British, American, and Japanese ministers in Peking, requesting foreign pressure to "save" Kuang-hsu.[17] Probably the most striking manifestation of protest was a mass telegram sent from Shanghai to Peking on January 26 and signed by 1231 individuals.[18]

These events, I would argue, symbolized a key stage in the evolution of China's political process. People and groups on the fringes of the traditional political structure, or outside it altogether, were beginning to constitute a nonbureaucratic public opinion. In the near future, the role of this force in Chinese politics would grow dramatically, in nationalistic protests and boycotts, rights recovery campaigns, and ultimately in the constitutional movement at the end of the dynasty.

The relevance of this new political development for our purposes is that its chief immediate beneficiary was Chang's rival, the *pao-huang* movement led by K'ang and Liang. Since 1898 the reformers' newspapers had consistently defended the emperor and attacked the Empress Dowager. Now other, more moderate, newspapers and newly activated groups within China and abroad joined the exiles in their longstanding protests against Tz'u-hsi's regime. A good example was Wang K'ang-nien and his Shanghai *Chung-wai jih-pao*.

Wang K'ang-nien had remained a stalwart spokesman for the moderate reform position of Chang Chih-tung through most of 1898, and his paper even welcomed the resumption of power by Tz'u-hsi. But Wang became increasingly impatient over the lack of reform initiative at the top of the Peking government, and by the late summer of 1899 he began to advocate returning active power to the emperor. By the end of 1899, Wang was backing the activities and programs of the reform exiles and decrying the court's efforts to have K'ang and Liang captured or assassinated. In late January 1900, the *Chung-wai jih-pao* unreservedly backed the mass Shanghai telegraph petition, and an editorial hinted that violence would be justified to protect the emperor's person.[19]

If the reformers-in-exile were finding new allies among elements of an emerging nonbureaucratic public opinion by early 1900, Chang Chih-tung, the symbol of moderate dynastic reform, was taking a corresponding public relations beating. By this time Chang, too, was probably hoping for more vigorous leadership in reform from Peking and deploring the dominance at court of men for whom he had little respect.[20] He was undoubtedly surprised at the widespread public outcry of late January and February 1900—and unpleasantly so when he realized that many of those protesting classified him together with the obscurantists at court.

A year earlier, in 1899, Chang had been eager to avoid charges in the reform press that he had been an early ally of the radicals of 1898. Now he showed himself eager to refute charges in the same press that he was a reactionary. Soon after the January 24 edict, Liang Ch'i-ch'ao's *Ch'ing-i pao* charged that Chang had been consulted in advance about the alleged plot against Kuang-hsu and that he had approved it happily.[21] Other papers reprinted and embellished the accusation.

Chang reacted vigorously. Already on February 10, 1900, he telegraphed the supervisor of Hupeh students in Japan, ordering him to go directly to the Japanese Foreign Ministry and raise a fuss about the newspapers in Chinese treaty ports which were technically registered in Japanese names but were disseminating the propaganda of the K'ang–Liang group. He specifically mentioned the charge that he had been consulted in advance on the new heir apparent as the kind of nonsense that had to be stopped.[22] Chang identified Yen Fu's Tientsin *Kuo-wen pao* and Wang K'ang-nien's *Chung-wai jih-pao* among the papers that he demanded be curbed, although these two papers were representative of the emerging nonbureaucratic public opinion in the treaty ports, not simply mouthpieces for the K'ang–Liang political group. In addition, Chang appealed to the foreign consuls in Hankow, requesting them to urge their governments to suppress seditious Chinese newspapers which were springing up under foreign protection in the treaty-port concession areas.[23] Chang also took more direct action. On March 7, 1900, he ordered customs officials in his jurisdiction to confiscate copies of the *Ch'ing-i pao* and other seditious newspapers and to do a thorough check on the backgrounds of any persons who wanted to start new publications.[24]

In the end, however, little headway was made by Chang in his efforts to prevent the dissemination of unwelcome reading matter. Too many newspapers and bookstores were under the legal ownership of foreigners, and the fact was that, without foreign cooperation, their permanent suppression was almost impossible.[25] Indeed, the circulation of the worst offender, the *Ch'ing-i pao,* probably continued to increase.

Thus in early 1900 the Ch'ing government was coming into increasing disrepute with a fledgling Chinese public opinion outside the bureaucracy and centered in the treaty ports. Chang Chih-tung, as a loyal servant of the central government, could not help but be tarnished along with it, and among the new reform constituency he lost ground to the K'ang–Liang party. In March 1900, Liang Ch'i-ch'ao wrote a confident editorial for the *Ch'ing-i pao* in the form of a long letter addressed to Chang Chih-tung.[26] Liang again castigated Chang for supposedly conniving in the emperor's deposition. The tone was that of a pretender to power with victory in sight, lording it over his defeated rival.

During the next few months, over the fateful Boxer summer, matters would get much worse both for the central government in Peking and for Chang Chih-tung, its defender in central China. For a flickering moment there was even a possibility that the reformers-in-exile might return to lead a new government. Yet, in the upshot, the K'ang–Liang group's own actions, especially their involvement with secret societies in backing T'ang Ts'ai-ch'ang and his Tzu-li hui revolt in Hankow during the summer of 1900, lost them much of the support they had won in the new reform constituency early in 1900.[27] And in the end, after 1900, Chang Chih-tung wound up victorious over the exiled reformers, a leading figure in an accelerated program of dynastic reform, and indeed for several years inheritor of both the bureaucratic pre-1898 and the nonbureaucratic post-1898 reform constituencies.

DISCUSSION

Roger Des Forges asked John Schrecker if he could clarify the relationship between the sale of offices and the reform movement. Mr. Schrecker replied that the *ch'ing-i* opposition was against the sale of offices and favored local reform, and that the logic of this link-up lay in the fact that many of those who purchased office were assigned to local posts. Li Hung-chang tended to use people who purchased office, but Chang Chih-tung usually used those who rose through the regular route. The reform proposals of the opposition were designed to increase gentry power and would have given more local power to *sheng-yuan* and other gentry out of office.

Daniel Bays noted that Chang Chih-tung personally developed an aversion to giving too much power to the local gentry. On this point Chang was in opposition to the reformers, including some of his own *mu-yu.*

Kwang-Ching Liu said that he was prepared to accept the argument for continuity between the *ch'ing-i* movement and the radical reformers. He insisted, however, on the difference that Western ideas made in 1898. There was intellectual change as well as intellectual continuity.

James Polachek raised the question of how xenophobia changed so radically to a reformist impulse inspired to a degree by Western ideas. Paul Cohen suggested that there might be a parallel with the Meiji Restoration. Many samurai who, in the late *bakumatsu* period, were identified with a policy of expelling the barbarians abruptly shifted in 1868 to advocating Western-inspired changes. W. G. Beasley and others had shown how, in the political context of the time, this was often not as radical a change as it appeared to be.

Saundra Sturdevant mentioned that in the 1875 telegraph controversy, the censor Ch'en I submitted two memorials on the same day, one impassioned, the other rational and logical, but both opposing the telegraph. Li Ho-nien, during the Taiwan crisis in 1874, proposed the introduction of the telegraph. Later he became angry over the practices of the telegraph company and switched positions. He chang from an advocate of a Western innovation to a violent opponent, but it was for political reasons. John Schrecker added that one's opinions sometimes changed also because of changes in status or age.

Marianne Bastid said that the intellectual changes caused by the Sino-French War were very significant. She questioned whether Chang Chih-tung should be considered a member of the *ch'ing-i* movement after 1885. He was no longer a patron of the group after that date and was trying to form his own faction. He sometimes opposed both the *ch'ing-i* movement and Li Hung-chang. John Schrecker said that he relied on the work of the Korean historian Min Tu-ki in placing Chang in the *ch'ing-i* camp. Mr. Schrecker added that there was some confusion over how to define the Ch'ing-liu p'ai. Sometimes it was defined broadly, sometimes narrowly.

Marianne Bastid said that age or generation was an important consideration in late Ch'ing politics. Many of K'ang's contemporaries held him in low regard simply because he was too young. Chang Chien mentioned this attitude in his diary.

Charlton Lewis raised the question of revolution, which had been touched upon in the presentations by Huang Chang-chien and Sung Shin. Mr. Lewis maintained that down to 1900 activities in Hunan were of a radical reform rather than a revolutionary nature. Among the several reasons he gave for reaching this conclusion was the content of the discussions that were carried on. The reformers talked about astronomy, for example, which was not generally a concern of revolutionaries. T'an Ssu-t'ung wrote about astronomy and expressed the conviction that science was common to all cultures.

Richard Shek said, with reference to the teaching of astronomy by the reformers, that the universalistic aspect was less important than the undermining of the cosmological myth referred to by Hao Chang. It had the Copernican effect of implying that no one planet or country could be considered the center. All was relative, and hierarchy was artificial. From an intellectual point of view, this was very significant.

Hao Chang pointed out that doctrine and politics were closely related. In Hunan in late 1897 and early 1898 the ideological component became more pronounced because of the exposure of gentry in Changsha to the ideas of K'ang Yu-wei, T'an Ssu-t'ung, and others. Many saw these ideas as subversive and attacked them. Mr. Chang also commented on Sung Shin's paper, disagreeing with Mr. Shin's implication that the struggle in Hunan was between conservatives and reformers. Actually it was a struggle of radicals versus moderates. Wang Hsien-ch'ien and others supported the self-strengtheners but opposed K'ang Yu-wei and Liang Ch'i-ch'ao. It was only in the course of time, as the struggle intensified, that moderates began lining up with conservatives.

Huang Chang-chien recalled that Liang, in his *Intellectual Trends in the Ch'ing Period,* stated that in Hunan the radicals had vigorously promoted revolution in the Nan hsueh-hui and in the *Hsiang-pao.* They secretly supported revolutionary activity, in spite of what may have been stated in the Nan hsueh-hui regulations. Noriko Kamachi added that after 1898 Liang and his associates were identified as *kakumeiha* (revolutionaries) in Japanese documents.

Hao Chang said that only after 1900 did a clear-cut distinction emerge between reformers and revolutionaries. Prior to this date Sun Yat-sen himself did not yet have a clear ideological position. Liang and his associates talked about *tzu-yu* (liberty) and *min-ch'üan* (people's rights)—ideas that were not too far from those of contemporary revolutionists. They even expressed vaguely anti-Manchu feelings. The reformist position was thus very complex. Undoubtedly it did contain elements of revolution. However, this did not make the reformers revolutionists.

James Polachek wondered to what extent the split between moderate reform and revolution was really visible in 1898. Was it an ideological split or merely one of factional alignment? John Schrecker replied that there were intellectual differences, but that the split was also a political one. There was a wide spectrum of political views.

Kwang-Ching Liu asked whether *ch'ing-i* memorials from censors and Hanlin members positively endorsed the K'ang–Liang position with regard to examination reform and opening the *yen-lu* to all. John Schrecker replied that although he could not yet answer that question, two other things about the memorials stood out. One was that they consciously attempted to display talent and emphasized the importance of giving more power to the literati as a whole. A second was that memorials sent by *sheng-yuan* were, from a Confucian point of view, very orthodox and doctrinally serious, not only in their style but also in the values expressed.

Nailene Chou observed that the more militant *ch'ing-i* officials, who had clamored for war at the time of the Sino-Japanese encounter, fared poorly after China's loss. Some, like Chang Chien, fell from favor; others shifted to a less militant line. Marianne Bastid said that it was true that Chang Chien left office and became a businessman in this period, but not as a result of his *ch'ing-i* stance on the war.

Paul Cohen said he was confused about the human structures of the *ch'ing-i* movement. He wondered what exactly was meant when one talked of the *ch'ing-i* "school," what it meant to be affiliated with or a member of the Ch'ing-liu "faction." Marianne Bastid said that one way of defining the group might simply be to include in it all those who thought of themselves as partisans of *ch'ing-i.* John Schrecker added that the term connoted both a specific group and a style.

Luke Kwong suggested that the role of the Kuang-hsu Emperor should be more closely examined. What influence did he have? John Schrecker was of the opinion that the emperor was very sincere in his policies. His concern with haste in carrying out the reforms was interesting. Certainly, it reflected in part his political struggle with the Empress Dowager. Then again, the two previous emperors had died very young, and there was a tendency toward weakness in the last few rulers of a dynasty. The Kuang-hsu Emperor might have thought that time was running out. This would be a psychological interpretation of his haste.

Daniel Bays said that the emperor might have been genuinely convinced by K'ang's ideas. He did not, however, think that the emperor was a puppet of K'ang. In fact, Kuang-hsu had read and

approved of Chang Chih-tung's *Exhortation to Study,* which
directly attacked K'ang.

Hao Chang pointed out that the emperor was in the process
of forming an attitude and that at any given time it was important
to consider what influences he was subject to. In the spring of
1898 Kuang-hsu was in close contact with K'ang Yu-wei and read
K'ang's writings. His edicts reflected the moderate side of K'ang.
There were, however, indications that he might have been moving
in a more radical direction when the coup took place. Mr. Chang
said that two events precipitated the crisis: the firing of two board
presidents and the appointment of T'an Ssu-t'ung to a responsible
position. Luke Kwong suggested that the appointment of T'an was
not, after all, such a radical action, since T'an was not given direct
daily access to the emperor.

Suzanne Barnett said that at this point a definition of reform
in the Chinese context would be helpful. Did reform imply a
specific, articulated program? Frank Lojewski spoke of proposals
to change the methods of collecting taxes. Was that reform? When
an official, in the course of performing his duties, introduced
certain innovations, was that reform?

Paul Cohen said that the motivation behind reform was an
important factor. Was reform undertaken in order to preserve
something—an essentially conservative orientation—or was it undertaken simply in order to meet a problem, without reference to the
"fall-out" effects of dealing with that problem—a potentially more
radical stance? John Schrecker suggested that in a time of dynastic
decline, just doing a good job might be considered reform. Paul
Cohen reminded the workshop of John Fairbank's observation that
the English word "reform" covered a number of different Chinese
concepts and terms.

Charles Peckham suggested that in the context of the nineteenth century it would be well to make a distinction between
reform and modernization. Modernization implied the adoption of
more up-to-date institutions, Western ideas, and science, whereas
reform signified any improvement in the existing situation. Hao
Chang said that intentionality was a very important element in

reform; modernization was a long-term process which might not involve intentionality. Thomas Kennedy disagreed, saying that, on the contrary, he saw modernization as the main constituent of reform and intentionality as an essential element in modernization. Hao Chang said that the relationship between modernization and reform was very problematic. You could have modernizing reform, but you could also have nonmodernizing reform.

Paul Cohen said that if one didn't bring in the concept of intentionality, reform became indistinguishable from change, which he saw as an impersonal process that might result from reform or from a variety of other forces that no one had consciously sought to bring into existence. Mr. Cohen also noted the possibility that when one tried to reform in one direction, one might end up with consequences in another direction, consequences that were unanticipated.

John Schrecker expressed some discomfort with these distinctions. He said that when he thought of reform, he thought of the dozens of real problems that faced China in the nineteenth century. *Ch'ing-i* people were not just looking for jobs. There were concrete problems which they felt the people in power were not really dealing with, and they went after these problems, certain individuals interesting themselves in certain kinds of problems. That was what reform was about.

CLOSING DISCUSSION

Esther Morrison said she would like to make a further attempt to define reform, focusing in particular on the political system. She felt that this could be done within the boundaries of James Liu's typology, which, she noted in passing, neglected to mention one crucial concept: *hsing-li ch'u-pi* (promote benefits and eradicate evils).

Ms. Morrison started out by identifying nature and scope as necessary elements in any definition of reform. In considering the former, she thought it useful to distinguish reform from innovation. Reform was the act of changing something that already existed— an idea, a process, or an institution. An innovation was an addition, the creation of something new. For example, the new regional armies and the likin taxes were domestic innovations arising out of the Taiping Rebellion, while the Tsungli Yamen, the Maritime Customs Service, and the treaty ports were innovations undertaken because of foreign initiative or pressure.

The comprehensiveness or scope of a given reform presented another important problem. The establishment of the T'ung-wen kuan, for example, had ramifications beyond the institution itself. Had this reform been more successful, there would have been the problem of finding positions for the graduates within the bureau- cracy and deciding what exactly their status should be. Problems of this sort, political in nature, permeated all phases of the reform process.

Finally, Ms. Morrison urged, we should examine the history of particular reforms. For example, likin began in response to a specific need, the need to finance the new armies, but it outlasted the new armies by many years.

Kwang-Ching Liu agreed that there was a distinction between innovation and reform and that innovation did not necessarily lead to reform, except perhaps to minor repairing reforms. Institutional innovation, however, did require full-scale reform. With reference to the T'ung-wen kuan, Mr. Liu said, Prince Kung would have become much more powerful had Hanlin scholars entered the new institution.

Esther Morrison, noting Mr. Liu's equation of "repairing reforms" with small scope, suggested that such reforms might actually be innovations. Mr. Liu said that in any event he would rank innovations below real *pien-fa* or institutional reform. First, you had innovations. Then the 1898 reformers came along and pushed for institutional reform. But this was not possible without political reform, without a new dispensation in politics, and that came only after 1901, after the Boxers, with the abolition of the examination system. Mr. Liu suggested that there were three sequential phases of intentional action which should be distinguished: innovation, reform of institutions, and finally political breakthrough.

John Schrecker said he thought that worrying about the definition of reform and then going back to the historical story was putting the cart before the horse. He pointed out that there were problems in China and different perspectives on how to solve them. That was what we should focus on, not how to define reform. One person's reform could be another's disaster. Mr. Schrecker also thought that in general we would have a great deal of difficulty, given the depth and breadth of the Confucian sense of politics, in crystallizing out a conception of reform that would be satisfactory.

Jonathan Ocko took issue with the implied premise that Confucianism was invariably the framework within which reform took place. The ideological impulse behind reform, he thought, was often Taoist, rather than Confucian. For most reformers, the perspective was local, and the concerns were reduction of scale, decentralization of power, lowering of the level of initiative, and equity—all themes associated with the Taoist approach to government. Mr. Ocko also pointed to a definite anti-Manchu theme in the activities of the gentry reformers. He said he thought that Paul Cohen's depiction of China as a Manchu colony in the nineteenth century was not all that far-fetched. Much of the effort of gentry reformers reflected a desire to return control of institutions to the local level, that is to Chinese hands.

Judith Whitbeck thought that a general distinction should be made between reformers like Li Hung-chang who were basically content with the existing system and wanted to shore it up and those like Kung Tzu-chen who were discontented and had a vision of a completely new society, based on new institutions and new modes of human interaction. Jeffrey Kinkley wondered to what extent the reformers of 1897–1898 had a vision of a new age and were preparing themselves for the founding of a new order, not necessarily according to the Kung-yang scheme.

Roger Des Forges said that an important new element in the history of the late Ch'ing period was the fact that China was not autonomous. It was no longer in a position of complete control over its own destiny. John Schrecker pointed out that one of the main impulses behind reform seemed to be the need to get the internal system in order before dealing with outside threats. Mr. Des Forges added that although people retained a sense that the really important things were within China, this attitude became harder to maintain in the nineteenth and twentieth centuries. It was difficult to separate the Taiping Revolution from the Western impact.

John Schrecker said that "reform" referred not only to institutional change in all of its aspects, but also to goals and to matters of technique and style. The word covered a broad range of things.

Paul Cohen added that there was great variation in the extent to which the different realms of a culture changed. When we compare China today with China in the late nineteenth century, he said, we find great changes in the intellectual realm. In the political realm, however, change seems to be far less pronounced. The political system has changed. But political style, the way in which politics tends to be carried on, appears not entirely different today from what it was a century ago.

NOTES

Definitions of Community by Ch'i Chi-kuang and Lü K'un/Joanna F. Handlin

SYY   Lü K'un, *Shen-yin yü*, ed. Kōda Rentarō (Tokyo, 1965).

CWCC   Lü K'un, *Ch'u-wei chai wen-chi* (Collected writings), in *Lü tzu i-shu* (The transmitted works of Lü; K'ai-fang ed., 1827), ed. Wang Ch'ing-lin and Sung Yü-mei.

LPSC   Ch'i Chi-kuang, *Lien ping shih chi* (True record of troop training; Shanghai, 1936).

CHHS   Ch'i Chi-kuang, *Chi hsiao hsin shu* (New manual of effectiveness; Changsha, 1938).

1.   Ch'eng Tsu-lo, "Memorial," *Lü tzu i-shu* (The transmitted works of Lü; 1827), pp. 1a–4b. This paper complements, and at times duplicates, Joanna F. Handlin, "Lü K'un Compromises with the Common People," a paper presented at the Association for Asian Studies meeting, San Francisco, March 1975, and published in *Ming Studies* (Fall 1975).

2.   Ch'eng Tsu-lo, "Preface," *Lü tzu i-shu*, p. 2a.

3.   Lo Jung-pang, ed., *K'ang Yu-wei: A Biography and a Symposium* (Tucson, University of Arizona Press, 1967), p. 23. For two of Lü's many statements on "sameness," see *SYY*, 5:649; 5:653.

4.   For Ch'i Chi-kuang's influence on nineteenth-century thought, see Philip A. Kuhn, *Rebellion and its Enemies in Late Imperial China* (Cambridge, Mass., Harvard University Press, 1970), pp. 126–127, 147–148; and James Ferguson Millinger, "Ch'i Chi-kuang: Chinese Military Official" (Ph.D. dissertation, Yale University, 1968), pp. 233–236. On Lü K'un, see Kuhn, p. 61. Also noteworthy are the plans for defense by Ch'i Piao-chia (1602–1645), ibid., pp. 33–34.

5.   *CWCC*, 5:7a.

6.   *SYY*, 3:410.

7.   *SYY*, 3:401.

8.   *SYY*, 2:350.

9.   *SYY*, 2:196; 2:213; 2:217; 2:225; 2:233; 3:424–425.

10. Lu Lung-ch'i, "Preface," *SYY*, pp. 18–19. For Lü's cynicism about "humaneness," see Lü K'un, *Wu-ju* (Nothing like it; n.d.), pp. 34b–35a.

11. *SYY*, 2:350. See also, *SYY*, 2:334. For Lü's use of the term *kuan*, see *SYY*, 1:48; 5:657. For a discussion of the late Ming preoccupation with "critical situations" (*kuan-t'ou*), see Heinrich Busch, "The Tung-lin Academy and its Political and Philosophical Significance," *Monumenta Serica* XIV (1949–1955), pp. 88, 112–113.

12. *CWCC*, 3:26b–27a.

13. *CWCC*, 7:49a; 7:20a; 7:37a. For a discussion of portions of Lü's manual, *Chiu-ming shu* (On saving lives), see Herbert Franke, "Siege and Defense of Towns in Medieval China," *Chinese Ways in Warfare*, ed., Frank A. Kierman, Jr. and John K. Fairbank (Cambridge, Mass., Harvard University Press, 1974), pp. 152–181.

14. *CWCC*, 7:21a.

15. Lü's selflessness was apparent to the author of the colophon to *Chiu-ming shu*, Ch'iao Yun-tun, who observed that "the lives of all, not simply the lives of Mr. [Lü's] own person or family," were being saved. *CWCC*, 7:52a.

16. Lü K'un, *Shih-cheng lu* (Records of practical government), in *Lü tzu i-shu* 2:34b. For a description of traditional forms of charity, see Hsu I-t'ang, "Social Relief during the Sung Dynasty," *Chinese Social History*, ed. and tr., E-tu Zen Sun and John de Francis (Washington, American Council of Learned Societies, 1956), pp. 207–215.

17. Thus even Li Tsu-t'ao (fl. 1800), who praised Ch'i's use of "favor and trust (*en hsin*) to unite his troops, emphasizes above all Ch'i's concept of "regulations" (*chieh-chih*) as an instrument for achieving collective action. Li Tsu-t'ao, *Mai-t'ang wen-lueh* (1865), 3:1a–b. See also Kuhn, p. 125.

18. *LPSC*, p. 170.

19. *LPSC*, p. 65.

20. *LPSC*, "Directions to the Reader," p. 1; p. 172. *CHHS*, p. 33. For a discussion of Lü's concessions to a popular audience, see Handlin, "Lü K'un Compromises with the Common People."

21. *LPSC*, p. 78; *CHHS*, p. 40.

22. *CHHS*, p. 48; *LPSC*, p. 81. See also *LPSC*, pp. 127, 131.

23. *LPSC*, p. 151.

24. *LPSC*, pp. 65–66.

25. See, for example, *SYY*, 5:755–756 and Lü K'un, *Shih-cheng lu* 3:5b.

26. Ibid., 3:7b. *LPSC*, "Directions to the Reader," p. 2. For information on T'ao Hsing-chih, see Howard Boorman, ed., *Biographical Dictionary of Republican China* (New York, Columbia University Press, 1967), III, 243–248.

27. *LPSC*, "Directions to the Reader," p. 2; p. 172.

28. *LPSC*, pp. 129, 151.

29. *LPSC*, p. 170; *CHHS*, p. 19.

30. *Ssu-k'u ch'üan-shu tsung-mu* (Catalogue to the complete treasury of four libraries; Taipei, 1964), 99:23b–24a. The comment also calls attention to Ch'i's emphasis on "trust" or "faith" (*hsin*).

31. *CHHS*, "Preface by the Author," p. 1.

32. *CHHS*, p. 40.

33. *CHHS*, "Preface by the Author," p. 1. See also *CHHS*, pp. 8, 18.

34. *CWCC*, 3:2a.

35. For further elaboration of these features see Wm. Theodore de Bary, "Individualism and Humanitarianism in Late Ming Thought," *Self and Society in Ming Thought*, ed., Wm. Theodore de Bary (New York, Columbia University Press, 1970), pp. 145–225; Etienne Balazs, *Political Theory and Administrative Reality in Traditional China* (London, School of Oriental and African Studies, University of London, 1965); and Joanna F. Handlin, "Lü K'un's New Audience: The Influence of Women's Literacy on Sixteenth-Century Thought," *Women in Chinese Society*, ed., Margery Wolf and Roxane Witke (Stanford University Press, 1975), pp. 13–38.

Merchant Investment, Commercialization, and Social Change in the Ningpo Area/Susan Mann Jones

CHHC   *Chen-hai hsien chih* (A gazetteer of Chen-hai district); suppl. *Hsin-chih pei-kao* (Complete draft of a new gazetteer), comp. Wang Jung-shang and Hung Hsi-fan, preface dated 1924, published 1931.

NCH   *North China Herald and Supreme Court and Consular Gazette*, illus. weekly (Shanghai, January 1870–November 1941).

1.   On Shen, see *Shang-hai hsien chih* (A gazetteer of Shanghai district), comp. Niu Yung-chien et al. (1935), 17:3b; *Gendai Shina jimmei kan* (Biographies of contemporary Chinese), ed. Gaimushō Jōhōbu (Tokyo, 1916), pp. 782–783; *NCH* (1895), Jan. 4, p. 13; (1901), Sept. 18, p. 563, Sept. 25, pp. 607–608; (1902), Apr. 9, pp. 706–707, June 18, p. 1211.

2.   Albert Feuerwerker, *China's Early Industrialization: Sheng Hsuan-huai (1844–1916) and Mandarin Enterprise* (Cambridge, Mass., Harvard University Press, 1958), pp. 13ff., points out the regional and local character of early Chinese industrialization, of which the Ningpo case is a good example.

3.   See P'eng Hsin-wei, *Chung-kuo huo-pi shih* (A history of money in China; Shanghai, 1958), pp. 647–648; Katō Shigeshi, "Shindai ni okeru sempo, senshō no hattatsu ni tsuite" (On the development of money-changing shops and native banks in the Ch'ing dynasty), *Tōyō gakuhō*, 31.3:344 (December 1947); Katō Shigeshi, "Shindai ni okeru sonchin no teiki-ichi" (Periodic marketing in the Ch'ing dynasty), *Tōyō gakuhō*, 23.2: 170 (February 1936); and Ping-ti Ho, *Studies in the Population of China, 1368–1953* (Cambridge, Mass., Harvard University Press, 1959), pp. 194, 198.

4.   See Nishizato Yoshiyuki, "Shinmatsu no Nimpō shōnin ni tsuite" (On the Ningpo merchants at the end of the Ch'ing dynasty), pt. 2, *Tōyōshi kenkyū*, 26.2:205 (September 1967); and *NCH* (1905), Dec. 15, pp. 595–596. On Hu, see C. John Stanley, *Late Ch'ing Finance: Hu Kuang-yung as an Innovator* (Cambridge, Mass., East Asian Research Center, Harvard University, 1961). On Yang, see Toyama Gunji, "Shanhai no shinshō Yan Bō" (Yang Fang, an official-merchant of Shanghai), *Tōyōshi kenkyū*, 9.4:17–35 (November 1945); and Jonathan Spence, *To Change China: Western Advisers in China, 1620–1960* (Boston, Little, Brown and Co., 1969), pp. 63, 70.

5. These figures, doubtless inflated, should be used only to suggest the relative magnitude of fluctuations. See Hatano Yoshihiro, *Chūgoku kindai kōgyōshi no kenkyū* (Studies on early industrialization in China; Kyoto, 1961), pp. 149-150; and Hallett Abend, *Treaty Ports* (Garden City, N.Y., Doubleday, Doran, 1944), p. 83.

6. The Ningpo Guild, founded in the late eighteenth century, was given tax-exempt status in Shanghai in 1844 by the prefect at the time, who was a native of Ting-hai district in Ningpo prefecture. See Negishi Tadashi, *Chūgoku shakai ni okeru shidōsō: kirō shinshi no kenkyū* (Elites in Chinese society: a study of elders and gentry; Tokyo, 1947), pp. 147-148. When the French Concession was created in 1849, the Guild property was incorporated into the concession. See Susan Mann Jones, "The Ningpo *pang* and Financial Power at Shanghai," in Mark Elvin and G. William Skinner, eds., *The Chinese City between Two Worlds* (Stanford University Press, 1974), pp. 86-88.

7. See *Yin hsien t'ung-chih* (A comprehensive gazetteer of Yin district), comp. Ch'en Hsun-cheng and Ma Ying (1936), *Shih-huo chih* (Monograph on economics), pp. 72b-73.

8. See Ōtani Kotarō, "Shanhai ni okeru dōkyō dantai oyobi dōgyō dantai" (Native-place associations and occupational associations in Shanghai), *Shina kenkyū,* 18:262-263, 275-278 (December 1928).

9. On transport, see Kwang-Ching Liu, *Anglo-American Steamship Rivalry in China, 1862-1874* (Cambridge, Mass., Harvard University Press, 1962), p. 88. On population, see *Shina keizai zensho* (The Chinese economy: a compendium; Tokyo, 1907-1908), II, 74.

10. *NCH* (1907), Mar. 15, pp. 548-549.

11. Kagawa Shun'ichirō, *Sensō shihon ron* (An essay on Chinese native banking capital; Tokyo, 1948), pp. 126 ff.

12. See Feng Kuei-fen's well-known disparaging reference to them in his *Chiao-pin-lu k'ang-i* (Straightforward words from the lodge of Early Chou studies; 1885), *chüan-hsia* (last): 99-101.

13. See *Shang-hai yen-chiu tzu-liao, hsu chi* (Materials for research on Shanghai, vol. 2), comp. Hsu Wei-nan et al. (Shanghai, 1935-1936), p. 154.

14. See *CHHC,* 12:3b–6. On charitable estates, see Denis Twitchett, "The Fan Clan's Charitable Estate, 1050–1760," in D. S. Nivison and A. F. Wright, eds., *Confucianism in Action* (Stanford University Press, 1959), pp. 97–133.

15. *Shina kaikojō shi* (Gazetteer of the treaty ports in China), ed. and publ. Tōa Dōbunkai Chōsa Hensambu (Tokyo, 1922), I, 1032–1033.

16. Milton T. Stauffer's survey of Christian missions, *The Christian Occupation of China* (Shanghai, China Continuation Committee of the World Missionary Conference, 1922), suggests the extent of Christian influence in the Ningpo area in Appendix Aiii.

17. *CHHC,* 12:2b.

18. *CHHC,* 12:2b–3b; 6b–9b.

19. *CHHC,* 11:1b–2b.

20. *CHHC,* 12:3b–6.

21. See *CHHC,* 45:21b–22.

Overseas Chinese Entrepreneurs as Reformers/Michael R. Godley

1. This paper is based on the author's dissertation research begun in Singapore at the Institute of Southeast Asian Studies in 1970. See "The Mandarin-Capitalists from Nanyang: Overseas Chinese Enterprise and the Modernization of China, 1893–1911" (Ph.D. dissertation, Brown University, 1973).

2. For details and citation of sources, consult the author's "Chang Pi-shih and Nanyang Chinese Involvement in South China's Railroads, 1896–1911," *Journal of Southeast Asian Studies* (March 1973), pp. 16–30.

3. There is very little written about Chang's career. The most easily available, but not always accurate, account is in Howard Boorman, ed., *Biographical Dictionary of Republican China* (New York, Columbia University Press, 1967), I, 90–92. The basic Chinese biography is that by Cheng Kuan-ying: *Chang Pi-shih chün sheng-p'ing shih-lueh* (A brief

biography of Chang Pi-shih; Taipei reprint: Chin-tai Chung-kuo shih-liao ts'ung-k'an, vol. 747, 1972).

4. "The Late Ch'ing Courtship of the Chinese in Southeast Asia," *Journal of Asian Studies* (February 1975), pp. 361–385.

5. See *Tung-hua hsu-lu* (The Tung-hua records continued for the Kuang-hsu period; Shanghai, 1909), 190:1–2 and *Ta Ch'ing li-ch'ao shih-lu* (Veritable records of successive reigns of the Ch'ing dynasty; Tokyo, 1937–1938), Kuang-hsu, 517:66–67.

6. Quoted in *Penang Sin Poe,* 18 December 1905.

Imperialism, Sovereignty, and Self-Strengthening/Saundra Sturdevant

1. Paraphrased from the *North China Daily News,* enclosed in a dispatch from George Seward to Hamilton Fish, July 10, 1876, United States Congress, House Miscellaneous Document no. 31, II:375–376, 45 Cong., 2 Sess. (Washington, U.S. Government Printing Office, 1878).

2. *Hai-fang-tang* (Archives of maritime defense), 9 vols. (Taipei, 1957), vol. 6, nos. 20, 22, 23.

3. Great Britain, British Foreign Office (Public Record Office, London), F.O. 17/672, No. 3 Inclosure: W. F. Mayers' Memorandum of an Inter-view with Li Hung-chang, Sept. 1865.

4. U.S. Congress, House Miscellaneous Document no. 31, I:285–286.

5. Paul A. Cohen, "Ch'ing China: Confrontation with the West, 1850–1900," in James Crowley, ed., *Modern East Asia: Essays in Interpretation* (New York, Harcourt, Brace, and World, 1970), p. 41.

6. Albert Feuerwerker, *China's Early Industrialization: Sheng Hsuan-huai (1844–1916) and Mandarin Enterprise* (Cambridge, Mass., Harvard University Press, 1958.

7. Mary C. Wright, *The Last Stand of Chinese Conservatism: The T'ung-chih Restoration, 1862–1874* (New York, Atheneum, 1967), p. 42.

Reform and the Tea Industry and Trade in Late Ch'ing China/Robert P.
Gardella

1.   Evelyn S. Rawski, *Agricultural Change and the Peasant Economy of
      South China* (Cambridge, Mass., Harvard University Press, 1972).

2.   See H. B. Morse, *The Trade and Administration of the Chinese Empire*
      (Taipei, Ch'eng-wen reprint, 1966), pp. 290–291; and Albert Feuer-
      werker, *The Chinese Economy, ca. 1870–1911* (Ann Arbor, Center for
      Chinese Studies, University of Michigan, 1969), p. 53.

3.   Sun Yü-t'ang, *Chung-Jih chia-wu chan-cheng ch'ien wai-kuo tzu-pen
      tsai Chung-kuo ching-ying te chin-tai kung-yeh* (Foreign capitalist
      control of modern industry in China before the Sino-Japanese War of
      1894–1895; Peking, 1955), p. 70.

4.   See Li Kuo-chi, "Yu Min-Che ch'ü-yü yen-chiu k'an Ch'ing-tai chieh-
      chueh jen-k'ou ya-li te chung-yao fang-fa: tsai-p'ei ching-chi tso-wu"
      (An important way to deal with overpopulation in Fukien and Chekiang
      in the Ch'ing: The cultivation of economic crops), *Shih-huo,* 4.10:421–
      441 (January 1975).

5.   Rawski, pp. 96–100.

6.   See Louis Dermigny, *La Chine et l'Occident, le Commerce à Canton au
      XVIIIe siècle: 1719–1833* (Paris, 1964), III, 1015. The Fukien export
      figure represents the writer's extrapolation based on types of tea
      exported from Canton to England.

7.   These figures have been arrived at by comparing the all-China statistics
      available in Hsiao Liang-lin, *China's Foreign Trade Statistics, 1864–
      1949* (Cambridge, Mass., East Asian Research Center, Harvard University,
      1974), p. 117, with Foochow tea exports as recorded in British consular
      reports and Chinese maritime customs reports (full citations available
      from the author; all figures converted from piculs to pounds).

8.   See Sun Yü-t'ang, pp. 20–21; and ibid., p. 117 (figures converted from
      piculs to pounds).

9.   Taiwan Tea Exporter's Association, *The Historical Brevities of Taiwan
      Tea Export, 1865–1965* (Taipei, 1965), table facing p. 58 (figures con-
      verted from kilograms to pounds); Edgar B. Wickberg, "Late Nineteenth

Century Land Tenure in North Taiwan," in Leonard H. D. Gordon, ed., *Taiwan: Studies in Chinese Local History* (New York, Columbia University Press, 1970), pp. 78–92; and Ramon Myers, "Taiwan under Ch'ing Imperial Rule, 1684–1895: The Traditional Economy," *The Journal of the Institute of Chinese Studies of the Chinese University of Hong Kong*, 5.2:373–409 (December 1972).

10. Rev. Justus Doolittle, *Social Life of the Chinese* (New York, 1876), I, 46; and China, Imperial Maritime Customs, *Tea, 1888,* 2-Special Series no. 11 (Shanghai, 1889), English text, pp. 139–140.

11. See Jen-min ta-hsueh Chung-kuo li-shih chiao-yen-shih, comp., *Ming-Ch'ing she-hui ching-chi hsing-t'ai te yen-chiu* (Research on the state of the Ming-Ch'ing society and economy; Shanghai, 1957), p. 301; Imperial Maritime Customs, *Tea, 1888,* Chinese text, p. 95; Yen-p'ing Hao, *The Comprador in Nineteenth Century China: Bridge between East and West* (Cambridge, Mass., Harvard University Press, 1971), p. 177; and James W. Davidson, *The Island of Formosa: Past and Present* (Yokohama, 1903), p. 379.

12. Imperial Maritime Customs, *Tea, 1888,* Chinese text, p. 95, referring to Yang-k'ou village. Similar high prices are reported for the Shao-wu and Foochow areas, and for northern Formosa.

13. China, Imperial Maritime Customs, *Reports on Trade, 1875* (Shanghai, 1876), p. 197.

14. On the deflation, see Yeh-chien Wang, *Land Taxation in Imperial China, 1750–1911* (Cambridge, Mass., Harvard University Press, 1973), pp. 114–115. Specie imports are described in Yen-p'ing Hao, pp. 75–81.

15. See Wang Hsiao-ch'üan, comp., *Fu-chien ts'ai-cheng shih-kang* (An outline history of Fukien financial administration; Foochow, 1935–1936), II, 394–395.

16. Yeh-chien Wang, pp. 12, 80–81.

17. Author's estimate from figures provided in Lo Yü-tung, *Chung-kuo li-chin shih* (A history of the likin tax in China; Shanghai, 1936), II, 562–563.

18. This total is derived from multiplying annual Foochow tea exports during the 1860s and 70s by 2.50 taels, the rate of export duty per picul stipulated by treaty tariff provisions.

19. Tso Tsung-t'ang, *Tso wen-hsiang kung tsou-kao* (Draft memorials of Tso Tsung-t'ang), *chüan* 19:61a.

20. Lo Yü-tung, I, 326.

21. See E. H. Parker, "A Journey from Foochow to Wenchow through Central Fukien," *Journal of the North China Branch, Royal Asiatic Society,* 19:1–19 (1883), and Rev. Justus Doolittle, *A Vocabulary and Hand-book of the Chinese Language Romanized in the Mandarin Dialect* (Foochow, 1872), II, 437–438, the latter reproducing an official pronouncement of April 24, 1872, prohibiting malpractices by Chinese tea merchants at Foochow.

22. See Lo Yü-tung, I, 337–338; Chu Wen-djang, *The Moslem Rebellion in Northwest China, 1862–1876* (The Hague, Mouton, 1966), pp. 112–113; John L. Rawlinson, *China's Struggle for Naval Development, 1839–1895* (Cambridge, Mass., Harvard University Press, 1967), pp. 53, 99–102; and Kobayashi Kazumi, "Chūgoku han-shokuminchika no keizai katei to minshū no tatakai—rikin o megutte, jūkyūseiki kōhan" (The economic process of China's semi-colonization and popular struggle—with reference to the likin in the second half of the nineteenth century), *Rekishigaku kenkyū,* 369:1–18 (February 1971), summarized in K. H. Kim, *Japanese Perspectives on China's Early Modernization* (Ann Arbor, Center for Chinese Studies, University of Michigan, 1974), pp. 95–96.

23. See Sir Percival Griffiths, *The History of the Indian Tea Industry* (London, Weidenfeld and Nicholson, 1967); and Donald R. Snodgrass, *Ceylon: An Export Economy in Transition* (Homewood, Ill., Richard D. Irwin, 1966).

24. Griffiths, p. 125.

25. See Ramon Myers, "Some Issues on Economic Organization during the Ming and Ch'ing Periods: A Review Article," *Ch'ing-shih wen-t'i,* 3.2:77–97 (December 1974).

26. Imperial Maritime Customs, *Tea, 1888,* English text, pp. 1–6.

27. Ibid., p. 5.

28. Ibid., Chinese text, p. 106. According to O. E. Nepomnin, *Genezis kapitalizma v sel'skom khoziaistve Kitaia* (1966), pp. 55–62, the tea

boom and bust resulted in the proletarianization, pauperization, and gradual breakdown of the closed character of peasant villages in Fukien. The writer is indebted to Professor Gilbert Rozman of Princeton University for a summation of Nepomnin's work.

29. China, Imperial Maritime Customs, *Decennial Reports, 1892–1901* (Shanghai, 1906), II, 99.

30. Ibid., pp. 124–125; Boris P. Torgasheff, *China as a Tea Producer* (Shanghai, 1926), pp. 35–36; and C. F. Remer, *The Foreign Trade of China* (Taipei, Ch'eng-wen reprint, 1967), p. 142.

31. Imperial Maritime Customs, *Decennial Reports, 1892–1901,* II, 99; and Sun Yü-t'ang, p. 21.

32. Pien Pao-ti, *Pien chih-chün cheng-shu* (Official writings of Pien Pao-ti), *chüan* 4:1a–3a.

33. Ibid., 2a–3b.

34. See Liu Kuang-ching, "Cheng Kuan-ying *I-yen:* Kuang-hsu ch'u-nien chih pien-fa ssu-hsiang" (Cheng Kuan-ying's *I-yen:* Reform proposals of the early Kuang-hsu period), *Tsing Hua Journal of Chinese Studies,* n. s. 8, nos. 1 and 2:398–407, 422–423; and Yen-p'ing Hao, "Cheng Kuan-ying: The Comprador as Reformer," *Journal of Asian Studies,* 29.1:20 (November 1969).

35. See Ma's "Fu-min shuo," in his collected essays entitled *Shih-k'o-chai chi-yen* (Peking reprint, 1960), pp. 1–4; and also Hayashi Yōzō, "Ba Ken-chū no keizai shisō: 'fumin' shisō no seiritsu oyobi sono yakuwari" (The economic thought of Ma Chien-chung: The development and role of the concept of "enriching the people"), *Tezukayama daigaku kiyō,* 2:191–219 (1966), summarized in K. H. Kim, pp. 80–81.

36. Kuo-chia tang-an chü, Ming-Ch'ing tang-an kuan-pien, *Wu-hsu pien-fa tang-an shih-liao* (Archival sources on the reform movement of 1898; Peking, 1958), pp. 397–399, 404–406.

37. "Min-ch'a chien-li shih" (Likin reduction on Fukien tea), *Nung-hsueh pao,* no. 35:1a–1b (June–July 1898; Kuang-hsu 24/5); and Lo Yü-tung, I, 325.

38.   Remer, pp. 142–143.

39.   See "Chung-kuo k'ao-ch'a Yin-Hsi ch'a-yeh te ti-i-jen" (The first Chinese investigator of the Indian and Ceylonese tea industries), *Ch'a-pao,* 1.2:26 (May 1937); "Lu Yung hsien-sheng wu-t'an chi" (A chat with Mr. Lu Yung), *Ch'a-pao,* 1.3:24 (June 1937); and H. S. Brunnert and V. V. Hagelstrom, *Present Day Political Organization of China* (Shanghai, 1912), pp. 246, 360.

40.   Lü Wei-ying, "Min-sheng ch'a-yeh mu-chih ch'ing-hsing" (The condition of the tea industry and lumbering in Fukien), *Shang-wu kuan-pao* (Jan. 12, 1908; Kuang-hsu, 33/12/15), p. 15a.

Politics, Intellectual Outlook, and Reform/Kwang-Ching Liu

1.   James B. Crowley, ed., *Modern East Asia: Essays in Interpretation* (New York, Harcourt, Brace, and World, 1970), p. 48.

2.   *Harvard Journal of Asiatic Studies,* 30:5–45 (1970).

3.   John E. Schrecker, *Imperialism and Chinese Nationalism: Germany in Shantung* (Cambridge, Mass., Harvard University Press, 1971), pp. 56–57.

4.   Hsu Shih-ch'ang, ed., *Ch'ing ju hsueh-an* (The records of Ch'ing scholars; 208 *chüan,* preface dated 1938), 107:19. Although Ch'i praised the scholarship of the Han dynasty scholars Hsu Shen and Cheng K'ang-ch'eng, he emphasized the crucial importance of the Neo-Confucianists, Chou Tun-i, Ch'eng I, Chang Tsai, and Chu Hsi. Ch'i believed that the classical commentaries by these Sung scholars "fully explain the ethical principles, scholarship, and the human mind and are quite adequate as models and restraints for the later generations. The effort to achieve rectified mind and sincerity of intentions as taught in the *Great Learning* must therefore be based on the investigation of things and the extension of knowledge."

5.   See Wu Hsiang-hsiang, *Wan-Ch'ing kung-t'ing shih-chi* (True account of palace politics during the late Ch'ing; rev. ed., Taipei, 1961), plate 10 and pp. 102–111.

6.   See Li Tsung-t'ung and Liu Feng-han, *Li Hung-tsao hsien-sheng nien-p'u*

(A chronological biography of Mr. Li Hung-tsao), 2 vols. (Taipei, 1969), I, 154–160.

7. *Ch'ing-tai ch'ou-pan i-wu shih-mo* (Complete record of the Ch'ing dynasty's management of barbarian affairs; 100 *chüan* for the T'ung-chih period; Peiping 1930), 46:47 (esp. line 3) and 48b (line 5). This memorial was followed by one on February 25 recommending that Hsu Chi-yü, the aging author of *Ying-huan chih-lueh* (A brief geography of the globe) be made commissioner (*ta-ch'en*) in charge of the T'ung-wen kuan.

8. Hao Chang [Chang Hao], "The Anti-foreignist Role of Wo-jen (1804–1871)," *Papers on China*, 14:1–29 (East Asian Research Center, Harvard University, 1960).

9. *Ch'ing-tai ch'ou-pan i-wu shih-mo*, T'ung-chih, 47:24a (line 10) and 24b (line 2).

10. Ibid., 48:4a (line 6).

11. Publication from the Grand Council archive of the T'ung-chih period (the bulk of which for this reign is in Peking) includes a memorial dated May 1, 1867, by Yü Ling-ch'en, commissioner of the Transmission Office (*t'ung-cheng shih*, of 3A rank), opposing the expansion of the T'ung-wen kuan chiefly on the ground that the new department of Western learning would create two factions among the scholar-officials. See Chung-kuo shih-hsueh hui (Chinese Historical Association) et al., eds., *Yang-wu yun-tung* (The Western affairs movement), 8 vols. (Peking 1961), II, 39–40. This seems to be the only memorial unequivocally supporting Wo-jen before a vitriolic memorial attacking the T'ung-wen kuan was received by the throne on June 30 from a candidate for *chou* magistrate, Yang T'ing-hsi, transmitted by the Censorate (*Ch'ing-tai ch'ou-pan i-wu shih-mo*, T'ung-chih, 49:13–24).

12. Ibid., 48:14a (lines 3–5); *Yang-wu yun-tung*, II, 39.

13. Cited in Knight Biggerstaff, *The Earliest Modern Government Schools in China* (Ithaca, Cornell University Press, 1961), p. 119, n. 47.

14. Weng T'ung-ho, *Weng Wen-kung kung jih-chi* (Weng T'ung-ho's diaries; typeset ed., 5 vols., Taipei, 1970), I, 370, 372, 377 (lines 15–16).

15.   Ibid., p. 369.

16.   *Ch'ing-tai ch'ou-pan i-wu shih-mo,* T'ung-chih, 48:15b.

17.   *Ta-Ch'ing li-ch'ao shih-lu* (Veritable records of successive reigns of the
      Ch'ing dynasty; Mukden, 1937), T'ung-chih, 238:17 (lines 7–9). The
      edict was addressed generally to all metropolitan as well as provincial
      officials, exhorting them to make greater efforts in governmental
      affairs now that both the Niens and the Taipings had been suppressed.

18.   *Ch'ing-tai ch'ou-pan i-wu shih-mo,* T'ung-chih, 49:25 (lines 9–10).

19.   Cf. Lloyd E. Eastman, *Throne and Mandarins: China's Search for a
      Policy during the Sino-French Controversy, 1880–1885* (Cambridge,
      Mass., Harvard University Press, 1967).

20.   I am grateful to Mr. I-fan Ch'eng for this useful phrase.

21.   See Wo-jen, *Wo Wen-tuan kung i-shu* (Writings of the late Wo-jen), 11
      chüan (2nd ed., 1894), *chüan-shou hsia:*22b–23b.

22.   *Ch'ing-tai ch'ou-pan i-wu shih-mo,* T'ung-chih, 48:11b (lines 7–8).

23.   Ibid., 48:11a (lines 3–4).

24.   Ibid., 46:45b (lines 7–8).

25.   Ibid., 46:46a (lines 6–7).

26.   See *inter alia* Li Tsung-t'ung and Liu Feng-han, *Li Hung-tsao hsien-
      sheng nien-p'u,* I, 172–173.

The Image of the Empress Dowager Tz'u-hsi/ Sue Fawn Chung

KCT   *Kung-chung tang Kuang-hsu ch'ao tsou-che* (Secret palace memorials
        of the Kuang-hsu period), ed. Kuo-li ku-kung po-wu yuan (Taipei,
        Kuo-li ku-kung po-wu yuan, 1973–1975).
SL   *Ch'ing Te-tsung Ching huang-ti shih-lu* (The veritable records of the
        Ch'ing Kuang-hsu emperor), ed. Ch'en Pao-shen et al. (Taiwan, Hua-
        wen shu chü, 1963–1964 photographic reduction of Tokyo 1937–
        1938 ed.).

TH   *Tung-hua hsu-lu, Kuang-hsu ch'ao* (Continuation of the official
        documents recorded at the Tung-hua Gate for the Kuang-hsu reign),
        ed. Chu Shou-p'eng (Shanghai, Ch'i-ch'eng tu-shu kung-ssu, 1909).
WHPF   *Wu-hsu pien-fa* (1898 reform movement), ed. Chien Po-tsan et al.
        (Shanghai, Chung-kuo hsin-shih-hsueh yen-chiu hui, 1953).

1. Chester C. Tan, *The Boxer Catastrophe* (New York, Columbia University
    Press, 1967) and Hsiao I-shan, *Ch'ing-tai t'ung-shih* (A comprehensive
    history of the Ch'ing dynasty; Taiwan, Shang-wu yin-shu-kuan, 1963),
    for example, both rely upon the writings of these men.

2. Charles Denby, *China and Her People* (Boston, L. C. Page, 1906), I,
    248. See also Isaac Taylor Headland, *Court Life in China* (New York,
    Fleming H. Revell Company, 1909), p. 156.

3. MacDonald to Salisbury, "Memo of conversation with K'ang Yu-wei on
    voyage from Shanghae to Hongkong, September 27–30, 1898," by
    Henry Cockburn, *China Blue Books* (Oct. 13, 1898), China No. 1 (1899),
    Doc. 401, p. 306.

4. See, for example, Wang Chao, *Shui-tung ch'üan-chi* (Complete works
    from Wang Chao's studio), ed. Yen I-p'ing (Taipei, I-wen yin-shu kuan,
    1964); *Ch'ing-i pao* (May 10, 1899), 1b; *SL* 476:8a–b, dated Jan. 29,
    1901; and Liang Ch'i-ch'ao, *Wu-hsu cheng-pien chi* (Account of the
    coup d'etat of 1898; Taipei, Wen-hai ch'u-pan she, 1970; first published
    in book form in Yokohama and Shanghai, 1899), chap. 2.

5. Fei Hsing-chien, "Tz'u-hsi chuan hsin-lu" (A true record of the Empress
    Dowager Tz'u-hsi), in *WHPF*, I, 464.

6. This is discussed in detail in my dissertation, "The Much Maligned
    Empress Dowager: A Revisionist Study of the Empress Dowager Tz'u-
    hsi," University of California, Berkeley, 1975, chap. 2.

7. Liu K'un-i, *Liu Chung-ch'eng Kung (K'un-i) i-chih* (The works of Liu
    K'un-i), ed. Ou-yang Fu-chih (Taipei, Wen-hai ch'u-pan she, 1970), *shu-
    tu* (letters), 12:66b–67a, dated Sept. 13, 1898 and 13:1a–2a, dated
    Nov. 11, 1898.

8. For more details, see chap. 4 of my dissertation. See also the emperor's
    notations of secret memorials on Sept. 24, 1898, *KCT,* 12:161–166,
    169–170.

9. *SL,* 427:1a–b and *TH,* 148:7a. Even Weng T'ung-ho felt that the basic policy of the new regime was "to strike a balance between extremes and not to be bound by previous commitments." Entry in *Weng Wen-kung-kung jih-chi* (The diary of Weng T'ung-ho; Shanghai, Commercial Press, 1925), dated Sept. 29, 1898, 37:92a. See Kung-ch'üan Hsiao, "Weng T'ung-ho and the Reform Movement of 1898," *Tsing Hua Journal of Chinese Studies,* n.s. 1.2:189–190 (April 1957).

10. See, for example, Nov. 5, 1898, *SL,* 430:7b–8a.

11. Dec. 30, 1898, *SL,* 434:3a–4a and *TH,* 150:19a–b.

12. *SL,* 431:4b–5a and *TH,* 150:1b–2a. Part of this edict has been translated by Kung-ch'üan Hsiao, pp. 190–191. He incorrectly dated the edict Nov. 3, 1898.

13. Nov. 5, 1898, *SL,* 430:8b–9a and *TH,* 149:16b–17a.

14. Nov. 8, 1898, *SL,* 430:12a–13a and *TH,* 149:18a–b.

15. *SL,* 428:11b–12a and *TH,* 148:19b–20a. See also Dec. 7, 1898, *SL,* 432:12a–b and *TH,* 150:8b–9a; MacDonald to Salisbury, *China Blue Books* (Dec. 20, 1898), China No. 1 (1900), Doc. 21, pp. 14–15; Ralph L. Powell, *The Rise of Chinese Military Power, 1895–1912* (Princeton University Press, 1955).

16. For a discussion on military funding, see Powell, p. 104. The annual military budget was presented on May 29, 1899, *SL,* 443:6a–b.

17. For more details on this subject, see chap. 3 of my dissertation.

18. Jan. 7, 1900, *SL,* 456:8a–b.

19. Powell, pp. 108–109.

20. Ibid.

21. Ibid., pp. 116–118.

22. Oct. 13, 1899, *SL,* 450:11a (Yü's report) and Nov. 22, 1899, *SL,* 453:8a (Hsu's report).

23. For more details, see chap. 3 of my dissertation.

24. Nov. 13, 1898, *SL,* 430:19b–20b. See also Oct. 9, 1898, *SL,* 428:7a–8b and *TH,* 148:19a; Kung-ch'üan Hsiao, pp. 190–191.

25. Ibid.

26. For example, see edicts of Oct. 8, 1898, *TH,* 148:17a–18a and Nov. 1, 1898, *SL,* 430:2b–3a and *TH,* 149:15b–16a.

27. For more details, see *SL,* 458:14a–15a and *TH,* 158:4a–5b. See also Ch'en K'uei-lung, *Meng-chiao t'ing tsa-chi* (Miscellaneous writings of Ch'en K'uei-lung), ed. Shen Yun-lung (Taiwan, Wen-hai ch'u-pan-she, 1970 reproduction of a 1925 ed.).

28. *SL,* 476:8a–10b. See also Kung-ch'üan Hsiao, pp. 193–194.

29. For a discussion and translation of this joint memorial, see Ssu-yü Teng and John K. Fairbank, *China's Response to the West: A Documentary Survey, 1839–1923* (Cambridge, Mass., Harvard University Press, 1954), pp. 196–198.

30. Yun Yü-ting, "Ch'ung-ling chuan-hsin lu" (The true story of the Kuang-hsu emperor), *Yung-yen* (The justice), vol. 2 (1914); reprinted in *Chung-kuo chin-pai-nien-shih tzu-liao, ch'u-pien* (Materials on Chinese history of the last century), ed. Tso Shun-sheng (Shanghai, Commercial Press, 1931), II, 454–488.

Local Reform and Its Opponents/Frank A. Lojewski

HCTK   Feng Kuei-fen, *Hsien-chih-t'ang kao* (Collected essays of the Hall of Manifest Aspirations; 1876).

CFCA   *Chiang-su sheng chien-fu ch'üan-an* (Complete records of the tax reduction in Kiangsu; preface dated 1866).

1. K'o Wu-ch'i, *Lou-wang yü-yü chi* (A collection of the gasps of a fish that escaped the net [diary 1836–1867]; Shanghai, 1959), p. 18; *HCTK,* 5:33.

2. *HCTK,* 9:23; Kung-ch'üan Hsiao, *Rural China: Imperial Control in the*

Nineteenth Century (Seattle, University of Washington Press, 1960), p. 599, n. 188.

3.   For example, see *Ta Ch'ing li-ch'ao shih-lu, Shih-tsung* (Veritable records of the Ch'ing dynasty, Yung-cheng reign), 16:21b–22, edict dated Yung-cheng 2/2/14 (1724); T'ung-tsu Ch'ü, *Local Government in China under the Ch'ing* (Stanford University Press, 1962), p. 332, n. 127.

4.   *HCTK*, 5:31–32b, 9:23–24; *CFCA*, 4:3b; Frank A. Lojewski, "Confucian Reformers and Local Vested Interests: The Su-Sung-T'ai Tax Reduction of 1863 and its Aftermath" (Ph.D. dissertation, University of California at Davis, 1973), p. 60.

5.   *Ta Ch'ing hui-tien shih-li* (Statutes and precedents of the Ch'ing dynasty; 1899 ed.), 173:1–12b; *CFCA*, 4:3b; *HCTK*, 9:21, 9:23, 10:1b.

6.   *HCTK*, 4:6b; Arthur W. Hummel, ed., *Eminent Chinese of the Ch'ing Period, 1644–1912* (Washington, D.C., United States Government Printing Office, 1943, 1944), p. 243. On the influence of parental entreaties, see Ping-ti Ho, *The Ladder of Success in Imperial China* (New York, Columbia University Press, 1962), esp. the comments on cases, pp. 272, 294–295.

7.   *HCTK*, 4:6b, 5:31–40, 43–46.

8.   *HCTK*, 9:2; James Legge, *The Chinese Classics* (Hong Kong, 1960), 3rd ed., I, 373–374, III, 92–127; *Chou-li* (Ritual of Chou; Ssu-pu ts'ung-k'an ed., 1920–1922), 1:14–15, 4:6a–b.

9.   *Ta Ch'ing li-ch'ao shih-lu, Shih-tsung,* 16:21b–22.

10. *HCTK*, 9:23–24b.

11. *HCTK*, 9:25; *Ta Ch'ing hui-tien* (Collected statutes of the Great Ch'ing; 1899 ed.), 32:11b; T'ung-tsu Ch'ü, *Law and Society in Traditional China* (Paris, 1961, 1965), pp. 178–180.

12. *HCTK*, 9:25; T'ung-tsu Ch'ü, *Local Government in China under the Ch'ing,* p. 173.

13. Feng Kuei-fen, *Chiao-pin-lu k'ang-i* (Straightforward words from the Lodge of Early Chou Studies; 1898 ed.), 1:10b.

14. *HCTK*, 9:23b.

15. *HCTK*, 5:33.

16. *HCTK*, 9:23a–b.

17. *HCTK*, 5:33, 9:23–25.

18. *HCTK*, 5:38, 9:24a–b.

19. Frank A. Lojewski, "Confucian Reformers and Local Vested Interests," pp. 188–195, 227–254.

20. Ibid., pp. 63–68.

21. Ibid., pp. 56–58.

The Ideal of Universality in Late Ch'ing Reformism/Young-tsu Wong

1. Frederic Wakeman, Jr., *History and Will: Philosophical Perspectives of Mao Tse-tung's Thought* (Berkeley, University of California Press, 1973), p. 115.

2. Kung-chuan Hsiao, *A Modern China and a New World: K'ang Yu-wei, Reformer and Utopian, 1858–1927* (Seattle, University of Washington Press, 1975), p. 409.

3. See, for example, Wang T'ao's comments in his *T'ao-yuan wen-lu wai-pien* (Collected essays of Wang T'ao; Hong Kong, 1883), 1:2b.

4. See Wang's unpublished letter quoted in Ch'en Chen-kuo, " 'Ch'ang-mao chuang-yuan' Wang T'ao" (Wang T'ao, "Senior Scholar of the Taiping Kingdom"), *I-ching*, no. 33:43 (July 1937). See also Wang Yung-tsu, "T'ien-nan tun-sou Wang T'ao" (Wang T'ao), *Hsin-chih tsa-chih*, 4.1:62 (February 1974).

5. Lu Hsiang-shan, quoted in Fung Yu-lan, *A History of Chinese Philosophy*, tr. Derk Bodde (Princeton University Press, 1953), II, 573.

6.   See Wang T'ao, *Man-yu sui-lu* (Notes on my trips), in *Hsiao-fang hu-chai yü-ti ts'ung-ch'ao,* comp. Wang Hsi-ch'i (Shanghai, 1897), 11.8:543. For a recent scholar's discussion of Wang's view see Paul A. Cohen, *Between Tradition and Modernity: Wang T'ao and Reform in Late Ch'ing China* (Cambridge, Mass., Harvard University Press, 1974), pp. 68–69.

7.   Wang T'ao, *T'ao-yuan wen-lu wai-pien,* 1:4b–5a; 5:18a–b, 4a–b.

8.   K'ang Yu-wei, *Ch'un-ch'iu Tung-shih hsueh* (Tung Chung-shu's interpretation of the *Ch'un-ch'iu*), reprint edition (Taipei, The Commercial Press, 1969), 6:44b–45a. Wang T'ao made similar remarks in *T'ao-yuan wen-lu wai-pien,* 5:20a.

9.   Donald W. Treadgold, *The West in Russia and China* (Cambridge, Eng., Cambridge University Press, 1973), II, 104–107.

10. Ch'en Chih, *Yung-shu* (A practical book; 1896), *wai-p'ien* II, 50a.

11. Wang T'ao, *T'ao-yuan wen-lu wai-pien,* 1:1b–2a.

12. For a discussion of the Jesuits' syncretism see Treadgold, II, 30–34.

13. Karl Mannheim, *Ideology and Utopia: An Introduction to the Sociology of Knowledge* (New York, Harcourt, Brace & World Inc., 1936), pp. 219–229.

14. Joseph R. Levenson, "History and Value: The Tensions of Intellectual Choice in Modern China," in Arthur F. Wright, ed., *Studies in Chinese Thought* (University of Chicago Press, 1953), pp. 146–194. For a critical review of Levenson's thesis see Michael Gasster, "The Death and Transfiguration of Confucianism," in *Philosophy East and West: A Journal of Oriental and Comparative Thought,* 18.3:205–213 (July 1968).

15. Benjamin I. Schwartz, *In Search of Wealth and Power: Yen Fu and the West* (Cambridge, Mass., Harvard University Press, 1964), pp. 205–213.

16. See Yen Fu's marginal commentaries in *Hou-kuan Yen-shih p'ing-tien Lao-tzu* (Yen Fu's annotated edition of the *Lao-tzu;* Chengtu, 1932), *shang-p'ien,* pp. 1b, 14a.

17.   Yen Fu, *Yen Chi-tao wen-ch'ao* (Essays of Yen Fu; Taipei, Shih-chieh shu-chü, 1971), pp. 206-207.

18.   Yen Fu, *Hou-kuan Yen-shih p'ing-tien Chuang-tzu* (Yen Fu's annotated edition of the *Chuang-tzu;* Chengtu, 1932), 1:6b-7a, 10a; 2:16b; 3:4a, 9a, 11a-b, 13b. See also Yen Fu, *P'ing-tien Lao-tzu, shang-p'ien,* pp. 5b-6a, 7a, 16b, 17a, 21a.

19.   For a recent scholar's interpretation of Yen's interest in Taoism see Schwartz, p. 236.

20.   Wang T'ao, *Weng-yu yü-t'an* (Superfluous talk; Shanghai, 1875), 5:2a-b.

21.   See, e.g., T'ang Chen, *Wei-yen* (Words of warning), in *Chih-hsueh ts'ung-shu ch'u-chi* (1890), 3:30a; Ch'en Chih, *Yung-shu, wai-p'ien* I, p. 6a.

22.   Ch'en Chih, *Yung-shu, nei-p'ien* II, pp. 3a-b.

23.   T'ang Chen, *Wei-yen,* 1:8b.

24.   Hsueh Fu-ch'eng, *Hai-wai wen-pien* (Overseas essays; 1901), 3:10a.

25.   Joseph Needham, in collaboration with Wang Ling, *Science and Civilization in China* (Cambridge, Eng., Cambridge University Press, 1959), III, 449.

26.   Hsueh Fu-ch'eng, *Ch'u-shih ssu-kuo jih-chi* (The diary concerning my diplomatic mission to four European nations; 1901), 2:12a; 5:12a; 1:10a, 3b-4a, 11a; 2:6a.

27.   Wang T'ao, *T'ao-yuan wen-lu wai-pien,* 7:18a. Wang's view has been incidentally supported by Joseph Needham: "It is vital today that the world should recognize that seventeenth-century Europe did not give rise to essentially 'European' or 'Western' science, but to universally valid world science, that is to say, 'modern' science as opposed to the ancient and medieval science." See Needham, *Science and Civilization in China,* III, 448.

28.   A handy volume on *ta-t'ung* thought in Chinese history may be found in Chung-kuo k'o-hsueh yuan che-hsueh yen-chiu so, ed., *Chung-kuo ta-t'ung ssu-hsiang tzu-liao* (Source materials on Chinese utopian thought; Shanghai, Chung-hua shu-chü, 1959).

29.   See Feng Kuei-fen, *Chiao-pin-lu k'ang-i* (Plain words from the Chiao-pin Studio; 1897), pp. 14b–15a, 100a–b, 102a.

30.   Kung-chuan Hsiao, p. 506.

31.   For details see ibid., pt. 4. For an English translation of K'ang's own writing see Lawrence G. Thompson, *Ta-t'ung Shu: The One-World Philosophy of K'ang Yu-wei* (London, G. Allen and Unwin, 1958).

32.   For a discussion of the late Ch'ing reformers' view of the nation-state world, see Wang Erh-min, *Wan-Ch'ing cheng-chih ssu-hsiang shih-lun* (Essays on late Ch'ing political thought; Taipei, Hsueh-sheng shu-chü, 1969), pp. 166–181. For a discussion of Wang T'ao's view see Cohen, pp. 91–109.

33.   Ch'en Chih, *Yung-shu, wai-p'ien* I, p. 13a.

34.   Wang T'ao, *T'ao-yuan wen-lu wai-pien,* 5:7b–9a. For a different interpretation of Wang's remark see Cohen, p. 138.

35.   Hu Li-yuan, *Hu I-nan hsien-sheng ch'üan-chi* (The complete works of Hu Li-yuan; Hong Kong, n.d.), 59:12a.

36.   Ibid., 59:9b–14b; 60:5b–6b, 18b–21a.

37.   See Kung-chuan Hsiao, p. 481.

38.   Wakeman, p. 134.

39.   Kenneth E. Boulding, *The Meaning of the Twentieth Century: The Great Transition* (New York and London, Harper and Row, 1964), p. 18.

40.   Arnold Toynbee, *Civilization on Trial and the World and the West* (Cleveland and New York, The World Publishing Co., 1955), p. 85.

National Image/Suzanne Wilson Barnett

1.   D. Z. Sheffield, "The Influence of the Western World on China: Progress, Mistakes, and Responsibilities," *The Century Magazine,* 60:785 (September 1900).

2. As in W. A. P. Martin, *The Awakening of China* (New York, Doubleday, Page and Company, 1907).

3. Sheffield, p. 785.

4. "Wai-kuo lieh-chuan" (Chapters on overseas countries), *Ming-shih* (History of the Ming dynasty), comp. Chang T'ing-yü et al. (Taipei, 1963), *chüan* 320–328.

5. See Chang Wei-hua, *Ming-shih Fo-lang-chi Lü-sung Ho-lan I-ta-li-ya ssu-chuan chu-shih* (A commentary on the four chapters on Portugal, Spain, Holland and Italy in the history of the Ming dynasty; Peiping, 1934).

6. *Chin-tai Chung-kuo tui Hsi-fang chi lieh-ch'iang jen-shih tzu-liao hui-pien* (Collected materials on modern Chinese views of the West and national power; Taipei, 1972), comp. Chung-yang yen-chiu-yuan Chin-tai-shih yen-chiu-so.

7. Wang Ta-hai, *Hai-tao i-chih* (Treatise on the islands of the sea), abridged version in Wang Hsi-ch'i, comp., *Hsiao-fang-hu-chai yü-ti ts'ung-ch'ao* (Collected copies of works on geography, from the Hsiao-fang-hu study; Taipei, 1964), *chih* 10, pp. 479–489b; excerpts in *Chin-tai Chung-kuo tui Hsi-fang chi lieh-ch'iang jen-shih tzu-liao hui-pien,* II, 751–753. For Yü Cheng-hsieh, see for example his *Kuei-ssu ts'un-kao* (Additional essays collected in 1833; Taipei, 1963), 5:148; see also references in Ch'eng Hung-chao, *Yu-heng-hsin-chai wen* (1872–1881), 2:6, 8:5b.

8. Examples: Ch'en Feng-heng, *Ying-chi-li chi-lueh* (A brief account of England; Edo, 1853); Wang Wen-t'ai, *Hung-mao-fan Ying-chi-li k'ao-lueh* (A brief account of England and the red-haired English barbarians), in Wang Ch'ao-tsung, comp., *Hai-wai fan-i lu* (Record of the barbarians beyond the seas; Peking, 1844), *ts'e* 2.

9. See for example Feng Ch'eng-chün, *Hai-lu chu* (Annotated edition of the *Hai-lu;* Taipei, 1962), p. 73. See also Wang Wen-t'ai, pp. 2b, 14b; Wei Yuan, comp., *Hai-kuo t'u-chih* (Illustrated treatise on the maritime countries; Kao-yu chou, 1852), 53:21b.

10. As in Wei Yuan, 53:23b, 71:2a–b; Wang Wen-t'ai, pp. 9b–10. Inspiration for these references came in part from a much earlier, quite perceptive account, Ch'en Lun-chiung, *Hai-kuo wen-chien lu* (A record of things

seen and heard among the maritime countries), completed ca. 1730 (Taipei, 1958), 1:27.

11. See for example Huang Chün-tsai, *Lang-mo* (Pieces written while wandering), 2:2b–4b, in his *Chin-hu ch'i-mo* (Seven sets of literary pieces; Sung-chiang-fu, 1873).

12. Yü Cheng-hsieh, *Kuei-ssu lei-kao* (Miscellaneous essays collected in 1833; Taipei, 1965), 15:585.

13. Huang Chün-tsai, 2:2b–3b.

14. See Liang T'ing-nan, *Yueh-tao kung-kuo shuo* (Discussion of countries trading at Canton; Taipei, 1968), 5:2–3. See also Hsien Yü-ch'ing, "Liang T'ing-nan chu-shu lu yao" (On the writings of Liang T'ing-nan), *Ling-nan hsueh-pao* (Lingnan journal), 4.1:144–145 (April 1935); Wei Yuan, 60:1–2.

15. For references to Wei Yuan and other early Chinese students of the West, see Suzanne Wilson Barnett, "Practical Evangelism: Protestant Missions and the Introduction of Western Civilization into China, 1820–1850" (Ph.D. dissertation, Harvard University, 1973), chap. 6.

16. Ibid., chaps. 1–5.

17. As, for example, in Kao-li-wen (Elijah Coleman Bridgman), *Mei-li-ko ho-sheng-kuo chih-lueh* (A brief geographical history of the United States of America; Singapore, 1838), 1:3; and as cited in Wei Yuan, for example, 59:23b, 32b–40. See also "Tzu-li chih li" (The principle of individual rights), *Tung-Hsi-yang k'ao mei-yueh t'ung-chi-chuan* (A general monthly record examining the Eastern and Western ocean [regions]), ed. Ai-han-che (K. F. A. Gützlaff), 1838.3:42–44b, 51b; and "Ying-chi-li kuo-cheng-hui" (The British parliament), *Tung-Hsi-yang k'ao*, 1838.4:63–65b, 1838.5:81–83.

18. Wei Yuan completed *Hai-kuo t'u-chih* in 1842; the first published version was in 50 *chüan*, 1844; subsequent expanded editions were in 60 *chüan* (1847) and 100 *chüan* (1852).

19. See the review of *"Hai Kwoh Tu chi,"* *Chinese Repository*, 16.9:417–424 (September 1847).

20. Robert Hart, *These from the Land of Sinim: Essays on the Chinese Question* (London, Chapman and Hall, 1903), esp. pp. 6, 49–55, 161–166.

21. S. Wells Williams, *The Middle Kingdom,* 3rd printing (New York, 1851), II, 371.

22. As discussed in Hao Chang, *Liang Ch'i-ch'ao and Intellectual Transition in China, 1890–1907* (Cambridge, Mass., Harvard University Press, 1971), esp. p. 307.

Kung as an Ethos in Late Nineteenth-Century China/I-fan Ch'eng

1. Mary C. Wright, *The Last Stand of Chinese Conservatism: The T'ung-chih Restoration, 1862–1874* (New York, Atheneum, 1969), p. 300.

2. Albert Feuerwerker, *China's Early Industrialization: Sheng Hsuan-huai (1844–1916) and Mandarin Enterprise* (Cambridge, Mass., Harvard University Press, 1958), p. 242.

3. For Wang's conservative activities, see Charlton M. Lewis, "The Hunanese Elite and the Reform Movement, 1895–1898," *Journal of Asian Studies,* 29.1:40–42 (November 1969).

4. In an earlier version of this paper I used the term "moralism" to connote Wang's ardent belief in the necessity of commitment to certain values. Such a total commitment made possible the intensity with which Wang held the value "*kung.*"

5. A core member of the Ch'ing-liu coterie (1875–1884), Chang P'ei-lun was one of the most outspoken advocates of war during the Sino-French controversy (1880–1885). See Lloyd E. Eastman, *Throne and Mandarins: China's Search for a Policy during the Sino-French Controversy, 1880–1885* (Cambridge, Mass., Harvard University Press, 1967).

6. Wang Hsien-ch'ien, *K'uei-yuan tzu-ting nien-p'u* (Chronological autobiography of Wang Hsien-ch'ien; Changsha, 1918), *chüan-shang:* 12a–14b; reprinted in Shen Yun-lun, comp., *Chin-tai chung-kuo shih-liao ts'ung-k'an,* No. 51 (Taiwan, Wen-hai ch'u-pan-she, n.d.), pp. 25–30. In another memorial, which was presented in 1880, Wang tried to alert the throne to

the danger of indecisiveness and delay in policy-formulating in diplomatic emergencies. Again, he proposed curbing the *ch'ing-i* influence
and enhancing the throne's own initiative. See ibid., *chüan-shang:* 34b-
35a (original ed.), or pp. 70–71 (reprint). A short biography of Wang,
depending heavily on Wang's own autobiography, is available in English:
Yi-t'ung Wang, "Biographic Sketches of 29 Classical Scholars of the
Late Manchu and Early Republican Era" (mimeographed and distributed
by author, 1963), pp. 70–74.

7. David Nivison, "Ho-shen and His Accusers: Ideology and Political
    Behavior in the Eighteenth Century," in David Nivison and Arthur F.
    Wright, eds., *Confucianism in Action* (Stanford University Press, 1959),
    pp. 209–243.

8. Wang Hsien-ch'ien, *Nien-p'u, chüan-chung:* 1a–2b (original ed.), or pp.
    179–182 (reprint).

9. Ibid., *chüan-chung:* 14a–15a, or pp. 205–207.

10. Joseph R. Levenson, *Confucian China and Its Modern Fate: A Trilogy*
    (Berkeley and Los Angeles, University of California Press, 1968), vol. 2,
    pt. 2, pp. 25–73.

11. Wang Hsien-ch'ien, *Hsu-shou-t'ang shu-cha* (Collected correspondence
    of Wang Hsien-ch'ien; 1907), 1:25b.

12. Frederic Wakeman, Jr., "The Price of Autonomy: Intellectuals in Ming
    and Ch'ing Politics," *Daedalus* (Spring 1972), pp. 35–70.

13. Wang Hsien-ch'ien, *Nien-p'u, chüan-shang:* 35b (original ed.), or p. 72
    (reprint).

14. Ibid., *chüan-shang:* 38b, or p. 78.

15. Thomas A. Metzger, *The Internal Organization of Ch'ing Bureaucracy:
    Legal, Normative, and Communicative Aspects* (Cambridge, Mass.,
    Harvard University Press, 1973), p. 267.

16. Nivison, pp. 209–243.

17. See my *"T'ien-hsia* vs. *T'ien-tzu:* The Formation of Ku Yen-wu's
    Localism," a paper delivered at the annual meeting of ASPAC (Asian

Studies on the Pacific Coast), San Diego, June 14–16, 1974.

18. *Lü-shih ch'un-ch'iu* (Spring and Autumn of Mr. Lü), commented by
     Kao Yu, printed by Ling-yen shan-kuan, 1788, *meng-ch'un-chi* (Record
     of the First Month), *ti-i, chüan* 1, sec. 5, "Ch'ü-ssu" (To get rid of
     selfishness), p. 11b.

19. Wang Hsien-ch'ien, *Shu-cha,* 2:75a–76a; an English translation of this
     discussion is in Ssu-yü Teng and John K. Fairbank, *China's Response
     to the West: A Documentary Survey, 1839–1923* (New York,
     Atheneum, 1967), pp. 181–182.

20. Wang Hsien-ch'ien, *Hsu-shou-t'ang wen-chi* (Collected works of Wang
     Hsien-ch'ien; 1900), 6:13a–14a.

21. Ibid., 5:28a–b.

22. Ibid., 5:28b. See also Wang Hsien-ch'ien, *Hsun-tzu chi-chieh* (Compre-
     hensive annotations of *Hsun-tzu;* 1891), 12:6a, for the source of the
     quotation from *Hsun-tzu;* or Homer H. Dubs, tr., *The Works of
     Hsüntze* (Taipei, Ch'eng-wen Publishing Co., 1966), p. 195.

23. Wang Hsien-ch'ien, *Hsun-tzu chi-chieh,* 3:6b–7a, 4:17a–18a.

24. Wang Hsien-chien, *Wen-chi,* 5:28a.

25. Ibid., 1:1a–2a.

26. Wang Hsien-ch'ien, *Nien-p'u, chüan-shang:*47a–48b (original ed.), or
     pp. 95–98 (reprint).

27. Wang Hsien-ch'ien, *Wen-chi,* 1:9b–10a.

28. Yen Fu, "Lun shih-pien chih chi" (On the crisis resulting from world
     change), first published in the Tientsin newspaper *Chih-pao* in 1895;
     cited in Benjamin Schwartz, *In Search of Wealth and Power: Yen Fu
     and the West* (New York, Evanston, and London, Harper Torchbooks,
     1969), p. 62.

29. Ibid., pp. 69–70.

30. Ibid., pp. 17–19.

31.   Wang Hsien-ch'ien, *Wen-chi,* 5:38b.

32.   This view was first enunciated by K'ang in 1903. Cited in Frederic
      Wakeman, Jr., *History and Will: Philosophical Perspectives of Mao
      Tse-tung's Thought* (Berkeley, Los Angeles, London, University of
      California Press, 1973), p. 140.

33.   Hao Chang, *Liang Ch'i-ch'ao and Intellectual Transition in China, 1890–
      1907* (Cambridge, Mass., Harvard University Press, 1971).

Reflections on an Aspect of Modern China in Transition/Luke S. K. Kwong

TC   T'an Ssu-t'ung, *T'an Ssu-t'ung ch'üan-chi* (The complete works of
         T'an Ssu-t'ung), ed. Ts'ai Shang-ssu et al. (Peking, 1954).
HLT   *Hu-nan li-shih tzu-liao* (Source materials on the history of Hunan),
         1958, no. 3 (July) and no. 4 (December); 1959, no. 1 (March), no.
         3 (September) and no. 4 (December); 1960, no. 1 (March).

1.   Liang's biography of T'an was first published in *Ch'ing-i pao* (The China
      discussion), no. 4 (Jan. 22, 1899), Taiwan reprint, 1:205–212 (1967),
      and later incorporated into Liang's *Wu-hsu cheng-pien chi* (An account
      of the coup in 1898). Liang's account has ever since dominated the
      interpretation of the life and thought of T'an. For a critique of Liang's
      reliability in this case, see Chang Te-chün, "Liang Ch'i-ch'ao chi T'an
      Ssu-t'ung shih shih-shih pien" (Clarification of Liang Ch'i-ch'ao's account
      of T'an Ssu-t'ung), *Wen-shih* (Literature and history), 1:81–85 (1962).

2.   See T'an's biography of Liu Yun-t'ien in *TC,* p. 171; also, T'an to Shen
      Hsiao-i, ca. 1893, *TC,* p. 431.

3.   See his "San-shih tzu-chi" (Autobiography at 30), *TC,* pp. 205–206.

4.   See T'an Yen-k'ai's remark in *Chin-tai Hsiang-hsien sou-cha* (The cor-
      respondence of eminent Hunanese in recent times), comp. Lung Po-
      chien (1934 reprint), p. 89. Also, see the diary entry of T'an Chi-hsun
      quoted in T'an Hsun-ts'ung, *Hsien-tsu Ssu-t'ung kung nien-p'u ch'u-kao*
      (A draft chronological biography of my ancestor, T'an Ssu-t'ung), p. 8,
      in *T'an Ssu-t'ung T'ang Ts'ai-ch'ang liang hsien-sheng chi ping-wu nien
      P'ing-Liu-Li ke-ming shih-liao* (Historical materials on the two gentle-
      men, T'an Ssu-t'ung and T'ang Ts'ai-ch'ang, and on the uprisings in P'ing-
      Liu-Li in 1906; Taipei, 1965 [?]), for private circulation only.

5.   T'an to Ou-yang Chung-ku, June 1895, *TC,* p. 288.

6.   Cf. T'an to Ou-yang Chung-ku, Jan. 21, 1895, *TC,* pp. 286–287.

7.   See *The Four Books,* tr. J. Legge (Hong Kong, The International Publication Society, reprint, n.d.), bk. 2, chap. 4, pp. 7–8.

8.   E. H. Erikson, *Young Man Luther* (New York, W. W. Norton & Company, Inc., 1962), p. 201; also pp. 171, 176. For a brief report on recent findings on this issue, see "Behavior," *Time* (Apr. 28, 1975), p. 43.

9.   T'an to Chi-yun, Feb. 20, 1895, *HLT,* no. 3:78 (1958).

10.   T'an to Pei Yuan-cheng, ca. 1894, *TC,* p. 388.

11.   T'an to Liu Sung-fu, ca. 1894, *TC,* p. 384.

12.   See his preface to the collection of his poems, *TC,* p. 154.

13.   *TC,* p. 204.

14.   T'an himself considered his thirtieth *sui* a significant divide in his personal and intellectual development. See his letter to T'ang Ts'ai-ch'ang, June 1897, *HLT,* no. 4:124–125 (1959).

15.   See E. H. Erikson, "Ego Identity and the Psychosocial Moratorium," in *New Perspectives for Research on Juvenile Delinquency,* ed. H. L. Witmer and R. Kotinsky (Washington, D.C., Children's Bureau, U.S. Department of Health, Education and Welfare, 1956), pp. 1–23; also, see his *Young Man Luther,* pp. 43, 100 ff; *Identity: Youth and Crisis* (New York, W. W. Norton & Company, Inc., 1968), pp. 156–157.

16.   T'an to Ou-yang Chung-ku, Mar. 11, 1896, *TC,* p. 331. In late 1893, T'an may have written to Ou-yang, who was in Peking, on this matter. See *TC,* p. 305. But the reference is too cryptic to permit a positive identification of its import.

17.   T'an to Ou-yang Chung-ku, Aug. 31, 1896, *TC,* pp. 316–329.

18.   H. Welch, *The Buddhist Revival in China* (Cambridge, Mass., Harvard University Press, 1968), pp. 2–10.

19. See Sun Pao-hsuan's diary entry, Sept. 20, 1896, in *Wu-hsu pien-fa* (The 1898 reform), ed. Chien Po-tsan et al. (Shanghai, 1953), 1:539.

20. The translation of this title, tentatively given here, is a trying problem that cannot be discussed in the present context. *Jen-hsueh* was published after T'an's execution in thirteen installments in Liang Ch'i-ch'ao's *Ch'ing-i pao* (nos. 2, 3, 4, 5, 7, 9, 10, 12, 14, 44, 45, 46 and 100, between 1898 and 1901). A comparison of the *Ch'ing-i pao* edition of *Jen-hsueh* with that in *T'an Liu-yang ch'üan-chi* (The complete works of T'an Ssu-t'ung of Liu-yang), ed. Ch'en Nai-ch'ien (1925), pp. 197–325, shows that Liang Ch'i-ch'ao did tamper with the text of the work when it first appeared in *Ch'ing-i pao*. Liang's editorial policy, sanctioned by K'ang Yu-wei, seems to have been in line with the *pao-huang* (protect the emperor) campaigns which they organized after the coup in 1898.

21. See his essay, "Chih-yen" (On governing the world), written about 1889, in *TC*, pp. 103–109. T'an later came to regret that he had ever professed the views contained therein. See his introductory remarks, *TC*, p. 103; also, his letter to Pei Yuan-cheng, ca. late 1895, *TC*, p. 427.

22. T'an to Ou-yang Chung-ku, Nov. 17, 1897, *TC*, pp. 304–305; also, see Sheng Hsuan-huai, *Sheng Hsuan-huai wei-k'an hsin-kao* (The unpublished correspondence of Sheng Hsuan-huai), ed. Shao Hsun-cheng et al. (Peking 1960); Sheng to Ch'en San-li, Nov. 22, 1897, pp. 44–45; to Huang Tsun-hsien, Nov. 22, 1897, p. 45; to Ch'en Pao-chen, Nov. 23, 1897, pp. 47–48; to Chiang Shao-mu and Hsiung Hsi-ling, Nov. 23, 1897, pp. 48–49. A letter from Liang Ch'i-ch'ao to Ch'en San-li and Hsiung Hsi-ling, November 1897 (*Wu-hsu pien-fa*, 2:592), also confirms this.

23. T'an to Ch'en Pao-chen, January 1898, *HLT*, no. 4:132–135 (1959).

24. T'an to wife, June 20, 1898, *HLT*, no. 3:78 (1959).

25. See *Yü-che hui-ts'un* (Reprints from the *Peking Gazette*), Taiwan reprint, 8:6127.

26. See, for example, *TC*, pp. 167–168 and p. 97.

27. P'i Hsi-jui, "Shih-fu-t'ang wei-k'an jih-chi" (The unpublished diary of P'i Hsi-jui), Apr. 4, 1898, in *HLT*, no. 1:82–83 (1959).

28. *TC*, pp. 3–4; also, T'an to T'ang Ts'ai-ch'ang, ca. October 1896, *TC*,

p. 446; T'an to Wang K'ang-nien, Feb. 19, 1897, *TC,* p. 343. Cf. T'an to T'ang Ts'ai-ch'ang, August 1897, *HLT,* no. 4:129 (1959).

29.   T'an to Wang K'ang-nien, Dec. 17, 1896, *TC,* p. 342.

30.   For examples of T'an's apparent acceptance of his father's interference with his career plans and activities, see T'an to Ou-yang Chung-ku, Mar. 11, 1896, *TC,* pp. 330–331; T'an to Wang K'ang-nien, June 13, 1897, *TC,* p. 353; T'an to Liu Chü-ch'ing, Feb. 11, 1898, *HLT,* no. 1:101 (1960).

31.   T'an to Ou-yang Chung-ku, Aug. 31, 1896, *TC,* p. 329.

32.   For another example of T'an's *yang-wu* activities, see T'an to Ou-yang Chung-ku, May 17 and 19, 1898, *TC,* pp. 314–315; Ou-yang to T'an, May 16, 1898, in *T'an Ssu-t'ung shu-chien* (The correspondence of T'an Ssu-t'ung), ed. Ou-yang Yü-ch'ien (Shanghai, 1948), pp. 131–132; also, T'an to Tsou Yueh-sheng, June 22, 1898, *HLT,* no. 1:77 (1959).

33.   Between 1895 and 1898, T'an conceived of a number of publication and study society projects. Although only a few of these ever got beyond the paper stage, extant documents show the wide range of T'an's interests in reform, extending from basic amendments of the examination system to the expansion of agricultural and industrial know-how, from the promotion of "equal status" and literacy for women to the cultivation of a balanced and disciplined way of life.

34.   A concept borrowed from A. D. Smith, *Theories of Nationalism* (New York, Harper & Row, 1972), pp. 236–254.

35.   See Jose Ortega y Gasset, *The Modern Theme* (New York, Harper & Row, 1961), pp. 3–18.

36.   T'an to T'u Chih-ch'u, August 1897, *HLT,* no. 4:136 (1959). Cf. T'an to T'ang Ts'ai-ch'ang, ca. August 1897, *HLT,* p. 127, and T'an's statement in *Jen-hsueh,* in *T'an Liu-yang ch'üan-chi,* p. 297.

37.   This radical side of T'an did, however, have important implications for his developing style in public affairs and for his changing conception of political ideals.

38.   T'an to wife, Aug. 27, 1898, *HLT,* no. 1:77 (1959).

Some Western Influences on T'an Ssu-t'ung's Thought/Richard H. Shek

CHM   *Chih-hsin mien ping fa* (The prevention of disease through mental
        healing; Shanghai, Ko-chih shu-shih, 1896).
TSTCC   *T'an Ssu-t'ung ch'üan-chi* (The collected works of T'an Ssu-t'ung),
        ed. Ts'ai Shang-ssu (Peking, San-lien shu-tien, 1954).
WKKP   *Wan-kuo kung-pao* (The globe magazine; later renamed Review of
        the times), 1874–1883; 1889–1907 (Taiwan photolithographic
        reprint, Chinese Materials and Research Aids Service Center, 1968).

1.   Liang Ch'i-ch'ao, *Intellectual Trends in the Ch'ing Period,* tr. Immanuel
      Hsu (Cambridge, Mass., Harvard University Press, 1959), p. 108.

2.   *TSTCC,* p. 525.

3.   Liang Ch'i-ch'ao, *Hsi-hsueh shu mu piao* (Bibliography of Western
      learning; Shanghai, Shih-wu pao-kuan, 1896).

4.   *TSTCC,* p. 295.

5.   *TSTCC,* pp. 74, 318, 320.

6.   *WKKP,* 10:635a (July 6, 1878).

7.   *WKKP,* 5:21 (June 1889).

8.   *WKKP,* 7:19 (August 1889).

9.   *WKKP,* 10:635a (July 6, 1878).

10.   *WKKP,* 10:635a (July 6, 1878).

11.   *WKKP,* 10:617b (June 29, 1878).

12.   *WKKP,* 9:38a–b (Sept. 2, 1876).

13.   *WKKP,* 14:68a (Oct. 1, 1881).

14.   *TSTCC,* p. 65.

15.   *TSTCC,* p. 51.

16. *TSTCC*, p. 55.

17. *TSTCC*, p. 67.

18. *TSTCC*, p. 55.

19. Chang Chih-tung, *Ch'üan-hsueh p'ien* (Exhortation to learning; Peking, T'ung-wen kuan, 1898), *nei-p'ien,* 22a.

20. Ibid., 22b.

21. Wang Erh-min, *Wan-Ch'ing cheng-chih ssu-hsiang-shih lun* (History of political thought in the late Ch'ing; Taipei, 1969), pp. 227, 238. Also by the same author, "Ch'ing-chi chih-shih fen-tzu ti tzu-chueh" (The awakening of late Ch'ing intellectuals), in *Chung-yang yen-chiu-yuan chin-tai-shih yen-chiu-so chi-k'an* (Bulletin of the Institute of Modern History, Academia Sinica), no. 2:16 (June 1971).

22. Hao Chang, "The Confucian Cosmological Myth and the Political Culture of Early Modern China," paper delivered at the 27th Annual Meeting of the Association for Asian Studies in San Francisco, March 24–26, 1975.

23. *TSTCC*, p. 320.

24. *CHM, chüan-shang:* 12a.

25. *TSTCC*, p. 319.

26. *CHM, chüan-shang:* 13a–b.

27. *TSTCC*, p. 11.

28. *CHM, chüan-hsia:* 21a.

29. *TSTCC*, p. 11.

30. *CHM, chüan-hsia:* 25a.

The Formation of a Province/Nailene Chou

1.   Nailene Chou, "Frontier Studies and Changing Frontier Administration in Late Ch'ing China" (Ph.D. dissertation, University of Washington, 1976).

2.   *Yang-jen* here is used metaphorically to denote a technical superiority. See Nailene Chou, "Changing Image of the Russians from *Hu-jen* to *Yang-jen*" (paper prepared for the Association for Asian Studies Western Conference, Tempe, Arizona, Dec. 8, 1974).

3.   Mary C. Wright, *The Last Stand of Chinese Conservatism: The T'ung-chih Restoration, 1862–1874* (New York, Atheneum, 1967), p. 221.

Local Reform Currents in Chekiang before 1900/Mary Backus Rankin

1.   On the Chang family (main figure Chang Sung-hsien) see *Nan-hsun chih*, Chou Ching-yun, comp. (1922), 21:13b–14a; Chang Chien, *Chang Chi-tzu chiu-lu* (The nine records of Chang Chien; Shanghai, 1935), *wen-lu*, 13:17a; Chung-li Chang, *The Income of the Chinese Gentry* (Seattle, University of Washington Press, 1962), pp. 159–160.
      On the Chou Family (Chou Chang-fu and Chou Chang-chih) see *Nan-hsun chih*, 21:19b–20b, 27b.
      On the Liu family (Liu Yung): *Nan-hsun chih*, 14:1b–2b, 21:18a–19a; Chang Chien, *wen-lu*, 14:2b.
      On the Chiang family (Chiang T'ang): *Nan-hsun chih*, 14:11b, 21:2b–¢ 10a–12a, 27:8a.

2.   On the Yeh family (Yeh Ch'eng-chung): *Chen-hai hsien-chih*, Wang Jung-shang, comp., Hung Hsi-fan, rev. (1931), 27:40a–41a; Chung-kuo jen-min yin-hang Shang-hai-shih fen-hang, *Shang-hai ch'ien-chuang shih-liao* (Historical materials on native banks in Shanghai; Shanghai, 1961), pp. 743–744; Chung-li Chang, p. 159.

3.   On the Yen family (Yen Hsing-hou): Wang Ching-yu, ed., *Chung-kuo chin-tai kung-yeh shih tzu-liao* (Historical materials on modern Chinese industry; Peking, 1957), pt. 2, vol. 2, pp. 929–930; Chung-li Chang, p. 178. Numerous other examples exist, although there are also merchant-gentry families whose prominence goes back further. One other relatively well-known example is Hu Kuang-yung, but I do not know what, if any, his family's activities in Hangchow were.

4. *Wu-Ch'ing chen-chih,* Lu Hsueh-p'u, comp. (1936), 29:25a.

5. *Nan-hsun chih,* 25:8a, *chüan* 7, passim.

6. *Hang-chou fu-chih,* Wu Ch'ing-ti, comp., Chi Yao-shan, rev. (1922–1926), 16:13a–25a, *chüan* 52.

7. *E.g.,* ibid., 52:5b; 67:24a.

8. Ibid., 16:17a, 18a; 53:17b, 19a–b, 35b; Arthur W. Hummel, ed., *Eminent Chinese of the Ch'ing Period* (Washington, D.C., 1943–1944), II, 726–727. Ting Ping's son was active in the railway and constitutionalist movements and in educational reform in Hangchow in the 1900s.

9. Philip A. Kuhn, *Rebellion and its Enemies in Late Imperial China* (Cambridge, Mass., Harvard University Press, 1970).

10. *Nan-hsun chih,* 2:16a. This institution supported various subsidiary charitable organizations. It was linked to the likin bureau, but was definitely a nonofficial organization. It is listed with guilds in the gazetteer.

11. *Shao-hsing hsien-chih tzu-liao, ti-i chi* (Materials for a gazetteer of Shaohsing, first collection; 1937), biographies, p. 163b.

12. Negishi Tadashi, *Shanhai no girodo* (The guilds of Shanghai; Tokyo, 1951), p. 263.

13. *Nan-hsun chih,* 21:21a.

14. *Wu-Ch'ing chen-chih,* 7:8a, 23:9b.

15. Here I am restricting consideration to elite mobility, thereby excluding two other important examples of population mobility: the post-Taiping *k'o-min,* and lower class mobility resulting from vagrancy, occupation, trade, etc.

16. *Nan-hsun chih,* 33:3b.

17. Chiang Monlin, *Tides from the West* (New Haven, Yale University Press, 1947), pp. 17, 31–39.

18.   *Shao-hsing hsien-chih tzu-liao,* biographies, 163b–164a, 176a.

19.   *Wu-Ch'ing chen-chih,* 14:11a–12b; 29:19b, 25a–b, 28a, 29b–30a, 33a, 34b–35a.

20.   *Shao-hsing hsien-chih tzu-liao,* biographies, 163b–164a; *Chen-hai hsien-chih,* 27:23b–24b; *Chen-hai hsien-chih pei-kao* (Draft for a gazetteer of Chen-hai), Tung Tsu-hsi, comp. (1924), 2:14b–17b.

21.   *Chen-hai hsien-chih pei-kao,* 2:5a. In contrast, Chiang Monlin says the Sino-French War elicited practically no interest in his home village in Yü-yao. Chiang Monlin, p. 7.

22.   An excellent source on this group is Ch'en Mi, *Ch'en Chieh-shih hsien-sheng nien-p'u* (A chronological biography of Ch'en Fu-ch'en; 1934). See also Lloyd Eastman, "Political Reformism in China Before the Sino-Japanese War," *Journal of Asian Studies,* 27.4:695–710 (August 1968); Hummel, I, 343; II, 677–679; Chu Fang-pu, *Sun I-jang nien-p'u* (A chronological biography of Sun I-jang; Shanghai, 1934); *P'ing-yang hsien-chih,* Liu Shao-k'uan, et al., comps. (1925), 39:12a–15b; Su Yuan-lei, *Sung P'ing-tzu p'ing chuan* (A critical biography of Sung Heng; Shanghai, 1947).

23.   Connections between reformers and previous militant groups within the bureaucracy can be illustrated in a number of instances. For example, T'ang Shou-ch'ien had been associated with Weng T'ung-ho and the emperor's party.

24.   On the *ching-shih* influence see Ch'en Mi, pp. 5b, 23a. Articles by Sun I-yen (Sun I-jang's father) were included in Sheng K'ang, comp., *Huang-ch'ao ching-shih wen hsu-pien* (A supplement to essays on statecraft of the Ch'ing dynasty; 1897), and Huang T'i-fang (Huang Shao-chi's father) was included in both that compilation and in Ko Shih-chün, comp., *Huang-ch'ao ching-shih wen hsu-pien* (1888). Essays by Ch'en Ch'iu appear in Ch'en Chung-i, ed., *Huang-ch'ao ching-shih wen san-pien* (A third collection of essays on statecraft of the Ch'ing dynasty; 1901).

25.   On this point see Ch'en Mi, pp. 24b–25a.

26.   Huang Shao-chi was a member of the Ch'iang-hsueh hui and Ch'en Ch'iu a member of the Pao-huang hui. Sung Heng was a friend of Liang Ch'i-ch'ao. Sun I-jang and Ch'en Fu-ch'en had plans (which fell through)

to publish a journal with Wang K'ang-nien. Huang Shao-chi was chancel-
lor of Peking University in 1898 and helped K'ang Yu-wei escape Peking.

27. Ch'en Mi, pp. 25a–b. This group was also friendly with T'ang Shou-
ch'ien and Chang Ping-lin.

28. Wang Chih-nien, ed. *Wang Jang-ch'ing (K'ang-nien) hsien-sheng chuan-
chi i-wen* (The biography and collected works of Wang K'ang-nien; 1966,
Taipei reprint), p. 66; *Hang-chou fu-chih,* 17:1a–3a. Sung Heng taught
in this school.

29. Wang Chih-nien, p. 69; *Hang-chou fu-chih,* 17:9a–b.

30. *Hang-chou fu-chih,* 175:21b.

31. Yu-chuan pu, *Kuei-cheng chi-yao tse-pien* (Second collection of documents concerning China's railway affairs), 2:62–63.

32. *Shao-hsing hsien-chih tzu-liao,* biographies, 163b; Chiang Monlin, p. 41.

33. *Chen-hai hsien-chih hsin-chih pei-kao,* 2:15a.

34. *Nan-hsun chih,* 3:2a. T'ang Shou-ch'ien was invited to teach in this
academy. Two of the men responsible for introducing the study of current affairs were scholar-reformers from families previously described as
having accumulated wealth during the mid-nineteenth century. They
were friends of T'ang Shou-ch'ien.

35. Edward Rhoads, *China's Republican Revolution* (Cambridge, Mass.,
Harvard University Press, 1975), chap. 3, passim. Other references in
this paragraph are to Chūzō Ichiko, "The Role of the Gentry: An
Hypothesis," in Mary C. Wright, ed., *China in Revolution* (New Haven,
Yale University Press, 1968), and to Mary Wright's introduction to this
book. See also the article by Mark Elvin, "The Administration of
Shanghai, 1905–1914," in Mark Elvin and William G. Skinner, eds.,
The Chinese City between Two Worlds (Stanford University Press, 1974).
Many of the other articles in this volume, particularly those by Jones,
Murphey, Buck, and Garrett, indirectly either support or challenge some
of my views.

Chihli Academies and Other Schools in the Late Ch'ing/Richard A. Orb

1. The precise figures and provincial rankings in this paragraph are from
    the Hsueh-pu tsung-wu-ssu (Ministry of Education, Department of
    General Affairs) editions, *Kuang-hsu san-shih-san nien fen, Ti-i-tz'u
    chiao-yü t'ung-chi t'u-piao* (The first statistical survey of education,
    1907), *ko-sheng* (provinces), pp. 17–18 (1910); and *Hsuan-t'ung yuan
    nien fen, Ti-san-tz'u chiao-yü t'ung-chi t'u-piao* (The third statistical
    survey of education, 1909), *ko-sheng* (provinces), pp. 1–2 (1911). A
    general summary of these statistics is provided in Table 1 of this paper,
    with gaps filled in from the second (1908) educational survey. These
    three surveys, giving detailed information district by district, reveal
    important trends in late Ch'ing educational development and not a
    few surprises. The relative positions, for example, of Chihli, Szechwan,
    Kwangtung, Chekiang, Hunan, and Fengtien in 1907 raise a number of
    questions about the realities of educational reform in areas thought
    to be relatively advanced or retarded in the last decade of the Ch'ing.
    The poor showing of Kwangtung and Chekiang in numbers of schools
    and students and amount of expenditure, compared with their large
    school property holdings, awaits explanation.

2. *Chi-fu t'ung-chih* (Chihli provincial history), 1884 (1923 ed.), pp.
    4483–4671.

3. Ibid.

4. The following sources have been used for the short profile of Shu-lu
    district: Chih-li hsueh-wu kung-so (Chihli Office of Education), ed.,
    Chung-hua min-kuo yuan nien, Chih-li chiao-yü t'ung-chi t'u-piao
    (Chihli statistical survey of education, 1912), Appendix following
    p. 371 (Tientsin, 1914); *Shu-lu hsiang-t'u chih* (Gazetteer of Shu-lu),
    9:2b–10b (1905); and *Chi-fu t'ung-chih*, pp. 4528–4530.

5. See Gilbert Rozman, *Urban Networks in Ch'ing China and Tokugawa
    Japan* (Princeton University Press, 1973), p. 167. An important question
    is the effect of urbanization and market structure on the development
    of the new schools. Rozman's study of Hopei is very useful in this
    regard. My impression at the moment, however, is that there is little
    correlation between urbanization and districts with relatively large
    numbers of new schools and students, aside from the fact that the
    cities of Peking, Tientsin, and Paoting were leading centers of technical
    and specialized education. The example of Shu-lu district suggests this

observation and also argues that there was little if any gap between district city and outlying villages in the formation of lower primary schools.

6. As indicated, Shu-lu district had an unusually high number of *i-hsueh*. Most Chihli districts had between three and four, a few had none, and some had only one. The total number of extant *i-hsueh* in late Ch'ing for all of Chihli (838) is very small and hardly compares with the 30,000 clan charitable schools reported for Yunnan in the 1730s. (Ping-ti Ho, *The Ladder of Success in Imperial China* [New York, Columbia University Press, 1962], p. 210.) This situation in Chihli must be included in the discussion of literacy in the Ch'ing. (See F. W. Mote, "China's Past in the Study of China Today—Some Comments on the Recent Work of Richard Solomon," *Journal of Asian Studies,* 32.1:111–112 [November 1972].) Either Chihli was very atypical as a province and had an extremely weak traditional school base, or the argument that other provinces had an elaborate network of semipublic schools at the local level has been overstated. In either case the combined total of *i-hsueh* and *she-hsueh* in Chihli (974) in the late nineteenth century is a small percentage of the 8723 new schools and offices reported for 1907. (See Table 1.)

7. For 1906 see Shang Ping-ho, *Hsin-jen ch'un-ch'iu* (Spring and autumn annals: 1911–1912; 1924, Taipei reprint), pp. 246–247. For 1907 through 1912 see the statistical surveys cited in notes 1 and 4 above.

8. See *Kuang-hsu san-shih-san,* Chihli, pp. 22–23, for a detailed breakdown of school revenue, district by district.

9. *Chi hsien chih* (Gazetteer of Chi district; 1929, Taipei reprint), pp. 1130–1132, 1148.

10. Kuo Li-chih, ed., *T'ung-ch'eng Wu hsien-sheng (Ju-lun) nien-p'u* (Chronological biography of Mr. Wu Ju-lun from T'ung-ch'eng; 1943, Taipei reprint), p. 324 and passim.

11. Sheng Lang-hsi's *Chung-kuo shu-yuan chih-tu* (The system of traditional academies in China; Shanghai, 1934) is a classic if somewhat dated work on academies. The only book-length study of a specific province, to my knowledge, is Liu Po-chi's *Kuang-tung shu-yuan chih-tu yen-ko* (The evolution of traditional academies in Kwangtung; 1939). Adam Lui, Lu Kuang-huan, and Tilemann Grimm have recently devoted attention to academies in the Ch'ing.

12.   The sources for my treatment of Chihli academies are *Chi-fu t'ung-chih;*
       Wang Lan-yin, "Ho-pei sheng shu-yuan chih ch'u kao" (A record of
       academies in Hopei province: initial draft), *Shih-ta yueh k'an,* no. 25
       (February 1936), pp. 1–62 and no. 29 (September 1936), pp. 1–105;
       and the personal examination of 71 gazetteers which have information
       on academy transformations and which are mostly of Republican
       provenance. Wang Lan-yin consulted 185 gazetteers for his survey and
       reported a total of 255 academies in Hopei. I found 10 additional *shu-
       yuan* in several Hopei districts and used the *Chi-fu t'ung-chih* as my
       main source for another 34 academies in areas which later became parts
       of Chahar and Jehol, for a total of 299 academies. It is worth noting
       that studies that speak of Chihli in the Ch'ing and limit their geographical
       coverage to Hopei in the Republican period ignore Ch'eng-te and Hsuan-
       hua prefectures and the K'ou-pei area, which comprised 20 additional
       administrative units at least. Hopei is not the same as Chihli.

13.   The *"shu-yuan* era" periodization (1733–ca. 1800) is from Ch'en Tung-
       yuan, *Chung-kuo chiao-yü shih* (A history of education in China; 1936,
       Taipei reprint), p. 450.

The New Coastal Reformers/Paul A. Cohen

1.   Paul A. Cohen, *Between Tradition and Modernity: Wang T'ao and
       Reform in Late Ch'ing China* (Cambridge, Mass., Harvard University
       Press, 1974), pp. 258–259.

2.   Rhoads Murphey, *The Treaty Ports and China's Modernization: What
       Went Wrong?* (Ann Arbor, Center for Chinese Studies, University of
       Michigan, 1970), p. 6.

3.   Cohen, p. 243.

Foreign Policy Interests and Activities of the Treaty-Port Chinese Community/
Louis T. Sigel

1.   John E. Schrecker, *Imperialism and Chinese Nationalism* (Cambridge, Mass
       Harvard University Press, 1971), chaps. 2, 7.

2.   Liu Kuang-ching, "Cheng Kuan-ying *I-yen:* Kuang-hsu ch'u-nien chih
       pien-fa ssu-hsiang" (Cheng Kuan-ying's *I-yen:* Reform proposals of the

early Kuang-hsu period), *Ch'ing-hua hsueh-pao,* n.s., 8.1–2:386–387 (August 1970).

3. *Ch'ing-chi Chung-Jih-Han kuan-hsi shih-liao* (Materials on Sino-Japanese-Korean diplomatic history of the Ch'ing period; Taipei, 1971), doc. 554, p. 910.

4. Ibid., doc. 584, app. 1, pp. 968–970.

5. Great Britain, Foreign Office. *FO 405. Confidential Prints on China and Korea,* no. 33, Affairs of Corea 1883. Nov. 25, 1882, T. G. Grosvenor to Lord Granville; Apr. 7, 1883, Sir Harry Parkes to Earl Granville.

6. Rosalie von Mollendorff, *P. G. von Moellendorff Ein Lebensbild* (Leipzig, 1930), pp. 50–51.

7. *Chung-Jih-Han,* doc. 1507, pp. 2734–2740.

8. Ibid., doc. 1725, pp. 3038–3040.

9. *Chung-Fa Yueh-nan chiao-she-tang* (Sino-French diplomatic documents concerning Vietnam; Taipei, 1962), doc. 126, p. 208.

10. Ibid., doc. 137, app. 1, pp. 247–253.

11. Ibid., doc. 140, app. 2, pp. 267–268.

12. Ibid., doc. 532, app. 1, pp. 1071–1080.

13. Ibid., pp. 1076–1077.

14. Ibid., p. 1079.

15. Ibid., doc. 532, app. 3, p. 1081.

16. Ibid., doc. 532, app. 2, p. 1080.

The Reform Movement of 1898 and the Ch'ing-i/John E. Schrecker

1. The most crucial article by Professor Min is "Musul pyŏnpŏp undong ŭi . paegyŏng e taehayŏ t'ŭkhi ch'ŏngnyup'a wa yangmup'a rŭl chungsim ŭro"

(On the background of the reform movement of 1898 with special reference to the Ch'ing-liu p'ai and Yang-wu p'ai), *Tongyang sahak yon'gu,* no. 5:101-151 (1971). Among T'ang Chih-chün's many works, particularly useful are *Wu-hsu pien-fa shih lun-ts'ung* (Collected essays on the reform movement of 1898; Wuhan, Hupei Jen-min ch'u-pan she, 1957); and *Wu-hsu pien-fa jen-wu chuan-kao* (Draft biographies of personalities in the reform movement of 1898), 2 vols. (Peking, Chung-hua shu-chü, 1961). Professor Huang's most relevant work is *Wu-hsu pien-fa shih yen-chiu* (Studies on the reform movement of 1898; Taipei, Academia Sinica, Institute of Philology Monographs, no. 54, 1970). I should also note Hsiao Kung-ch'üan's classic article on "Weng T'ung-ho and the Reform Movement of 1898," *Tsing Hua Journal of Chinese Studies,* n.s., 1.2:111-245 (April 1957), which is still very useful.

2.   Richard Howard, "The Chinese Reform Movement of the 1890s: A Symposium," *Journal of Asian Studies,* 29.1:13 (November 1969).

3.   K'ang Yu-wei, *Chronological Autobiography,* tr. Lo Jung-pang, in Lo Jung-pang, ed., *K'ang Yu-wei: A Biography and a Symposium* (Tucson, University of Arizona Press, 1967), p. 50.

4.   Byon Jae-hyon, "The Ch'iang-hsueh hui: The Initiation of an Organized Reform Movement" (M.A. thesis, University of Washington, 1970), p. 24.

5.   *Wu-hsu pien-fa* (The reform movement of 1898), ed. Chien Po-tsan et al. (Shanghai, 1953), IV, 384-385.

6.   The first is cited by Min Tu-ki, p. 101 and is to be found in *T'an Ssu-t'ung ch'üan-chi* (Collected works of T'an Ssu-t'ung; Peking, 1954), p. 334. The second is quoted in Howard, p. 13.

7.   Quoted in Min, p. 101.

8.   *Wu-hsu cheng-pien chi* (Taipei, Chung-hua, 1959), p. 20.

9.   *Wu-hsu pien-fa,* II, 188 ff.

10.   Ibid., pp. 482 ff.

11.   T'ang Chih-chün, *Lun-ts'ung,* p. 19.

12. *Wu-hsu pien-fa tang-an shih-liao* (Archival materials on the reform movement of 1898), comp. National Bureau of Archives, Office of Ming and Ch'ing Archives (Peking, 1958), pp. 1 ff.

13. *Wu-hsu pien-fa,* II, 335 ff.

Reform through Study Societies in the Late Ch'ing Period / Sung Wook Shin

1. T'an Ssu-t'ung and T'ang Ts'ai-ch'ang, comps., *Hsiang-pao lei-tsuan* (Classified compilation of the *Hsiang daily;* Shanghai, 1902), *chia-chung,* p. 14. I have used the reprint published in Taiwan in 1969.

2. Ibid., *ping shang,* p. 5.

3. Ibid., *chia shang,* p. 9.

4. Ibid., *ting shang,* p. 5.

5. Ibid., pp. 1–3.

6. Ibid., pp. 8–10.

7. T'ang Chih-chün, *Wu-hsu pien-fa jen-wu chuan-kao* (Draft of the biographies of the 1898 reformers; Peking, 1961), 2 vols., p. 81.

8. *Hsiang-pao lei-tsuan, ting shang,* pp. 5–6.

9. Wang Erh-min, "Nan hsueh-hui" (Southern study society), *Ta-lu tsa-chih* 23.5:19 (September 1961).

10. Liang Ch'i-ch'ao, *Wu-hsu cheng-pien chi* (Record of the coup d'etat of 1898; Peking, 1954), 9:18. I have used the Korean translation published in Seoul in 1900, but I have checked the translation against the original.

11. *Hsiang-pao lei-tsuan, ting shang,* pp. 6–8.

12. T'ang Chih-chün, *Wu-hsu pien-fa-shih lun-ts'ung* (Collected essays on the history of the reform movement of 1898; Hupei, 1957), pp. 302–321.

Chang Chih-tung after the "100 Days"/Daniel H. Bays

1.   *K'ang Yu-wei: A Biography and a Symposium,* ed. Lo Jung-pang (Tucson, University of Arizona Press, 1967), p. 172, n. 69.

2.   Kuo T'ing-i, *Chin-tai Chung-kuo shih-shih jih-chih* (Daily record of events in modern Chinese history), 2 vols. (Taipei, 1963), pp. 1027 ff., has the most convenient summary of the edicts of late 1898, culled from the *Shih-lu.*

3.   This is also the interpretation of Hsiao Kung-ch'üan in his "Weng T'ung-ho and the Reform Movement of 1898," *Tsing Hua Journal of Chinese Studies,* n.s., 1.2:111–245 (April 1957).

4.   Issue of Sept. 23, 1898, in *wu-hsu pien-fa* (The reform movement of 1898), ed. Chien Po-tsan, 4 vols. (Shanghai, 1953), III, 324–326.

5.   Wang Shu-huai, *Wai-jen yü wu-hsu pien-fa* (Foreigners and the 1898 reforms; Nankang, 1965), pp. 191–219. As Sue Fawn Chung argues in her contribution to this volume, however, it is debatable to what extent there were real moves against Kuang-hsu and to what extent these were fabricated by the exiled reformers' press.

6.   For example, Tseng-ho, the Manchu appointed governor of Hupeh in November 1898, in January 1899 requested that the edicts rescinding many of the "100 days" decrees be canceled, allowing the summer measures to come back into effect. He was immediately denounced, dismissed from office, and denied future employment. Kuo T'ing-i, p. 1039.

7.   Hsu T'ung-hsin, *Chang Wen-hsiang-kung nien-p'u* (Chronological biography of Chang Chih-tung; Chungking, 1944), p. 122. The consul-general was Odagiri Masunosuke, with whom Chang had extensive communications in the last few months of 1898. His report of December 21, 1898, in *Nihon gaikō bunshō* (Diplomatic documents of Japan), vol. 31, pt. 1, p. 725.

8.   Wang Shu-huai, pp. 225–226.

9.   See Hsu T'ung-hsin, pp. 110, 112–113, 122.

10. For a general account, see Wang Shu-huai, pp. 231–233. Also *Nihon gaikō bunshō,* vol. 31, pt. 1, pp. 723–724.

11. Aoki's telegram in *Nihon gaikō bunshō,* vol. 31, pt. 1, p. 724; the Japanese government paid K'ang $9,000 to finance his trip to North America.

12. Ralph Powell, *The Rise of Chinese Military Power 1895–1912* (Princeton University Press, 1955), pp. 120–121; Kuo T'ing-i, pp. 1051–1053; the total of 27 is compiled from the tables in Fang Chao-ying, *Ch'ing-mo Min-ch'u yang-hsueh hsueh-sheng t'i-ming lu, ch'u-chi* (Name registers of students abroad in the late Ch'ing and early Republic, first collection; Taipei, 1962).

13. Wang Shu-huai, p. 235.

14. Ibid., p. 239.

15. Ibid., pp. 240–241; *Wu-hsu pien-fa,* II, 619–620.

16. See Wang Shu-huai, pp. 218–221. A special message emphasizing the poor health of the emperor accompanied the delivery of the decree to each foreign embassy. It is possible, as Sue Fawn Chung's research has indicated, that there was no actual plot to dethrone Kuang-hsu. But many believed there was such a plot and acted accordingly.

17. Ibid., p. 219.

18. Ibid. For a contemporary Chinese newspaper account of the mass telegram incident, see *Wu-hsu pien-fa,* III, 474.

19. For the information in this paragraph, see Li Shou-k'ung, "T'ang Ts'ai-ch'ang yü Tzu-li chün" (T'ang Ts'ai-ch'ang and the independence army), in *Chung-kuo hsien-tai shih ts'ung-k'an* (Selected articles on the contemporary history of China), ed. Wu Hsiang-hsiang, 6:41–159 (1964).

20. Hsu T'ung-hsin, pp. 126–127.

21. Wang Shu-huai, p. 241.

22. *Wu-hsu pien-fa,* II, 620.

23. Public Record Office, London, FO 228/1361, Fraser's quarterly intelligence report, April 4, 1900.

24. *Wu-hsu pien-fa,* II, 621–622.

25.   Wang Shu-huai, p. 241. Yen Fu's Tientsin paper was, however, closed down on Feb. 23, 1900.

26.   Liang was in Hawaii at this time. The editorial was dated March 25 and appeared in no. 42:2729–2734 (Apr. 20, 1900; reprint ed.).

27.   See my Ph.D. dissertation, "Chang Chih-tung and the Politics of Reform in China, 1895–1905" (The University of Michigan, 1971), chap. 5.

GLOSSARY

Names of people with biographies in Hummel, *Eminent
Chinese of the Ch'ing Period* or Boorman, *Biographical Dictionary
of Republican China* are not included here.

ch'a-chuang 茶莊

ch'a-wu hsueh-t'ang 茶務學堂

Chang-chia-k'ou 張家口

Chang Chü-cheng 張居正

Chang Hsiao-ch'ien 張孝謙

Chang Pi-shih 張弼士

Chang Sheng-tsao 張盛藻

Chang Sung-hsien 張頌賢

Chang T'ing-hsiang 張廷湘

Ch'ang-shu 常熟

Chao K'uang-yin 趙匡胤

Chao-shang-chü 招商局

ch'e-p'iao 折票

Chen-hai 鎮海

chen tzu-yu 箴自由

Ch'en Chih 陳熾

Ch'en Ch'iu 陳虬

Ch'en Fu-ch'en 陳黻宸

Ch'en I 陳彝

Ch'en K'uei-lung 陳夔龍

Ch'en Liang 陳亮

Ch'en Pao-chen 陳寶箴

Ch'en Pao-ch'en 陳寶琛

Ch'en San-li 陳三立

cheng 正

cheng-chih 整飭

Cheng I-sao 鄭一嫂

Cheng Kuan-ying 鄭觀應

Cheng-ting 正定

cheng-tun 整頓

Ch'eng-Chu 程朱

chi-ch'iao 技巧

Chi-chou 冀州

Chi-fu t'ung-chih 畿輔通志

Ch'i Chi-kuang 戚繼光

Chia I 賈誼

chia-shu 家塾

Chia-ting 嘉定

chiang-i 講義

Chiang T'ang 蔣堂

Ch'iang-hsueh hui 強學會

Chiao-hui hsin-pao 教會新報

chieh 節

chieh-chih 節制

chien 建

ch'ien-chuang 錢莊

Chih-hsin mien ping fa 治心免病法

chih hsing 志行

chih-shen chü-wai 置身局外

chin 衿

chin-shih 進士

chin-wen 今文

Ching-hua yuan 鏡花緣

Ching-pao 京報

ching-shih 經世

Ching Su 景甦

ch'ing-i 清議

Ch'ing-i pao 清議報

ch'ing-kuan 清官

Ch'ing-liu p'ai 清流派

Ch'ing-p'u 青浦

Ch'ing Te-tsung Ching huang-ti shih-lu 清德宗景皇帝實錄

Ch'ing-yuan 清苑

Ch'ing-yü 慶裕

chiu-shih huo-kuo 救時活國

Ch'iu-shih shu-yuan 求是書院

chou 宙

Chou Ch'ang-chih 周昌熾

Chou Ch'ang-fu 周昌福

Chou Tsu-p'ei 周祖培

Chu Hsi 朱熹

Chu Yuan-chang 朱元璋

ch'u-neng 儲能

ch'u-teng hsiao-hsueh-t'ang 初等小學堂

Ch'u-ts'ai hsueh-t'ang 儲才學堂

chuang 莊

Chuang-fei 壯飛

ch'uang 劇

Chueh-mi yao-lu 覺迷要錄

chung-hsing 中興

chung-tien 重典

Chung-t'u 中土

Chung-wai hsin-pao 中外新報

Chung-wai jih-pao 中外日報

Ch'ü T'ing-shao 瞿廷韶

Ch'üan-hsueh p'ien 勸學篇

ch'üan-hsueh-so 勸學所

ch'üan-mou 權謀

chün-p'ing 均平

chün-tzu 君子

ch'ün-ch'i 群氣

ch'ün-ch'ing 群情

ch'ün-hsin 群心

ch'ün-ts'ai 群材

en 恩

Fan Chung-yen 范仲淹

Fan Fen 樊棻

fen-chia 分家

Feng Chün-kuang 馮焌光

feng-i wei-shih 奉夷為師

feng-shui 風水

fu-ch'iang 富強

fu-ku keng-hua 復古更化

"Fu-min shuo" 富民說

Fu-nü yueh-k'an 婦女月刊
Fu-she 復社

Hai-fang-tang 海防檔
Han-hsueh 漢學
hao-hsia 豪俠
Ho Fu-t'ang 何福堂
Ho Hsin-yin 何心隱
Ho Kai (Ho Ch'i) 何啟
Ho Miao-ling 何妙靈
Hsi-hsueh 西學
Hsi-hsueh shu-mu piao 西學書目表
Hsiang-pao 湘報
hsiang-tung 鄉董
hsiao-hu 小戶
Hsieh Fu-tien 謝輔坫
hsin 信 (trust)
hsin 新 (new)
Hsin-chih pei-kao 新志備稿
Hsin-hsueh wei-ching k'ao 新學偽經考
hsin-ting 新定
Hsin-tu 信都
hsing-li ch'u-pi 興利除弊
hsiu-shen 修身
Hsiung Hsi-ling 熊希齡
Hsu Chih-ching 徐致靖
Hsu Jun 徐潤
Hsu Nai-chao 許乃釗
Hsu Shu-lan 徐樹蘭

Hsu Ying-ch'i 許應騤
Hsu Yu-lan 徐友蘭
Hsuan-wu 宣武
hsueh-shu 學術
hsueh-t'ang 學堂
Hu-ch'iang-ying 虎槍營
hu-jen 胡人
Hu Kuang-yung 胡光墉
Hu Li-yuan 胡禮垣
Hua-tzu jih-pao 華字日報
Huai-jou 懷柔
Huang-ch'ao ching-shih wen pien 皇朝經世文編
Huang Chün-tsai 黃鈞宰
Huang Shao-chi 黃紹箕
Huang T'i-fang 黃體芳
hui-kuan 會館
Hui-pao 匯報
Hung-mao 紅毛

i-cheng wang 議政王
i-chih 壹旨
I-chih shu-hui 益智書會
i-chuang 義莊
i-hsia chih pien 夷夏之辨
i-hsin 一心
i-hsueh 義學
i-p'ien kung-ch'eng chih hsin 一片公誠之心
i-t'ung chih t'ien-hsia 一統之天下

i-yuan 議院

jen 仁
jen-hsin 人心
Jen-hsueh 仁學
jen tzu wei chan 人自為戰
jen-wu i-t'i 人物一體

kai 改
kai-chin 改進
kai-ko 改革
kai-liang 改良
kai-liang p'ai 改良派
kai-pien 改變
kai-shan 改善
kai-tsao 改造
kakumeiha 革命派
kan-shih pu 幹事部
k'an-shu p'ing-tan 看書憑單
kao-teng hsiao-hsueh-t'ang
　　　高等小學堂
keng 更
keng-hua 更化
ko-hsin 革新
ko-wai yu-pao 格外優保
k'o 科
k'o-min 客民
Ku-shih kou-ch'en lun
　　　古史鉤沉論
kuan 關
kuan-shang ho-pan 官商合辦

kuan-shu jen 管書人
kuan-t'ou 關頭
kuan-tu shang-pan
　　　官督商辦
Kuang-fang yen-kuan
　　　廣方言館
"Kuang-hsu hsiang-yung K'ang
　　shih-mo" 光緒嚮用康
　　始末
"Kuang-hsu sheng-te chi"
　　　光緒聖德記
Kuang-hsueh hui 廣學會
kung 公
kung-cheng 公正
Kung-Ch'in-Chieh 鞏秦階
Kung-chung tang Kuang-hsu
　　ch'ao tsou-che 宮中檔光
　　朝奏摺
Kung-chü shang-shu
　　　公車上書
kung-fu 工夫
kung-hsin 公心
kung-i wei chu-i
　　　公益為主義
kung-li 公立
kung-shan i-yuan 公善醫院
kung-te 公德
Kung-yang 公羊
kuo-chih 國制
kuo-shih chin-kuang
　　　國勢寖廣
Kuo-wen pao 國聞報

le-chüan 樂捐

li 利 (profit)

li 禮 (rites, ceremony, propriety)

li 力 (force)

Li-chi 禮記

Li Chih 李贄

li-ch'üan 利權

Li Fan 李璠

Li Ho-nien 李鶴年

li-hsueh 理學

li-ting 釐定

Li Tuan-fen 李端棻

Liang Ju-hao 梁如浩

Liang Ting-fen 梁鼎棻

lieh-kuo 列國

Lien-ch'ih 蓮池

ling-hun 靈魂

"Liu-ho chiang ho wei-i" 六合將合為一

Liu Hsi-hung 劉錫鴻

Liu Hsun-kao 劉郇膏

Liu Kuang-ti 劉光第

Liu Yung 劉鏞

Lo Tun-jung 羅惇曧

Lu Chien-ying 陸建瀛

Lu Lung-ch'i 陸隴其

Lun-ts'un 掄村

Lü K'un 呂坤

Lü Wei-ying 呂渭英

Ma Chien-chung 馬建忠

Mei-ch'i shu-yuan 梅溪書院

min 民

min-chih 民智

min-chu 民主

min-ch'üan 民權

min-tsu chu-i 民族主義

Min Tu-ki 閔斗基

ming-fa 明法

Ming-liang lun 明良論

mu-fu 幕府

mu-yu 幕友

Nan hsueh-hui 南學會

nei-wai 內外

neng-li 能力

Nguyen Van Tuong 阮文祥

Nieh Shih-ch'eng 聶士成

niu yü mu-ch'ien 狃於目前

nü-hsia 女俠

Odagiri Masunosuke 小田切萬壽

Ou Chü-chia 歐榘甲

Ou-yang Chung-ku 歐陽中鵠

Ou-yang Hsiu 歐陽修

pa-ku wen 八股文

Pan-ch'iao 板橋

pao-chiao 保教

pao-huang 保皇

pao-kuo 保國
Pao-ting 保定
Pei-ling 北嶺
pen-yin chih-hsien 本隱至現
p'eng-tang 朋黨
Pi Yung-nien 畢永年
pien 變
pien-fa 變法
pien-hsiu 編修
Pien Pao-ti 卞寶第
p'ing-chün 平均
P'ing-shan 平山
p'ing-tan 憑單
p'ing-teng 平等
p'ing t'ien-hsia 平天下
p'o chuan-chih 破專制
pu tang ch'üan p'ai

　　不當權派
P'u-chün 溥儁

sai-tung 塞董
san-kang 三綱
San-shih erh li 三十而立
San-shih tzu-chi 三十自紀
san-tai 三代
shang-chan 商戰
she-hsueh 社學
shen 紳
Shen-chi-ying 神機營
shen-ch'üan 紳權
shen-shang 紳商

shen-shih 紳士
Shen Tseng-chih 沈曾植
Shen Tun-ho 沈敦和
Sheng Chih-hsing 盛植型
Sheng Ping-chi 盛炳紀
Sheng Ping-wei 盛炳緯
sheng-p'ing shih 升平世
Sheng-wu-chi 聖武記
sheng-yuan 生員
shih 市
shih-cheng 實政
shih-feng 士風
shih-hsin jen-shih 實心任事
shih-hsueh 實學
shishi 志士
shu-fu 束縛
Shu-lu 束鹿
shu-shu 術數
shu-yuan 書院
ssu chih chü 私之局
ssu-li 私立
Ssu-ming kung-so 四明公所
ssu-shu 私塾
ssu-te 私德
Ssu-yeh kung-so 絲業公所
sui-kung-sheng 歲貢生
Sun I-yen 孫衣言
Sun Yü-wen 孫毓文
Sung Heng 宋衡
Sung-yun an 松筠庵

ta-hu 大戶
Ta-ming 大明
ta-t'ung 大同
ta-t'ung shih 大同世
t'ai-p'ing 太平
T'an Chi-hsun 譚繼洵
T'ang Chen 湯震
T'ang Chih-chün 湯志鈞
T'ang En-t'ung 唐恩桐
T'ang Shao-yi 唐紹儀
T'ang Shou-ch'ien 湯壽潛
T'ang T'ing-keng 唐廷庚
T'ang T'ing-shu 唐廷樞
T'ang Ts'ai-ch'ang 唐才常
tao 道
T'ao-yuan 桃園
Teng Ch'eng-hsiu 鄧承修
ti-fang tzu-chih 地方自治
ti-pao 地保
t'i-yung 體用
T'ien-chu-chiao 天主教
t'ien-hsia 天下
t'ien-hsia wei kung 天下為公
t'ien-hsin 天心
t'ien-i 天意
T'ien-kuei 天桂
t'ien-kuo 天國
t'ien-ti chien kung-kung chih li 天地間公共之理
t'ien-ti pu-jen 天地不仁

Ting-hsing 定興
Ting Ping 丁丙
Tōa Dōbunkai 東亞同文會
Tong King-sing (T'ang Ching-hsing) 唐景星
tou-p'i-kai 鬥批改
Ts'ai Erh-k'ang 蔡爾康
Ts'ai Shao-chi 蔡紹基
Ts'ai-shih-k'ou 菜市口
ts'ang-shu ch'u 藏書處
ts'ao-liang 漕糧
Tseng Lien 曾廉
Tsou Tai-chün 鄒代鈞
ts'un 村
ts'un-tung 村董
tsung chiao-hsi 總教習
tsung-hui chang-ch'eng 總會章程
T'u Jen-shou 屠仁守
t'u-tung 土董
t'uan 疃
t'uan-lien 團練
t'ui-chien chih-yin 推見至隱
t'ui-hsieh 推卸
Tung Chung-shu 董仲舒
Tung Fu-hsiang 董福祥
Tung-hua hsu-lu 東華續錄
Tung-lin 東林
tung-shih 董事
t'ung 同 (sameness)

t'ung 通 (linkage, communication)

T'ung-ch'eng 桐城

T'ung-chien kang-mu
通鑑綱目

T'ung-chou 通州

t'ung-hsiang 同鄉

T'ung-wen kuan 同文館

Tzu-cheng hsin-pien
資政新編

Tzu-chih t'ung-chien
資治通鑑

tzu-chu chih ch'üan
自主之權

tzu-i chü 咨議局

Tzu-li hui 自立會

tzu-li keng-sheng 自力更生

tzu neng tso chu chih ch'üan
自能作主之權

tzu-yu 自由

Tz'u-ch'i 慈谿

tz'u-shan 慈善

wan-kuo ho-hui 萬國和會

Wan-kuo kung-pao
萬國公報

Wan-mu ts'ao-t'ang
萬木草堂

Wang An-shih 王安石

Wang K'ang-nien 汪康年

Wang Lan-yin 王蘭蔭

wang-lo 網羅

Wang Mang 王莽

Wang Ta-hai 王大海

Wang Ta-hsieh 汪大燮

Wang Wen-shao 王文韶

Wang Yang-ming 王陽明

wei-hsin 維新

wei-wo 為我

Wen-t'i 文悌

Wen-yang 溫陽

Wu-i 武夷

Wu-pei hsueh-t'ang
武備學堂

wu-ssu 無私

Wu-wei chün 武衛軍

Yang Chi-sheng 楊繼盛

Yang Ch'ung-i 楊崇伊

Yang Fang 楊坊

yang-jen 洋人

Yang Jui 楊銳

Yang Shen-hsiu 楊深秀

Yang T'ing-hsi 楊廷熙

Yang Wen-hui 楊文會

yang-wu 洋務

yang-wu p'ai 洋務派

Yeh Ch'eng-chung 葉成忠

Yeh Shih 葉適

Yeh-su-chiao 耶蘇教

yen-hsing 嚴刑

yen-lu 言路

Yen-p'ing 延平
Yen Sung 嚴嵩
Yin 鄞
yin-liang 銀兩
Ying-chi-li 英吉利
yu-hsia 游俠
Yuan-shih 元氏

Yun Yü-ting 惲毓鼎
Yung-yen 庸言
yü 宇
Yü Hung-ch'ao 余鴻潮
Yü Lien-san 俞廉三
Yü Ling-ch'en 于凌辰
yü-ying t'ang 育嬰堂

PARTICIPANTS IN WORKSHOP ON REFORM IN NINETEENTH-CENTURY CHINA
East Asian Research Center, Harvard University
July 7–18, 1975

Suzanne Wilson Barnett
University of Puget Sound
Marianne Bastid
Centre National de la
Recherche Scientifique
Paris
Daniel H. Bays
University of Kansas
Adrian A. Bennett
Iowa State University
Ellsworth Carlson
Oberlin College
Hao Chang
The Ohio State University
Peter Ch'en
Harvard University
Joseph Cheng
Harvard University
I-fan Ch'eng
University of California
Berkeley
Nailene Chou
Pacific Lutheran University
Sue Fawn Chung
University of Nevada
Las Vegas
Paul A. Cohen
Wellesley College
Maryruth Coleman
Harvard University

Roger Des Forges
State University of New York
Buffalo
John K. Fairbank
Harvard University
Albert Feuerwerker
University of Michigan
Ann Arbor
Robert P. Gardella
University of Washington
Michael R. Godley
Beloit College
Kent Guy
Harvard University
Joanna F. Handlin
University of Rochester
Andrew Hsieh
Skidmore College
Immanuel C. Y. Hsu
University of California
Santa Barbara
Chang-chien Huang
Institute of History and
Philology
Academia Sinica
Susan Mann Jones
University of Chicago
Noriko Kamachi
University of Michigan
Dearborn

Thomas L. Kennedy
  Washington State University
Jeffrey Kinkley
  Harvard University
Luke S. K. Kwong
  University of Toronto
Charlton M. Lewis
  Brooklyn College
Lillian Li
  Swarthmore College
Peter Li
  Rutgers University
James T. C. Liu
  Princeton University
Kwang-Ching Liu
  University of California
  Davis
Wai-fong Loh
  Harvard University
Frank A. Lojewski
  Indiana University
  Kokomo
Esther Morrison
  Howard University
Dian Murray
  Cornell University
Jonathan Ocko
  Clark University
Richard A. Orb
  University of Michigan
  Ann Arbor
Charles A. Peckham
  University of Kansas
James Polachek
  Columbia University
David Pong
  University of Delaware

Don Price
  University of California
  Davis
Mary Backus Rankin
  Washington, D.C.
John E. Schrecker
  Brandeis University
Richard H. Shek
  University of California
  Berkeley
Linda P. Shin
  California State College
  Dominguez Hills
Sung Wook Shin
  University of California
  Berkeley
Louis T. Sigel
  Australian National University
  Canberra
Saundra Sturdevant
  University of California
  Berkeley
Hoyt Tillman
  Arizona State University
  Tempe
Yeh-chien Wang
  Kent State University
Judith Whitbeck
  University of California
  Berkeley
Roxane Witke
  State University of New York
  Binghamton
Young-tsu Wong
  Virginia Polytechnic Institute
  and State University
Shui-yuen Yim
  University of Cambridge

INDEX

Bruce, Sir Frederick, 68
Buddhism, 153, 188; and T'an Ssu-t'ung, 194, 203, 251; Ch'an Buddhism, 227
Bureau of Book Collection (ts'ang-shu ch'u), public library, 313
Bureaucrats: businessmen as equals of, 56; Wang Hsien-ch'ien's attacks on, 172-173
Businessmen: status of, with Chang Pi-shih, 56; role of in treaty ports, 280. See also Merchants

Canton: growth of foreign trade in, 42; foreign-language school at, 91; in littoral culture, 255-257
Capitalists, overseas Chinese vs. home Chinese as, 61
Carlson, Ellsworth: on missionary and opium, 80; in discussion, 82; on littoral-hinterland, 284-285
Ceylon, tea production in, 75, 78
Chang Chien, 293, 294, 297, 327, 329
Chang Chih-tung, 52, 107, 108, 121, 181, 326; on t'i-yung, 147; bibliography of, 148; sociopolitical stand of, 149; and T'an Ssu-t'ung, 185; on disruptive power of people's rights, 199; and new coastal reformers, 259; in ch'ing-i movement, 291, 293, 294, 296, 327; patron of Ch'iang-hsueh hui, 297, 298; in reform of 1898, 299, 305, 310; after the Hundred Days, 317-325
Chang Chü-cheng, 16; and system-reorienting reform, 12; dysfunction in reform of, 14
Chang Chung-li, 117, 120
Chang Hao, 17, 32, 93, 145-149, 247; on ideology, 112-113, 114, 328; in discussion, 181, 182, 183, 205, 284; on cosmological myth, 200, 327;

on democratic participation, 204; on Kuang-hsu, 330; on intentionality and reform, 330
Chang Hsiao-ch'ien, 297
Chang Hsueh-ch'eng, 28
Chang P'ei-lun, 172
Chang Pi-shih, 49, 51-59; role in development of China, 52; reform suggestions of, 53-55; appointments of, 55-56; status of as entrepreneur, 56-58
Chang Ping-lin, 299
Chang Sheng-tsao, 93
Chang T'ing-hsiang, 234, 235
Changsha, 283; influence of littoral culture on, 284
Chao K'uang-yin, system-founding reforms of, 11
Charitable or endowed schools (i-hsueh), 232, 234, 238; converted into lower primary, 232-233. See also Schools
ch'e-p'iao ("chop loans"), 43
Chekiang: local reform in, 221-230; changes in elite society of, 222-224; introduction of reform at local level, 224-226; traditional scholarship and reform, 226-228; coalescence of reform efforts in, 228-230
Chen-hai, 46-48
Ch'en Ai-t'ing, 267
Ch'en Chih, 155, 157; director of Ch'iang-hsueh hui, 297
Ch'en Ch'iu, 227, 228
Ch'en Fu-ch'en, 227, 228
Ch'en I, 326
Ch'en K'uei-lung, memorial on old examination system by, 108, 109
Ch'en Lan-pin, 267
Ch'en Liang, 14
Ch'en Pao-chen, 189, 190, 314, 319

Chou, Duke of, 26
Chou Ch'ang-chih, 224
Chou dynasty, lack of historian-chronicler in, 29
Chou, Nailene, 183, 217–220, 241; on *ch'ing-i* officials, 329
Chou system, 155
Chou Tsu-p'ei, 89, 90–91
Christianity: of overseas Chinese, 61; and principle of universality, 151–152; studied by T'an Ssu-t'ung, 195; Williamson on, 197–198; and sanction of autonomy, 199. *See also* Missionaries
Chu Hsi, 14
Chu, Richard, 205
Chu Yuan-chang, system-founding reforms of, 11
Ch'ü T'ing-shao, 319
Ch'üan Han-sheng, 39
Ch'üan-hsueh p'ien (Chang Chih-tung), 318
Chuang-tzu, 29, 154, 194
chün-tzu (ruling class), 3, 174
ch'ün (grouping), 173
Chung-Hsi hsueh-t'ang, established in Shaohsing, 228
chung-hsing, 5
Chung, Sue Fawn, 101–110; in discussion, 60; on Tz'u-hsi as woman ruler, 249
Chung-wai jih-pao, Shanghai daily, 318, 323; Chang Chih-tung's demand for curb on, 324
Chūzō Ichiko, 229
Cities, economy of Chinese, 38–39. *See also* Urban development
Clan ties, importance of in spread of reform, 229
Clarifying Goodness (Ming-liang lun), 27–28
Classes, social, Ch'ing changes in, 37.

See also Gentry; Elite; Literati
Cliometric study: of economic history of the Ch'ing, 35; data for, 35–36
Clubs, and the reform movement, 298
Cockburn, Henry, 101
Cohen, Paul A., 41, 268; on modernization, 67; in discussion, 80, 83, 137, 205, 206, 242, 282; on power struggles, 87, 99; on ideology, 112, 114; on littoral vs. hinterland, 148, 283–284, 284–285; on new coastal reformers, 255–264; on acceptance of Western ideas, 326; on *ch'ing-i,* 329; on motivation for reform, 330–331; on cultural change, 337
Coleman, Maryruth, 60
Colonialism: of Hong Kong, 263; Wu T'ing-fang's attitude toward, 268–271. *See also* Semicolonialism
Collaboration: of littoral reformers with West, 259–260; and acculturation, 260
Commerce: littoral geared to, 256; development of Sino-Western, 258
Commoners: in government, 3; spread of literacy to, 16; Ch'i Chi-kuang on unification of, 22–23; responsiveness of Confucianism to, 24; in Ming period, 32
Communal or village schools (*she-hsueh*), 232, 234, 238. *See also* Schools
Communication: problem of, 241–242; to the throne (*yen-lu*), 291–292
Communism, Chinese, roots of in *ch'ing-i* movement, 305
Comprador-merchants, influence of

advantages of, over foreigners, 55–56; status of as entrepreneurs, 56–58

pao-huang (protect the emperor) group, 319, 323
Pao-kuo hui (Society to Preserve the Nation), 299
Pao Shih-ch'en, 145; reformist thought of, 146
Paoting fu, primary schools in, 233
Peace, universal, goal of reform, 150
Peckham, Charles, 330
Perkins, Dwight, 35–36
Philanthropy: of merchant class, 45; in Ningpo, 47–48
Pi Yung-nien, 200, 316
P'i Hsi-jui, 200, 311, 313, 314
Pien Pao-ti, on tea in Fukien, 77
p'ing-chün (equalization), 26
p'ing t'ien-hsia, 3
Pirates, woman as leader of, 249
Plato, 159
Plotinus, 159
Polachek, James, 16, 32, 211–214, 242, 255; on role of ideology, 111–112, 114; on local elite, 215; in discussion, 241, 326, 328
Politics: reform as involutionary, 9; linked with intellectual outlook, 87–100
Pong, David, 60–61, 83, 113
Pope-Hennessy, Sir John, 269
Popular rights: as significant trend, 309; in Hunan, 310
Population, shifts in during Taiping Rebellion, 43
Power, relation to virtue, 291; struggle for in 1898, 299–305
Pragmatism in statecraft, Tseng Kuo-fan on, 146–147
Price, Don, 182–183, 242

Primary schools. See Higher primary schools; Lower primary schools
Private or family schools (ssu-shu and chia-shu), 233–234
Proletariat, growth of as consequence of reform, 125
Protestantism: in China, 165; T'an Ssu-t'ung on, 199. See also Missionaries
Provinces: modernization of forces of, 105–106; reform at level of, 211, 310; gentry-official conflict in Kiangsu, 215–216; reform in Sinkiang, 217–220, 242; reform in Chekiang, 221–230; educational statistics for, 239; assemblies as expression of min-ch'üan, 316
Psychotherapy, Wood on, 200–203
P'u-chün, as heir apparent, 322

Railways: Shanghai-Wusung, 63; opposition to, 65–66; as intrusion on sovereignty, 68; failure of central government on, 211; local participation in decisions on, 213–214
Rankin, Mary Backus, 221–230; in discussion, 62, 241; on women in reform movement, 248
Rawski, Evelyn, 39, 138
Reform: a Western concept, 3; modern tied with past, 5; Chinese concepts included in, 9–10; types of, 10–12; economic aspects of, 35–40; and Chang Pi-shih, 51–59; relation of imperialism and sovereignty to, 63–70; and agrarian economy, 71–79; relation of politics and intellectual outlook to, 87–100; and the Empress Dowager, 101–110; social context of, 117–127; social antecedents of,

HARVARD EAST ASIAN MONOGRAPHS

Frank H.H. King (ed.) and Prescott Clarke, *A Research Guide to China-Coast Newspapers, 1822-1911*

Ellis Joffe, *Party and Army: Professionalism and Political Control in the Chinese Officer Corps, 1949-1964*

Toshio G. Tsukahira, *Feudal Control in Tokugawa Japan: The Sankin Kōtai System*

Kwang-Ching Liu, ed., *American Missionaries in China: Papers from Harvard Seminars*

George Moseley, *A Sino-Soviet Cultural Frontier: The Ili Kazakh Autonomous Chou*

Carl F. Nathan, *Plague Prevention and Politics in Manchuria, 1910-1931*

Adrian Arthur Bennett, *John Fryer: The Introduction of Western Science and Technology into Nineteenth-Century China*

Donald J. Friedman, *The Road from Isolation: The Campaign of the American Committee for Non-Participation in Japanese Aggression, 1938-1941*

Edward Le Fevour, *Western Enterprise in Late Ch'ing China: A Selective Survey of Jardine, Matheson and Company's Operations, 1842-1895*

Charles Neuhauser, *Third World Politics: China and the Afro-Asian People's Solidarity Organization, 1957-1967*

Kungtu C. Sun, assisted by Ralph W. Huenemann, *The Economic Development of Manchuria in the First Half of the Twentieth Century*

Shahid Javed Burki, *A Study of Chinese Communes, 1965*

John Carter Vincent, *The Extraterritorial System in China: Final Phase*

Madeleine Chi, *China Diplomacy, 1914-1918*

Clifton Jackson Phillips, *Protestant America and the Pagan World: The First Half Century of the American Board of Commissioners for Foreign Missions, 1810-1860*